GRAPHIC GUIDE TO

Frame
Construction

DETAILS FOR BUILDERS AND DESIGNERS

GRAPHIC GUIDE TO

Frame Construction

DETAILS FOR BUILDERS AND DESIGNERS

ROB THALLON

COMPLETELY REVISED AND UPDATED

The Taunton Press

Cover illustrator: Scott Wolf

Author's drawings rendered as follows:
Illustrations 6B (right), 23C, 25C, 30 (third from top on left), 33D, 44A–D, 45B, 61 (top left),
62B–D, 74, 75A & B, 76A, C & D, 82, 83, 84, 85A & B, 86A–D, 87A–D, 94B (top and center),
106B, 119, 120 (top right), 122–125, 152A & D, 153C, 157B (right), 160, 161A–D, 198, 199A–D,
204A & B, 205C, 215B & C rendered by Anthony Baron.
All other illustrations rendered by Scott Wolf.

Publisher: Jim Childs
Acquisitions Editor: Steve Culpepper
Assistant Editor: Jennifer Renjilian
Copy Editor: Daphne Hougham
Indexer: Catherine Goddard
Cover Designer: Steve Hughes
Interior Designer: Lynne Phillips
Layout Artist: Lisa DeFeo

The Taunton Press
Inspiration for hands-on living™

Printed in the United States of America
10 9 8 7 6 5 4 3 2

For Pros / By Pros® is a trademark of The Taunton Press, Inc.,
registered in the U.S. Patent and Trademark Office.

The Taunton Press, Inc., 63 South Main Street, P.O. Box 5506, Newtown, CT 06470-5506
e-mail: tp@taunton.com

Distributed by Publishers Group West

Library of Congress Cataloging-in-Publication Data
Thallon, Rob
    For Pros / By Pros®: Graphic guide to frame construction : details for builders and designers / Rob Thallon
        p.   cm
    Includes index.
    ISBN 1-56158-636-6
    1. Wooden-frame buildings—Design and construction.
    2. Wooden-frame buildings—Drawings. 3. Framing (Building).
        TH1101.T48   2000
        694.2—dc21

TO DEE

ACKNOWLEDGMENTS

This book has been enriched immeasurably by the contributions of consultants throughout the country. The first edition was reviewed in its entirety by the following architects and builders:

Ed Allen, South Natick, Mass.; Judith Capen, Washington, D.C.; Steve Kearns, Ketchum, Idaho; Scott McBride, Sperryville, Va.; Jud Peake, Oakland, Calif.; Dan Rockhill, LeCompton, Kans.; Joel Schwartz, Princeton, N.J.; Stephen Suddarth, Miami Beach, Fla.; Blaine Young, Santa Fe, N.Mex.

In addition, portions of this new edition were reviewed by:

Ed Allen, South Natick, Mass.; John Carmody, Minneapolis, Minn.; Walter Grondzik, Tallahassee, Fla.; Christine Theodoropolous, Eugene, Oreg.

The participation of all these reviewers has made the book more comprehensive and the process of writing it more enjoyable.

Also, I gratefully acknowledge invaluable contributions to the first edition by the following people:

Paul Bertorelli, for helping to define the scope of the book and the method of producing it; Joanne Bouknight, for patient and skillful editing with just the right touch of humor; David Edrington, my architectural partner, for his patience and understanding; Dee Etwiler, my wife, for her research assistance, her loving support, and her patience; Lloyd Kahn, for inspiration and support for this project long before it was realized; Chuck Miller, for listening to my ideas and suggesting the project to the publishers in the first place; Don Peting, for valuable assistance in articulating my thoughts about structural relationships in early chapters; Scott Wolf, for insightful assistance with the format and for putting as much energy into rendering the original drawings as humanly possible.

And for this edition I sincerely thank:

Steve Culpepper, for his unwavering belief in the importance of the *Graphic Guide* series and his deft facilitation of this second edition; Jennifer Renjilian, my editor, for gracious management and astute tuning of the writing; David McClean, my assistant, for helpful suggestions about and multiple drafts of most of the new drawings; Anthony Baron, for skillful rendering of the new drawings in the style of the originals; and all the other professionals whose contributions large and small have added quality to this volume.

CONTENTS

INTRODUCTION

Light wood-frame construction originated in this country over 150 years ago and quickly evolved into the predominant construction system for houses and other small-scale buildings. Today, over 90% of all new buildings in North America are made using some version of this method. Remodeling projects follow the same track.

There are many reasons why this system has been the choice of professional and amateur builders alike over the years. A principal reason is its flexibility. Because the modules are small, virtually any shape or style of building can be built easily with the studs, joists, and rafters that are the primary components of wood-frame construction. In addition, the pieces are easily handled, the material is readily available, and the skills and tools required for assembly are easily acquired.

Given the popularity of the system, it was surprising to find that, as recently as nine years ago, before the first edition of this book was published, no detailed reference book existed. Now nearly 100,000 copies of *Graphic Guide to Frame Construction* have found their way into the libraries of architects, contractors, owner-builders, and students—filling the void that previously existed. It is gratifying to know that so many people interested in designing and constructing quality wood-frame buildings have found the book to be a useful reference.

This second edition has been developed to keep pace with the changes in the building industry in the past nine years and to expand the information presented in the first edition.

The most obvious changes in the building industry have to do with the materials used to construct buildings. Sheathing, which used to be predominantly plywood, is now usually oriented strand board (OSB). Wood I-joists, which were relatively rare nine years ago, are now common. Vinyl windows, which were just being introduced, are now the standard. These and other, smaller changes are reflected in the drawings and descriptions of this new edition.

In addition, I have expanded the book to include more information about resisting lateral forces such as earthquakes and hurricanes, and about energy conservation techniques that exceed code minimums. The inclusion of both of these areas reflects the intention of the original edition to assist people to design and build for durability and resource efficiency. The new sections on lateral forces include several pages on shear walls, diaphragms, and high-wind roofs. The new sections on energy conservation include advanced framing, upgraded wall insulation, and upgraded ceiling insulation.

THE SCOPE OF THE BOOK

To provide a detailed reference, the scope of the book had to be limited. I decided to focus on the parts of a building that contribute most significantly to its longevity. Virtually all the drawings, therefore, describe details relating to the structural shell or to the outer protective layers of the building. Plumbing, electrical, and mechanical systems are described only as they affect the foundation and framing of the building. Interior finishes and details are not covered because they are the subject of a companion volume, *Graphic Guide to Interior Details* (The Taunton Press, 1996). The process of construction, covered adequately in many references, has here been stripped away so as to expose the details themselves as much as possible. Design, although integral with the concerns of this book, is dealt with only at the level of the detail.

The details shown here employ simple, standard materials. With this type of information, it should be possible to build a wood building in any shape and in any style. Many local variations are included.

A FOCUS ON DURABILITY

Although the details in this book have been selected partly on the basis of their widespread use, the primary focus is on durability. I believe that wood-frame buildings can and should be built to last for 200 years or more. To accomplish this, a building must be built on a solid foundation; it must be designed and built to resist moisture; it must be protected from termites, ants, and other insect pests; it must be structurally stable; and it must be reasonably protected from the ravages of fire. All these criteria may be met with standard construction details if care is taken in both the design and the building process.

There are some accepted construction practices, however, that I do not think meet the test of durability. For example, the practice in some regions of building foundations without rebar is not prudent. The small investment of placing rebar in the foundation to minimize the possibility of differential settlement is one that should be made whether or not it is required by code. The stability of a foundation affects not only the level of the floors but also the integrity of the structure above and the ability of the building to resist moisture. Another common practice that I discourage is the recent overreliance on caulks and sealants for waterproofing. This practice seems counterproductive in the long run because the most sophisticated and scientifically tested sealants are warranted for only 20 to 25 years. Should we be investing time, money, and materials in buildings that could be se-riously damaged if someone forgets to recaulk? It is far better, I believe, to design buildings with adequate overhangs or with flashing and drip edges that direct water away from the structural core by means of the natural forces of gravity and surface tension.

Durability, however, does not depend entirely upon material quality and construction detailing. Durability also depends heavily upon the overall design of the building and whether its usefulness over time is sufficient to resist the wrecking ball. The more intangible design factors such as the quality of the space and the flexibility of the plan are extremely important but are not a part of this book.

ON CODES

Every effort has been made to ensure that the details included in this book conform to building codes. Codes vary, however, so local codes and building departments should always be consulted to verify compliance.

HOW THE BOOK WORKS

The book's five chapters follow the approximate order of construction, starting with the foundation and working up to the roof (stairs follow roofs, however). Each chapter begins with an introduction that describes general principles. The chapters are divided into subsections, also roughly ordered according to the sequence of construction. Subsections, usually with another more specific introduction and an isometric reference drawing, lead to individual drawings or notes.

Chapter titles and subsections are called out at the top of each page for easy reference. Each drawing has a title and sometimes a subtitle. The pages are numbered at the top outside corner, and the drawings are lettered. With this system, all the drawings may be cross-referenced. The callout "see 42A," for example, refers to drawing A on page 42.

As many details as possible are drawn in the simple section format found on architectural working drawings. Most are drawn at the scale of 1 in. equals 1 ft. or 1½ in. equals 1 ft., although the scale is not noted on the drawings. This format should allow the details to be transferred to architectural drawings with minor adjustments. (Details will usually have to be adjusted to allow for different size or thickness of material, for roof pitch, or for positional relationships.) Those details that are not easily depicted in a simple section drawing are usually drawn isometrically in order to convey the third dimension.

Any notes included in a detail are intended to describe its most important features. By describing the relationship of one element to another, the notes sometimes go a little further than merely naming an element. Materials symbols are described on page 226. Abbreviations are spelled out on page 227.

A FINAL NOTE

My intention in writing and now in revising this book has been to assist designers and builders who are attempting to make beautiful buildings that endure. With the drawings I have tried to describe the relationship among the parts of every common connection. Alternative approaches to popular details have been included as well. I have relied primarily on my own experiences but have also drawn significantly on the accounts of others. In order to build upon this endeavor, I encourage you, the reader, to let me know of your own observations and critical comments. Please send them to me care of The Taunton Press, P.O. Box 5506, Newtown, CT 06470-5506.

CHAPTER 1

FOUNDATIONS

A foundation system has two functions. First, it supports the building structurally by keeping it level, minimizing settling, preventing uplift from the forces of frost or expansive soils and resisting horizontal forces such as winds and earthquakes. Second, a foundation system keeps the wooden parts of the building above the ground and away from the organisms and moisture in the soil that both eat wood and cause it to decay.

The foundation is the part of a building that is most likely to determine its longevity. If the foundation does not support the building adequately, cracks and openings will occur over time, even in the most finely crafted structure. No amount of repair on the structure above the foundation will compensate for an inadequate foundation; once a foundation starts to move significantly, it will continue to move. We now have developed the knowledge to design and construct durable foundations, so there is no reason to invest in a modern building that is not fully supported on a foundation that will endure for the life of the structure.

In the United States, there are three common foundation types. Each performs in different ways, but all rely on a perimeter foundation, i.e., a continuous support around the outside edge of the building.

SLAB-ON-GRADE FOUNDATIONS
Slab-on-grade systems are used mostly in warm climates, where living is close to the ground and the frost line is close to the surface. The footing is usually shallow, and the ground floor is a concrete slab.

Many slab-on-grade systems allow the concrete footing, foundation and subfloor to be poured at the same time.

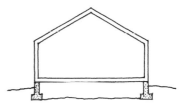

CRAWL SPACES
Crawl spaces are found in all climates but predominate in temperate regions. In this system, the insulated wooden ground floor is supported above grade on a foundation wall made of concrete or concrete block. The resulting crawl space introduces an accessible zone for ductwork, plumbing and other utilities, and allows for simple remodeling.

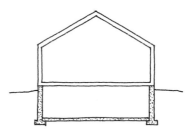

BASEMENTS
Basements are the dominant foundation system in the coldest parts of the country, where frost lines mandate deep footings in any case. Like crawl spaces, basements are accessible, and in addition they provide a large habitable space. Basement foundation systems are usually constructed of concrete or concrete-block foundation walls. Drainage and waterproofing are particularly critical with basement systems.

CHOOSING A FOUNDATION

Each foundation system has many variations, and it is important to select the one best suited to the climate, the soil type, the site, and the building program. With all foundations, you should investigate the local soil type. Soil types, along with their bearing capacities, are often described in local soil profiles based on information from the U.S. Geological Survey (USGS). If there is any question about matching a foundation system to the soil or to the topography of the site, consult a soil or structural engineer before construction begins. This small investment may save thousands of dollars in future repair bills.

DESIGN CHECKLIST

Because the foundation is so important to the longevity of the building and because it is so difficult to repair, it is wise to be conservative in its design and construction. Make the foundation a little stronger than you think you need to. As a minimum, even if not required by code, it is recommended that you follow this rule-of-thumb checklist:

1. Place the bottom of the footing below the frost line on solid, undisturbed soil that is free of organic material. (Local codes will prescribe frost-line depth.)

2. Use continuous horizontal rebar in the footing and at the top of foundation walls (joint reinforcing may be allowable in concrete-block walls). Tie the footing and wall together with vertical rebar.

3. Use pressure-treated or other decay-resistant wood in contact with concrete. Use a moisture barrier between all concrete and untreated wood.

4. Tie wood members to the foundation with bolts or straps embedded in the foundation. Anchoring requirements in hurricane and severe earthquake zones are shown in the following chapters, but specific requirements should be verified with local codes.

5. Provide adequate drainage around the foundation. Slope backfill away from the building and keep soil 6 in. below all wood.

Many codes and many site conditions require measures beyond these minimum specifications. In addition, there are several other considerations important to a permanent foundation system, and these are discussed in this chapter. They include support of loads that do not fall at the perimeter wall, such as footings for point loads within the structure and at porches and decks; insulation and moisture barriers; waterproofing and drainage; protection against termites, other insects and wood-decaying organisms; and precautions against radon gas.

ABOUT THE DRAWINGS

The sizes of building elements indicated in the drawings in this section are for the purposes of illustrating principles and reminding the designer and the builder to consider their use carefully. These drawings should therefore be used only for reference.

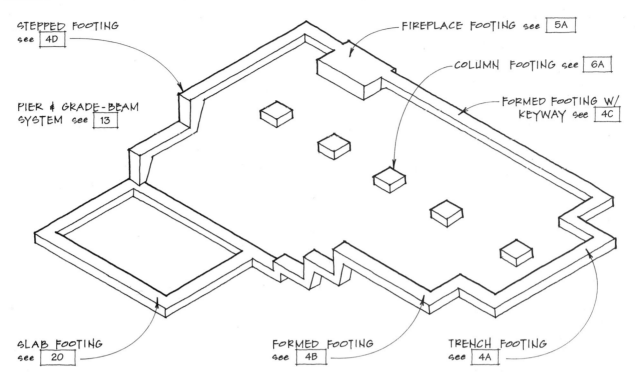

STEPPED FOOTING see 4D

FIREPLACE FOOTING see 5A

COLUMN FOOTING see 6A

PIER & GRADE-BEAM SYSTEM see 13

FORMED FOOTING W/ KEYWAY see 4C

SLAB FOOTING see 20

FORMED FOOTING see 4B

TRENCH FOOTING see 4A

Footings are the part of a foundation that transfers the building's loads—its weight in materials, contents, occupants, and snow, and possibly wind and earthquake loads—directly to the ground. Consequently, the size and type of footing should be matched carefully to the ground upon which it bears.

Soil type—Concrete footings should be placed on firm, undisturbed soil that is free from organic material. Soil types are tested and rated as to their ability to support loads (bearing capacity).

Soil type	Bearing capacity (psf)
Soft clay or silt	do not build
Medium clay or silt	1,500–2,200
Stiff clay or silt	2,200–2,500
Loose sand	1,800–2,000
Dense sand	2,000–3,000
Gravel	2,500–3,000
Bedrock	4,000 and up

Compaction of soil may be required before footings are placed. Consult a soil engineer if the stability of the soil at a building site is unknown.

Reinforcing—Most codes require steel reinforcing rods (called rebar) in footings. Rebar is a sound investment even if it is not required, because it gives tensile strength to the footing, thereby minimizing cracking and differential settling. Rebar is also the most common way to connect the footing to the foundation wall. For rebar rules of thumb, see 5B.

Size—Footing size depends mainly on soil type and the building's weight. The chart below shows footing sizes for soils with bearing capacities of 2,000 pounds per square foot (psf).

No. of stories	H	W
1	6 in.	12 in.
2	7 in.	15 in.
3	8 in.	18 in.

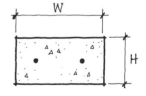

A rule of thumb for estimating the size of standard footings is that a footing should be 8 in. wider than the foundation wall and twice as wide as high.

Frost line—The base of the footing must be below the frost line to prevent the building from heaving as the ground swells during freezing. Frost lines range from 0 ft. to 6 ft. in the continental United States. Check local building departments for frost-line requirements.

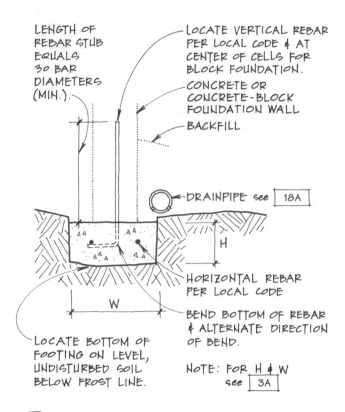

LENGTH OF REBAR STUB EQUALS 30 BAR DIAMETERS (MIN.).

LOCATE VERTICAL REBAR PER LOCAL CODE & AT CENTER OF CELLS FOR BLOCK FOUNDATION.

CONCRETE OR CONCRETE-BLOCK FOUNDATION WALL

BACKFILL

DRAINPIPE see 18A

H

HORIZONTAL REBAR PER LOCAL CODE

BEND BOTTOM OF REBAR & ALTERNATE DIRECTION OF BEND.

W

LOCATE BOTTOM OF FOOTING ON LEVEL, UNDISTURBED SOIL BELOW FROST LINE.

NOTE: FOR H & W see 3A

A TRENCH FOOTING

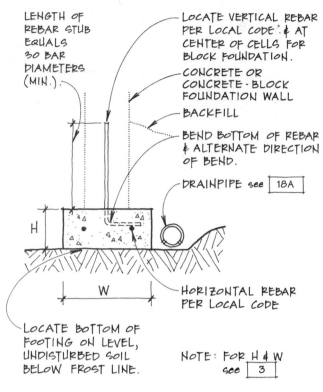

LENGTH OF REBAR STUB EQUALS 30 BAR DIAMETERS (MIN.).

LOCATE VERTICAL REBAR PER LOCAL CODE & AT CENTER OF CELLS FOR BLOCK FOUNDATION.

CONCRETE OR CONCRETE-BLOCK FOUNDATION WALL

BACKFILL

BEND BOTTOM OF REBAR & ALTERNATE DIRECTION OF BEND.

DRAINPIPE see 18A

H

W

HORIZONTAL REBAR PER LOCAL CODE

LOCATE BOTTOM OF FOOTING ON LEVEL, UNDISTURBED SOIL BELOW FROST LINE.

NOTE: FOR H & W see 3

B TYPICAL FORMED FOOTING

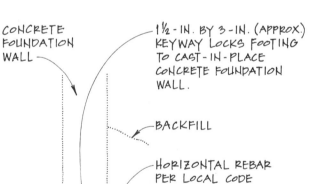

CONCRETE FOUNDATION WALL

1½-IN. BY 3-IN. (APPROX.) KEYWAY LOCKS FOOTING TO CAST-IN-PLACE CONCRETE FOUNDATION WALL.

BACKFILL

HORIZONTAL REBAR PER LOCAL CODE

DRAINPIPE see 18A

NOTE: USE KEYWAY FOOTINGS ONLY WITH CONCRETE FOUNDATION WALLS WHERE LATERAL LOADS ON FOUNDATION ARE NOT SIGNIFICANT. USE FOOTINGS DOWELED WITH VERTICAL REBAR FOR LATERAL LOADS.

LOCATE BOTTOM OF FOOTING ON LEVEL, UNDISTURBED SOIL BELOW FROST LINE.

C FOOTING W/ KEYWAY

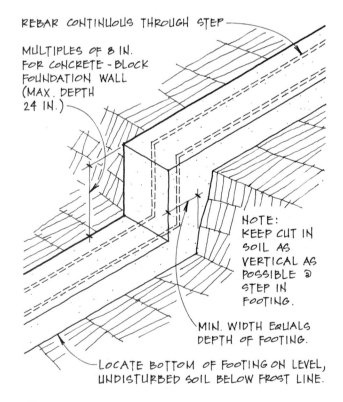

REBAR CONTINUOUS THROUGH STEP

MULTIPLES OF 8 IN. FOR CONCRETE-BLOCK FOUNDATION WALL (MAX. DEPTH 24 IN.)

NOTE: KEEP CUT IN SOIL AS VERTICAL AS POSSIBLE @ STEP IN FOOTING.

MIN. WIDTH EQUALS DEPTH OF FOOTING.

LOCATE BOTTOM OF FOOTING ON LEVEL, UNDISTURBED SOIL BELOW FROST LINE.

D STEPPED FOOTING

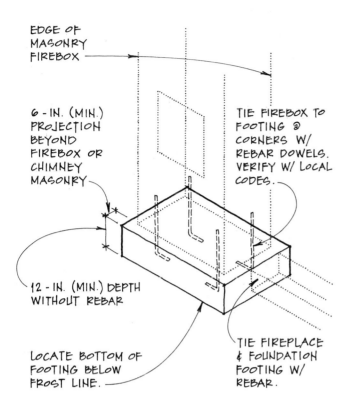

EDGE OF MASONRY FIREBOX

6 - IN. (MIN.) PROJECTION BEYOND FIREBOX OR CHIMNEY MASONRY

TIE FIREBOX TO FOOTING @ CORNERS W/ REBAR DOWELS. VERIFY W/ LOCAL CODES.

12 - IN. (MIN.) DEPTH WITHOUT REBAR

LOCATE BOTTOM OF FOOTING BELOW FROST LINE.

TIE FIREPLACE & FOUNDATION FOOTING W/ REBAR.

$\overset{\displaystyle A}{\bigcirc}$ **FIREPLACE FOOTING**

Code requirements for rebar use may vary, but a few rules of thumb can be helpful guidelines. Verify with local codes first.

Sizes—Rebar is sized by diameter in ⅛-in. increments: #3 rebar is ⅜-in. dia., #4 is ½-in. dia., #5 is ⅝-in. dia., etc. The most common sizes for wood-frame construction foundations are #3, #4, and #5.

Overlapping—Rebar is manufactured in 20-ft. lengths. When rebar must be spliced to make it continuous or joined at corners, the length of the lap should equal 30 bar diameters, as shown below.

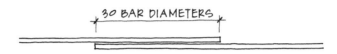

30 BAR DIAMETERS

Clearance—The minimum clearance between rebar and the surface of the concrete is 3 in. for footings, 2 in. for formed concrete exposed to backfill or weather, and ¾ in. for formed concrete protected from the weather.

$\overset{\displaystyle B}{\bigcirc}$ **REBAR RULES OF THUMB**

Column footings (also called pier pads) support columns in crawl spaces and under porches and decks. Place all footings on unfrozen, undisturbed soil free of organic material. The bottom of the footing must be located below the frost line unless it is within a crawl space. Columns may need to be anchored to column footings to prevent uplift caused by wind or earthquake forces (see 6B).

Typical sizes are 12 in. to 14 in. for square footings or 16-in. to 18-in. diameter for round footings.

Extreme loads may require oversize footings. The vertical load divided by the soil bearing capacity equals the area of footing, e.g.,

$$6,000 \text{ lb.} \div 2,000 \text{ psf} = 3 \text{ sq. ft.}$$

To prevent moisture in the footing from damaging the column, use a pressure-treated wood column or place a 30-lb. felt moisture barrier between an untreated wood column and a concrete footing, or use steel connectors where required (see 6B).

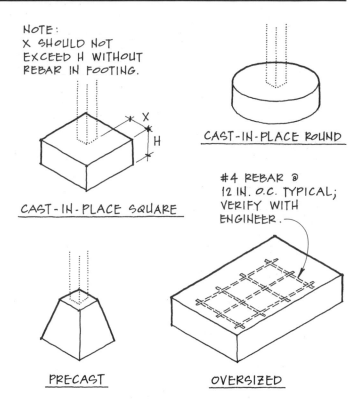

NOTE:
X SHOULD NOT EXCEED H WITHOUT REBAR IN FOOTING.

CAST-IN-PLACE SQUARE

CAST-IN-PLACE ROUND

#4 REBAR @ 12 IN. O.C. TYPICAL; VERIFY WITH ENGINEER.

PRECAST

OVERSIZED

(A) **COLUMN FOOTINGS**

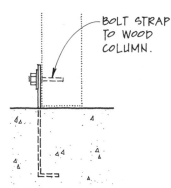

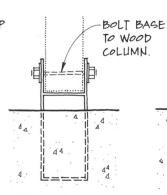

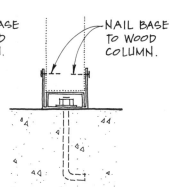

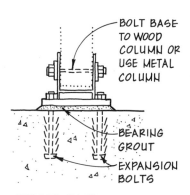

BOLT STRAP TO WOOD COLUMN.

BOLT BASE TO WOOD COLUMN.

NAIL BASE TO WOOD COLUMN.

BOLT BASE TO WOOD COLUMN OR USE METAL COLUMN

BEARING GROUT

EXPANSION BOLTS

SINGLE STRAP
GALVANIZED STEEL STRAP IS OFTEN USED IN CRAWL SPACES OR UNDER PORCHES.

NOTE:
USE P.T. WOOD COLUMN OR PLACE 30-LB. FELT MOISTURE BARRIER BETWEEN UNTREATED POST & CONCRETE.

WET BASE
THIS GALVANIZED STEEL BASE PROVIDES THE CLEANEST CONNECTION. IT MUST BE PRECISELY LOCATED IN WET CONCRETE.

ADJUSTABLE BASE
MULTIPLE-PIECE GALVANIZED STEEL ASSEMBLY ALLOWS FOR SOME LATERAL ADJUSTMENT BEFORE NUT IS TIGHTENED. BASE ELEVATES WOOD COLUMN ABOVE CONCRETE FOOTING.

DRILLED BASE
EXPANSION BOLTS ARE DRILLED INTO FOOTING OR SLAB AFTER CONCRETE IS FINISHED, ALLOWING FOR PRECISE LOCATION OF COLUMN

(B) **COLUMN BASE CONNECTORS**
IN COLUMN FOOTING OR SLAB

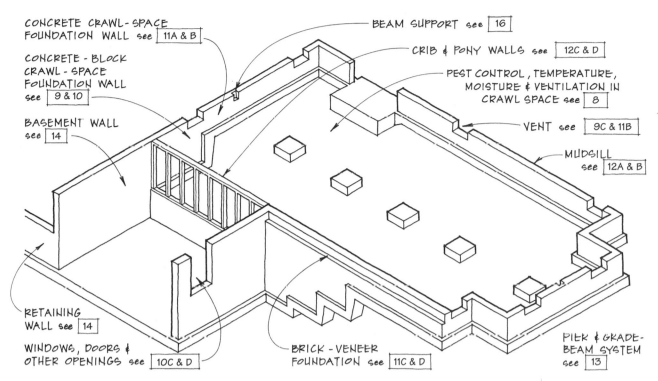

CONCRETE CRAWL-SPACE FOUNDATION WALL see 11A & B

CONCRETE-BLOCK CRAWL-SPACE FOUNDATION WALL see 9 & 10

BASEMENT WALL see 14

RETAINING WALL see 14

WINDOWS, DOORS & OTHER OPENINGS see 10C & D

BRICK-VENEER FOUNDATION see 11C & D

BEAM SUPPORT see 16

CRIB & PONY WALLS see 12C & D

PEST CONTROL, TEMPERATURE, MOISTURE & VENTILATION IN CRAWL SPACE see 8

VENT see 9C & 11B

MUDSILL see 12A & B

PIER & GRADE-BEAM SYSTEM see 13

Foundation walls act integrally with the footings to support the building. They also raise the building above the ground. The primary decision to make about foundation walls is what material to make them of. There are several choices:

Concrete block—Also known as concrete masonry unit or CMU construction, concrete block is the most common system for foundation walls. Its primary advantage is that it needs no formwork, making it appropriate in any situation, but especially where the foundation is complex. Concrete masonry will be used most efficiently if the foundation is planned in 8-in. increments, based on the dimensions of standard concrete blocks (8 in. by 8 in. by 16 in.).

Cast concrete—Concrete can be formed into almost any shape, but formwork is expensive. The most economical use of cast concrete, therefore, is where the formwork is simple or where the formwork can be used several times. Cast-in-place concrete is used for forming pier and grade-beam systems, which are especially appropriate for steep sites or expansive soils (see 13).

Reinforcing—Some local codes do not require reinforcing of foundation walls. Codes in severe earthquake zones are at the other extreme. As a prudent minimum, all foundation walls should be tied to the footing with vertical rebar placed at the corners, adjacent to all major openings, and at regular intervals along the wall. There should be at least one continuous horizontal bar at the top of the wall. Joint reinforcing may be an adequate substitute (see 10B).

Width—The width of the foundation wall depends on the number of stories it supports and on the depth of the backfill, which exerts a lateral force on the wall. With minimum backfill (2 ft. or less), the width of the wall can be determined from the chart below.

No. of stories	Foundation width
1	6 in.
2	8 in.
3	10 in.

The design of basement walls and foundation walls retaining more than 2 ft. of backfill should be verified by an engineer or an architect.

The minimum height of a foundation wall should allow for the adequate clearance of beams and joists from the crawl-space floor. A 12-in. to 18-in. clearance usually requires 12-in. to 24-in. foundation walls, depending on the type of floor system.

Pests—Rodents and other large burrowing pests can be kept out of crawl spaces by means of a "rat slab," which is a 1-in. thick layer of concrete poured over the ground in a crawl space. A concrete-rated moisture barrier should be placed below this slab (see 20). Termites and other insect pests are most effectively controlled by chemical treatment of the soil before construction begins.

Temperature—Heated crawl spaces must be insulated at the foundation wall. The insulation can be installed using the same details as for a basement wall (see 15C).

If the foundation wall is insulated on the inside, most codes require that the insulation be protected if it is a flammable type (such as polystyrene), or that it be a nonflammable type (such as rigid fiberglass or mineral wool).

Moisture—Even with the best drainage, the soil under crawl spaces always carries some ground moisture, which will tend to migrate up to the crawl space in the form of vapor. This vapor can be controlled with a barrier laid directly on the ground, which must first be cleared of all organic debris. In vented, unheated crawl spaces, the circulation of air through the vents will remove any excess moisture. In heated crawl spaces, the heated air that circulates through the building will absorb the excess moisture.

Crawl-space vapor barriers should be 6-mil (min.) black polyethylene. The dark plastic retards plant growth by preventing daylight from reaching the soil.

Ventilation—In an unheated crawl space, ventilation minimizes the buildup of excess moisture under the structure. In some regions, ventilation is also required to remove radon gas.

The net area of venting is related to the under-floor area and to the climatic and groundwater conditions. Most codes require that net vent area equals $\frac{1}{150}$ of the under-floor area with a reduction to $\frac{1}{1500}$ if a vapor barrier covers the ground in the crawl space. Screened vents should be rated for net venting area.

Vents should supply cross-ventilation to all areas of the crawl space. Locating vents near corners and on opposite sides of the crawl space is most effective.

Access doors can provide a large area of ventilation. Wells allow vents to be placed below finished grade.

As shown in the drawing below, screened vents are available for installing in masonry, cast concrete, and wood. They are available in metal or plastic, and some have operable doors for closing off the crawl space temporarily. Operable doors should be closed only during extreme weather conditions. Closing the vents for an entire season will increase moisture in the crawl space and can significantly increase the concentration of radon gas.

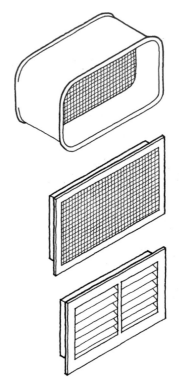

AN 8-IN. OR 10-IN. DEEP SCREENED VENT MADE TO BE CAST IN PLACE IN CONCRETE BLOCK OR CONCRETE FOUNDATION WALL

AN 8-IN. × 16-IN. SCREENED VENT THAT FITS IN PLACE OF ONE CONCRETE BLOCK

ONE OF VARIOUS PLASTIC OR METAL VENTS MADE TO VENT THROUGH THE RIM JOIST AND FASTEN TO WOOD SIDING. CARE MUST BE TAKEN TO INSTALL PROPER FLASHING.

Recent research has found that foundation vents may be eliminated altogether when accompanied by the complete sealing of the crawl-space floor and the foundation walls. In fact, this may be the best way to keep moisture levels low and eliminate the insidious damage caused by fungus and other organisms dependent on moisture. Reflecting this trend, the American Society of Heating, Refrigerating and Air-Conditioning Engineers (ASHRAE) has eliminated crawl-space ventilation as a requirement from its 1997 *Handbook of Fundamentals*. Some states have also made moves in this direction.

A   CRAWL-SPACE CONTROLS

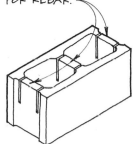

KNOCK OUT WEBS OF BOND BLOCKS TO FORM CHANNEL FOR REBAR.

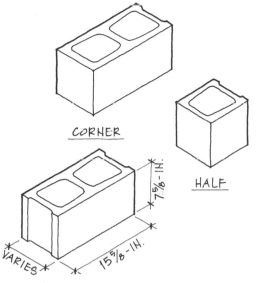

CORNER

HALF

7⅞-IN.

VARIES

15⅝-IN.

JAMB

JAMB BLOCKS ARE AVAILABLE IN HALF (SHOWN) AND STRETCHER SIZES. IN ONE SIDE A SLOT LOCKS BASEMENT WINDOWS IN PLACE.

BOND OR LINTEL

CUT HALF, CORNER AND OTHER BLOCKS ON SITE TO CONTINUE BOND BEAMS TO THE END OF WALLS AND AROUND CORNERS.

STRETCHER OR REGULAR

STANDARD WIDTHS ARE 3⅝-IN., 5⅝-IN., 7⅝-IN., 9⅝-IN. AND 11⅝-IN. ALL DIMENSIONS ARE ACTUAL.

NOTE:
ALMOST ANY SIZE OR SHAPE OF MASONRY WALL CAN BE BUILT WITH BASIC BLOCK TYPES. CONSULT NCMA FOR CONSTRUCTION TECHNIQUES AND FOR SPECIAL BLOCKS WITH SPECIAL EDGE CONDITIONS, TEXTURES, COLORS AND SIZES.

(A) CONCRETE - BLOCK TYPES

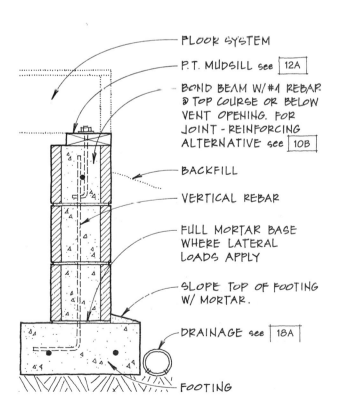

- FLOOR SYSTEM
- P.T. MUDSILL see [12A]
- BOND BEAM W/ #4 REBAR @ TOP COURSE OR BELOW VENT OPENING. FOR JOINT - REINFORCING ALTERNATIVE see [10B]
- BACKFILL
- VERTICAL REBAR
- FULL MORTAR BASE WHERE LATERAL LOADS APPLY
- SLOPE TOP OF FOOTING W/ MORTAR.
- DRAINAGE see [18A]
- FOOTING

(B) CRAWL - SPACE FOUNDATION WALL
CONCRETE BLOCK

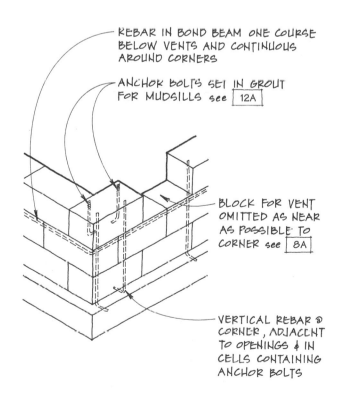

- REBAR IN BOND BEAM ONE COURSE BELOW VENTS AND CONTINUOUS AROUND CORNERS
- ANCHOR BOLTS SET IN GROUT FOR MUDSILLS see [12A]
- BLOCK FOR VENT OMITTED AS NEAR AS POSSIBLE TO CORNER see [8A]
- VERTICAL REBAR @ CORNER, ADJACENT TO OPENINGS & IN CELLS CONTAINING ANCHOR BOLTS

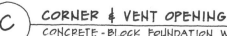

(C) CORNER & VENT OPENING
CONCRETE-BLOCK FOUNDATION WALL

NOTE:
HORIZONTAL REBAR SHOULD BE CONTINUOUS IN A BOND BEAM AT THE TOP COURSE, OR AT THE SECOND COURSE IF FOUNDATION VENTS ARE LOCATED IN THE TOP COURSE. HORIZONTAL REBAR MAY ALSO BE LOCATED IN INTERMEDIATE BOND BEAMS IF THE HEIGHT, WIDTH & FUNCTION OF THE WALL REQUIRE IT.

NOTE:
TO REINFORCE A JOINT, A WELDED HEAVY-WIRE TRUSS MAY BE SUBSTITUTED FOR HORIZONTAL REBAR IN MANY CASES. IT IS EMBEDDED IN THE MORTAR JOINTS BETWEEN COURSES OF MASONRY.

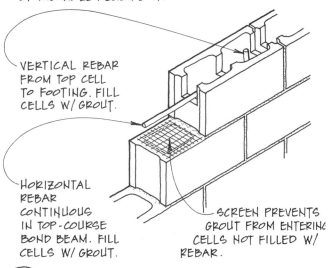

VERTICAL REBAR FROM TOP CELL TO FOOTING. FILL CELLS W/ GROUT.

HORIZONTAL REBAR CONTINUOUS IN TOP-COURSE BOND BEAM. FILL CELLS W/ GROUT.

SCREEN PREVENTS GROUT FROM ENTERING CELLS NOT FILLED W/ REBAR.

(A) CONCRETE-BLOCK FOUNDATION
REBAR PLACEMENT

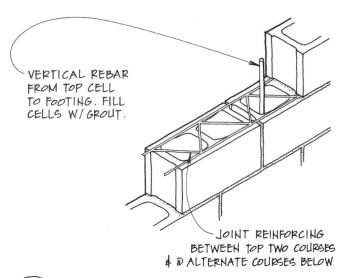

VERTICAL REBAR FROM TOP CELL TO FOOTING. FILL CELLS W/ GROUT.

JOINT REINFORCING BETWEEN TOP TWO COURSES & @ ALTERNATE COURSES BELOW

(B) CONCRETE-BLOCK FOUNDATION
JOINT-REINFORCING ALTERNATIVE

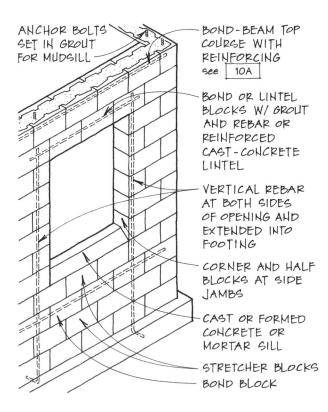

ANCHOR BOLTS SET IN GROUT FOR MUDSILL

BOND-BEAM TOP COURSE WITH REINFORCING see 10A

BOND OR LINTEL BLOCKS W/ GROUT AND REBAR OR REINFORCED CAST-CONCRETE LINTEL

VERTICAL REBAR AT BOTH SIDES OF OPENING AND EXTENDED INTO FOOTING

CORNER AND HALF BLOCKS AT SIDE JAMBS

CAST OR FORMED CONCRETE OR MORTAR SILL

STRETCHER BLOCKS

BOND BLOCK

(C) CONCRETE-BLOCK BASEMENT
OPENING WITHIN WALL

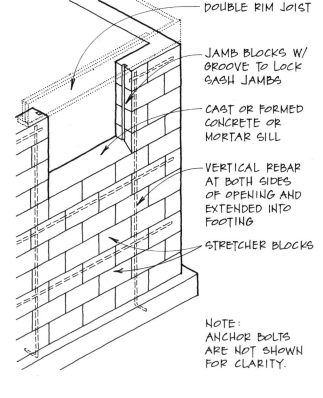

DOUBLE RIM JOIST

JAMB BLOCKS W/ GROOVE TO LOCK SASH JAMBS

CAST OR FORMED CONCRETE OR MORTAR SILL

VERTICAL REBAR AT BOTH SIDES OF OPENING AND EXTENDED INTO FOOTING

STRETCHER BLOCKS

NOTE:
ANCHOR BOLTS ARE NOT SHOWN FOR CLARITY.

(D) CONCRETE-BLOCK BASEMENT
OPENING @ TOP OF WALL

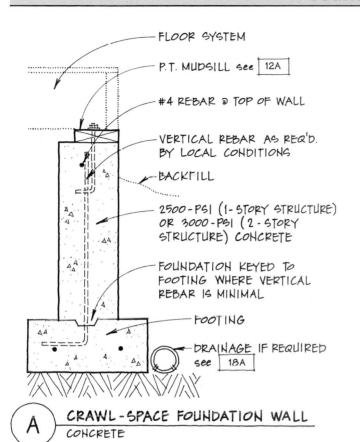

- FLOOR SYSTEM
- P.T. MUDSILL see 12A
- #4 REBAR @ TOP OF WALL
- VERTICAL REBAR AS REQ'D. BY LOCAL CONDITIONS
- BACKFILL
- 2500-PSI (1-STORY STRUCTURE) OR 3000-PSI (2-STORY STRUCTURE) CONCRETE
- FOUNDATION KEYED TO FOOTING WHERE VERTICAL REBAR IS MINIMAL
- FOOTING
- DRAINAGE IF REQUIRED see 18A

A CRAWL-SPACE FOUNDATION WALL
CONCRETE

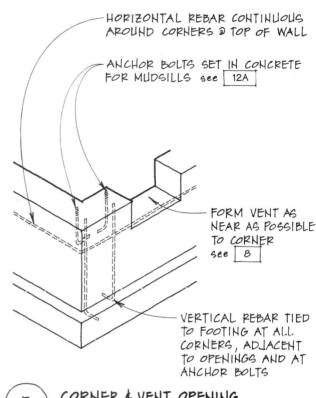

- HORIZONTAL REBAR CONTINUOUS AROUND CORNERS @ TOP OF WALL
- ANCHOR BOLTS SET IN CONCRETE FOR MUDSILLS see 12A
- FORM VENT AS NEAR AS POSSIBLE TO CORNER see 8
- VERTICAL REBAR TIED TO FOOTING AT ALL CORNERS, ADJACENT TO OPENINGS AND AT ANCHOR BOLTS

B CORNER & VENT OPENING
CONCRETE FOUNDATION WALL

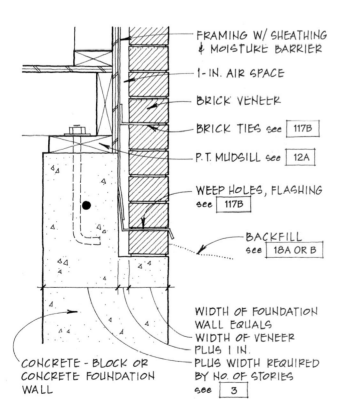

- FRAMING W/ SHEATHING & MOISTURE BARRIER
- 1-IN. AIR SPACE
- BRICK VENEER
- BRICK TIES see 117B
- P.T. MUDSILL see 12A
- WEEP HOLES, FLASHING see 117B
- BACKFILL see 18A OR B
- WIDTH OF FOUNDATION WALL EQUALS WIDTH OF VENEER PLUS 1 IN. PLUS WIDTH REQUIRED BY NO. OF STORIES see 3

CONCRETE-BLOCK OR CONCRETE FOUNDATION WALL

C BRICK-VENEER FOUNDATION
BRICK BELOW MUDSILL

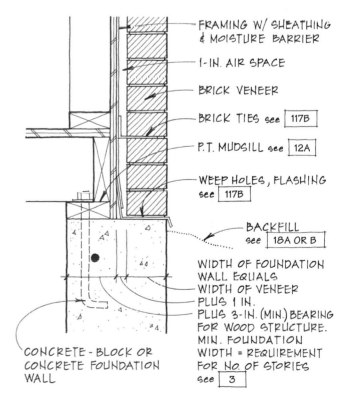

- FRAMING W/ SHEATHING & MOISTURE BARRIER
- 1-IN. AIR SPACE
- BRICK VENEER
- BRICK TIES see 117B
- P.T. MUDSILL see 12A
- WEEP HOLES, FLASHING see 117B
- BACKFILL see 18A OR B
- WIDTH OF FOUNDATION WALL EQUALS WIDTH OF VENEER PLUS 1 IN. PLUS 3-IN. (MIN.) BEARING FOR WOOD STRUCTURE. MIN. FOUNDATION WIDTH = REQUIREMENT FOR NO. OF STORIES see 3

CONCRETE-BLOCK OR CONCRETE FOUNDATION WALL

D BRICK-VENEER FOUNDATION
BRICK LEVEL W/ MUDSILL

½-IN. STEEL ANCHOR BOLT @ 4 FT. OR 6 FT. O.C. (MAX.) & 12-IN. (MAX.) FROM END OF EACH PIECE OF MUDSILL. VERIFY W/ LOCAL CODES.

½-IN. STEEL NUT W/ STEEL WASHER

2×4 OR 2×6 P.T. WOOD MUDSILL

SILL GASKET OF CAULK OR FIBERGLASS @ BASEMENTS OR OTHER LIVING SPACE

CONTINUOUS TERMITE SHIELD IN TERMITE REGIONS

CONCRETE OR CONCRETE-BLOCK FOUNDATION WALL

REBAR

7-IN. MIN. DEPTH OF ANCHOR BOLT INTO FOUNDATION WALL

NOTE: SOME CODES REQUIRE LONGER BOLTS FOR MASONRY WALLS.

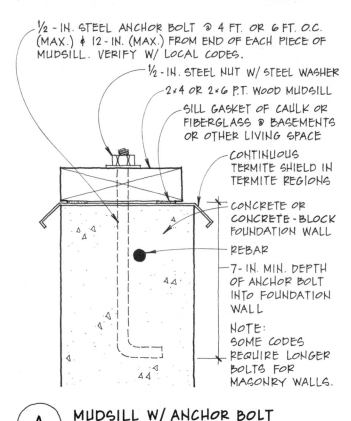

A   MUDSILL W/ ANCHOR BOLT

BEND DOUBLE-STRAP ANCHOR AROUND MUDSILL & NAIL @ SIDE & TOP, OR NAIL ONE STRAP TO MUDSILL & OTHER TO FACE OF STUD.

2×4 OR 2×6 P.T. WOOD MUDSILL

SILL GASKET OF CAULK OR FIBERGLASS AT BASEMENTS OR OTHER LIVING SPACE

PLACE SLAB ANCHORS INTO FRESH CONCRETE OR NAIL TO FORM BEFORE PLACING CONCRETE.

SLAB W/ TURNED-DOWN FOOTING see │22│

NOTE: VERIFY ACCEPTABILITY OF SLAB ANCHOR W/ LOCAL BUILDING CODE. THE SLAB ANCHOR ALLOWS THE ABILITY TO FINISH SLAB TO THE EDGE BUT IT IS DIFFICULT TO USE W/ TERMITE SHIELD.

B   MUDSILL W/ SLAB ANCHOR

A CRIB WALL IS AN ALTERNATIVE TO COLUMNS & A BEAM SUPPORT FOR JOISTS IN A CRAWL SPACE. IT ALLOWS MORE CLEARANCE FOR DUCTS AND EQUIPMENT & AVOIDS THE POTENTIAL PROBLEM OF CROSS-GRAIN SHRINKAGE IN BEAMS.

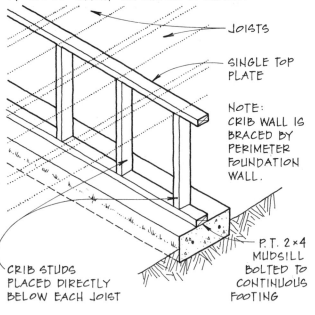

JOISTS

SINGLE TOP PLATE

NOTE: CRIB WALL IS BRACED BY PERIMETER FOUNDATION WALL.

P.T. 2×4 MUDSILL BOLTED TO CONTINUOUS FOOTING

CRIB STUDS PLACED DIRECTLY BELOW EACH JOIST

C   CRIB WALL

A PONY WALL IS USEFUL IN A STEPPED FOUNDATION WALL OR IN A SLOPING PIER & GRADE-BEAM FOUNDATION. THE PONY WALL PROVIDES A LEVEL SURFACE FOR CONSTRUCTION OF THE FIRST FLOOR.

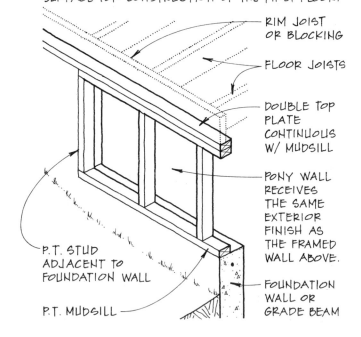

RIM JOIST OR BLOCKING

FLOOR JOISTS

DOUBLE TOP PLATE CONTINUOUS W/ MUDSILL

PONY WALL RECEIVES THE SAME EXTERIOR FINISH AS THE FRAMED WALL ABOVE.

P.T. STUD ADJACENT TO FOUNDATION WALL

FOUNDATION WALL OR GRADE BEAM

P.T. MUDSILL

D   PONY WALL

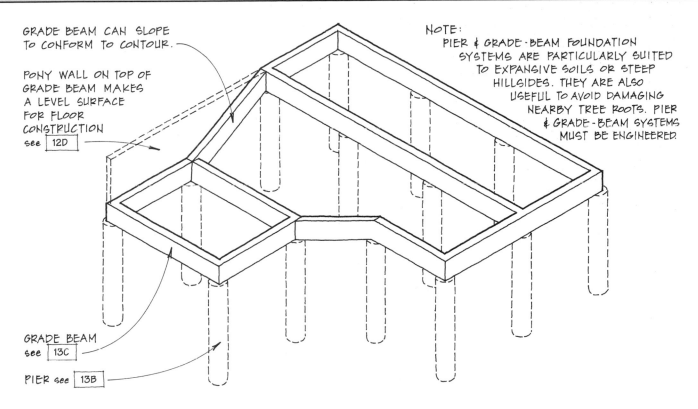

GRADE BEAM CAN SLOPE TO CONFORM TO CONTOUR.

PONY WALL ON TOP OF GRADE BEAM MAKES A LEVEL SURFACE FOR FLOOR CONSTRUCTION see 12D

NOTE:
PIER & GRADE-BEAM FOUNDATION SYSTEMS ARE PARTICULARLY SUITED TO EXPANSIVE SOILS OR STEEP HILLSIDES. THEY ARE ALSO USEFUL TO AVOID DAMAGING NEARBY TREE ROOTS. PIER & GRADE-BEAM SYSTEMS MUST BE ENGINEERED.

GRADE BEAM see 13C

PIER see 13B

 A   PIER & GRADE-BEAM SYSTEMS

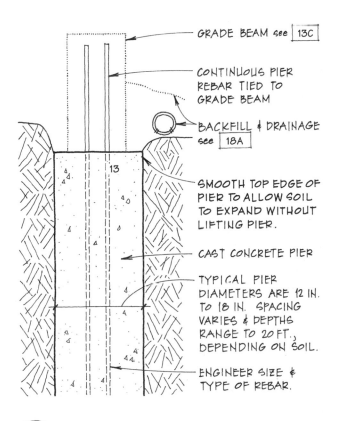

GRADE BEAM see 13C

CONTINUOUS PIER REBAR TIED TO GRADE BEAM

BACKFILL & DRAINAGE see 18A

SMOOTH TOP EDGE OF PIER TO ALLOW SOIL TO EXPAND WITHOUT LIFTING PIER.

CAST CONCRETE PIER

TYPICAL PIER DIAMETERS ARE 12 IN. TO 18 IN. SPACING VARIES & DEPTHS RANGE TO 20 FT., DEPENDING ON SOIL.

ENGINEER SIZE & TYPE OF REBAR.

B   PIERS FOR GRADE BEAM

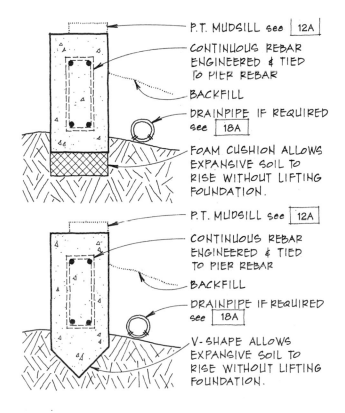

P.T. MUDSILL see 12A

CONTINUOUS REBAR ENGINEERED & TIED TO PIER REBAR

BACKFILL

DRAINPIPE IF REQUIRED see 18A

FOAM CUSHION ALLOWS EXPANSIVE SOIL TO RISE WITHOUT LIFTING FOUNDATION.

P.T. MUDSILL see 12A

CONTINUOUS REBAR ENGINEERED & TIED TO PIER REBAR

BACKFILL

DRAINPIPE IF REQUIRED see 18A

V-SHAPE ALLOWS EXPANSIVE SOIL TO RISE WITHOUT LIFTING FOUNDATION.

 **C**   GRADE BEAMS
TWO TYPES FOR EXPANSIVE SOILS

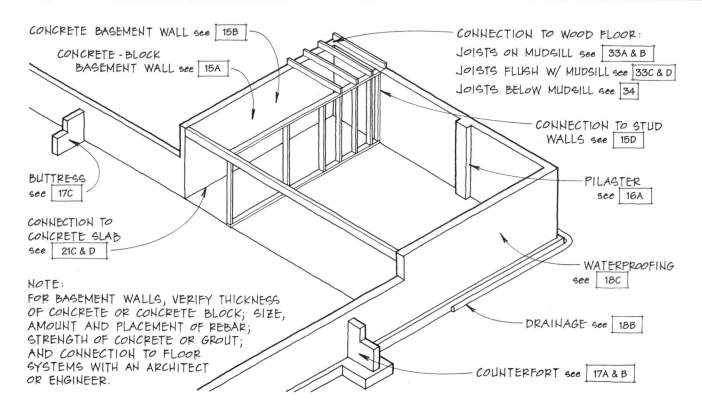

CONCRETE BASEMENT WALL see [15B]

CONCRETE - BLOCK BASEMENT WALL see [15A]

CONNECTION TO WOOD FLOOR:
JOISTS ON MUDSILL see [33A & B]
JOISTS FLUSH W/ MUDSILL see [33C & D]
JOISTS BELOW MUDSILL see [34]

CONNECTION TO STUD WALLS see [15D]

BUTTRESS see [17C]

CONNECTION TO CONCRETE SLAB see [21C & D]

PILASTER see [16A]

WATERPROOFING see [18C]

DRAINAGE see [18B]

COUNTERFORT see [17A & B]

NOTE:
FOR BASEMENT WALLS, VERIFY THICKNESS OF CONCRETE OR CONCRETE BLOCK; SIZE, AMOUNT AND PLACEMENT OF REBAR; STRENGTH OF CONCRETE OR GROUT; AND CONNECTION TO FLOOR SYSTEMS WITH AN ARCHITECT OR ENGINEER.

Basement walls—Basement walls are one story in height (7 ft. to 9 ft.) and are generally backfilled to at least 4 ft. A basement wall must resist the lateral pressure of the backfill at both the top and bottom of the wall. Basement walls are therefore usually designed as if they were a beam spanning in the vertical direction, with the rebar located at the inside (tension) side of the wall. Because the floor must resist the lateral force of the backfill against the basement wall, the connection between the wood floor and the basement wall is especially important (see 33–34). When basement wall backfill exceeds 4 ft. in height, an engineer should be consulted about this connection. The floor system should always be in place before backfilling. Basement walls can be strengthened with pilasters (see 16), which allow the wall to be designed to span between pilasters in the horizontal (as well as the vertical) direction. Pilasters are also useful as beam supports.

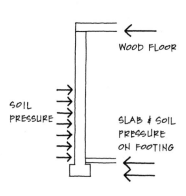

WOOD FLOOR

SOIL PRESSURE

SLAB & SOIL PRESSURE ON FOOTING

Retaining walls—Retaining walls resist lateral loads from the bottom only. They rely on friction at the base of the footing and soil pressure at the outside

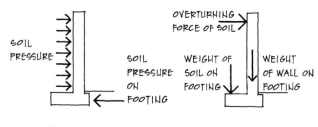

SOIL PRESSURE

OVERTURNING FORCE OF SOIL

SOIL PRESSURE ON FOOTING

WEIGHT OF SOIL ON FOOTING

WEIGHT OF WALL ON FOOTING

FOOTING

SLIDING FORCES   OVERTURNING FORCES

face of the footing to resist sliding. The weight of the wall and the weight of soil on the footing resist overturning.

Buttresses and counterforts strengthen retaining walls in much the same way that pilasters strengthen basement walls (see 17). Buttresses help support retaining walls from the downhill side, and counterforts from the uphill side.

Technically, freestanding retaining walls are not a part of the building, but they are included here because they are typical extensions of the building components (foundation and basement walls) into the landscape.

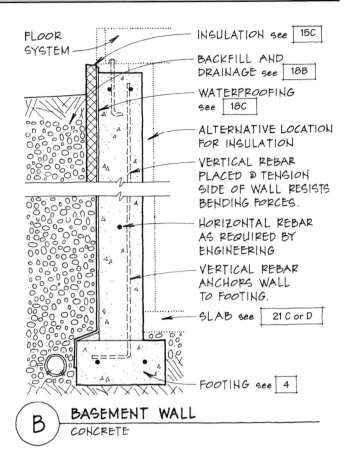

FLOOR SYSTEM
INSULATION see 15C
BACKFILL AND DRAINAGE see 18B
WATERPROOFING see 18C
ALTERNATIVE LOCATION FOR INSULATION
VERTICAL REBAR PLACED @ TENSION SIDE OF WALL RESISTS BENDING FORCES.
BOND BEAMS AS REQUIRED BY ENGINEERING
VERTICAL REBAR ANCHORS WALL TO FOOTING.
SLAB see 21C OR D
FULL MORTAR JOINT ON ROUGHENED FOOTING
FOOTING see 4

A BASEMENT WALL
CONCRETE BLOCK

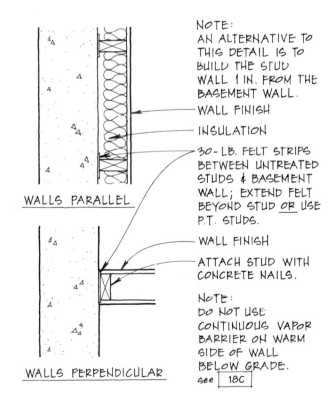

FLOOR SYSTEM
INSULATION see 15C
BACKFILL AND DRAINAGE see 18B
WATERPROOFING see 18C
ALTERNATIVE LOCATION FOR INSULATION
VERTICAL REBAR PLACED @ TENSION SIDE OF WALL RESISTS BENDING FORCES.
HORIZONTAL REBAR AS REQUIRED BY ENGINEERING
VERTICAL REBAR ANCHORS WALL TO FOOTING.
SLAB see 21 C or D
FOOTING see 4

B BASEMENT WALL
CONCRETE

Heated basements must be insulated at their perimeter walls. The amount of insulation required depends on the climate. There are two ways to insulate basement walls—from the exterior or from the interior.

Exterior—Exterior insulation should be a closed-cell rigid insulation (extruded polystyrene or polyisocyanurate) that will not absorb moisture. This insulation, available in 2-ft. or 4-ft. by 8-ft. sheets, is attached directly to the basement wall with adhesive or mechanical fasteners. It may be applied either under or over the waterproofing, depending on the type.

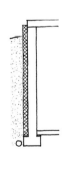

Interior—Interior insulation may be either rigid or batt type. Petroleum-based rigid types must be covered for fire protection when used in an interior location. Other rigid insulation, such as rigid mineral fiber, need not be fire-protected. Building a stud wall with batt insulation has the advantage of providing a nailing surface for interior finishes.

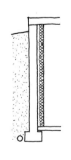

C BASEMENT INSULATION

WALLS PARALLEL

WALLS PERPENDICULAR

NOTE:
AN ALTERNATIVE TO THIS DETAIL IS TO BUILD THE STUD WALL 1 IN. FROM THE BASEMENT WALL.

WALL FINISH
INSULATION
30-LB. FELT STRIPS BETWEEN UNTREATED STUDS & BASEMENT WALL; EXTEND FELT BEYOND STUD OR USE P.T. STUDS.

WALL FINISH
ATTACH STUD WITH CONCRETE NAILS.

NOTE:
DO NOT USE CONTINUOUS VAPOR BARRIER ON WARM SIDE OF WALL BELOW GRADE.
see 18C

D BASEMENT WALL / STUD WALL
PLAN VIEWS

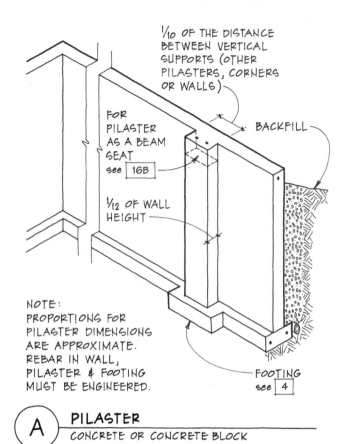

1/10 OF THE DISTANCE BETWEEN VERTICAL SUPPORTS (OTHER PILASTERS, CORNERS OR WALLS)

FOR PILASTER AS A BEAM SEAT see 16B

BACKFILL

1/12 OF WALL HEIGHT

NOTE: PROPORTIONS FOR PILASTER DIMENSIONS ARE APPROXIMATE. REBAR IN WALL, PILASTER & FOOTING MUST BE ENGINEERED.

FOOTING see 4

A PILASTER
CONCRETE OR CONCRETE BLOCK

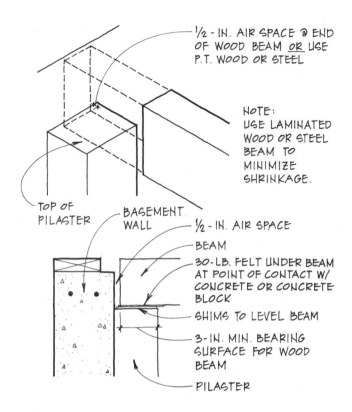

1/2 - IN. AIR SPACE @ END OF WOOD BEAM OR USE P.T. WOOD OR STEEL

NOTE: USE LAMINATED WOOD OR STEEL BEAM TO MINIMIZE SHRINKAGE.

TOP OF PILASTER

BASEMENT WALL

1/2 - IN. AIR SPACE

BEAM

30-LB. FELT UNDER BEAM AT POINT OF CONTACT W/ CONCRETE OR CONCRETE BLOCK

SHIMS TO LEVEL BEAM

3-IN. MIN. BEARING SURFACE FOR WOOD BEAM

PILASTER

B PILASTER BEAM SEAT
CONCRETE OR CONCRETE BLOCK

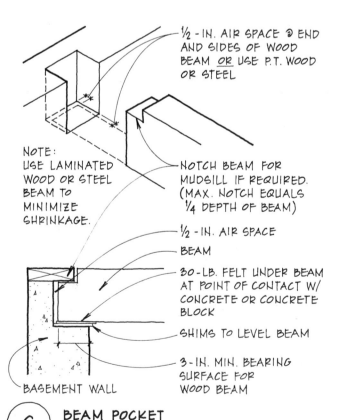

1/2 - IN. AIR SPACE @ END AND SIDES OF WOOD BEAM OR USE P.T. WOOD OR STEEL

NOTE: USE LAMINATED WOOD OR STEEL BEAM TO MINIMIZE SHRINKAGE.

NOTCH BEAM FOR MUDSILL IF REQUIRED. (MAX. NOTCH EQUALS 1/4 DEPTH OF BEAM)

1/2 - IN. AIR SPACE

BEAM

30-LB. FELT UNDER BEAM AT POINT OF CONTACT W/ CONCRETE OR CONCRETE BLOCK

SHIMS TO LEVEL BEAM

3-IN. MIN. BEARING SURFACE FOR WOOD BEAM

BASEMENT WALL

C BEAM POCKET
CONCRETE OR CONCRETE BLOCK

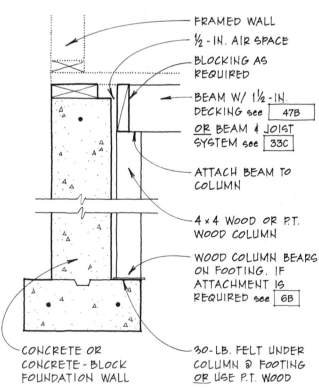

FRAMED WALL

1/2 - IN. AIR SPACE

BLOCKING AS REQUIRED

BEAM W/ 1 1/2 - IN. DECKING see 47B

OR BEAM & JOIST SYSTEM see 33C

ATTACH BEAM TO COLUMN

4 x 4 WOOD OR P.T. WOOD COLUMN

WOOD COLUMN BEARS ON FOOTING. IF ATTACHMENT IS REQUIRED see 6B

CONCRETE OR CONCRETE-BLOCK FOUNDATION WALL

30-LB. FELT UNDER COLUMN @ FOOTING OR USE P.T. WOOD

D WOOD-COLUMN BEAM SUPPORT
BASEMENT OR CRAWL - SPACE WALL

NOTE:
COUNTERFORT MUST BE PROFESSIONALLY
ENGINEERED. REINFORCEMENT IS REQUIRED
FOR TENSION AND SHEAR.

COUNTERFORT REBAR TIED TO
RETAINING WALL & FOOTING

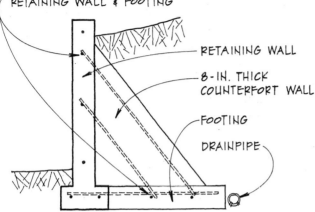

RETAINING WALL

8-IN. THICK
COUNTERFORT WALL

FOOTING

DRAINPIPE

NOTE:
FOOTING IS LARGE AND REINFORCED BECAUSE
COUNTERFORT USES ITS OWN WEIGHT PLUS
WEIGHT OF SOIL ABOVE FOOTING TO RESIST
THE HORIZONTAL FORCE ON THE WALL.

(A) CONCRETE COUNTERFORT

NOTE:
COUNTERFORT MUST BE PROFESSIONALLY
ENGINEERED.

COUNTERFORT REBAR TIED
TO RETAINING WALL
& FOOTING

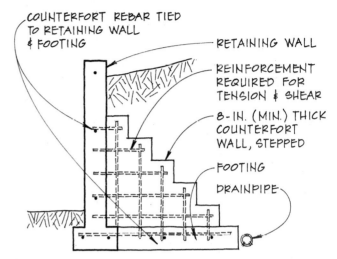

RETAINING WALL

REINFORCEMENT
REQUIRED FOR
TENSION & SHEAR

8-IN. (MIN.) THICK
COUNTERFORT
WALL, STEPPED

FOOTING

DRAINPIPE

NOTE:
FOOTING IS LARGE AND REINFORCED BECAUSE
COUNTERFORT USES ITS OWN WEIGHT PLUS
WEIGHT OF SOIL ABOVE FOOTING TO RESIST
THE HORIZONTAL FORCE ON THE WALL.

(B) CONCRETE-BLOCK COUNTERFORT

NOTE:
BUTTRESS & RETAINING WALL MUST BE
PROFESSIONALLY ENGINEERED.

RETAINING WALL

8-IN. (MIN.) THICK
BUTTRESS WALL,
STEPPED (SHOWN)
OR SLOPED

BUTTRESS REBAR
REQUIRED FOR SHEAR
IS TIED TO RETAINING
WALL & FOOTING.

BUTTRESS FOOTING
REINFORCED &
CONTINUOUS W/
WALL FOOTING

DRAINPIPE

(C) BUTTRESS
CONCRETE OR CONCRETE BLOCK

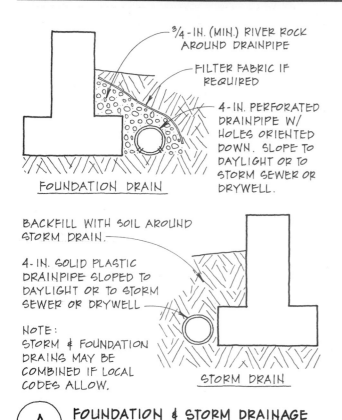

3/4-IN. (MIN.) RIVER ROCK AROUND DRAINPIPE

FILTER FABRIC IF REQUIRED

4-IN. PERFORATED DRAINPIPE W/ HOLES ORIENTED DOWN. SLOPE TO DAYLIGHT OR TO STORM SEWER OR DRYWELL.

FOUNDATION DRAIN

BACKFILL WITH SOIL AROUND STORM DRAIN.

4-IN. SOLID PLASTIC DRAINPIPE SLOPED TO DAYLIGHT OR TO STORM SEWER OR DRYWELL

NOTE: STORM & FOUNDATION DRAINS MAY BE COMBINED IF LOCAL CODES ALLOW.

STORM DRAIN

(A) FOUNDATION & STORM DRAINAGE

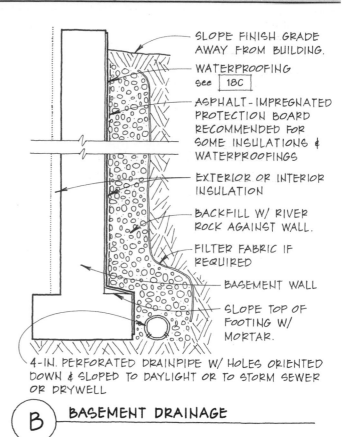

SLOPE FINISH GRADE AWAY FROM BUILDING.

WATERPROOFING see 18C

ASPHALT-IMPREGNATED PROTECTION BOARD RECOMMENDED FOR SOME INSULATIONS & WATERPROOFINGS

EXTERIOR OR INTERIOR INSULATION

BACKFILL W/ RIVER ROCK AGAINST WALL.

FILTER FABRIC IF REQUIRED

BASEMENT WALL

SLOPE TOP OF FOOTING W/ MORTAR.

4-IN. PERFORATED DRAINPIPE W/ HOLES ORIENTED DOWN & SLOPED TO DAYLIGHT OR TO STORM SEWER OR DRYWELL

(B) BASEMENT DRAINAGE

Drainage is essential in protecting a basement from groundwater, but waterproofing the basement wall from the outside is also vital. In selecting a waterproofing material, consider the method of application, the elasticity, and the cost. Below are common waterproofing and drainage materials.

Bituminous coatings—Tar or asphalt can be rolled, sprayed, troweled, or brushed on a dry surface. Often applied over a troweled-on coating of cement plaster that is called parging, some bituminous coatings may be fiberglass reinforced. They have minimal elasticity, and thin coats may not be impervious to standing water.

Modified portland-cement plaster—Plaster with water-repellent admixtures can look exactly like stucco. It is usually applied with a brush or a trowel to a moistened surface. It is inelastic, and unlike parging, it is waterproof.

Bentonite—A natural clay that swells when moistened to become impervious to water, bentonite is available as panels, in rolls, or in spray-on form. It is applied to a dry surface, and is extremely elastic.

Membranes—Rubberized or plastic membranes that are mechanically applied or bonded to a moist or dry surface are moderately elastic.

Bitumen-modified urethane—The most recent development in waterproof coatings, bitumen-modified urethane is applied with a brush to a dry surface. It is elastic, protecting cracks up to ⅛ in.

Plastic air-gap materials—These drainage materials create a physical gap between the basement wall and the soil. A filter fabric incorporated in the material allows water to enter the gap and drop to the bottom of the wall. These systems are expensive, but they eliminate the need for gravel backfill.

Although waterproofing and drainage will prevent water from entering the basement, water vapor may migrate into the basement through the footing and basement wall. It's important not to trap this vapor in an insulated wall, so a vapor barrier on the warm side of a basement wall is not recommended. More common and more practical is to allow the vapor to enter the space, and to remove the vapor with ventilation or a dehumidifier.

(C) WATERPROOFING
PRINCIPLES & MATERIALS

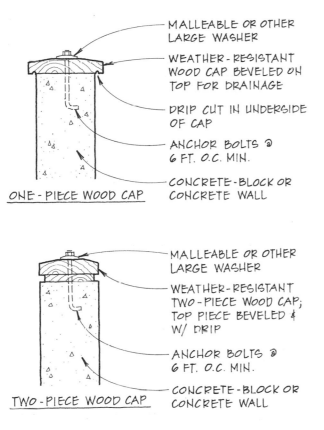

ONE-PIECE WOOD CAP

- MALLEABLE OR OTHER LARGE WASHER
- WEATHER-RESISTANT WOOD CAP BEVELED ON TOP FOR DRAINAGE
- DRIP CUT IN UNDERSIDE OF CAP
- ANCHOR BOLTS @ 6 FT. O.C. MIN.
- CONCRETE-BLOCK OR CONCRETE WALL

MASONRY CAP

- ROWLOCK BRICK OR PAVER CAP
- MASONRY TIES @ 2 FT. O.C.
- CONCRETE-BLOCK OR CONCRETE WALL

TWO-PIECE WOOD CAP

- MALLEABLE OR OTHER LARGE WASHER
- WEATHER-RESISTANT TWO-PIECE WOOD CAP; TOP PIECE BEVELED & W/ DRIP
- ANCHOR BOLTS @ 6 FT. O.C. MIN.
- CONCRETE-BLOCK OR CONCRETE WALL

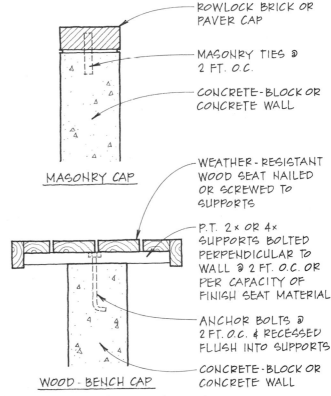

WOOD-BENCH CAP

- WEATHER-RESISTANT WOOD SEAT NAILED OR SCREWED TO SUPPORTS
- P.T. 2x OR 4x SUPPORTS BOLTED PERPENDICULAR TO WALL @ 2 FT. O.C. OR PER CAPACITY OF FINISH SEAT MATERIAL
- ANCHOR BOLTS @ 2 FT. O.C. & RECESSED FLUSH INTO SUPPORTS
- CONCRETE-BLOCK OR CONCRETE WALL

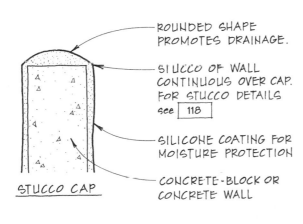

STUCCO CAP

- ROUNDED SHAPE PROMOTES DRAINAGE.
- STUCCO OF WALL CONTINUOUS OVER CAP. FOR STUCCO DETAILS see 118
- SILICONE COATING FOR MOISTURE PROTECTION
- CONCRETE-BLOCK OR CONCRETE WALL

NOTES:
THESE DETAILS ARE FOR THE TOPS OF RETAINING WALLS, WHICH ARE USUALLY EXPOSED TO THE WEATHER. WOOD CAPS WILL ULTIMATELY DECAY, SO THEY ARE DESIGNED FOR RELATIVE EASE OF REPLACEMENT. THERE IS NOT MUCH POINT IN MOISTURE BARRIERS, SINCE THEY WILL ONLY TRAP RAINWATER AGAINST THE WOOD. RETAINING-WALL SURFACES SHOULD BE PROTECTED FROM MOISTURE PENETRATION TO PREVENT DAMAGE FROM THE FREEZE-THAW CYCLE. SEAL W/ CLEAR ACRYLIC OR SILICONE, OR WATERPROOF W/ MODIFIED PORTLAND-CEMENT PLASTER OR BITUMEN-MODIFIED URETHANE see 18C

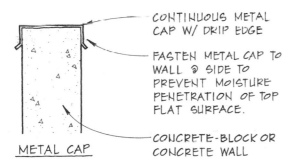

METAL CAP

- CONTINUOUS METAL CAP W/ DRIP EDGE
- FASTEN METAL CAP TO WALL @ SIDE TO PREVENT MOISTURE PENETRATION OF TOP FLAT SURFACE.
- CONCRETE-BLOCK OR CONCRETE WALL

(A) CONCRETE & CONCRETE-BLOCK WALL CAPS

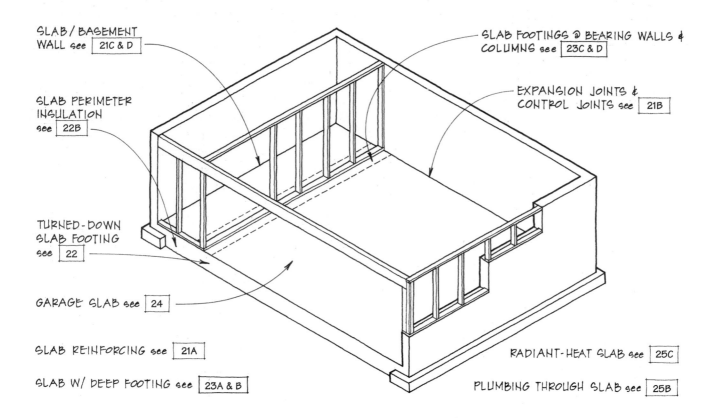

SLAB/BASEMENT WALL see | 21C & D |

SLAB PERIMETER INSULATION see | 22B |

TURNED-DOWN SLAB FOOTING see | 22 |

GARAGE SLAB see | 24 |

SLAB REINFORCING see | 21A |

SLAB W/ DEEP FOOTING see | 23A & B |

SLAB FOOTINGS @ BEARING WALLS & COLUMNS see | 23C & D |

EXPANSION JOINTS & CONTROL JOINTS see | 21B |

RADIANT-HEAT SLAB see | 25C |

PLUMBING THROUGH SLAB see | 25B |

Preparation before pouring a slab is critical to the quality of the slab itself. The primary goals in preparing for a slab are to provide adequate and even support, and to control ground moisture.

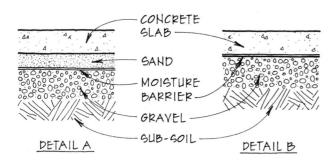

DETAIL A   DETAIL B

CONCRETE SLAB
SAND
MOISTURE BARRIER
GRAVEL
SUB-SOIL

Soil—Soil is the ultimate support of the slab. Soil must be solid and free of organic material. Some soils require compaction. In termite areas, the soil is often treated chemically. Verify compaction and soil treatment practices in your local area.

Gravel—Gravel is a leveling device that provides a porous layer for groundwater to drain away from the slab. A minimum of 4 in. of gravel is recommended. Gravel must be clean and free from organic matter.

Crushed and ungraded gravels must be compacted. Graded gravels such as pea gravel composed entirely of similar-sized round particles cannot and need not be compacted.

Moisture barrier—Moisture barriers prevent moisture (and retard vapor) from moving upward into a slab. Six-mil polyethylene is common and works well in Detail A. Overlap joints 12 in. and tape the joints in areas of extreme moisture. A more substantial concrete-rated moisture barrier is necessary for Detail B because the moisture barrier is in direct contact with the concrete slab. Polyethylene may deteriorate within a very short period in this situation, and it is easily punctured during slab preparation and pouring. A more substantial concrete-rated barrier is a fiber-reinforced bituminous membrane, sandwiched between two layers of polyethylene.

Sand—Sand (shown only in Detail A), allows water to escape from concrete in a downward direction during curing. This produces a stronger slab. The American Concrete Institute recommends a 2-in. layer of sand below slabs.

Welded wire mesh—Welded wire mesh (WWM) is the most common reinforcement for light-duty slabs. The most common size is 6x6 (w1.4 x w1.4)—adequate for a residential garage, which requires a stronger slab than a house. One disadvantage to WWM is that the 6-in. grid is often stepped on and forced to the bottom of the slab as the concrete is poured.

Rebar—Rebar is stronger than welded wire mesh. A grid of #3 rebar at 24 in. o.c is also adequate for a residential garage.

Fiber reinforcement—Fiber reinforcement is a recent development in slab reinforcement. Polypropylene fiber reinforcement is mixed with the concrete at the plant and poured integrally with the slab, thereby eliminating difficulties with placement of the reinforcing material. The addition of 1.5 lb. of fiber per cubic yard of concrete produces flexural strength equal to WWM in a slab. The appearance of the slab is affected by the presence of fibers exposed at the surface.

Expansion joints—Expansion joints allow slabs to expand and contract slightly with temperature changes. They also allow slabs to act independently of building elements with which they interface. Expansion joints are appropriate at the edges of slabs that are not heated (not in the living space) or that, for some other reason, are expected to change temperature significantly over their lifetimes. Expansion joints are also used to isolate building elements that penetrate slabs such as structural columns, walls, or plumbing (see 25B).

Control joints—Control joints induce cracking to occur at selected locations. They are troweled or cut into the surface of a slab to about one-quarter of the slab depth and at 20-ft. intervals. Cold joints, which automatically occur between sections of a slab poured separately, can act as control joints.

A CONCRETE-SLAB REINFORCING

B CONCRETE-SLAB JOINTS

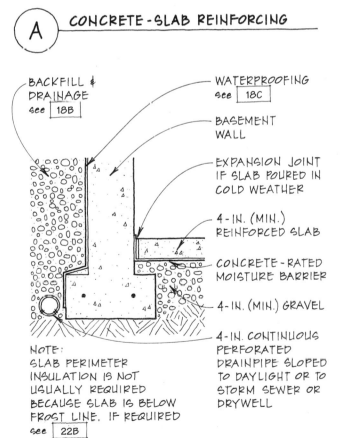

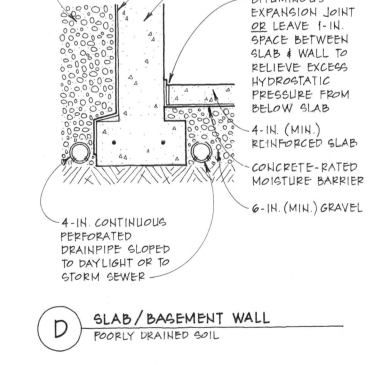

C SLAB / BASEMENT WALL
WELL-DRAINED SOIL

D SLAB / BASEMENT WALL
POORLY DRAINED SOIL

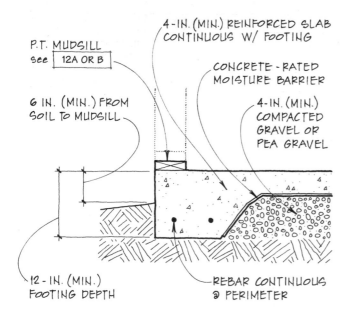

P.T. MUDSILL
see [12A OR B]

6 IN. (MIN.) FROM
SOIL TO MUDSILL

4-IN. (MIN.) REINFORCED SLAB
CONTINUOUS W/ FOOTING

CONCRETE-RATED
MOISTURE BARRIER

4-IN. (MIN.)
COMPACTED
GRAVEL OR
PEA GRAVEL

12-IN. (MIN.)
FOOTING DEPTH

REBAR CONTINUOUS
@ PERIMETER

NOTE:
AN UNINSULATED & EXPOSED PERIMETER SLAB IS
APPROPRIATE ONLY @ UNHEATED SPACES OR IN
VERY WARM CLIMATES.

A SLAB W/ TURNED-DOWN FOOTING
WARM CLIMATE, WELL-DRAINED SOIL

NOTE:
SLABS LOSE HEAT MOST READILY AT THEIR
PERIMETERS, WHERE THEY ARE EXPOSED TO THE
AIR, SO SLABS MUST BE PROTECTED FROM HEAT
LOSS BY A CLOSED-CELL RIGID INSULATION PLACED
AT THEIR EDGES. THE AMOUNT OF INSULATION
REQUIRED WILL DEPEND ON THE CLIMATE AND ON
WHETHER THE SLAB IS HEATED.
THE POSITION OF THE INSULATION WILL DEPEND
PRIMARILY ON THE FOUNDATION TYPE. SLABS
INTEGRAL WITH TURNED-DOWN FOOTINGS ARE
INSULATED @ THE OUTSIDE BUILDING EDGE. SLABS
WITH DEEP FOOTINGS ARE OFTEN INSULATED @
THE INSIDE FACE OF THE FOUNDATION, ALTHOUGH
THEY MAY ALSO BE INSULATED @ THE OUTSIDE
BUILDING EDGE.

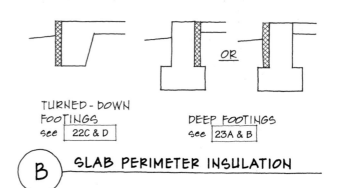

TURNED-DOWN
FOOTINGS
see [22C & D]

OR

DEEP FOOTINGS
see [23A & B]

B SLAB PERIMETER INSULATION

WALL FINISH:
STUCCO-WRAPPED
INSULATION
OR
SIDING STOPPED @
TOP OF INSULATION
W/ FLASHING &
PROTECTIVE
COATING OVER
INSULATION

4-IN. (MIN.) SLAB
CONTINUOUS W/
FOOTING

CONCRETE-RATED
MOISTURE
BARRIER

4-IN. (MIN.)
COMPACTED
GRAVEL OR
PEA GRAVEL

P.T. MUDSILL
see [12A OR B]

CLOSED-CELL
RIGID INSULATION
TO BELOW FROST LINE

FOOTING BELOW
FROST LINE

REBAR CONTINUOUS
@ PERIMETER

C SLAB W/ TURNED-DOWN FOOTING
INSULATION OUTSIDE FRAMING

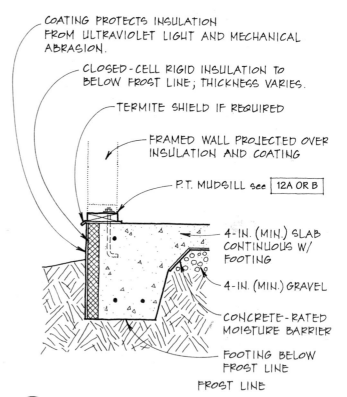

COATING PROTECTS INSULATION
FROM ULTRAVIOLET LIGHT AND MECHANICAL
ABRASION.

CLOSED-CELL RIGID INSULATION TO
BELOW FROST LINE; THICKNESS VARIES.

TERMITE SHIELD IF REQUIRED

FRAMED WALL PROJECTED OVER
INSULATION AND COATING

P.T. MUDSILL see [12A OR B]

4-IN. (MIN.) SLAB
CONTINUOUS W/
FOOTING

4-IN. (MIN.) GRAVEL

CONCRETE-RATED
MOISTURE BARRIER

FOOTING BELOW
FROST LINE

FROST LINE

D SLAB W/ TURNED-DOWN FOOTING
INSULATION FLUSH W/ FRAMING

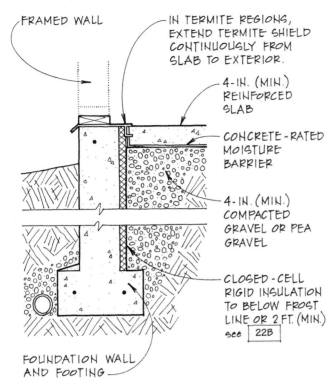

FRAMED WALL

IN TERMITE REGIONS, EXTEND TERMITE SHIELD CONTINUOUSLY FROM SLAB TO EXTERIOR.

4-IN. (MIN.) REINFORCED SLAB

CONCRETE-RATED MOISTURE BARRIER

4-IN. (MIN.) COMPACTED GRAVEL OR PEA GRAVEL

CLOSED-CELL RIGID INSULATION TO BELOW FROST LINE OR 2 FT. (MIN.) see 22B

FOUNDATION WALL AND FOOTING

A SLAB ON GRADE / DEEP FOOTING
VERTICAL INTERIOR INSULATION

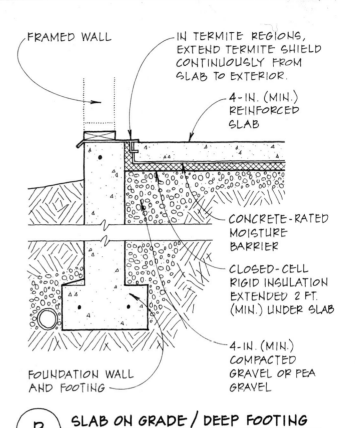

FRAMED WALL

IN TERMITE REGIONS, EXTEND TERMITE SHIELD CONTINUOUSLY FROM SLAB TO EXTERIOR.

4-IN. (MIN.) REINFORCED SLAB

CONCRETE-RATED MOISTURE BARRIER

CLOSED-CELL RIGID INSULATION EXTENDED 2 FT. (MIN.) UNDER SLAB

4-IN. (MIN.) COMPACTED GRAVEL OR PEA GRAVEL

FOUNDATION WALL AND FOOTING

B SLAB ON GRADE / DEEP FOOTING
HORIZONTAL INTERIOR INSULATION

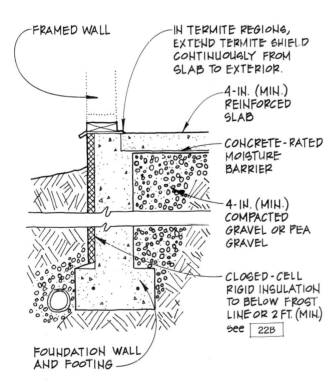

FRAMED WALL

IN TERMITE REGIONS, EXTEND TERMITE SHIELD CONTINUOUSLY FROM SLAB TO EXTERIOR.

4-IN. (MIN.) REINFORCED SLAB

CONCRETE-RATED MOISTURE BARRIER

4-IN. (MIN.) COMPACTED GRAVEL OR PEA GRAVEL

CLOSED-CELL RIGID INSULATION TO BELOW FROST LINE OR 2 FT. (MIN.) see 22B

FOUNDATION WALL AND FOOTING

C SLAB ON GRADE / DEEP FOOTING
VERTICAL EXTERIOR INSULATION

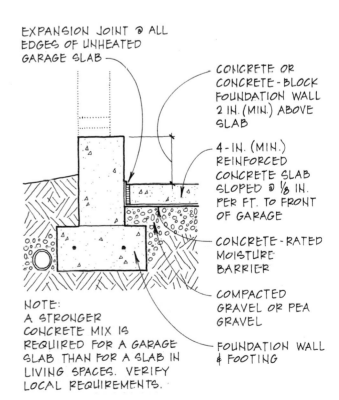

EXPANSION JOINT @ ALL EDGES OF UNHEATED GARAGE SLAB

CONCRETE OR CONCRETE-BLOCK FOUNDATION WALL 2 IN. (MIN.) ABOVE SLAB

4-IN. (MIN.) REINFORCED CONCRETE SLAB SLOPED @ 1/8 IN. PER FT. TO FRONT OF GARAGE

CONCRETE-RATED MOISTURE BARRIER

COMPACTED GRAVEL OR PEA GRAVEL

FOUNDATION WALL & FOOTING

NOTE:
A STRONGER CONCRETE MIX IS REQUIRED FOR A GARAGE SLAB THAN FOR A SLAB IN LIVING SPACES. VERIFY LOCAL REQUIREMENTS.

D GARAGE SLAB / FOUNDATION WALL

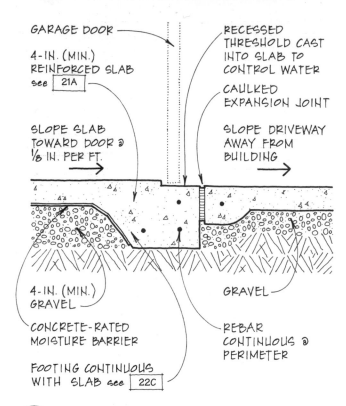

GARAGE DOOR

4-IN. (MIN.) REINFORCED SLAB see 21A

SLOPE SLAB TOWARD DOOR @ 1/8 IN. PER FT.

RECESSED THRESHOLD CAST INTO SLAB TO CONTROL WATER

CAULKED EXPANSION JOINT

SLOPE DRIVEWAY AWAY FROM BUILDING

4-IN. (MIN.) GRAVEL

CONCRETE-RATED MOISTURE BARRIER

FOOTING CONTINUOUS WITH SLAB see 22C

GRAVEL

REBAR CONTINUOUS @ PERIMETER

A **TURNED-DOWN FOOTING**
AT GARAGE DOOR

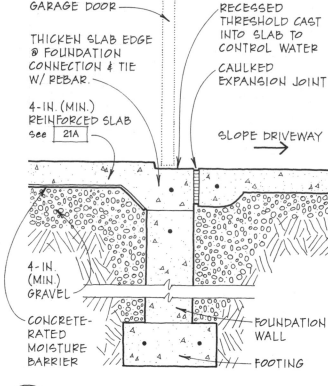

GARAGE DOOR

THICKEN SLAB EDGE @ FOUNDATION CONNECTION & TIE W/ REBAR.

4-IN. (MIN.) REINFORCED SLAB see 21A

RECESSED THRESHOLD CAST INTO SLAB TO CONTROL WATER

CAULKED EXPANSION JOINT

SLOPE DRIVEWAY

4-IN. (MIN.) GRAVEL

CONCRETE-RATED MOISTURE BARRIER

FOUNDATION WALL

FOOTING

B **DEEP FOOTING**
AT GARAGE DOOR

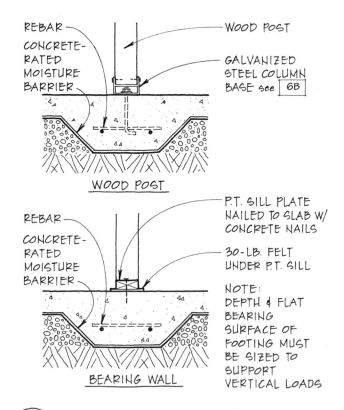

REBAR

CONCRETE-RATED MOISTURE BARRIER

WOOD POST

GALVANIZED STEEL COLUMN BASE see 6B

WOOD POST

REBAR

CONCRETE-RATED MOISTURE BARRIER

P.T. SILL PLATE NAILED TO SLAB W/ CONCRETE NAILS

30-LB. FELT UNDER P.T. SILL

NOTE: DEPTH & FLAT BEARING SURFACE OF FOOTING MUST BE SIZED TO SUPPORT VERTICAL LOADS

BEARING WALL

C **INTEGRAL SLAB FOOTING**
WOOD POST & BEARING WALL

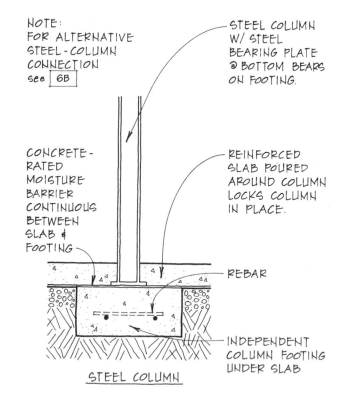

NOTE: FOR ALTERNATIVE STEEL-COLUMN CONNECTION see 6B

STEEL COLUMN W/ STEEL BEARING PLATE @ BOTTOM BEARS ON FOOTING.

CONCRETE-RATED MOISTURE BARRIER CONTINUOUS BETWEEN SLAB & FOOTING

REINFORCED SLAB POURED AROUND COLUMN LOCKS COLUMN IN PLACE.

REBAR

INDEPENDENT COLUMN FOOTING UNDER SLAB

STEEL COLUMN

D **UNDER-SLAB FOOTING**
STEEL COLUMN

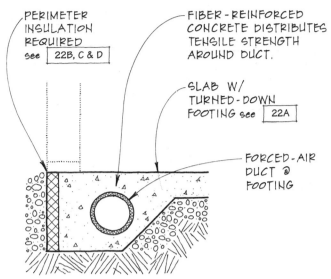

PERIMETER INSULATION REQUIRED see [22B, C & D]

FIBER-REINFORCED CONCRETE DISTRIBUTES TENSILE STRENGTH AROUND DUCT.

SLAB W/ TURNED-DOWN FOOTING see [22A]

FORCED-AIR DUCT @ FOOTING

NOTE:
AIR DUCTS MUST BE INSULATED AND MUST BE STRUCTURALLY CAPABLE OF SUPPORTING WET CONCRETE. AN UNREINFORCED DUCT MAY BE ALLOWED IF A LIGHT COATING OF CONCRETE IS USED TO STRENGTHEN IT BEFORE THE MAIN CONCRETE POUR.

(A) FORCED-AIR DUCT IN SLAB

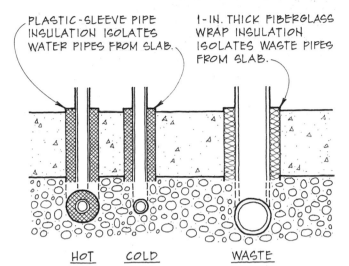

PLASTIC-SLEEVE PIPE INSULATION ISOLATES WATER PIPES FROM SLAB.

1-IN. THICK FIBERGLASS WRAP INSULATION ISOLATES WASTE PIPES FROM SLAB.

HOT   COLD   WASTE

NOTE:
USE TYPE K OR TYPE L COPPER SUPPLY PIPES. MINIMIZE BRAZED FITTINGS BELOW SLAB. HOT-PIPE INSULATION IS RECOMMENDED.

NOTE:
USE ABS PLASTIC WASTE LINES. NO CLEANOUTS ARE ALLOWED BELOW SLAB. SET CLOSET FLANGE AT F.F.L. AND ANCHOR DIRECTLY & SECURELY TO SLAB.

(B) PLUMBING THROUGH SLAB

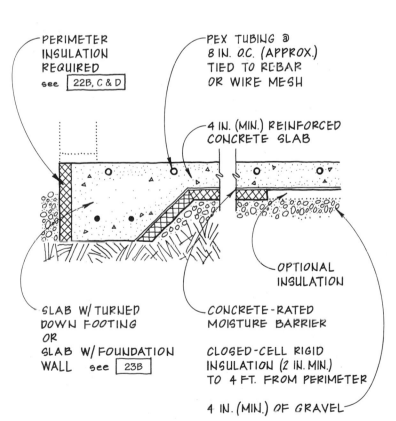

PERIMETER INSULATION REQUIRED see [22B, C & D]

PEX TUBING @ 8 IN. O.C. (APPROX.) TIED TO REBAR OR WIRE MESH

4 IN. (MIN.) REINFORCED CONCRETE SLAB

OPTIONAL INSULATION

SLAB W/ TURNED DOWN FOOTING OR SLAB W/ FOUNDATION WALL see [23B]

CONCRETE-RATED MOISTURE BARRIER

CLOSED-CELL RIGID INSULATION (2 IN. MIN.) TO 4 FT. FROM PERIMETER

4 IN. (MIN.) OF GRAVEL

NOTE:
CROSS-LINKED POLYETHYLENE TUBING (PEX) HAS REPLACED COPPER TUBING AS THE CONVEYOR OF HOT WATER FOR RADIANT SLABS. THIS ELASTIC TUBING IS SUPPLIED IN LONG ROLLS & CAN COVER ABOUT 200 SQ. FT. WITHOUT ANY JOINTS BELOW THE SURFACE. THE ADDITION OF INSULATION BELOW THE SLAB WILL IMPROVE THE PERFOMANCE OF THE SYSTEM.

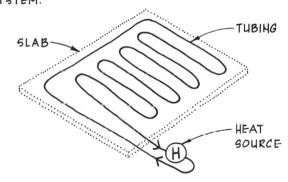

SLAB   TUBING

HEAT SOURCE

DIAGRAM OF RADIANT-HEAT TUBING

(C) RADIANT-HEAT SLAB

CHAPTER 2

FLOORS

The floor is the part of the building with which we have most contact. We walk on the floor and, on occasion, dance, wrestle, or lie on it. We can easily tell if the floor is not level, if it is bouncy or squeaky, and this tells us something about the overall quality of the building. The floor carries the loads of our weight, all our furniture, and most of our other possessions. It also acts as a diaphragm to transfer lateral loads (e.g., wind, earthquake, and soil) to the walls, which resist these loads. Floors insulate us from beneath and often hold ductwork, plumbing, and other utilities. So a floor must be carefully designed as a system that integrates with the other systems of a wood-frame building—the foundation, walls, stairs, insulation, and utilities. Once designed, the floor must be carefully built because so many subsequent parts of the construction process depend on a level and solid floor construction.

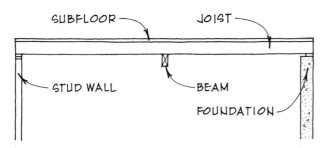

ELEMENTS OF A FLOOR SYSTEM

There are several floor-construction systems, and all of them are composed of variations of the same basic elements: support, joists, and a subfloor.

Support—Wood floor systems usually span between parallel supports. These supports may be a foundation wall, a stud bearing wall, or a beam. The first two are covered in Chapters 1 and 3, and beams are a subject of this chapter (see 29-31).

Joists—The primary structural members of a floor system are the joists, which span between the supports. Joists can be made of a variety of materials and usually are placed on 12-in., 16-in. or 24-in. centers.

Subfloor—The planar structural surface attached to the top of the joists is called the subfloor. The subfloor provides the level surface to which the finish floor is applied, and it also acts as a diaphragm to transfer lateral loads to the walls. Subfloors are usually made of plywood or oriented strand board (OSB) but may also be made of other materials. Some subfloors also provide mass for passive-solar heating.

FLOORS AND WALLS

It is essential to coordinate the details of a floor-framing system with those of the wall framing. There are two wall-framing systems from which to choose:

Balloon framing—Balloon framing is a construction system in which the studs are continuous through the floor levels. It is a mostly archaic system, but there are some situations where balloon framing is appropriate. These situations are discussed in the introduction to Chapter 3 (see 65-66). Balloon-framing details that pertain to floors are included in this chapter.

Platform framing—Platform framing is the dominant wood-floor construction system in this country. The platform frame floor is so named because the stud-wall structure stops at each level, where the floor structure provides a platform for the construction of the walls of the next level. This chapter concentrates on platform framing, which has two basic variations: joists with structural panels (OSB or plywood), and girders with decking.

Dimension-lumber joists with a structural-panel subfloor is the more straightforward and generally the less expensive of the platform frame systems and is therefore the more widely used. The details in this chapter all illustrate this system (except where noted), but the details may be extrapolated to incorporate other materials, such as composite joists. Composite joists are floor trusses, wood I-joists and other composite members that are used in conjunction with structural subfloor panels, often to handle long spans or heavy loads. Composite joists are more dimensionally stable than dimension-lumber joists and are deeper, which allows them to accommodate more utilities, but they are also more expensive. Composite joists are most useful when the form of the building is simple.

In areas where timber is plentiful, 4x girders with 2-in. tongue-and-groove subfloor decking that spans 4 ft. are often used as a floor system (see 46-47). Lower grades of decking on girders make a very economical floor over crawl spaces, and appearance grades of decking are often used for exposed ceilings. The decking itself does not technically act as a diaphragm to resist lateral loads, so it may require additional diagonal structure, especially at upper levels.

Also included in this chapter are porch and deck floors, floor insulation, and vapor barriers.

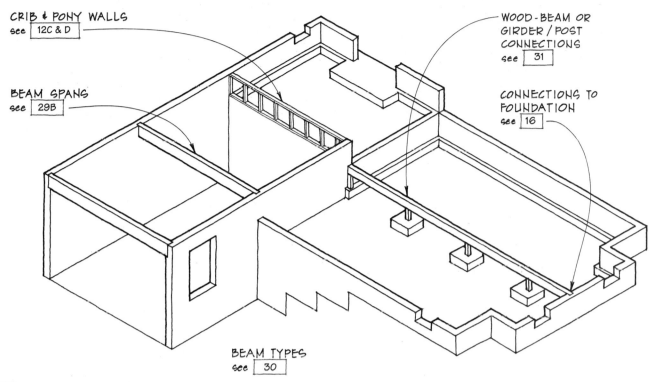

CRIB & PONY WALLS
see 12C & D

BEAM SPANS
see 29B

WOOD-BEAM OR
GIRDER / POST
CONNECTIONS
see 31

CONNECTIONS TO
FOUNDATION
see 16

BEAM TYPES
see 30

A FLOOR BEAMS

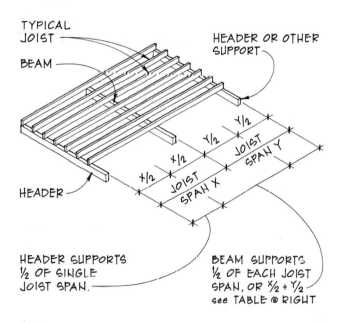

TYPICAL JOIST

BEAM

HEADER

HEADER OR OTHER SUPPORT

Y/2   Y/2
X/2   Y/2   JOIST SPAN Y
X/2   X/2   JOIST SPAN X

HEADER SUPPORTS
½ OF SINGLE
JOIST SPAN.

BEAM SUPPORTS
½ OF EACH JOIST
SPAN, OR X/2 + Y/2
see TABLE @ RIGHT

NOTE:
THE DRAWING ABOVE AND THE TABLE AT RIGHT ARE
FOR UNIFORM FLOOR LOADS ONLY. ROOF LOADS,
POINT LOADS & OTHER LOADS MUST BE ADDED
TO FLOOR LOADS WHEN CALCULATING BEAMS &
HEADERS.

Beam Span Comparison				
	Joist span $(\frac{X}{2} + \frac{Y}{2})$			
	8ft.	10ft.	12ft.	14ft.
Beam type	Beam Span (ft.)			
(2) 2x8 built-up beam	6.8	6.1	5.3	4.7
4x8 timber	7.7	6.9	6.0	5.3
3⅛ in. x 7½ in. glue-laminated beam	9.7	9.0	8.3	7.7
3½ in. x 7½ in. PSL beam	9.7	9.0	8.5	8.0
(2) 1¾ in. x 7½ in. LVL (unusual depth)	10.0	9.3	8.8	8.3
4x8 steel beam (W8 x 13 A36)	17.4	16.2	15.2	14.1

This table assumes a 40-psf live load and a 15-psf
dead load. The table is intended only for estimating
beam sizes and comparing beam types. For calculation tables, consult the national or regional organiza-
tions listed on pp. 228–229.

A FLOOR BEAMS

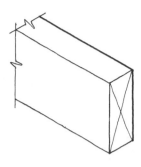

CUT TIMBER

TIMBER BEAMS ARE AVAILABLE IN A VARIETY OF SPECIES & GRADES; DOUGLAS-FIR IS THE STRONGEST. ACTUAL WIDTHS ARE 3½ IN. AND 5½ IN.; ACTUAL HEIGHTS ARE 5½ IN., 7½ IN., ETC., TO 13½ IN.

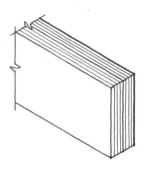

LAMINATED-VENEER LUMBER (LVL) BEAM

VERTICAL FACTORY-LAMINATED SECTIONS ARE NAILED TOGETHER. ACTUAL WIDTHS ARE MULTIPLES OF 1¾ IN. (TWO PIECES MATCH THICKNESS OF 2×4 WALL). ACTUAL HEIGHTS RANGE FROM 5½ IN. TO 18 IN.

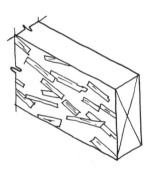

PARALLEL-STRAND LUMBER (PSL) BEAM

FACTORY-GLUED COMPOSITE BEAM MADE WITH LONG NARROW STRIPS OF VENEER ORIENTED ALONG BEAM LENGTH. ACTUAL WIDTHS ARE 3½ IN., 5¼ IN., & 7 IN. HEIGHTS RANGE FROM 9¼ IN. TO 18 IN.

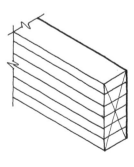

LAMINATED LUMBER BEAM

HORIZONTAL FACTORY-GLUED LAMINATIONS MAKE A KNOT-FREE & VERY STABLE BEAM. ACTUAL WIDTHS ARE 3⅛ IN., 5⅛ IN., 7⅛ IN., ETC. HEIGHTS ARE IN MULTIPLES OF 1½ IN.

NOTE:
BEAMS & JOISTS MUST BE DESIGNED AS A SYSTEM. CONNECTIONS BETWEEN JOISTS & BEAMS ARE SIMILAR FOR ALL WOOD-BEAM TYPES see 36

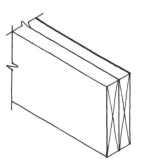

BUILT-UP BEAM

DIMENSION LUMBER IS NAILED TOGETHER TO FORM A SINGLE BEAM (4 PIECES MAX.). WIDTHS ARE MULTIPLES OF 1½ IN. HEIGHT FOLLOWS DIMENSION LUMBER.

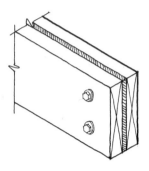

FLITCH BEAM

A STEEL PLATE SANDWICHED BETWEEN TWO PIECES OF LUMBER ADDS STRENGTH WITHOUT SUBSTANTIALLY INCREASING THE BEAM SIZE. THE LUMBER PREVENTS BUCKLING OF THE STEEL & PROVIDES A NAILING SURFACE. WIDTHS ARE 3 IN. TO 3½ IN. HEIGHTS FOLLOW DIMENSION LUMBER.

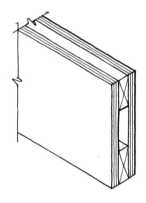

BOX BEAM

2×4 LUMBER IS SANDWICHED BETWEEN TWO PLYWOOD SKINS. PLYWOOD IS BOTH NAILED & GLUED TO 2×4s & AT ALL EDGES. PLYWOOD JOINTS MUST BE OFFSET.

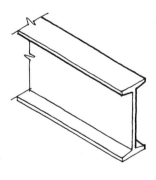

STEEL BEAM

THE STRONGEST OF THE BEAMS FOR A GIVEN SIZE, STEEL BEAMS ARE COMMONLY AVAILABLE IN VARIOUS SIZES FROM 4 IN. WIDE & 4 IN. HIGH TO 12 IN. WIDE & 36 IN. HIGH. THEY MAY BE PREDRILLED FOR BOLTING WOOD PLATE TO TOP FLANGE OR TO WEB.

FOR CONNECTIONS TO STEEL BEAMS see 37

(A) BEAM TYPES

NOTE:
WOOD BEAMS MAY BE SPLICED OVER VERTICAL SUPPORTS & OFTEN MAY BE ATTACHED TO THE SUPPORT BY MEANS OF TOENAILING. SOME SITUATIONS & CODES, HOWEVER, REQUIRE A POSITIVE CONNECTION OF BEAM TO POST SUCH AS A PLYWOOD GUSSET OR METAL CONNECTOR. SPLICE BEAMS ONLY OVER VERTICAL SUPPORTS UNLESS ENGINEERED. SPLICE WILL DEPEND ON TYPE OF BEAM & TYPE OF SUPPORT.

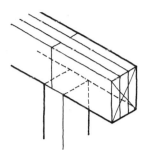
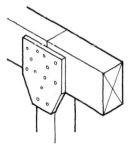
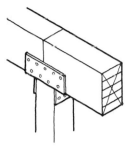
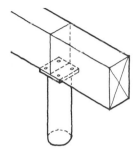

BUILT-UP BEAM

KEEP ONE MEMBER CONTINUOUS OVER POSTS. POSITION JOINTS OVER POST
OR
SPLICE ONE MEMBER WITHIN FIRST 30% OF SPAN FROM POST.

PLYWOOD GUSSET

PLYWOOD GUSSETS ARE APPLIED TO BOTH SIDES OF SPLICED BEAMS.

METAL CONNECTOR

METAL CONNECTORS ARE MANUFACTURED IN MANY CONFIGURATIONS FOR MOST TYPES OF WOOD BEAM & POST JOINTS.

METAL COLUMN

METAL LALLY COLUMN IS LAG-BOLTED TO BOTTOM SIDE OF SPLICED BEAM.

 A   WOOD BEAM OR GIRDER / POST CONNECTIONS

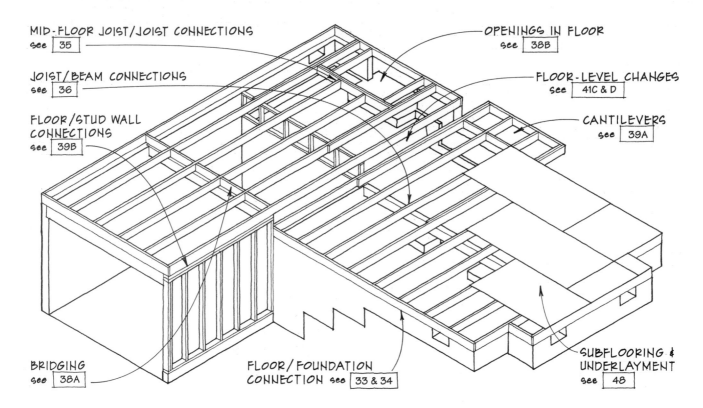

MID-FLOOR JOIST/JOIST CONNECTIONS
see 35

JOIST/BEAM CONNECTIONS
see 36

FLOOR/STUD WALL CONNECTIONS
see 39B

BRIDGING
see 38A

FLOOR/FOUNDATION CONNECTION see 33 & 34

OPENINGS IN FLOOR
see 38B

FLOOR-LEVEL CHANGES
see 41C & D

CANTILEVERS
see 39A

SUBFLOORING & UNDERLAYMENT
see 48

A dimension-lumber joist system is the most common floor structure in wood-frame buildings. The system is flexible and relatively inexpensive, and the materials are universally available. Species vary considerably from region to region, but sizes are uniform. The most common sizes for floors are 2x8, 2x10, and 2x12. Selection of floor-joist size depends on span; on spacing required for subflooring and ceiling finishes (usually 12 in., 16 in., or 24 in.); and on depth required for insulation (usually over a crawl space) and/or utilities (over basements and in upper floors).

The table at right compares spans at common on-center spacings for three typical species and grades of framing lumber at four different sizes of joist (2x6, 2x8, 2x10, and 2x12). For information on wood I-joists, see 43 and 44; for information on wood trusses, see 45A.

This table assumes a 40-psf live load, a 10-psf dead load and a deflection of L/360. The table is for estimating purposes only.

Floor-joist span comparison			
	Joist span (ft.)		
Joist size, species, and grade	12 in. o.c.	16 in. o.c.	24 in. o.c.
2x6 hem-fir #1	10.5	9.5	8.3
2x6 south. yellow pine #1	10.9	9.9	8.7
2x6 Douglas-fir #1	11.2	10.2	8.8
2x8 hem-fir #1	13.8	12.5	10.0
2x8 south. yellow pine #1	14.4	13.1	11.4
2x8 Douglas-fir #1	14.7	13.3	11.7
2x10 hem-fir #1	17.7	16.0	14.0
2x10 south. yellow pine #1	18.4	16.7	14.7
2x10 Douglas-fir #1	18.7	17.0	14.9
2x12 hem-fir #1	21.5	19.5	17.0
2x12 south. yellow pine #1	22.3	20.3	17.7
2x12 Douglas-fir #1	22.8	20.8	18.1

A JOIST-FLOOR SYSTEMS

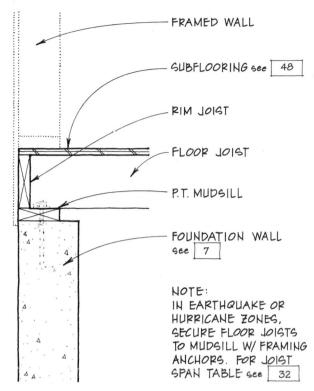

— FRAMED WALL

— SUBFLOORING see 48

— RIM JOIST

— FLOOR JOIST

— P.T. MUDSILL

— FOUNDATION WALL see 7

NOTE:
IN EARTHQUAKE OR HURRICANE ZONES, SECURE FLOOR JOISTS TO MUDSILL W/ FRAMING ANCHORS. FOR JOIST SPAN TABLE see 32

(A) JOISTS ON MUDSILL
⊥ TO WALL

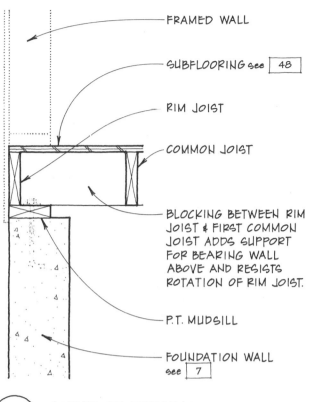

— FRAMED WALL

— SUBFLOORING see 48

— RIM JOIST

— COMMON JOIST

— BLOCKING BETWEEN RIM JOIST & FIRST COMMON JOIST ADDS SUPPORT FOR BEARING WALL ABOVE AND RESISTS ROTATION OF RIM JOIST.

— P.T. MUDSILL

— FOUNDATION WALL see 7

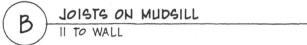

(B) JOISTS ON MUDSILL
∥ TO WALL

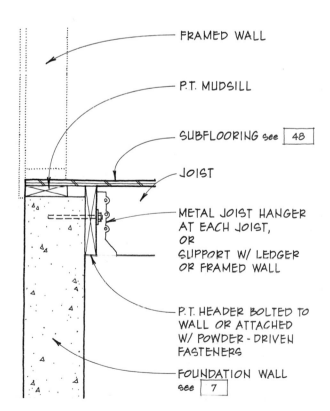

— FRAMED WALL

— P.T. MUDSILL

— SUBFLOORING see 48

— JOIST

— METAL JOIST HANGER AT EACH JOIST, OR SUPPORT W/ LEDGER OR FRAMED WALL

— P.T. HEADER BOLTED TO WALL OR ATTACHED W/ POWDER-DRIVEN FASTENERS

— FOUNDATION WALL see 7

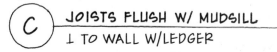

(C) JOISTS FLUSH W/ MUDSILL
⊥ TO WALL W/LEDGER

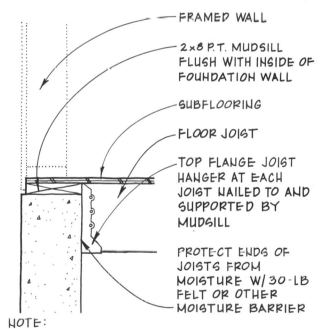

— FRAMED WALL

— 2×8 P.T. MUDSILL FLUSH WITH INSIDE OF FOUNDATION WALL

— SUBFLOORING

— FLOOR JOIST

— TOP FLANGE JOIST HANGER AT EACH JOIST NAILED TO AND SUPPORTED BY MUDSILL

— PROTECT ENDS OF JOISTS FROM MOISTURE W/ 30-LB FELT OR OTHER MOISTURE BARRIER

NOTE:
WALL SHEATHING ALIGNED FLUSH WITH FOUNDATION WHICH IS NATURAL WITH THIS DETAIL BUT ALSO POSSIBLE WITH ANY DETAIL ON THIS PAGE

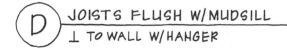

(D) JOISTS FLUSH W/MUDSILL
⊥ TO WALL W/HANGER

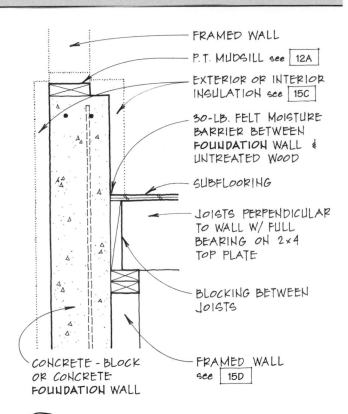

FRAMED WALL

P.T. MUDSILL see 12A

EXTERIOR OR INTERIOR INSULATION see 15C

30-LB. FELT MOISTURE BARRIER BETWEEN FOUNDATION WALL & UNTREATED WOOD

SUBFLOORING

JOISTS PERPENDICULAR TO WALL

BLOCKING BETWEEN JOISTS

P.T. 4× LEDGER BOLTED TO FOUNDATION WALL

CONCRETE - BLOCK OR CONCRETE FOUNDATION WALL

A JOISTS BELOW MUDSILL
⊥ TO WALL / LEDGER SUPPORT

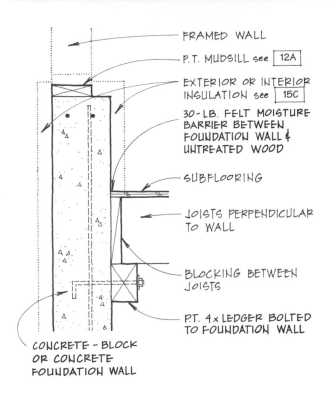

FRAMED WALL

P.T. MUDSILL see 12A

EXTERIOR OR INTERIOR INSULATION see 15C

30-LB. FELT MOISTURE BARRIER BETWEEN FOUNDATION WALL & UNTREATED WOOD

SUBFLOORING

JOISTS PERPENDICULAR TO WALL W/ FULL BEARING ON 2×4 TOP PLATE

BLOCKING BETWEEN JOISTS

CONCRETE - BLOCK OR CONCRETE FOUNDATION WALL

FRAMED WALL see 15D

B JOISTS BELOW MUDSILL
⊥ TO WALL / FRAMED WALL SUPPORT

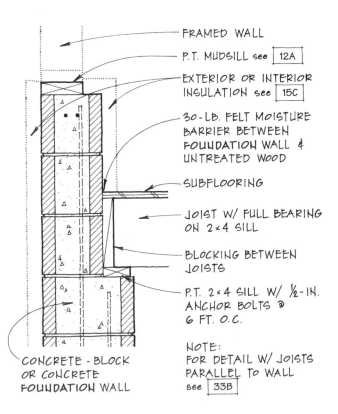

FRAMED WALL

P.T. MUDSILL see 12A

EXTERIOR OR INTERIOR INSULATION see 15C

30-LB. FELT MOISTURE BARRIER BETWEEN FOUNDATION WALL & UNTREATED WOOD

SUBFLOORING

JOIST W/ FULL BEARING ON 2×4 SILL

BLOCKING BETWEEN JOISTS

P.T. 2×4 SILL W/ ½-IN. ANCHOR BOLTS @ 6 FT. O.C.

NOTE:
FOR DETAIL W/ JOISTS PARALLEL TO WALL see 33B

CONCRETE - BLOCK OR CONCRETE FOUNDATION WALL

C JOISTS BELOW MUDSILL
⊥ TO WALL / STEPPED WALL SUPPORT

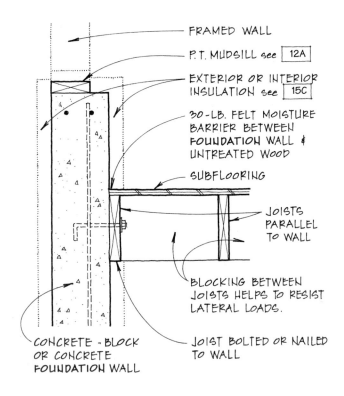

FRAMED WALL

P.T. MUDSILL see 12A

EXTERIOR OR INTERIOR INSULATION see 15C

30-LB. FELT MOISTURE BARRIER BETWEEN FOUNDATION WALL & UNTREATED WOOD

SUBFLOORING

JOISTS PARALLEL TO WALL

BLOCKING BETWEEN JOISTS HELPS TO RESIST LATERAL LOADS.

JOIST BOLTED OR NAILED TO WALL

CONCRETE - BLOCK OR CONCRETE FOUNDATION WALL

D JOISTS BELOW MUDSILL
∥ TO WALL / ALL SUPPORT SYSTEMS

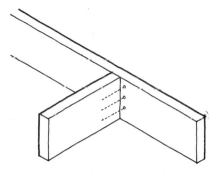

NAILED THROUGH JOIST

THE SIMPLEST BUT THE WEAKEST METHOD IS RECOMMENDED ONLY FOR BLOCKING.

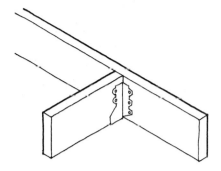

METAL JOIST HANGER

THIS IS THE STRONGEST OF THE STANDARD METHODS. EACH APPROVED HANGER IS RATED IN POUNDS.

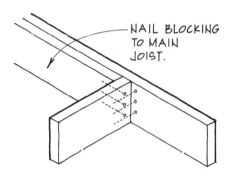

NAIL BLOCKING TO MAIN JOIST.

NAILED WITH BLOCKING

IN THIS FAIRLY STRONG & SIMPLE JOINT, NAILS AT RIGHT ANGLES EFFECTIVELY LOCK PERPENDICULAR JOISTS IN PLACE. IT IS RECOMMENDED ONLY FOR SHORT JOISTS.

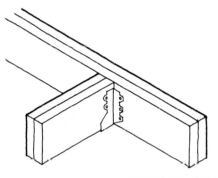

DOUBLED HANGER

DOUBLED HANGERS ARE SIZED TO HOLD TWO PIECES OF DIMENSION LUMBER.

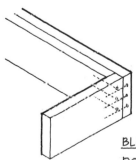

BLOCKED CORNER

DOUBLED JOISTS MAKE A STRONG OUTSIDE CORNER. FOR CANTILEVERS see 39A AND DECKS see 52

NOTES:
FOR ALL WOOD/WOOD CONNECTIONS, USE 16d NAILS (MIN.). FOR METAL HANGERS USE ONLY HARDENED HANGER NAILS UNLESS OTHERWISE SPECIFIED. FOR FLOOR OPENINGS see 38B

 JOIST/JOIST CONNECTIONS

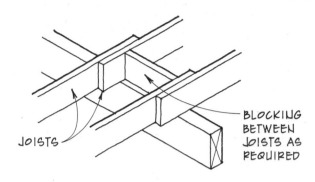

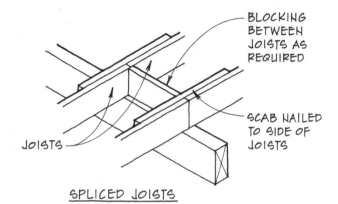

NOTE:
SCAB MUST BE LONG ENOUGH TO QUALIFY SPLICE AS A SINGLE JOIST SO THAT ADEQUATE BEARING ON BEAM IS ACHIEVED. VERIFY W/ LOCAL CODES.

JOISTS

BLOCKING BETWEEN JOISTS AS REQUIRED

BLOCKING BETWEEN JOISTS AS REQUIRED

JOISTS

SCAB NAILED TO SIDE OF JOISTS

LAPPED JOISTS

THIS COMMON JOINT REQUIRES SHIFTING THE SUBFLOOR LAYOUT 1½ IN. ON OPPOSITE SIDES OF THE BEAM TO ALLOW THE SUBFLOOR TO BEAR ON THE JOISTS.

SPLICED JOISTS

BUTT JOISTS TO MAINTAIN SAME SPACING FOR NAILING THE SUBFLOOR ON EACH SIDE OF THE BEAM.

NOTE:
LAPPED JOISTS & SPLICED JOISTS ARE COMMONLY USED OVER A CRAWL SPACE OR OTHER LOCATION WHERE HEAD CLEARANCE BELOW THE BEAM IS NOT REQUIRED.

 A JOIST / WOOD BEAM CONNECTIONS
BEAM BELOW JOISTS

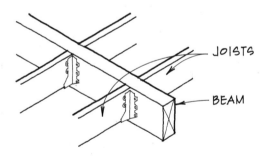

JOISTS

BEAM

JOIST HANGERS

ALIGN JOISTS ON EACH SIDE OF BEAM TO MAINTAIN SAME SPACING FOR SUBFLOOR NAILING.

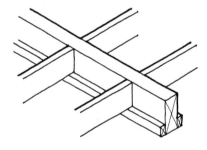

JOISTS ON LEDGER

A 2×2 OR 2×4 LEDGER NAILED TO THE BEAM SUPPORTS THE JOISTS. TOENAIL THE JOISTS TO THE BEAM OR BLOCK BETWEEN JOISTS. NOTCH JOISTS TO ⅓ OF DEPTH IF REQUIRED TO FIT OVER THE LEDGER.

NOTE:
JOIST HANGERS & JOISTS ON LEDGER ARE USED WHERE MAXIMUM HEAD CLEARANCE IS REQUIRED BELOW THE FLOOR. THEY WORK BEST IF THE JOISTS & BEAM ARE OF SIMILAR SPECIES & MOISTURE CONTENT SO THAT ONE DOES NOT SHRINK MORE THAN THE OTHER.

B JOIST / WOOD BEAM CONNECTIONS
BEAM FLUSH W/ JOISTS

2×2 WOOD STRAPS NAILED TO JOISTS OVER STEEL BEAM MAINTAIN JOIST ALIGNMENT.

JOIST

PROVIDE SPACE BETWEEN STRAP & BEAM TO ALLOW FOR JOIST SHRINKAGE.

STEEL BEAM

NAILING PLATES BOLTED TO LOWER BEAM FLANGE

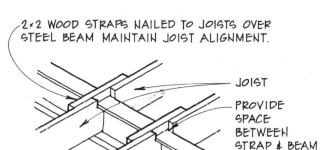

JOISTS BEARING ON STEEL FLANGE

2× NAILING PLATE BOLTED TO UPPER BEAM FLANGE

JOISTS

STEEL BEAM

NOTE: ALLOWABLE HANGER LOADS REDUCED DUE TO THICKNESS OF NAILING PLATE.

METAL HANGERS NAILED TO NAILING PLATE

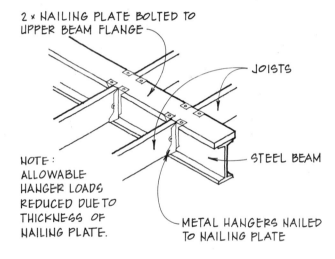

JOISTS HUNG FROM NAILING PLATE

JOISTS

JOIST HANGERS ATTACHED TO NAILERS

NAILERS BOLTED TO BOTH SIDES OF WEB

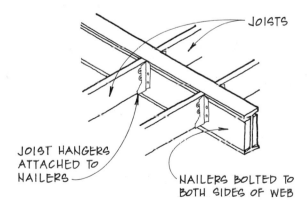

JOISTS HUNG FROM DOUBLE NAILER

BLOCKING BETWEEN JOISTS AS REQUIRED

2× NAILING PLATE BOLTED TO UPPER BEAM FLANGE

STEEL BEAM

SPLICED JOISTS see [36A]

BLOCKING BETWEEN JOISTS AS REQUIRED

2× NAILING PLATE BOLTED TO UPPER BEAM FLANGE

STEEL BEAM

LAPPED JOISTS see [36A]

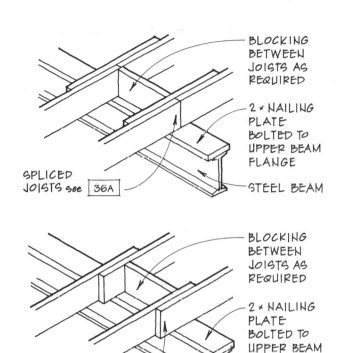

JOISTS ON NAILING PLATE

NOTE: USE ONLY IN CONDITIONS WITHOUT UPLIFT FORCES AND WHERE SCABS WILL NOT INTERFERE W/ CEILING.

1× BOARDS SCABBED TO UNDERSIDE OF JOISTS KEEP JOISTS ALIGNED & PREVENT LATERAL MOVEMENT OF STEEL BEAM.

JOISTS ON STEEL BEAM

NOTE:
THE DETAILS SHOWN IN 37A & B MAY BE ADJUSTED FOR USE WITH OTHER TYPES OF JOISTS & GIRDERS DISCUSSED IN THE FOLLOWING SECTIONS.

(A) **JOIST/STEEL BEAM CONNECTIONS**
BEAM FLUSH W/ JOISTS

(B) **JOIST/STEEL BEAM CONNECTIONS**
BEAM BELOW JOISTS

BLOCK BRIDGING

SOLID BLOCKING FROM
SAME MATERIAL AS
JOISTS IS STAGGERED
FOR EASE OF NAILING.

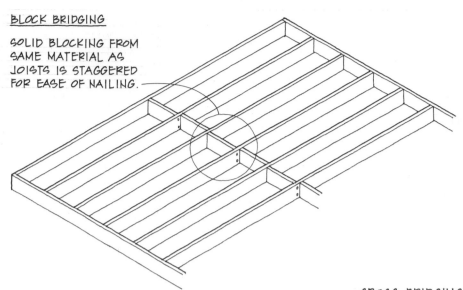

METAL BRIDGING

METAL PIECES SHOULD NOT
TOUCH EACH OTHER.

NOTE:
FOR DEEP JOISTS WITH LONG SPANS (OVER 10 FT.),
LOCAL CODES MAY REQUIRE BRIDGING TO PREVENT
ROTATION & TO DISTRIBUTE THE LOADING.

CROSS BRIDGING

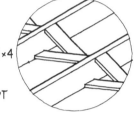

⁵⁄₄ × 3 OR ⁵⁄₄ × 4 OR 2×2 OR 1×4
BOARDS ARE NAILED IN A
CROSS PATTERN BETWEEN
JOISTS. PIECES SHOULD NOT
TOUCH EACH OTHER.

(A)   BRIDGING

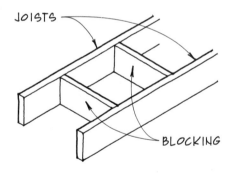

JOISTS

BLOCKING

SMALL OPENINGS

OPENINGS THAT FIT BETWEEN TWO
JOISTS FOR LAUNDRY CHUTES OR
HEATING DUCTS ARE SIMPLY MADE
BY NAILING BLOCKING BETWEEN
THE JOISTS.

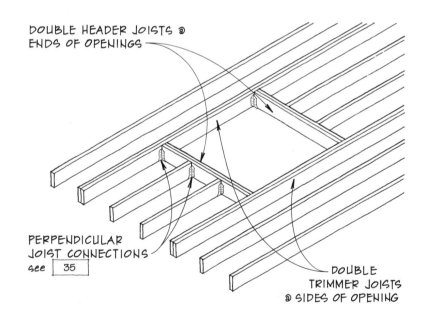

DOUBLE HEADER JOISTS @
ENDS OF OPENINGS

PERPENDICULAR
JOIST CONNECTIONS
see   35

DOUBLE
TRIMMER JOISTS
@ SIDES OF OPENING

LARGE OPENINGS

IN OPENINGS THAT ARE WIDER THAN THE JOIST SPACING, SUCH AS FOR STAIRWAYS &
CHIMNEYS, THE FLOOR STRUCTURE AROUND THE OPENING MUST BE STRENGTHENED.
FOR OPENINGS UP TO THREE JOIST SPACES WIDE, DOUBLING THE JOISTS AT THE SIDES &
ENDS OF THE OPENING MAY SUFFICE. WIDER OPENINGS SHOULD BE ENGINEERED.

(B)   OPENINGS IN JOIST-FLOOR SYSTEM

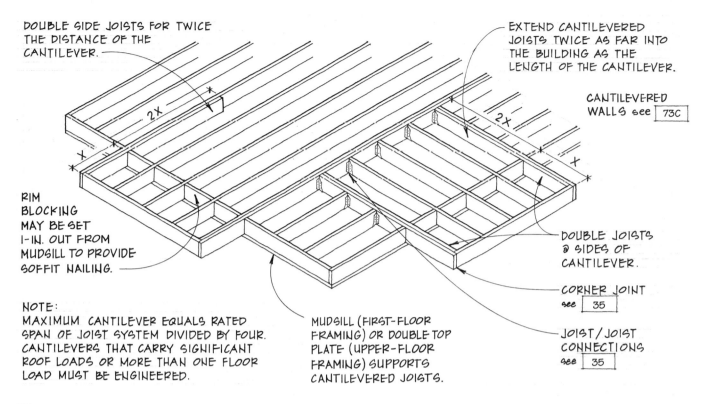

DOUBLE SIDE JOISTS FOR TWICE THE DISTANCE OF THE CANTILEVER.

2X

EXTEND CANTILEVERED JOISTS TWICE AS FAR INTO THE BUILDING AS THE LENGTH OF THE CANTILEVER.

CANTILEVERED WALLS see 73C

2X

RIM BLOCKING MAY BE SET 1-IN. OUT FROM MUDSILL TO PROVIDE SOFFIT NAILING.

DOUBLE JOISTS @ SIDES OF CANTILEVER.

CORNER JOINT see 35

JOIST/JOIST CONNECTIONS see 35

NOTE:
MAXIMUM CANTILEVER EQUALS RATED SPAN OF JOIST SYSTEM DIVIDED BY FOUR. CANTILEVERS THAT CARRY SIGNIFICANT ROOF LOADS OR MORE THAN ONE FLOOR LOAD MUST BE ENGINEERED.

MUDSILL (FIRST-FLOOR FRAMING) OR DOUBLE TOP PLATE (UPPER-FLOOR FRAMING) SUPPORTS CANTILEVERED JOISTS.

(A) FLOOR CANTILEVERS
II & ⊥ TO JOIST SYSTEM

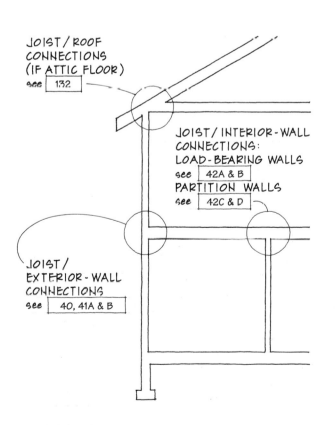

JOIST/ROOF CONNECTIONS (IF ATTIC FLOOR) see 132

JOIST/INTERIOR-WALL CONNECTIONS:
LOAD-BEARING WALLS see 42A & B
PARTITION WALLS see 42C & D

JOIST/ EXTERIOR-WALL CONNECTIONS see 40, 41A & B

Joist floor-system connections to exterior walls are straightforward. The wall framing may be one of two types.

Platform framing—Platform framing, the most common system in use today, takes advantage of standard materials and framing methods. The ground floor and all upper floors can be constructed using the same system.

Balloon framing—Balloon framing is rarely used because it is harder to erect and requires very long studs. It may be the system of choice, however, if the floor structure must work with the walls to resist lateral roof loads or if extra care is required to make the insulation and vapor barrier continuous from floor to floor.

Joist floor-system connections to interior walls depend on whether the walls are load-bearing walls or partition walls. The other factor to consider is whether edge nailing is required for the ceiling.

(B) JOIST / STUD-WALL CONNECTIONS

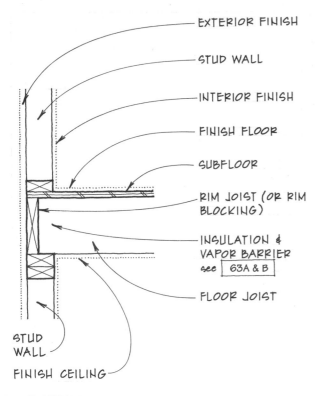

EXTERIOR FINISH

STUD WALL

INTERIOR FINISH

FINISH FLOOR

SUBFLOOR

RIM JOIST (OR RIM BLOCKING)

INSULATION & VAPOR BARRIER see [63A & B]

FLOOR JOIST

STUD WALL

FINISH CEILING

(A) JOISTS @ EXTERIOR WALL
JOISTS ⊥ TO WALL

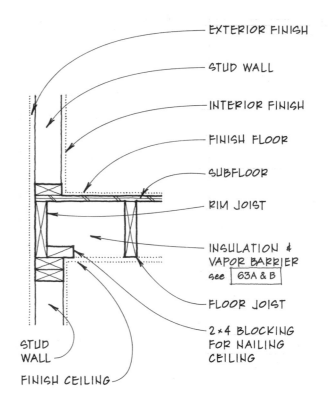

EXTERIOR FINISH

STUD WALL

INTERIOR FINISH

FINISH FLOOR

SUBFLOOR

RIM JOIST

INSULATION & VAPOR BARRIER see [63A & B]

FLOOR JOIST

2 × 4 BLOCKING FOR NAILING CEILING

STUD WALL

FINISH CEILING

(B) JOISTS @ EXTERIOR WALL
JOISTS ∥ TO WALL

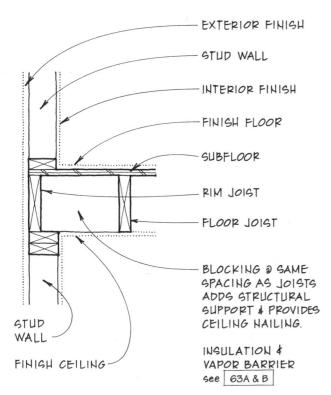

EXTERIOR FINISH

STUD WALL

INTERIOR FINISH

FINISH FLOOR

SUBFLOOR

RIM JOIST

FLOOR JOIST

BLOCKING @ SAME SPACING AS JOISTS ADDS STRUCTURAL SUPPORT & PROVIDES CEILING NAILING.

INSULATION & VAPOR BARRIER see [63A & B]

STUD WALL

FINISH CEILING

(C) JOISTS @ EXTERIOR WALL
JOISTS ∥ TO WALL, W/ BLOCKING

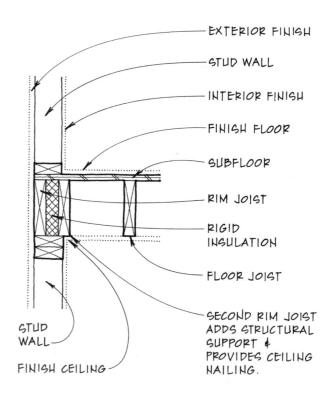

EXTERIOR FINISH

STUD WALL

INTERIOR FINISH

FINISH FLOOR

SUBFLOOR

RIM JOIST

RIGID INSULATION

FLOOR JOIST

SECOND RIM JOIST ADDS STRUCTURAL SUPPORT & PROVIDES CEILING NAILING.

STUD WALL

FINISH CEILING

(D) JOISTS @ EXTERIOR WALL
DOUBLED RIM JOISTS ∥ TO WALL

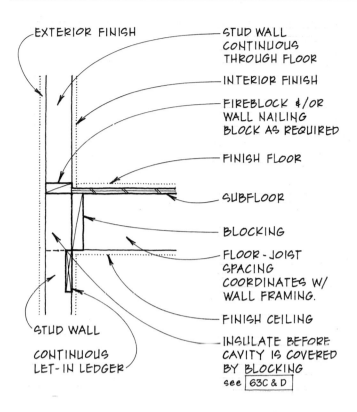

EXTERIOR FINISH

STUD WALL CONTINUOUS THROUGH FLOOR

INTERIOR FINISH

FIREBLOCK &/OR WALL NAILING BLOCK AS REQUIRED

FINISH FLOOR

SUBFLOOR

BLOCKING

FLOOR-JOIST SPACING COORDINATES W/ WALL FRAMING.

FINISH CEILING

INSULATE BEFORE CAVITY IS COVERED BY BLOCKING see 63C & D

STUD WALL

CONTINUOUS LET-IN LEDGER

A **JOISTS @ BALLOON-FRAMED WALL**
JOISTS ⊥ TO WALL

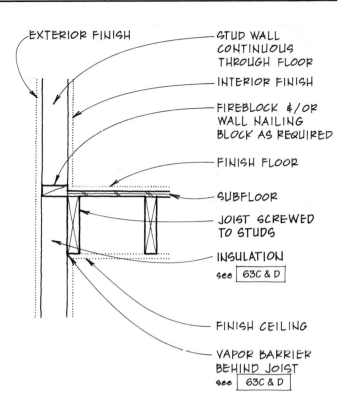

EXTERIOR FINISH

STUD WALL CONTINUOUS THROUGH FLOOR

INTERIOR FINISH

FIREBLOCK &/OR WALL NAILING BLOCK AS REQUIRED

FINISH FLOOR

SUBFLOOR

JOIST SCREWED TO STUDS

INSULATION see 63C & D

FINISH CEILING

VAPOR BARRIER BEHIND JOIST see 63C & D

B **JOISTS @ BALLOON-FRAMED WALL**
JOISTS ‖ TO WALL

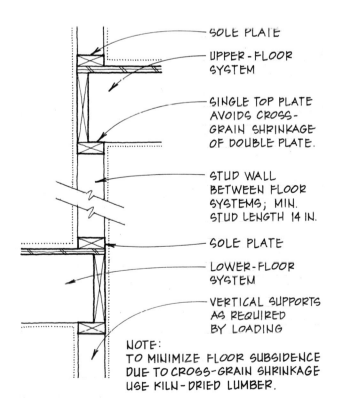

SOLE PLATE

UPPER-FLOOR SYSTEM

SINGLE TOP PLATE AVOIDS CROSS-GRAIN SHRINKAGE OF DOUBLE PLATE.

STUD WALL BETWEEN FLOOR SYSTEMS; MIN. STUD LENGTH 14 IN.

SOLE PLATE

LOWER-FLOOR SYSTEM

VERTICAL SUPPORTS AS REQUIRED BY LOADING

NOTE:
TO MINIMIZE FLOOR SUBSIDENCE DUE TO CROSS-GRAIN SHRINKAGE USE KILN-DRIED LUMBER.

C **LEVEL CHANGE**
PLATFORM FRAMING

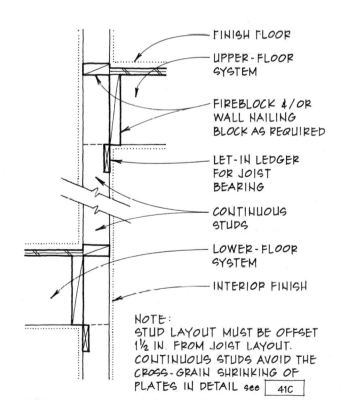

FINISH FLOOR

UPPER-FLOOR SYSTEM

FIREBLOCK &/OR WALL NAILING BLOCK AS REQUIRED

LET-IN LEDGER FOR JOIST BEARING

CONTINUOUS STUDS

LOWER-FLOOR SYSTEM

INTERIOR FINISH

NOTE:
STUD LAYOUT MUST BE OFFSET 1½ IN. FROM JOIST LAYOUT. CONTINUOUS STUDS AVOID THE CROSS-GRAIN SHRINKING OF PLATES IN DETAIL see 41C

D **LEVEL CHANGE**
BALLOON FRAMING

Interior walls are either bearings walls, which carry loads from the roof or from floors above, or partition walls, which do not support any loads from above. Both types of wall can be fastened directly to the subfloor, but bearing walls must have their loads distributed to or through the floor system with extra framing. Both types of wall may require extra framing where they attach to floor systems, but the framing in bearing walls will generally be more substantial.

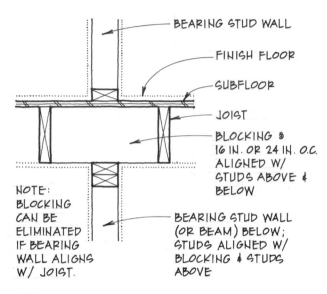

BEARING STUD WALL

FINISH FLOOR

SUBFLOOR

JOIST

BLOCKING @ 16 IN. OR 24 IN. O.C. ALIGNED W/ STUDS ABOVE & BELOW

NOTE: BLOCKING CAN BE ELIMINATED IF BEARING WALL ALIGNS W/ JOIST.

BEARING STUD WALL (OR BEAM) BELOW; STUDS ALIGNED W/ BLOCKING & STUDS ABOVE

(A) JOISTS @ BEARING WALL
JOISTS ∥ TO WALL

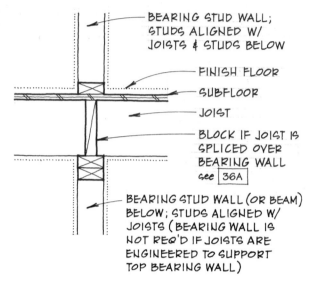

BEARING STUD WALL; STUDS ALIGNED W/ JOISTS & STUDS BELOW

FINISH FLOOR

SUBFLOOR

JOIST

BLOCK IF JOIST IS SPLICED OVER BEARING WALL
see 36A

BEARING STUD WALL (OR BEAM) BELOW; STUDS ALIGNED W/ JOISTS (BEARING WALL IS NOT REQ'D IF JOISTS ARE ENGINEERED TO SUPPORT TOP BEARING WALL)

(B) JOISTS @ BEARING WALL
JOISTS ⊥ TO WALL

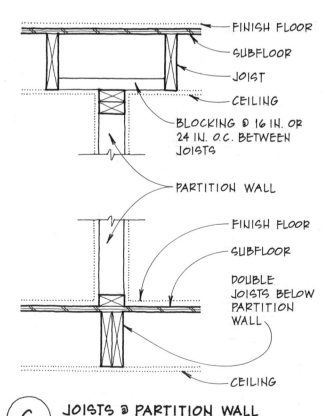

FINISH FLOOR

SUBFLOOR

JOIST

CEILING

BLOCKING @ 16 IN. OR 24 IN. O.C. BETWEEN JOISTS

PARTITION WALL

FINISH FLOOR

SUBFLOOR

DOUBLE JOISTS BELOW PARTITION WALL

CEILING

(C) JOISTS @ PARTITION WALL
JOISTS ∥ TO WALL

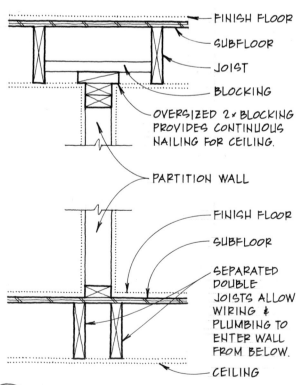

FINISH FLOOR

SUBFLOOR

JOIST

BLOCKING

OVERSIZED 2x BLOCKING PROVIDES CONTINUOUS NAILING FOR CEILING.

PARTITION WALL

FINISH FLOOR

SUBFLOOR

SEPARATED DOUBLE JOISTS ALLOW WIRING & PLUMBING TO ENTER WALL FROM BELOW.

CEILING

(D) JOISTS @ PARTITION WALL
ALTERNATIVE DETAILS

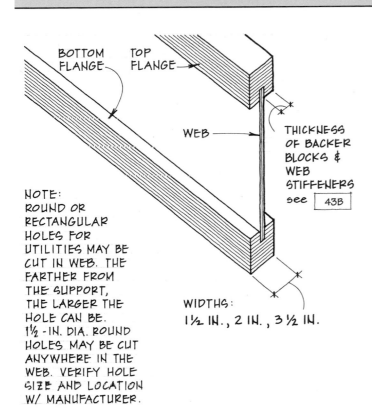

BOTTOM FLANGE

TOP FLANGE

WEB

THICKNESS OF BACKER BLOCKS & WEB STIFFENERS see 43B

NOTE:
ROUND OR RECTANGULAR HOLES FOR UTILITIES MAY BE CUT IN WEB. THE FARTHER FROM THE SUPPORT, THE LARGER THE HOLE CAN BE. 1½ -IN. DIA. ROUND HOLES MAY BE CUT ANYWHERE IN THE WEB. VERIFY HOLE SIZE AND LOCATION W/ MANUFACTURER.

WIDTHS:
1½ IN., 2 IN., 3½ IN.

Wood I-joists are designed to work efficiently, with most of the wood located at the top and bottom of the joist where the stresses are greatest. Called flanges, the top and bottom are generally made of laminated or solid wood; the slender central part of the joist, the web, is made of plywood or OSB. I-joists are straighter, drier, and more precise than dimension lumber and therefore make a flatter, quieter floor. Their spanning capacity is only slightly greater than that of dimension lumber, but because they can be manufactured much deeper and longer than lumber joists (up to 30 in. deep and 60 ft. long), they are the floor-framing system of choice when long spans are required.

Wood I-joists are designed to be part of a system composed of engineered beams, joists, and sheathing. Laminated strand lumber (LSL) rim joists and laminated veneer lumber (LVL) beams are sized to integrate with the joists. In cases of extreme loading, LVL beams may be substituted for I-joists. The system is completed with APA-rated tongue-and-groove sheathing nailed to the joists and reinforced with construction adhesive. Wood I-joists are valued by plumbers and electricians because they are often manufactured with precut holes.

A WOOD I-JOISTS

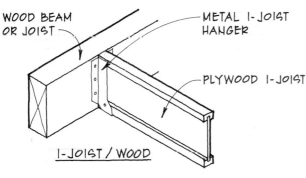

WOOD BEAM OR JOIST

METAL I-JOIST HANGER

PLYWOOD I-JOIST

I-JOIST / WOOD

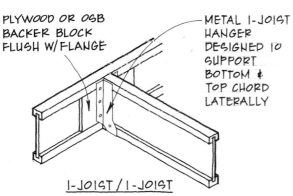

PLYWOOD OR OSB BACKER BLOCK FLUSH W/ FLANGE

METAL I-JOIST HANGER DESIGNED TO SUPPORT BOTTOM & TOP CHORD LATERALLY

I-JOIST / I-JOIST

B WOOD I-JOIST CONNECTIONS

Because the web is thin, I-joists are about 50% lighter than lumber joists. But the thin web also means I-joists do not have as much strength to resist vertical crushing forces. For this reason, the web often must be reinforced with plywood or OSB web stiffeners. Nailed to the web, these stiffeners occur at bearing walls, at connectors for deep joists, and in other conditions as required by manufacturers' specifications and local codes (see 44C). When vertical loads are extreme, I-joists can be reinforced by attaching sections of 2x framing lumber called squash blocks to their sides (see 44C).

When other framing members need to be attached to the side of an I-joist, backer blocks are added to the webs of the I-joists. Like web stiffeners, backer blocks are made of plywood or OSB, but their primary purpose is to provide a planar, thick nailing surface rather than to resist vertical loads (see 44D).

Wood I-joists are easily cut on site and can be attached to each other with metal straps and hangers, but, because of the need for web stiffeners and backer blocks, they take more time to install than dimension lumber joists.

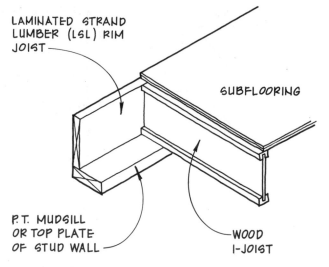

LAMINATED STRAND LUMBER (LSL) RIM JOIST

SUBFLOORING

P.T. MUDSILL OR TOP PLATE OF STUD WALL

WOOD I-JOIST

NOTE:
LSL RIM JOISTS ARE SIZED TO CORRESPOND WITH THE DEPTH OF WOOD I-JOISTS

A WOOD I-JOISTS @ RIM JOIST
JOISTS ON MUDSILL OR TOP PLATE

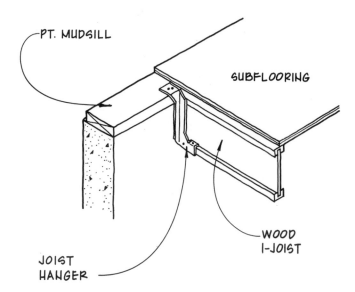

PT. MUDSILL

SUBFLOORING

JOIST HANGER

WOOD I-JOIST

B WOOD I-JOISTS @ RIM JOIST
JOISTS FLUSH WITH MUDSILL

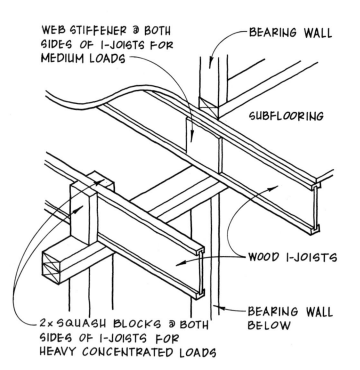

WEB STIFFENER @ BOTH SIDES OF I-JOISTS FOR MEDIUM LOADS

BEARING WALL

SUBFLOORING

WOOD I-JOISTS

2x SQUASH BLOCKS @ BOTH SIDES OF I-JOISTS FOR HEAVY CONCENTRATED LOADS

BEARING WALL BELOW

C WOOD I-JOISTS FOR LOADS
WEB STIFFENERS & SQUASH BLOCKS

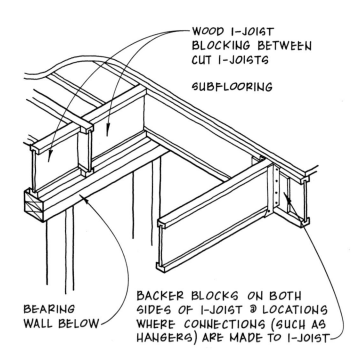

WOOD I-JOIST BLOCKING BETWEEN CUT I-JOISTS

SUBFLOORING

BEARING WALL BELOW

BACKER BLOCKS ON BOTH SIDES OF I-JOIST @ LOCATIONS WHERE CONNECTIONS (SUCH AS HANGERS) ARE MADE TO I-JOIST

D WOOD I-JOIST CONNECTIONS
BLOCKING & BACKER BLOCKS

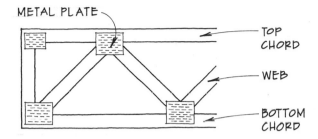

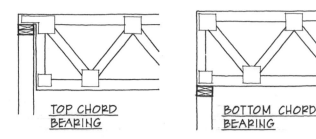

TOP CHORD
BEARING

BOTTOM CHORD
BEARING

Four-by-two wood floor trusses are made up of small members (usually 2x4s) that are connected so that they act like a single large member. The parallel top and bottom chords and the webs are made of lumber held together at the intersections with toothed metal plates.

The open web allows for utilities to run through the floor without altering the truss. Round ducts from 5 in. to 16 in. in diameter can be accommodated, depending on the depth of the truss. Truss depths vary from 10 in. to 24 in., with spans up to about 30 ft. Like plywood I-joists, floor trusses are practical for long spans and simple plans, but difficult for complicated buildings.

Floor trusses are custom manufactured for each job, and cannot be altered at the site. Bearing walls, floor openings, and other departures from the simple span should always be engineered by the manufacturer.

 WOOD FLOOR TRUSSES

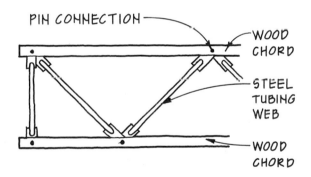

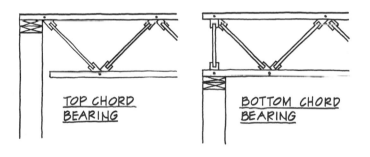

TOP CHORD
BEARING

BOTTOM CHORD
BEARING

Wood top and bottom chords are linked with steel tubing webs in the composite truss. The tubing is pressed flat at the ends and connected to the *wood* chords with a metal pin. Unlike wood trusses with metal plates (see 45A above), the webs of the composite truss are entirely free to rotate (on the pins) and therefore allow the truss to return to its original shape when the load is removed.

Composite trusses are generally more heavy duty than their all-wood cousins illustrated in 45A above. The largest composite trusses are capable of spanning over 100 ft. They are made with double 2x chords, which sandwich the webs. The lightest-duty composite trusses are made with single 2x4 chords oriented flat and dadoed to receive the webs.

Like wood floor trusses, composite trusses easily accommodate ducts and other utilities, which can be run through the open webs without altering the truss. Like all trusses, composite trusses are most practical for simple plans with long spans. Once engineered and installed, they are very difficult to alter.

 COMPOSITE FLOOR TRUSSES

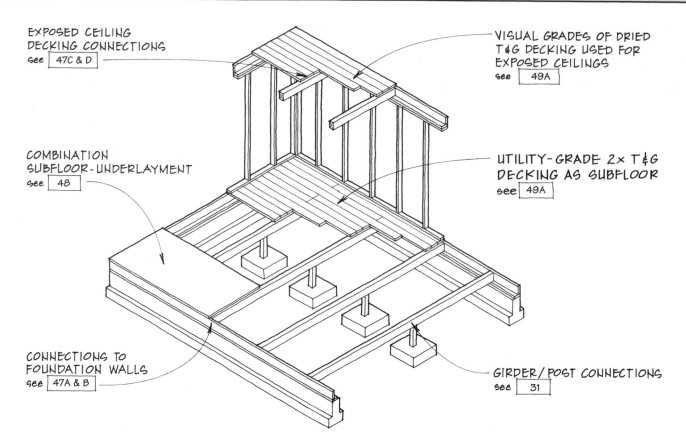

EXPOSED CEILING
DECKING CONNECTIONS
see [47C & D]

VISUAL GRADES OF DRIED
T&G DECKING USED FOR
EXPOSED CEILINGS
see [49A]

COMBINATION
SUBFLOOR-UNDERLAYMENT
see [48]

UTILITY-GRADE 2× T&G
DECKING AS SUBFLOOR
see [49A]

CONNECTIONS TO
FOUNDATION WALLS
see [47A & B]

GIRDER/POST CONNECTIONS
see [31]

Girder systems may be designed with either dimension or laminated lumber. They are most common in the Northwest, where dimension timber is plentiful. Girder floor systems are similar to joist floor systems except that girders, which are wider than joists, can carry a greater load for a given span and therefore can be spaced at wider intervals than joists. Girders are typically placed on 48-in. centers, so long-spanning subfloor materials such as 2-in. T&G decking or 1⅛-in. combination subfloor-underlayment are required (see 48).

When used over crawl spaces, girders may be supported directly on posts. Over a basement, a girder system may be supported on posts or may bear on a wall or a beam like a joist system. At upper floor levels, girder systems are often used in conjunction with an exposed T&G decking ceiling. These exposed ceilings can make wiring, plumbing, and ductwork difficult.

Girder spans	
Size, species, grade, & spacing	Span (ft.)
4x6 Douglas-fir #2 @ 48 in. o.c.	8.6
4x8 Douglas-fir #2 @ 48 in. o.c.	11.3
4x10 Douglas-fir #2 @ 48 in. o.c.	14.4
4x12 Douglas-fir #2 @ 48 in. o.c.	17.6

This table assumes a 40-psf live load, a 10-psf dead load, and a deflection of L/360. The table is for estimating purposes only. No. 2 Douglas-fir is most prevalent in regions where girder systems are most frequently used.

(A) GIRDER-FLOOR SYSTEMS

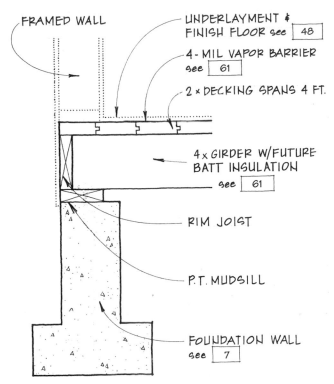

FRAMED WALL

UNDERLAYMENT &
FINISH FLOOR see 48

4- MIL VAPOR BARRIER
see 61

2 × DECKING SPANS 4 FT.

4 × GIRDER W/FUTURE
BATT INSULATION
see 61

RIM JOIST

P.T. MUDSILL

FOUNDATION WALL
see 7

A GIRDERS ON MUDSILL
GIRDERS ⊥ TO WALL

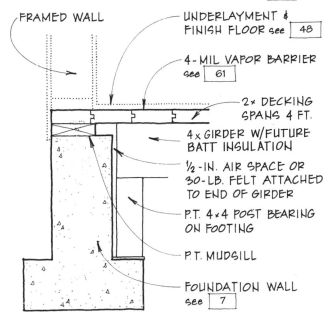

NOTE:
THIS DETAIL IS NOT RECOMMENDED FOR GIRDERS
OVER 4×8 BECAUSE OF POTENTIAL SHRINKAGE
PROBLEMS. FOR BEAM-POCKET DETAIL see 16C

FRAMED WALL

UNDERLAYMENT &
FINISH FLOOR see 48

4- MIL VAPOR BARRIER
see 61

2 × DECKING
SPANS 4 FT.

4 × GIRDER W/FUTURE
BATT INSULATION

½ -IN. AIR SPACE OR
30- LB. FELT ATTACHED
TO END OF GIRDER

P.T. 4 × 4 POST BEARING
ON FOOTING

P.T. MUDSILL

FOUNDATION WALL
see 7

B GIRDERS FLUSH W/ MUDSILL
GIRDERS ⊥ TO WALL

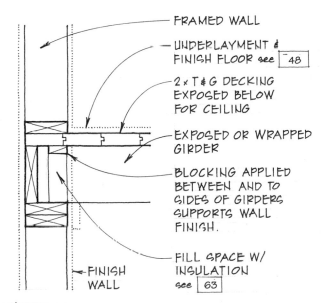

FRAMED WALL

UNDERLAYMENT &
FINISH FLOOR see 48

2 × T&G DECKING
EXPOSED BELOW
FOR CEILING

EXPOSED OR WRAPPED
GIRDER

BLOCKING APPLIED
BETWEEN AND TO
SIDES OF GIRDERS
SUPPORTS WALL
FINISH.

FILL SPACE W/
INSULATION
see 63

FINISH
WALL

NOTE:
2 × T&G DECKING MAY BE SANDED TO MAKE FINISH
FLOOR, BUT THIS IS ADVISABLE ONLY W/ VERY
DRY DECKING. DUST FILTRATION FROM UPPER TO
LOWER FLOOR & SOUND TRANSMISSION BETWEEN
FLOORS MAY OCCUR WITH THIS DETAIL.

C GIRDERS W/ EXPOSED DECKING
2 ND FLOOR : GIRDERS ⊥ TO WALL

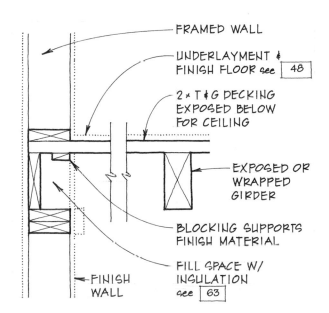

FRAMED WALL

UNDERLAYMENT &
FINISH FLOOR see 48

2 × T&G DECKING
EXPOSED BELOW
FOR CEILING

EXPOSED OR
WRAPPED
GIRDER

BLOCKING SUPPORTS
FINISH MATERIAL

FILL SPACE W/
INSULATION
see 63

FINISH
WALL

NOTE:
DECKING DOES NOT PROVIDE STRUCTURAL
DIAPHRAGM REQUIRED @ UPPER FLOORS. USE
PLYWOOD UNDERLAYMENT OR OTHER METHOD
TO TRANSFER LATERAL LOADS.

D GIRDERS W/ EXPOSED DECKING
2 ND FLOOR : GIRDERS ‖ TO WALL

Subflooring—Subflooring is the structural skin of a floor system. It spans between the joists and acts as a diaphragm to transfer horizontal loads to the walls of a structure. For joist systems, subflooring is typically tongue-and-groove (T&G) plywood, non-veneered panels such as oriented strand board (OSB) or T&G plywood combination subfloor/underlayment, which is a grade of T&G plywood that is plugged and sanded to a smooth underlayment-grade surface. In girder systems, the subflooring is typically T&G decking (see 49A).

Underlayment—Underlayment is not structural but provides a smooth surface necessary for some finish floors. It can also be used to fur up floors to match an adjacent finish floor of a different thickness. Underlayment is typically plywood, particleboard, or hardboard.

Spacing and nailing—Most plywood manufacturers specify a space of ⅛ in. between the edges of panels to allow for expansion. Panels that are sized ⅛ in. smaller in each direction are available to allow a space without compromising the 4-ft. by 8-ft. module. The procedure may be successfully avoided in dry climates. Check with local contractors for accepted local practice.

A common rule of thumb is to nail panels 6 in. o.c. at edges and 12 in. o.c. in the panel field. Glues and panel adhesives can minimize squeaks and reduce the nailing requirements for panel floor systems. Verify attachment methods with the specifications of the manufacturer. A typical plywood grade stamp is shown below.

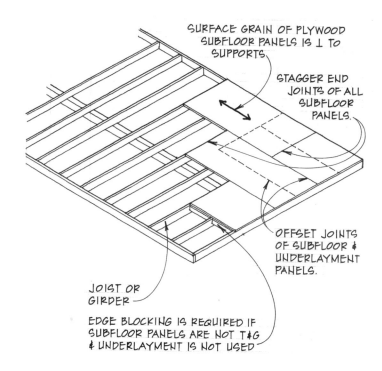

SURFACE GRAIN OF PLYWOOD SUBFLOOR PANELS IS ⊥ TO SUPPORTS

STAGGER END JOINTS OF ALL SUBFLOOR PANELS.

OFFSET JOINTS OF SUBFLOOR & UNDERLAYMENT PANELS.

JOIST OR GIRDER

EDGE BLOCKING IS REQUIRED IF SUBFLOOR PANELS ARE NOT T&G & UNDERLAYMENT IS NOT USED

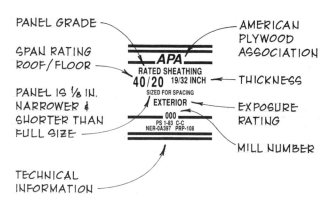

PANEL GRADE

SPAN RATING ROOF/FLOOR

PANEL IS ⅛ IN. NARROWER & SHORTER THAN FULL SIZE

AMERICAN PLYWOOD ASSOCIATION

APA RATED SHEATHING 40/20 19/32 INCH SIZED FOR SPACING EXTERIOR 000 PS 1-83 C-C NER-0A397 PRP-108

THICKNESS

EXPOSURE RATING

MILL NUMBER

TECHNICAL INFORMATION

Subflooring spans		
Subfloor type	**Thickness**	**Maximum span**
Plywood sheathing or combination subfloor underlayment	½ in. to ⅝ in.	16 in.
	⅝ in. to ¾ in.	20 in.
	¾ in. to ⅞ in.	24 in.
	1⅛ in.	48 in.
Non-veneered panels: OSB, waferboard, particleboard	⅝ in.	16 in.
	¾ in.	24 in.

The values in this table are based on information from the APA-The Engineered Wood Association and the Uniform Building Code (UBC). Values are for panels that are continuous over two or more spans, with the long dimension of the panel perpendicular to supports. Verify span with panel rating.

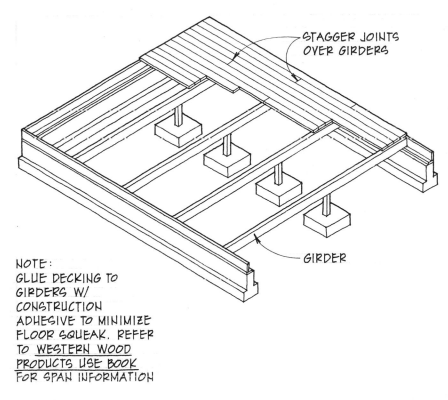

STAGGER JOINTS OVER GIRDERS

GIRDER

NOTE:
GLUE DECKING TO GIRDERS W/ CONSTRUCTION ADHESIVE TO MINIMIZE FLOOR SQUEAK. REFER TO WESTERN WOOD PRODUCTS USE BOOK FOR SPAN INFORMATION

TYPICAL T&G DECKING SECTIONS

2×6 V-JOINT IS MOST COMMONLY USED ON UPPER FLOORS TO MAKE EXPOSED CEILINGS BELOW. MOST SPECIES WILL SPAN 4 FT.

2×8 UTILITY IS USED PRIMARILY AS SUBFLOOR OVER CRAWL SPACES OR BASEMENTS, & IS OFTEN INSTALLED GREEN. IT WILL SPAN 4 FT. IN MOST FLOOR SITUATIONS.

3× & 4× LAMINATED IS USED MOSTLY AT ROOFS TO MAKE EXPOSED CEILINGS BELOW, BUT ALSO AS FLOORING. DECKING IS END MATCHED FOR RANDOM-LENGTH APPLICATION & IS AVAILABLE PREFINISHED IN 3×6, 3×8, 4×6 & 4×8 SIZES. IT SPANS UP TO 14 FT. FOR RESIDENTIAL FLOOR LOADS.

(A) SUBFLOORING
T&G DECKING

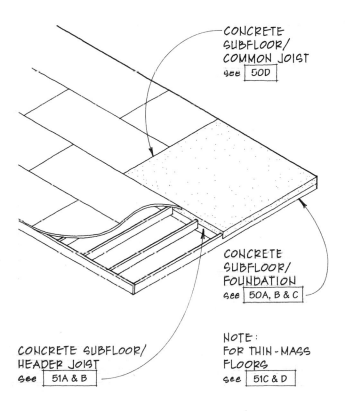

CONCRETE SUBFLOOR/ COMMON JOIST
see | 50D |

CONCRETE SUBFLOOR/ FOUNDATION
see | 50A, B & C |

CONCRETE SUBFLOOR/ HEADER JOIST
see | 51A & B |

NOTE:
FOR THIN-MASS FLOORS
see | 51C & D |

A small part of the subfloor may need to be concrete to support tiles or for a passive-solar mass floor at a south edge. The structure under the concrete must be lowered in order to accommodate the extra thickness of the concrete, typically 2¼ in. to 3 in. Use plywood that is rated to carry the load of wet concrete, usually ¾ in. (min.).

In the case of a tiled floor, the complications of adjusting the structure to accommodate a thick concrete subfloor may be avoided by using a ⁷⁄₁₆ in. thick glass-fiber–reinforced cement board over the surface of the typical wood subfloor. Check with the tile manufacturer for recommendations.

(B) SUBFLOORING
CONCRETE

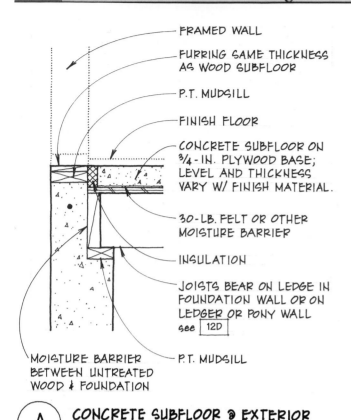

FRAMED WALL

FURRING SAME THICKNESS AS WOOD SUBFLOOR

P.T. MUDSILL

FINISH FLOOR

CONCRETE SUBFLOOR ON ¾-IN. PLYWOOD BASE; LEVEL AND THICKNESS VARY W/ FINISH MATERIAL.

30-LB. FELT OR OTHER MOISTURE BARRIER

INSULATION

JOISTS BEAR ON LEDGE IN FOUNDATION WALL OR ON LEDGER OR PONY WALL see [12D]

MOISTURE BARRIER BETWEEN UNTREATED WOOD & FOUNDATION

P.T. MUDSILL

(A) **CONCRETE SUBFLOOR @ EXTERIOR**
FULL-DEPTH JOISTS BELOW MUDSILL

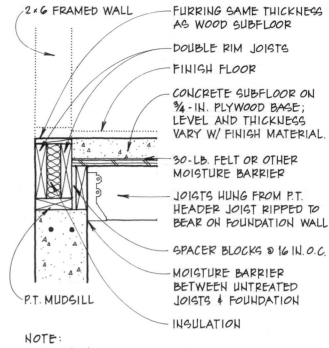

2×6 FRAMED WALL

FURRING SAME THICKNESS AS WOOD SUBFLOOR

DOUBLE RIM JOISTS

FINISH FLOOR

CONCRETE SUBFLOOR ON ¾-IN. PLYWOOD BASE; LEVEL AND THICKNESS VARY W/ FINISH MATERIAL.

30-LB. FELT OR OTHER MOISTURE BARRIER

JOISTS HUNG FROM P.T. HEADER JOIST RIPPED TO BEAR ON FOUNDATION WALL

SPACER BLOCKS @ 16 IN. O.C.

MOISTURE BARRIER BETWEEN UNTREATED JOISTS & FOUNDATION

INSULATION

P.T. MUDSILL

NOTE:
FOR 2×4 WALL, PLACE INSULATION BETWEEN DOUBLE RIM JOIST & P.T. HEADER JOIST.

(B) **CONCRETE SUBFLOOR @ EXTERIOR**
FULL-DEPTH JOISTS / ALTERNATIVE

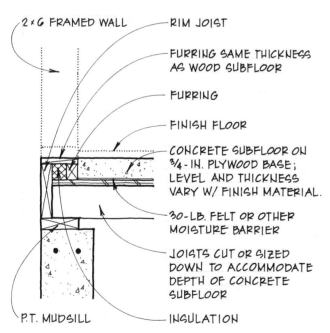

2×6 FRAMED WALL

RIM JOIST

FURRING SAME THICKNESS AS WOOD SUBFLOOR

FURRING

FINISH FLOOR

CONCRETE SUBFLOOR ON ¾-IN. PLYWOOD BASE; LEVEL AND THICKNESS VARY W/ FINISH MATERIAL.

30-LB. FELT OR OTHER MOISTURE BARRIER

JOISTS CUT OR SIZED DOWN TO ACCOMMODATE DEPTH OF CONCRETE SUBFLOOR

P.T. MUDSILL

INSULATION

NOTE:
DECREASE SPAN &/OR SPACING OF SIZED-DOWN JOISTS SUPPORTING CONCRETE.

(C) **CONCRETE SUBFLOOR @ EXTERIOR**
CUT-DOWN JOISTS ON MUDSILL

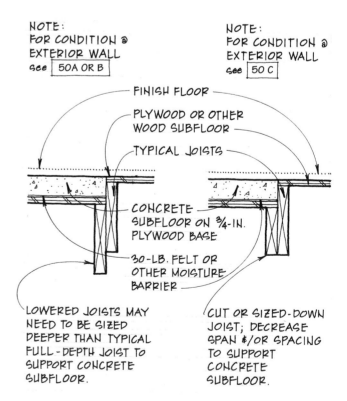

NOTE:
FOR CONDITION @ EXTERIOR WALL see [50A OR B]

NOTE:
FOR CONDITION @ EXTERIOR WALL see [50C]

FINISH FLOOR

PLYWOOD OR OTHER WOOD SUBFLOOR

TYPICAL JOISTS

CONCRETE SUBFLOOR ON ¾-IN. PLYWOOD BASE

30-LB. FELT OR OTHER MOISTURE BARRIER

LOWERED JOISTS MAY NEED TO BE SIZED DEEPER THAN TYPICAL FULL-DEPTH JOIST TO SUPPORT CONCRETE SUBFLOOR.

CUT OR SIZED-DOWN JOIST; DECREASE SPAN &/OR SPACING TO SUPPORT CONCRETE SUBFLOOR.

(D) **CONCRETE SUBFLOOR @ INTERIOR**
EDGE ‖ TO JOISTS / 2 DETAILS

NOTE:
FOR CONDITION @ EXTERIOR WALL
see 50A OR B

PLYWOOD OR OTHER
WOOD SUBFLOOR

FINISH FLOOR

CONCRETE SUBFLOOR
ON ¾-IN. PLYWOOD
BASE

30-LB. FELT OR OTHER
MOISTURE BARRIER

JOIST ON JOIST HANGER

DOUBLE HEADER JOIST

JOIST ON
JOIST
HANGER

SINGLE HEADER JOIST
NAILED TO DOUBLE
HEADER JOIST

VERTICAL SUPPORT
AS REQUIRED

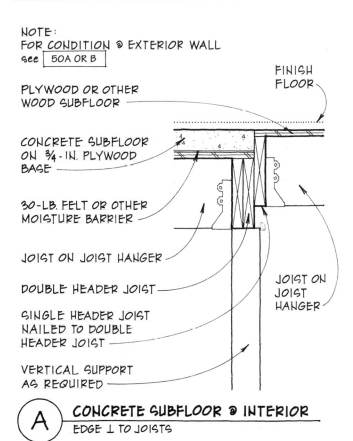

A **CONCRETE SUBFLOOR @ INTERIOR**
EDGE ⊥ TO JOISTS

FINISH FLOOR

CONCRETE
SUBFLOOR ON ¾-IN.
PLYWOOD BASE

CUT-DOWN JOIST

VERTICAL SUPPORT
AS REQUIRED

FINISH FLOOR

CONCRETE
SUBFLOOR ON ¾-IN.
PLYWOOD BASE

30-LB. FELT OR OTHER
MOISTURE BARRIER

NOTCHED JOIST

BLOCKING

BEAM OR STUD-WALL
SUPPORT AS REQUIRED

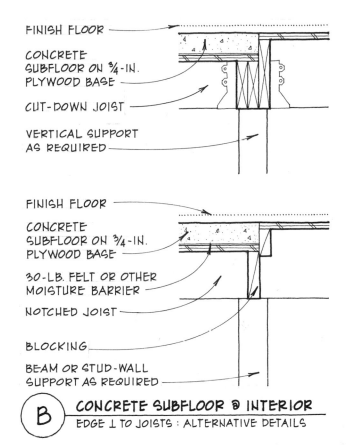

B **CONCRETE SUBFLOOR @ INTERIOR**
EDGE ⊥ TO JOISTS : ALTERNATIVE DETAILS

STUD WALL FRAMED
AFTER CONCRETE IS
FINISHED

DOUBLE 2× P.T. PLATE
SERVES AS SCREED.

3-IN. CONCRETE
SUBFLOOR ON ¾-IN.
PLYWOOD BASE

30-LB. FELT OR OTHER
MOISTURE BARRIER

JOIST

P.T. MUDSILL (OR TOP
PLATE IF THIN-MASS
SUBFLOOR IS AT
UPPER STORY)

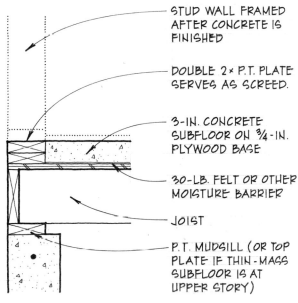

NOTE:
THIS DETAIL IS USED TO PROVIDE MASS TO A LARGE
AREA OF FLOOR FOR SOLAR GAIN.

C **THIN-MASS SUBFLOOR**
@ EXTERIOR WALL

STUD WALL FRAMED
AFTER CONCRETE IS
FINISHED

DOUBLE 2× P.T. PLATE
SERVES AS SCREED &
ALLOWS UTILITIES TO
PASS THROUGH FLOOR
SYSTEM @ WALL

3-IN. CONCRETE
SUBFLOOR ON ¾-IN.
PLYWOOD BASE

30-LB. FELT OR OTHER
MOISTURE BARRIER

JOIST

BLOCKING

STRUCTURE BELOW
AS REQUIRED

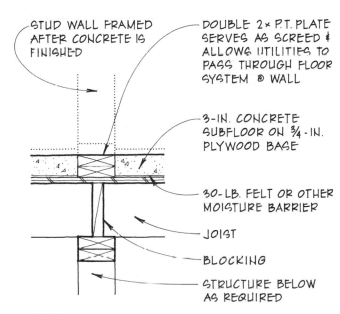

NOTE:
IF THE CONCRETE IS TO BE EXPOSED, THE DOUBLE
PLATE MAY BE OMITTED FOR EASE OF TROWELING.
THE STUD WALL MAY THEN BE SHOT TO CONCRETE
see 24C

D **THIN-MASS SUBFLOOR**
@ INTERIOR WALL

Porches and decks are traditional and useful additions to wood-frame structures. They provide a transition between indoors and out, allowing people to pause upon entering or leaving, and they extend the building to include the out-of-doors. Porch and deck floors must be constructed differently from interior floors in order to withstand the weather. The connection between porch and deck floors and the building itself is especially critical in keeping moisture out of the main structure. Because of constant exposure to the weather, this connection must be detailed in such a way that it can be repaired or replaced.

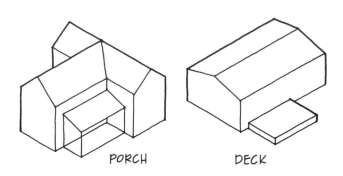

PORCH   DECK

The floors of porches and decks can be grouped into two major types: those that are waterproof and thus act as a roof protecting the area below, and those that are open and allow water to pass through.

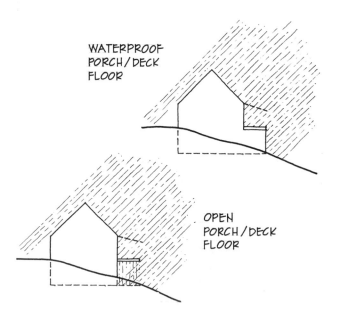

WATERPROOF PORCH/DECK FLOOR

OPEN PORCH/DECK FLOOR

Waterproof porch—A waterproof porch or deck floor can be treated like a flat roof. As shown in the drawing below, flashing (or the roofing material itself) must be tucked under the siding to catch water running down the side of the building, and the floor (roof) surface must be sloped away from the building (see 56A). The framing for waterproof decks over living spaces needs proper ventilation (see 205A).

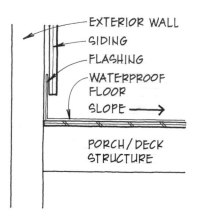

EXTERIOR WALL
SIDING
FLASHING
WATERPROOF FLOOR
SLOPE ⟶
PORCH/DECK STRUCTURE

Open porch—In an open porch or deck floor, the parts that connect it to the main structure are exposed to the weather, yet need to penetrate the skin of the wall. This connection can be accomplished by keeping the porch/deck structure away from the exterior wall and attaching it only at intervals with spaced connectors (see 54B & C).

Alternatively, a continuous ledger may be bolted to the wall and flashed (see 55A & B).

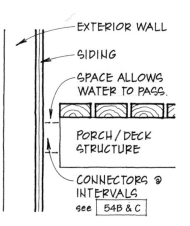

EXTERIOR WALL
SIDING
SPACE ALLOWS WATER TO PASS.
PORCH/DECK STRUCTURE
CONNECTORS @ INTERVALS
see 54B & C

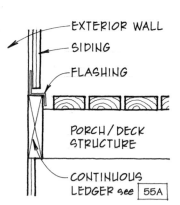

EXTERIOR WALL
SIDING
FLASHING
PORCH/DECK STRUCTURE
CONTINUOUS LEDGER see 55A

Porches and decks are exposed directly to the weather in ways that the main part of the structure is not. Consequently, the wood used in porches and decks is much more susceptible to expansion and contraction, twisting, checking, and rotting. A special strategy for building porches and decks is therefore appropriate.

Weather resistance—Elements of porches and decks that are likely to get wet should be constructed of weather-resistant materials. Virtually all the material required to make a new porch or deck is now available in pressure-treated lumber. Weather-resistant woods like cedar or redwood are also appropriate.

Connectors—At least once a year, joints that are exposed to the weather will shrink and swell, causing nails to withdraw and joints to weaken. Joints made with screws or bolts will therefore outlast those made with nails. For joist connections, use joist hangers or angle clips.

Joist hangers are made of galvanized steel, which should not be adversely affected by exposure to the weather. Galvanized steel deteriorates relatively quickly, however, when combined with pressure-treated lumber, especially when moisture is added to the mix. Consider the use of weather-resistant wood species for use with galvanized hangers.

Fasteners such as nails and deck screws should be galvanized. Stainless steel screws are also available and will give the longest life.

Framing—Areas between adjacent wood members collect moisture and are especially prone to rot. Even pressure-treated lumber can rot in this situation. Avoid doubling up members in exposed situations. It is better to use a single large timber where extra strength is required, as shown in the drawing at right.

POOR   GOOD

Where wood must touch another surface, make the area of contact as small as possible and allow for air circulation around the joint.

Wood decking—Because decking is oriented horizontally, it has a relatively large exposed surface to collect and absorb moisture. This moisture will tend to make the decking cup. Flat-grain decking (and rail caps) should be placed with the bark side up (as shown) so if they cup, the boards will shed water.

Synthetic decking—There is a new generation of synthetic decking made of reclaimed hardwood and recycled plastic. This material holds up in exposed conditions, is not harmed by rot or insects, and is extremely consistent and stable. Because the decking does not absorb water, thermal expansion is more of a concern than warping or cupping. The decking requires no sealers or preservatives and is manufactured with a nonskid surface. It is disposable (no toxins). The decking can be fastened to framing with conventional methods and is available in standard sizes from 1x6 to 2x8.

Painting—Sealers and preservatives will extend the life of porches and decks. Special attention should be given to end grain and to areas likely to hold moisture. Stains will outlast paints. Special porch and deck paints are available for use where exposure to the weather is not severe.

(A) PORCH & DECK CONSTRUCTION

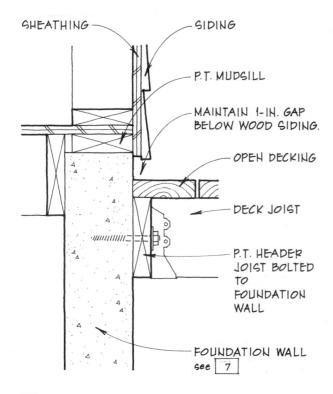

SHEATHING

SIDING

P.T. MUDSILL

MAINTAIN 1-IN. GAP BELOW WOOD SIDING.

OPEN DECKING

DECK JOIST

P.T. HEADER JOIST BOLTED TO FOUNDATION WALL

FOUNDATION WALL see ⊡ 7

 A   **OPEN DECK / FOUNDATION WALL**

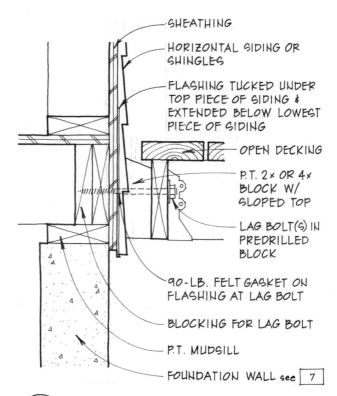

SHEATHING

HORIZONTAL SIDING OR SHINGLES

FLASHING TUCKED UNDER TOP PIECE OF SIDING & EXTENDED BELOW LOWEST PIECE OF SIDING

OPEN DECKING

P.T. 2× OR 4× BLOCK W/ SLOPED TOP

LAG BOLT(S) IN PREDRILLED BLOCK

90-LB. FELT GASKET ON FLASHING AT LAG BOLT

BLOCKING FOR LAG BOLT

P.T. MUDSILL

FOUNDATION WALL see ⊡ 7

 B   **OPEN DECK / WOOD WALL**
1ST FLOOR : HORIZONTAL SIDING OR SHINGLES

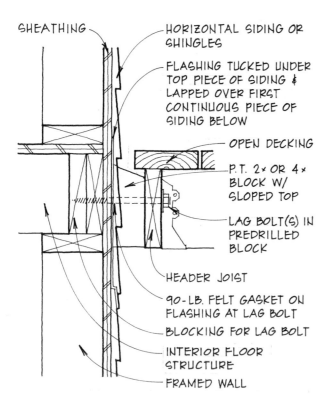

SHEATHING

HORIZONTAL SIDING OR SHINGLES

FLASHING TUCKED UNDER TOP PIECE OF SIDING & LAPPED OVER FIRST CONTINUOUS PIECE OF SIDING BELOW

OPEN DECKING

P.T. 2× OR 4× BLOCK W/ SLOPED TOP

LAG BOLT(S) IN PREDRILLED BLOCK

HEADER JOIST

90-LB. FELT GASKET ON FLASHING AT LAG BOLT

BLOCKING FOR LAG BOLT

INTERIOR FLOOR STRUCTURE

FRAMED WALL

NOTES :
FLASHING EXTENDS 8 IN. MIN. PAST BOTH SIDES OF BLOCK SPACERS. INSTALL SPACER BLOCKS SIMULTANEOUSLY W/ SIDING & FLASHING, THEN INSTALL DECK.

OPEN DECKING LAID DIAGONALLY ACROSS JOIST SYSTEM ACTS AS A DIAPHRAGM, WHICH MAY ELIMINATE THE NEED FOR BRACING PORCH SUPPORTS.

DETAILS SHOW LEVEL OF DECK SLIGHTLY BELOW LEVEL OF FINISH FLOOR. IN SNOW COUNTRY, ADJUST DECK LEVEL AND FLASHING HEIGHT TO ACCOUNT FOR SNOW BUILDUP.

C   **OPEN DECK / WOOD WALL**
2ND FLOOR : HORIZONTAL SIDING OR SHINGLES

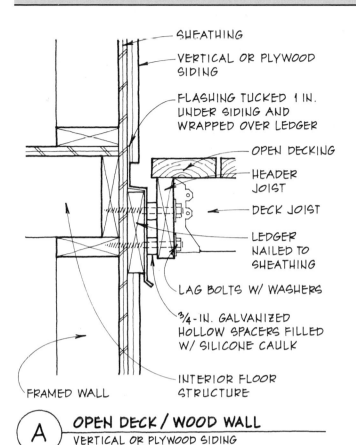

SHEATHING

VERTICAL OR PLYWOOD SIDING

FLASHING TUCKED 1 IN. UNDER SIDING AND WRAPPED OVER LEDGER

OPEN DECKING

HEADER JOIST

DECK JOIST

LEDGER NAILED TO SHEATHING

LAG BOLTS W/ WASHERS

¾-IN. GALVANIZED HOLLOW SPACERS FILLED W/ SILICONE CAULK

INTERIOR FLOOR STRUCTURE

FRAMED WALL

(A) OPEN DECK / WOOD WALL
VERTICAL OR PLYWOOD SIDING

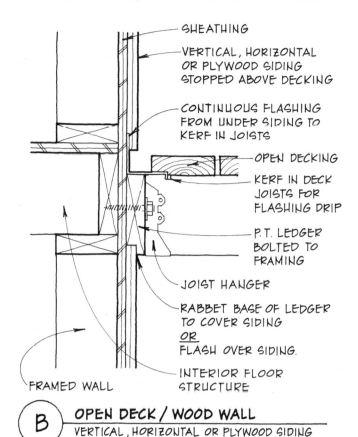

SHEATHING

VERTICAL, HORIZONTAL OR PLYWOOD SIDING STOPPED ABOVE DECKING

CONTINUOUS FLASHING FROM UNDER SIDING TO KERF IN JOISTS

OPEN DECKING

KERF IN DECK JOISTS FOR FLASHING DRIP

P.T. LEDGER BOLTED TO FRAMING

JOIST HANGER

RABBET BASE OF LEDGER TO COVER SIDING
OR
FLASH OVER SIDING.

INTERIOR FLOOR STRUCTURE

FRAMED WALL

(B) OPEN DECK / WOOD WALL
VERTICAL, HORIZONTAL OR PLYWOOD SIDING

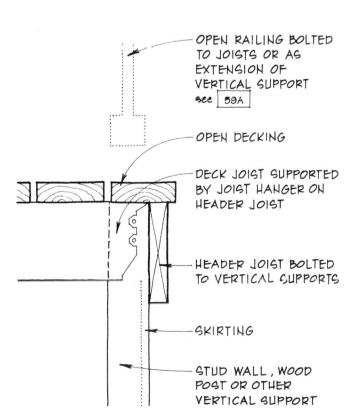

OPEN RAILING BOLTED TO JOISTS OR AS EXTENSION OF VERTICAL SUPPORT
see 59A

OPEN DECKING

DECK JOIST SUPPORTED BY JOIST HANGER ON HEADER JOIST

HEADER JOIST BOLTED TO VERTICAL SUPPORTS

SKIRTING

STUD WALL, WOOD POST OR OTHER VERTICAL SUPPORT

(C) OPEN DECK / OPEN RAILING

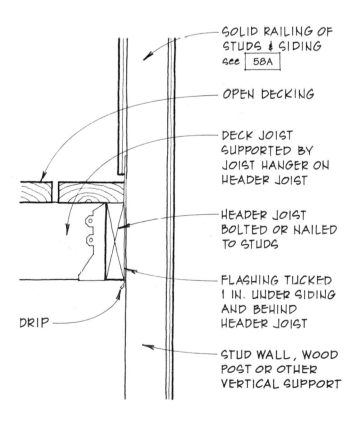

SOLID RAILING OF STUDS & SIDING
see 58A

OPEN DECKING

DECK JOIST SUPPORTED BY JOIST HANGER ON HEADER JOIST

HEADER JOIST BOLTED OR NAILED TO STUDS

FLASHING TUCKED 1 IN. UNDER SIDING AND BEHIND HEADER JOIST

STUD WALL, WOOD POST OR OTHER VERTICAL SUPPORT

DRIP

(D) OPEN DECK / SOLID RAILING

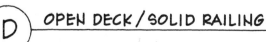

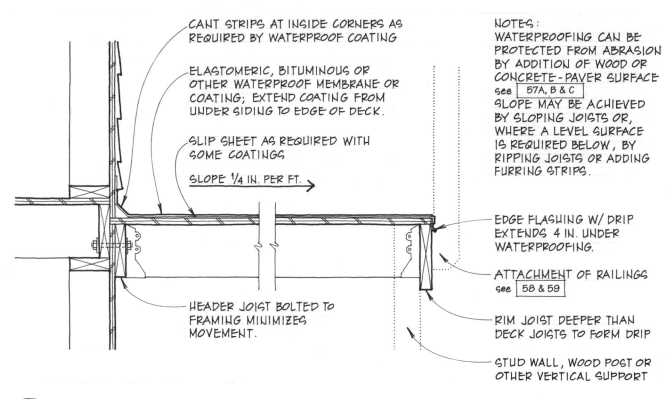

CANT STRIPS AT INSIDE CORNERS AS
REQUIRED BY WATERPROOF COATING

ELASTOMERIC, BITUMINOUS OR
OTHER WATERPROOF MEMBRANE OR
COATING; EXTEND COATING FROM
UNDER SIDING TO EDGE OF DECK.

SLIP SHEET AS REQUIRED WITH
SOME COATINGS

SLOPE ¼ IN. PER FT. →

NOTES:
WATERPROOFING CAN BE
PROTECTED FROM ABRASION
BY ADDITION OF WOOD OR
CONCRETE-PAVER SURFACE
see 57A, B & C
SLOPE MAY BE ACHIEVED
BY SLOPING JOISTS OR,
WHERE A LEVEL SURFACE
IS REQUIRED BELOW, BY
RIPPING JOISTS OR ADDING
FURRING STRIPS.

EDGE FLASHING W/ DRIP
EXTENDS 4 IN. UNDER
WATERPROOFING.

ATTACHMENT OF RAILINGS
see 58 & 59

HEADER JOIST BOLTED TO
FRAMING MINIMIZES
MOVEMENT.

RIM JOIST DEEPER THAN
DECK JOISTS TO FORM DRIP

STUD WALL, WOOD POST OR
OTHER VERTICAL SUPPORT

 A **WATERPROOF DECKS**
GENERAL CHARACTERISTICS

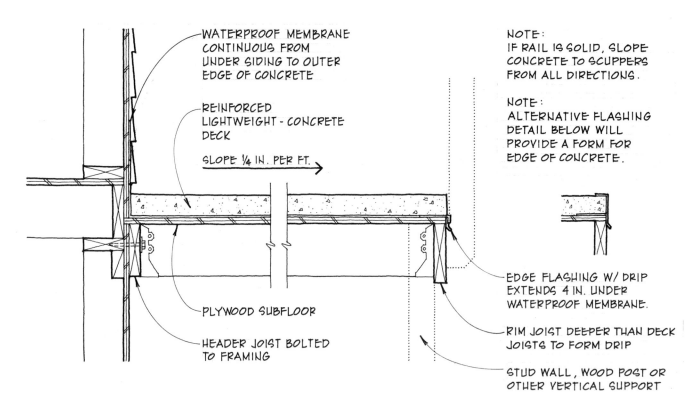

WATERPROOF MEMBRANE
CONTINUOUS FROM
UNDER SIDING TO OUTER
EDGE OF CONCRETE

REINFORCED
LIGHTWEIGHT-CONCRETE
DECK

SLOPE ¼ IN. PER FT. →

NOTE:
IF RAIL IS SOLID, SLOPE
CONCRETE TO SCUPPERS
FROM ALL DIRECTIONS.

NOTE:
ALTERNATIVE FLASHING
DETAIL BELOW WILL
PROVIDE A FORM FOR
EDGE OF CONCRETE.

EDGE FLASHING W/ DRIP
EXTENDS 4 IN. UNDER
WATERPROOF MEMBRANE.

PLYWOOD SUBFLOOR

HEADER JOIST BOLTED
TO FRAMING

RIM JOIST DEEPER THAN DECK
JOISTS TO FORM DRIP

STUD WALL, WOOD POST OR
OTHER VERTICAL SUPPORT

B **LIGHTWEIGHT-CONCRETE PORCH DECK**

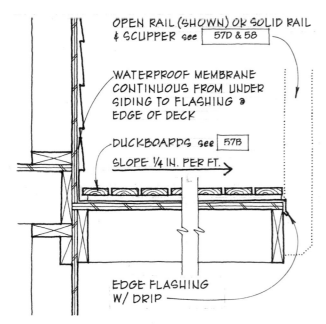

OPEN RAIL (SHOWN) OR SOLID RAIL & SCUPPER see 57D & 58

WATERPROOF MEMBRANE CONTINUOUS FROM UNDER SIDING TO FLASHING @ EDGE OF DECK

DUCKBOARDS see 57B

SLOPE 1/4 IN. PER FT.

EDGE FLASHING W/ DRIP

NOTE:
DUCKBOARD DECKS ARE GENERALLY HELD IN PLACE BY GRAVITY. THEY SHOULD NOT BE USED IN AREAS OF EXTREMELY HIGH WINDS.

 A DUCKBOARD DECK
OPEN RAIL SHOWN

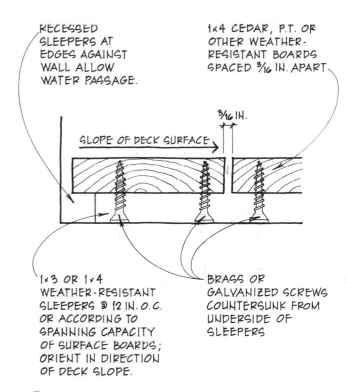

RECESSED SLEEPERS AT EDGES AGAINST WALL ALLOW WATER PASSAGE.

1×4 CEDAR, P.T. OR OTHER WEATHER-RESISTANT BOARDS SPACED 3/16 IN. APART

3/16 IN.

SLOPE OF DECK SURFACE

1×3 OR 1×4 WEATHER-RESISTANT SLEEPERS @ 12 IN. O.C. OR ACCORDING TO SPANNING CAPACITY OF SURFACE BOARDS; ORIENT IN DIRECTION OF DECK SLOPE.

BRASS OR GALVANIZED SCREWS COUNTERSUNK FROM UNDERSIDE OF SLEEPERS

B DUCKBOARD DECK
DETAIL

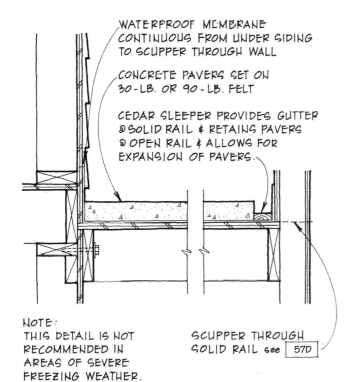

WATERPROOF MEMBRANE CONTINUOUS FROM UNDER SIDING TO SCUPPER THROUGH WALL

CONCRETE PAVERS SET ON 30-LB. OR 90-LB. FELT

CEDAR SLEEPER PROVIDES GUTTER @ SOLID RAIL & RETAINS PAVERS @ OPEN RAIL & ALLOWS FOR EXPANSION OF PAVERS.

NOTE:
THIS DETAIL IS NOT RECOMMENDED IN AREAS OF SEVERE FREEZING WEATHER.

SCUPPER THROUGH SOLID RAIL see 57D

 C CONCRETE-PAVER DECK
SOLID RAIL SHOWN

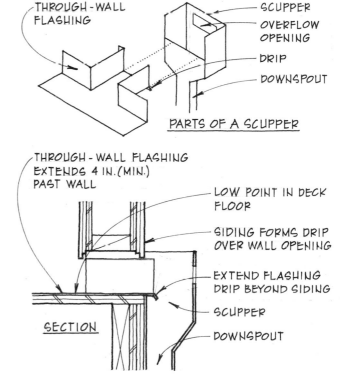

THROUGH-WALL FLASHING

SCUPPER

OVERFLOW OPENING

DRIP

DOWNSPOUT

PARTS OF A SCUPPER

THROUGH-WALL FLASHING EXTENDS 4 IN. (MIN.) PAST WALL

LOW POINT IN DECK FLOOR

SIDING FORMS DRIP OVER WALL OPENING

EXTEND FLASHING DRIP BEYOND SIDING

SCUPPER

DOWNSPOUT

SECTION

 D SCUPPER

Because they make continuous contact with the porch or deck floor, solid railings are relatively simple to design and construct to resist overturning due to lateral force. For short railings (up to 8 ft. long) supported at both ends by a column, a wall, or a corner, the simplest framing (see the drawing below) will suffice because the top edge may be made stiff enough to span between its two rigid ends.

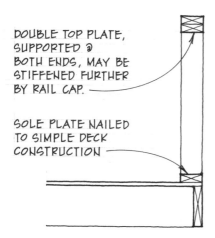

DOUBLE TOP PLATE, SUPPORTED @ BOTH ENDS, MAY BE STIFFENED FURTHER BY RAIL CAP.

SOLE PLATE NAILED TO SIMPLE DECK CONSTRUCTION

Longer railings or railings with one or both ends unsupported must be designed to resist lateral forces by means of a series of vertical supports firmly secured to the porch or deck floor framing (see the drawing below). This means, of course, that the porch floor framing itself must be solidly constructed.

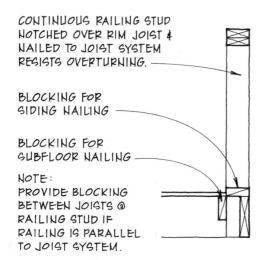

CONTINUOUS RAILING STUD NOTCHED OVER RIM JOIST & NAILED TO JOIST SYSTEM RESISTS OVERTURNING.

BLOCKING FOR SIDING NAILING

BLOCKING FOR SUBFLOOR NAILING

NOTE:
PROVIDE BLOCKING BETWEEN JOISTS @ RAILING STUD IF RAILING IS PARALLEL TO JOIST SYSTEM.

The same results may be achieved in a porch or deck built over a living space by using a balloon frame system with porch-rail studs continuous through to the wall below.

Waterproof deck with solid railing—Waterproof decks surrounded by a solid railing must be sloped to an opening in the railing. This opening can be a flashed hole in the wall, or scupper, as shown here, or it can be a gap in the wall that accommodates a stairway or walk. (Avoid directing water to walkways in climates with freezing temperatures.) The opening should be located away from the main structure of the building, and the floor should pitch toward the opening from all directions. In some cases, a second opening or overflow should be provided to guarantee that water won't build up if the primary drain clogs.

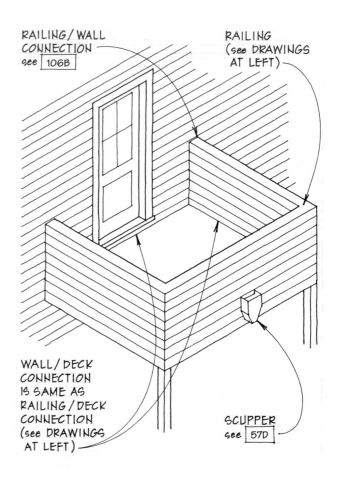

RAILING/WALL CONNECTION
see 106B

RAILING (see DRAWINGS AT LEFT)

WALL/DECK CONNECTION IS SAME AS RAILING/DECK CONNECTION (see DRAWINGS AT LEFT)

SCUPPER see 57D

Open deck with solid railing—Open decks surrounded by a solid railing are simple to drain since water will pass through the floor surface (see 55D). Care should be taken to provide adequate drainage from the surface below the deck.

SOLID RAILING @ PORCH OR DECK

Open railings are connected to the floor of a porch or deck only intermittently, where the vertical supports occur. It is through these supports that open railings gain their rigidity. When the end of the railing is supported at a wall or a column, no special connections are required. When the vertical support does not coincide with a rigid part of the structure, however, a rigid connection must be made with the floor system of the porch or deck. One logical place to locate this connection is at the inside edge of the rim joist (see the drawing below).

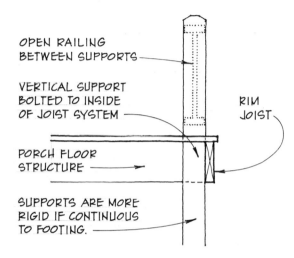

OPEN RAILING
BETWEEN SUPPORTS

VERTICAL SUPPORT
BOLTED TO INSIDE
OF JOIST SYSTEM

RIM
JOIST

PORCH FLOOR
STRUCTURE

SUPPORTS ARE MORE
RIGID IF CONTINUOUS
TO FOOTING.

Another logical place to secure the railing to the porch floor is at the outside of the rim joist (see the drawing below). This is usually the most practical choice for waterproof decks, since the railing does not have to penetrate the waterproof surface.

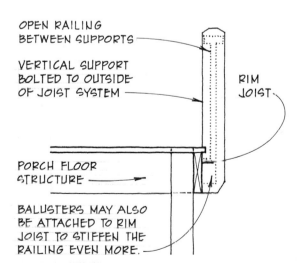

OPEN RAILING
BETWEEN SUPPORTS

VERTICAL SUPPORT
BOLTED TO OUTSIDE
OF JOIST SYSTEM

RIM
JOIST

PORCH FLOOR
STRUCTURE

BALUSTERS MAY ALSO
BE ATTACHED TO RIM
JOIST TO STIFFEN THE
RAILING EVEN MORE.

Waterproof deck with open railing—However the railing is attached to the porch, its rigidity depends ultimately on the solid construction of the porch framing. Pressure-treated joists will contribute to the floor's longevity, and metal hangers and clips will add rigidity. Block between joist bays when the railing is parallel to the joist system.

Waterproof decks surrounded by an open railing should be sloped away from the wall(s) of the building. Drainage may be distributed around all open edges, as shown below, or it can be collected in a scupper.

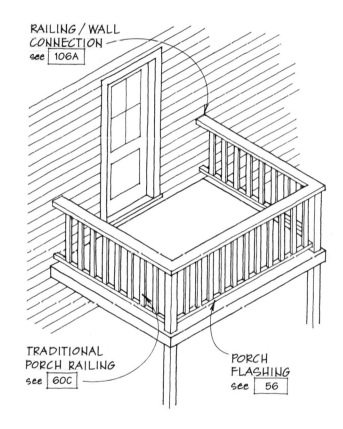

RAILING / WALL
CONNECTION
see 106A

TRADITIONAL
PORCH RAILING
see 60C

PORCH
FLASHING
see 56

Open deck with open railing—Open decks surrounded by an open railing are relatively simple to drain. Be sure to provide adequate drainage from the surface below the deck.

A wood porch with an open railing and a tongue-and-groove wood floor has been a tradition throughout the U.S. for the entire history of wood-frame construction and is still in demand. A tongue-and-groove porch floor is actually a hybrid between a waterproof deck and an open deck because although it is not waterproof, it is also not truly open like the spaced decking of open porch or deck floors. Moisture is likely to get trapped in the tongue-and-groove joint between floor boards and cause decay. To avoid this problem, the floors of these porches are often painted annually. Weather-resistant species or wood that has been pressure-treated will provide the most maintenance-free porch.

The tongue-and-groove wood porch was traditionally built without flashing. But for a longer lasting porch, the connection between the porch floor and the main structure should be flashed for the same reason as for all open porch and deck floors.

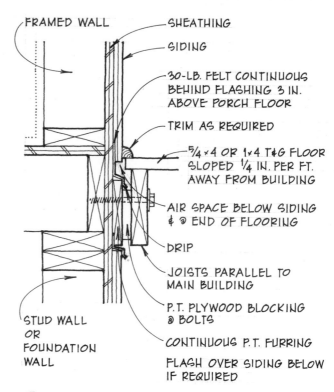

FRAMED WALL
SHEATHING
SIDING
30-LB. FELT CONTINUOUS BEHIND FLASHING 3 IN. ABOVE PORCH FLOOR
TRIM AS REQUIRED
⁵⁄₄ × 4 OR 1 × 4 T&G FLOOR SLOPED ¼ IN. PER FT. AWAY FROM BUILDING
AIR SPACE BELOW SIDING & @ END OF FLOORING
DRIP
JOISTS PARALLEL TO MAIN BUILDING
P.T. PLYWOOD BLOCKING @ BOLTS
CONTINUOUS P.T. FURRING
FLASH OVER SIDING BELOW IF REQUIRED
STUD WALL OR FOUNDATION WALL

Ⓐ TRADITIONAL WOOD PORCH
FLOOR CHARACTERISTICS

Ⓑ TRADITIONAL WOOD PORCH
CONNECTION TO MAIN STRUCTURE

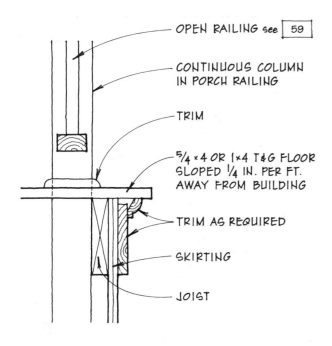

OPEN RAILING see [59]
CONTINUOUS COLUMN IN PORCH RAILING
TRIM
⁵⁄₄ × 4 OR 1 × 4 T&G FLOOR SLOPED ¼ IN. PER FT. AWAY FROM BUILDING
TRIM AS REQUIRED
SKIRTING
JOIST

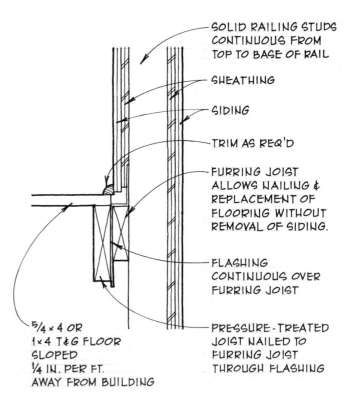

SOLID RAILING STUDS CONTINUOUS FROM TOP TO BASE OF RAIL
SHEATHING
SIDING
TRIM AS REQ'D
FURRING JOIST ALLOWS NAILING & REPLACEMENT OF FLOORING WITHOUT REMOVAL OF SIDING.
FLASHING CONTINUOUS OVER FURRING JOIST
PRESSURE-TREATED JOIST NAILED TO FURRING JOIST THROUGH FLASHING
⁵⁄₄ × 4 OR 1 × 4 T&G FLOOR SLOPED ¼ IN. PER FT. AWAY FROM BUILDING

Ⓒ TRADITIONAL WOOD PORCH
OPEN RAILING

Ⓓ TRADITIONAL WOOD PORCH
CLOSED RAILING

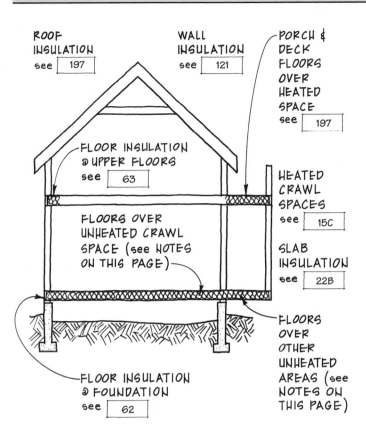

ROOF INSULATION see 197

WALL INSULATION see 121

PORCH & DECK FLOORS OVER HEATED SPACE see 197

FLOOR INSULATION @ UPPER FLOORS see 63

HEATED CRAWL SPACES see 15C

SLAB INSULATION see 22B

FLOORS OVER UNHEATED CRAWL SPACE (see NOTES ON THIS PAGE)

FLOORS OVER OTHER UNHEATED AREAS (see NOTES ON THIS PAGE)

FLOOR INSULATION @ FOUNDATION see 62

Floor insulation—Building codes in most climates require at least R-11 for floors over unheated spaces.

Installation—Floors over vented crawl spaces and other unheated areas are typically insulated with fiberglass batts because the ample depth of the floor structure can accommodate this cost-effective but relatively bulky type of insulation. The batts are easiest to install if weather and other considerations permit them to be dropped in from above. To support the batts, a wire or plastic mesh or wood lath can first be stapled to the underside of the joists, or plastic mesh can be draped very loosely over the joists.

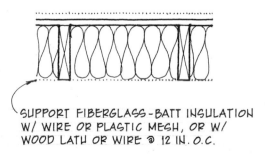

SUPPORT FIBERGLASS-BATT INSULATION W/ WIRE OR PLASTIC MESH, OR W/ WOOD LATH OR WIRE @ 12 IN. O.C.

When crawl-space floor insulation must be installed from below, spring wires are cheap, easy and effective.

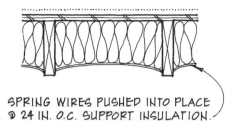

SPRING WIRES PUSHED INTO PLACE @ 24 IN. O.C. SUPPORT INSULATION.

Floor insulation over open areas that are exposed to varmints and house pets should be covered from below with solid sheathing.

Vapor barriers—A vapor barrier is not always required in the floor structure over a crawl space because the temperature differential between the interior space and the crawl space is not always enough to cause condensation. When conditions require a vapor barrier or when an air-infiltration barrier is desired, a 4-mil air/vapor barrier may be placed on the warm side of the insulation, as shown in the drawing below.

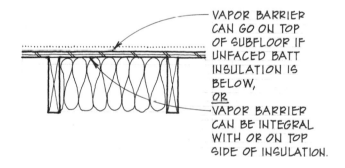

VAPOR BARRIER CAN GO ON TOP OF SUBFLOOR IF UNFACED BATT INSULATION IS BELOW, OR VAPOR BARRIER CAN BE INTEGRAL WITH OR ON TOP SIDE OF INSULATION.

A vapor barrier placed on the subfloor is more continuous than one on the top side of the batts, and it also will not trap rainwater during construction. For more on vapor barriers and air-infiltration barriers, see 120.

Perimeter insulation—Floors whose perimeter completes the thermal envelope, such as upper floors that are located over a heated space, need only be insulated at their perimeter, not throughout the entire floor. The continuity of insulation and air/vapor barriers at this location requires serious consideration (see 62B, C & D and 63).

Ⓐ FLOOR INSULATION

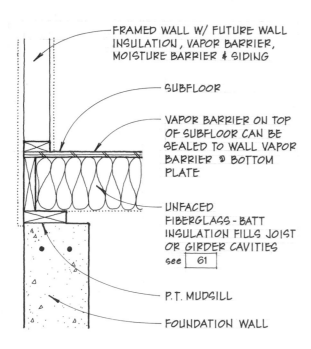

FRAMED WALL W/FUTURE WALL INSULATION, VAPOR BARRIER, MOISTURE BARRIER & SIDING

SUBFLOOR

VAPOR BARRIER ON TOP OF SUBFLOOR CAN BE SEALED TO WALL VAPOR BARRIER @ BOTTOM PLATE

UNFACED FIBERGLASS-BATT INSULATION FILLS JOIST OR GIRDER CAVITIES see [61]

P.T. MUDSILL

FOUNDATION WALL

(A) FLOOR INSULATION @ FOUNDATION
UNINSULATED BASEMENT OR CRAWL SPACE

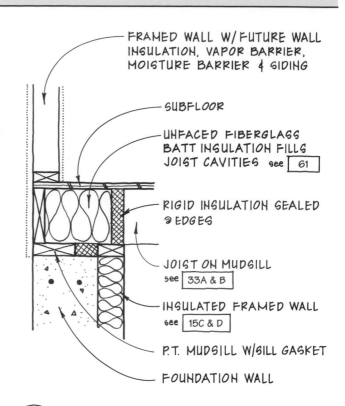

FRAMED WALL W/FUTURE WALL INSULATION, VAPOR BARRIER, MOISTURE BARRIER & SIDING

SUBFLOOR

UNFACED FIBERGLASS BATT INSULATION FILLS JOIST CAVITIES see [61]

RIGID INSULATION SEALED @ EDGES

JOIST ON MUDSILL see [33A & B]

INSULATED FRAMED WALL see [15C & D]

P.T. MUDSILL W/SILL GASKET

FOUNDATION WALL

(B) FLOOR INSULATION @ FOUNDATION
HEATED BASEMENT/JOIST ON MUDSILL

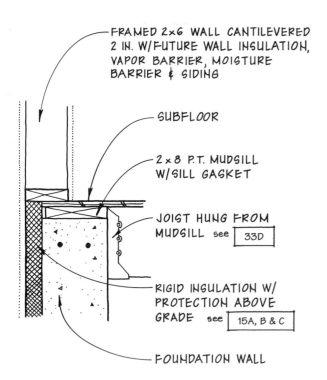

FRAMED 2×6 WALL CANTILEVERED 2 IN. W/FUTURE WALL INSULATION, VAPOR BARRIER, MOISTURE BARRIER & SIDING

SUBFLOOR

2×8 P.T. MUDSILL W/SILL GASKET

JOIST HUNG FROM MUDSILL see [33D]

RIGID INSULATION W/ PROTECTION ABOVE GRADE see [15A, B & C]

FOUNDATION WALL

(C) FLOOR INSULATION @ FOUNDATION
HEATED BASEMENT/JOIST FLUSH W/MUDSILL

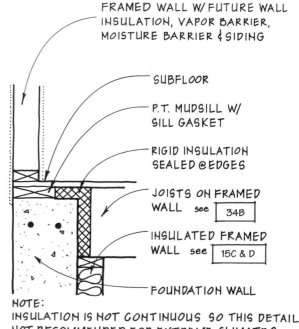

FRAMED WALL W/FUTURE WALL INSULATION, VAPOR BARRIER, MOISTURE BARRIER & SIDING

SUBFLOOR

P.T. MUDSILL W/ SILL GASKET

RIGID INSULATION SEALED @ EDGES

JOISTS ON FRAMED WALL see [34B]

INSULATED FRAMED WALL see [15C & D]

FOUNDATION WALL

NOTE:
INSULATION IS NOT CONTINUOUS SO THIS DETAIL NOT RECOMMENDED FOR EXTREME CLIMATES UNLESS WALLS ARE SUPERINSULATED see [121B]

(D) FLOOR INSULATION @ FOUNDATION
HEATED BASEMENT/JOISTS FLUSH W/MUDSILL

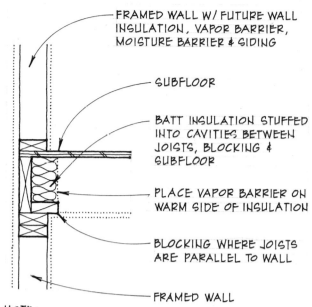

FRAMED WALL W/ FUTURE WALL INSULATION, VAPOR BARRIER, MOISTURE BARRIER & SIDING

SUBFLOOR

BATT INSULATION STUFFED INTO CAVITIES BETWEEN JOISTS, BLOCKING & SUBFLOOR

PLACE VAPOR BARRIER ON WARM SIDE OF INSULATION

BLOCKING WHERE JOISTS ARE PARALLEL TO WALL

FRAMED WALL

NOTE:
BECAUSE JOISTS PERPENDICULAR TO THE WALL PENETRATE THE WALL CAVITY, IT IS DIFFICULT TO GET A TIGHT SEAL AGAINST AIR INFILTRATION. FOR ALTERNATIVE DETAIL see 63B

A UPPER-FLOOR INSULATION
PLATFORM FRAMING

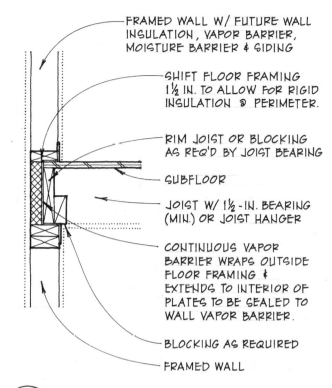

FRAMED WALL W/ FUTURE WALL INSULATION, VAPOR BARRIER, MOISTURE BARRIER & SIDING

SHIFT FLOOR FRAMING 1½ IN. TO ALLOW FOR RIGID INSULATION @ PERIMETER.

RIM JOIST OR BLOCKING AS REQ'D BY JOIST BEARING

SUBFLOOR

JOIST W/ 1½-IN. BEARING (MIN.) OR JOIST HANGER

CONTINUOUS VAPOR BARRIER WRAPS OUTSIDE FLOOR FRAMING & EXTENDS TO INTERIOR OF PLATES TO BE SEALED TO WALL VAPOR BARRIER.

BLOCKING AS REQUIRED

FRAMED WALL

B UPPER-FLOOR INSULATION
PLATFORM FRAME : ALTERNATIVE DETAIL

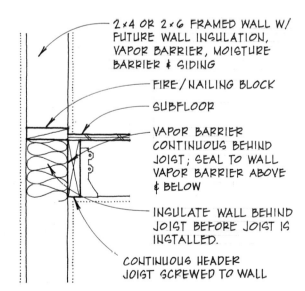

2 x 4 OR 2 x 6 FRAMED WALL W/ FUTURE WALL INSULATION, VAPOR BARRIER, MOISTURE BARRIER & SIDING

FIRE/NAILING BLOCK

SUBFLOOR

VAPOR BARRIER CONTINUOUS BEHIND JOIST; SEAL TO WALL VAPOR BARRIER ABOVE & BELOW

INSULATE WALL BEHIND JOIST BEFORE JOIST IS INSTALLED.

CONTINUOUS HEADER JOIST SCREWED TO WALL

NOTE:
BECAUSE THE JOISTS DO NOT PENETRATE THE WALL CAVITY, IT IS POSSIBLE TO PROVIDE A GOOD SEAL AGAINST AIR INFILTRATION. HOWEVER, THIS DETAIL DOES NOT PROVIDE THE LATERAL STRUCTURAL STRENGTH OF ALTERNATIVE DETAIL see 63D

C UPPER-FLOOR INSULATION
BALLOON FRAMING / JOISTS ⊥ TO WALL

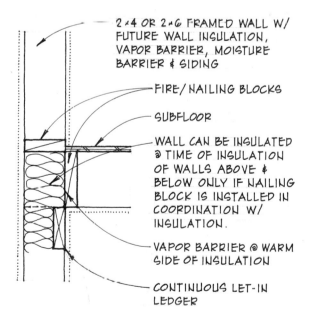

2 x 4 OR 2 x 6 FRAMED WALL W/ FUTURE WALL INSULATION, VAPOR BARRIER, MOISTURE BARRIER & SIDING

FIRE/NAILING BLOCKS

SUBFLOOR

WALL CAN BE INSULATED @ TIME OF INSULATION OF WALLS ABOVE & BELOW ONLY IF NAILING BLOCK IS INSTALLED IN COORDINATION W/ INSULATION.

VAPOR BARRIER @ WARM SIDE OF INSULATION

CONTINUOUS LET-IN LEDGER

NOTE:
BECAUSE JOISTS PERPENDICULAR TO THE WALL PENETRATE THE WALL CAVITY, IT IS DIFFICULT TO GET A TIGHT SEAL AGAINST AIR INFILTRATION. FOR ALTERNATIVE DETAIL see 63C

D UPPER-FLOOR INSULATION
BALLOON FRAME : ALTERNATIVE DETAIL

CHAPTER 3

WALLS

The walls of a building serve several important functions: They define the spaces within the building to provide privacy and zoning, and they enclose the building itself, keeping the weather out and the heat or cold in. Walls provide the vertical structure that supports the upper floors and roof of the building, and the lateral structure that stiffens the building. Walls also encase the mechanical systems (electrical wiring, plumbing, and heating). To incorporate all of this within a 4-in. or 6-in. deep wood-framed panel is quite an achievement, so numerous decisions need to be made in the course of designing a wall system for a wood-frame building. There are two preliminary decisions to make that establish the framework for the remaining decisions.

WALL THICKNESS

Should the walls be framed with 2x4s or 2x6s? The 2x6 wall has become increasingly popular in recent years, primarily because it provides more space for insulation and allows for other minor energy-saving advantages (such as the ability to run electricity in a notched base, as shown in 73A). These advantages all come at some cost. A 2x6 wall with studs spaced 24 in. o.c. (the maximum spacing allowed by codes) uses about 20% more material for studs and plates than a 2x4 wall with studs with a code-allowed spacing of 16 in. o.c. On the outside, the sheathing has to be ½ in. thick (⅛ in. thicker than sheathing on a standard 2x4 wall). Inside, the drywall also has to be ⅛ in. thicker to span the 24-in. spacing between 2x6 studs. Thicker insulation costs more too. So, overall, 2x6 framing makes a superior wall, but one that costs more. Framing the exterior walls with 2x6s and interior walls with 2x4s is a typical combination when the energy-efficient 2x6 wall is selected. Stud spacing of 2x4 and 2x6 walls may vary with loading, lumber grades, and finish materials; in this book, however, studs are assumed to be 16 in. o.c. in 2x4 walls and 24 in. o.c. in 2x6 walls unless noted otherwise.

FRAMING STYLE

Should the walls be built using platform framing or balloon framing? Balloon framing, with studs continuous from mudsill to top plate and continuous between floors, was developed in the 1840s and is the antecedent of the framed wall. In recent years, balloon framing has been almost completely superseded by the more labor-efficient and fire-resistant platform frame construction, with studs extending only between floors. There are still situations, however, where a variation of the balloon frame system is useful. One such situation is where the continuity of studs longer than the normal ceiling height is essential to the strength of a wall. Examples include parapet walls and eave (side) walls that must resist the lateral thrust of a vaulted roof (as in a 1½-story building).

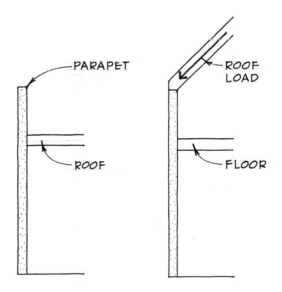

Balloon-framed gable-end walls also provide increased stability in high-wind areas (see 160).

Another reason for using balloon framing is to minimize the effects of shrinkage that occurs across the grain of joists in a platform-framed building. This could be important with continuous stucco siding that spans two floors without a control joint, or in a multiple-story hybrid building system where the floors in the balloon-framed part would not shrink equally with the floors in the platform-framed part.

DESIGNING A WALL SYSTEM

Once the stud size and spacing and the framing system have been selected, it is time to consider how to brace the building to resist the forces of wind, earthquakes, and eccentric loading. Will diagonal bracing be adequate, or should the building be braced with structural sheathing and/or shear walls? This question is best answered in the context of the design of the building as a whole, considering the other materials that complete the wall system. How is the wall to be insulated? Where are the openings in the wall for doors and windows? Will there be an air-infiltration barrier? What material will be used for the exterior finish? The details relating to these issues are addressed in this chapter, along with some suggestions for their appropriate use. How these various details are assembled into a complete wall system depends on local climate, codes, tradition, and the talent of the designer.

SIZING HEADERS

Header size depends on wood species and grade, loading, header design, and rough-opening span. Following is a rule of thumb for sizing a common header type, the 4x header (see 68B):

For a single-story building with a 30-lb. live load on the roof and 2x4 bearing walls, the span in feet of the rough opening should equal the depth (nominal) in inches of a 4x header. For example, openings up to 4 ft. wide require a 4x4 header.

ABOUT THE DRAWINGS

Construction terms vary regionally, and the names for the components that frame wall openings (see 68A) are the least cast in stone. Studs called "trimmer studs" in one locality are called "jack studs" in another; and the bottom plate may go by either "bottom plate" or "sole plate." Consult local builders and architects for common usage.

For clarity, insulation is not generally shown in the exterior walls except in the insulation section (120–125).

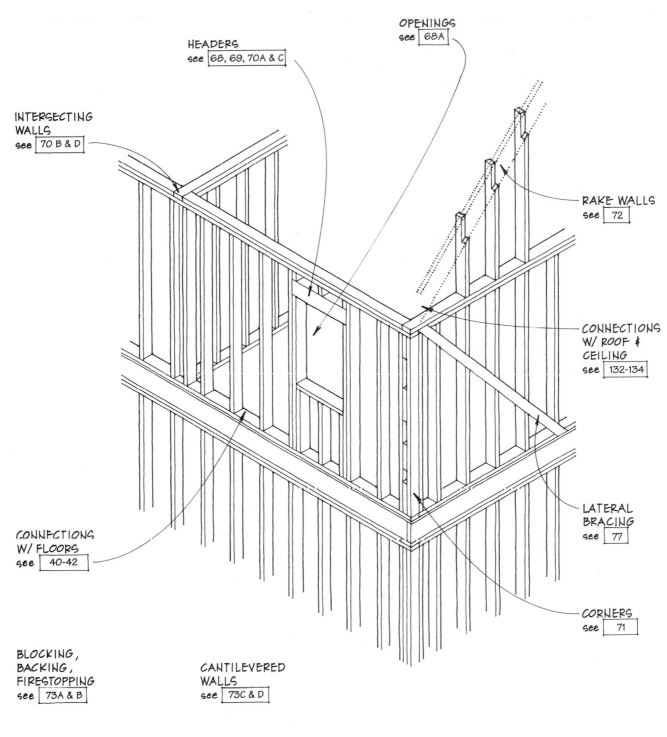

INTERSECTING
WALLS
see 70 B & D

HEADERS
see 68, 69, 70A & C

OPENINGS
see 68A

RAKE WALLS
see 72

CONNECTIONS
W/ ROOF &
CEILING
see 132-134

LATERAL
BRACING
see 77

CONNECTIONS
W/ FLOORS
see 40-42

CORNERS
see 71

BLOCKING,
BACKING,
FIRESTOPPING
see 73A & B

CANTILEVERED
WALLS
see 73C & D

RESOURCE-EFFICIENT
ADVANCED FRAMING
see 74

NOTE:
IN THIS CHAPTER ALL 2×4 WALLS ARE SHOWN
WITH STUDS @ 16 IN. O.C.; ALL 2×6 WALLS ARE
SHOWN WITH STUDS @ 24 IN. O.C.; UNLABELED
WALLS MAY BE EITHER 2×4 OR 2×6.

A WALL FRAMING

DOUBLE TOP PLATE

LAP DOUBLE TOP PLATE 4 FT. (MIN.)

CRIPPLE STUDS

DOOR ROUGH OPENING TYP. 6 FT. 10½ IN. FOR 6-FT. 8-IN. DOOR

HEADER

TRIMMER STUD

KING STUD

COMMON STUDS

SUBFLOOR

HEADER

TRIMMER STUD

KING STUD

SILL

WINDOW ROUGH OPENING

WINDOW HEADER TYP. ALIGNS W/ DOOR HEADER

CRIPPLE STUDS

DOOR ROUGH OPENING

SOLE PLATE

WINDOW ROUGH OPENING

(A) OPENINGS IN A STUD WALL

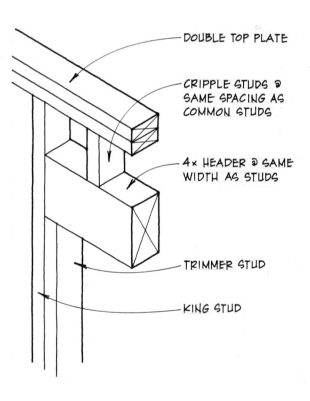

DOUBLE TOP PLATE

CRIPPLE STUDS @ SAME SPACING AS COMMON STUDS

4 × HEADER @ SAME WIDTH AS STUDS

TRIMMER STUD

KING STUD

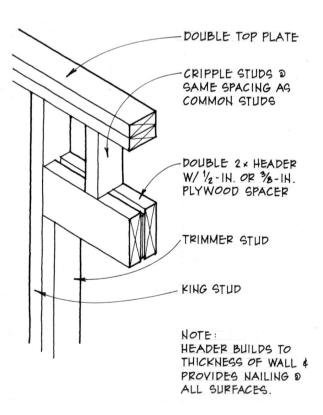

DOUBLE TOP PLATE

CRIPPLE STUDS @ SAME SPACING AS COMMON STUDS

DOUBLE 2 × HEADER W/ ½-IN. OR ⅜-IN. PLYWOOD SPACER

TRIMMER STUD

KING STUD

NOTE:
HEADER BUILDS TO THICKNESS OF WALL & PROVIDES NAILING @ ALL SURFACES.

(B) 4 × HEADER
2×4 BEARING WALL

(C) TYPICAL DOUBLE 2 × HEADER
2×4 BEARING WALL

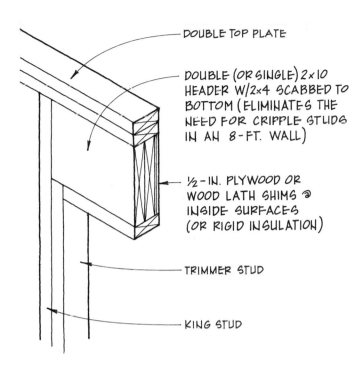

DOUBLE TOP PLATE

DOUBLE (OR SINGLE) 2×10 HEADER W/2×4 SCABBED TO BOTTOM (ELIMINATES THE NEED FOR CRIPPLE STUDS IN AN 8-FT. WALL)

½-IN. PLYWOOD OR WOOD LATH SHIMS @ INSIDE SURFACES (OR RIGID INSULATION)

TRIMMER STUD

KING STUD

A **2×10 HEADER**
2×4 BEARING WALL

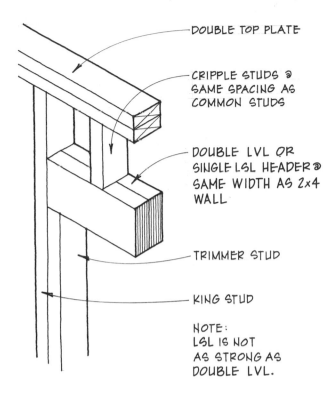

DOUBLE TOP PLATE

CRIPPLE STUDS @ SAME SPACING AS COMMON STUDS

DOUBLE LVL OR SINGLE LSL HEADER @ SAME WIDTH AS 2×4 WALL

TRIMMER STUD

KING STUD

NOTE: LSL IS NOT AS STRONG AS DOUBLE LVL.

B **DOUBLE LVL OR LSL HEADER**
2×4 BEARING WALL

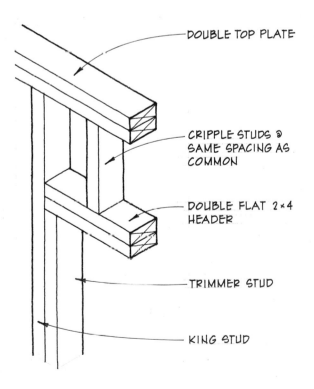

DOUBLE TOP PLATE

CRIPPLE STUDS @ SAME SPACING AS COMMON

DOUBLE FLAT 2×4 HEADER

TRIMMER STUD

KING STUD

C **FLAT 2×4 HEADER**
2×4 PARTITION WALL

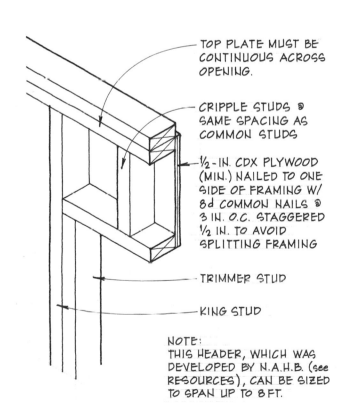

TOP PLATE MUST BE CONTINUOUS ACROSS OPENING.

CRIPPLE STUDS @ SAME SPACING AS COMMON STUDS

½-IN. CDX PLYWOOD (MIN.) NAILED TO ONE SIDE OF FRAMING W/ 8d COMMON NAILS @ 3 IN. O.C. STAGGERED ½ IN. TO AVOID SPLITTING FRAMING

TRIMMER STUD

KING STUD

NOTE: THIS HEADER, WHICH WAS DEVELOPED BY N.A.H.B. (see RESOURCES), CAN BE SIZED TO SPAN UP TO 8 FT.

D **OPEN-BOX PLYWOOD HEADER**
2×4 BEARING WALL

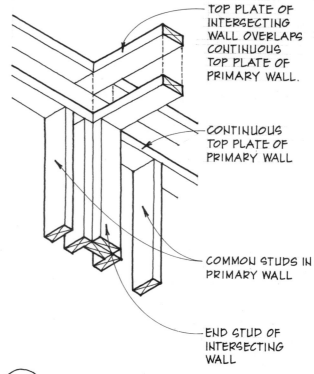

DOUBLE TOP PLATE

NOTCH CRIPPLE STUDS FOR 2× HEADER.

2× HEADER ⊘ OUTSIDE OF WALL

2-IN. OR 4-IN. SPACE ⊘ INSIDE OF HEADER FOR INSULATION

2×4 OR 2×6 HEADER PLATE

TRIMMER STUD

KING STUD

Ⓐ INSULATED HEADER
2×4 OR 2×6 EXTERIOR WALL

TOP PLATE OF INTERSECTING WALL OVERLAPS CONTINUOUS TOP PLATE OF PRIMARY WALL.

CONTINUOUS TOP PLATE OF PRIMARY WALL

COMMON STUDS IN PRIMARY WALL

END STUD OF INTERSECTING WALL

Ⓑ INTERSECTING 2× WALLS
⊘ DOUBLE TOP PLATE

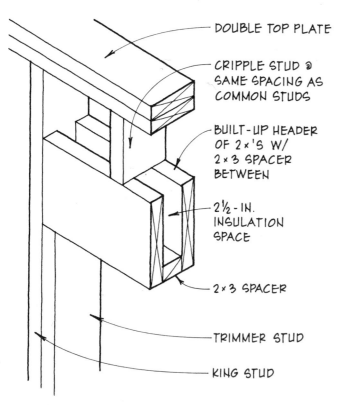

DOUBLE TOP PLATE

CRIPPLE STUD ⊘ SAME SPACING AS COMMON STUDS

BUILT-UP HEADER OF 2×'S W/ 2×3 SPACER BETWEEN

2½-IN. INSULATION SPACE

2×3 SPACER

TRIMMER STUD

KING STUD

Ⓒ INSULATED DOUBLE 2× HEADER
2×6 BEARING WALL/ALTERNATIVE DETAIL

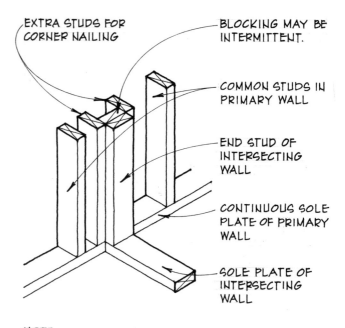

EXTRA STUDS FOR CORNER NAILING

BLOCKING MAY BE INTERMITTENT.

COMMON STUDS IN PRIMARY WALL

END STUD OF INTERSECTING WALL

CONTINUOUS SOLE PLATE OF PRIMARY WALL

SOLE PLATE OF INTERSECTING WALL

NOTE:
INSULATE CAVITY BEHIND INTERSECTING WALL BEFORE SHEATHING IS APPLIED IF PRIMARY

Ⓓ INTERSECTING 2× WALLS
⊘ SOLE PLATE

DOUBLE TOP PLATE OVERLAPS @ CORNERS TO LOCK TWO WALLS TOGETHER.

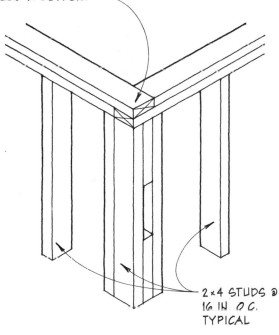

2×4 STUDS @ 16 IN. O.C. TYPICAL

A **2×4 CORNER**
@ DOUBLE TOP PLATE

DOUBLE TOP PLATE OVERLAPS @ CORNERS, LOCKING TWO WALLS TOGETHER.

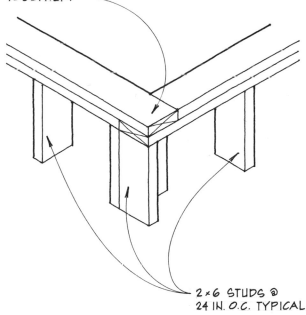

2×6 STUDS @ 24 IN. O.C. TYPICAL

B **2×6 CORNER**
@ DOUBLE TOP PLATE

CORNER STUDS BUILT UP W/ 2×4 BLOCKING BETWEEN PROVIDES NAILING @ INSIDE CORNER.

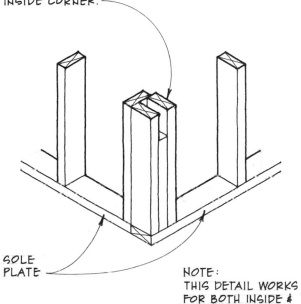

SOLE PLATE

NOTE:
THIS DETAIL WORKS FOR BOTH INSIDE & OUTSIDE CORNERS.

C **2×4 CORNER**
@ SOLE PLATE

EXTRA STUD ADDED PERPENDICULAR TO CORNER STUD PROVIDES NAILING @ INSIDE CORNER & ALLOWS SPACE FOR 4-IN. THICK INSULATION @ CORNER.

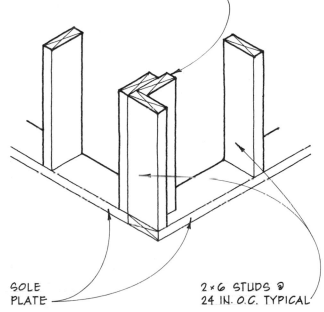

SOLE PLATE

2×6 STUDS @ 24 IN. O.C. TYPICAL

D **2×6 CORNER**
@ SOLE PLATE

A wall that extends to a sloped roof or ceiling is called a rake wall and may be built one of two ways:

Platform framing—Platform framing is commonly the method of choice when a horizontal structural element such as a floor or ceiling ties the structure together at the level of the top plate or when the top plate itself is short enough to provide the necessary lateral strength (see 72B).

Balloon framing—Balloon framing allows for ease of construction and economy of material and stabilizes a tall wall where there is no horizontal structure at the level of the top plate or where lateral forces are extreme, such as in high-wind areas (see 72C).

For details of rake walls with truss-framed roofs, see 157.

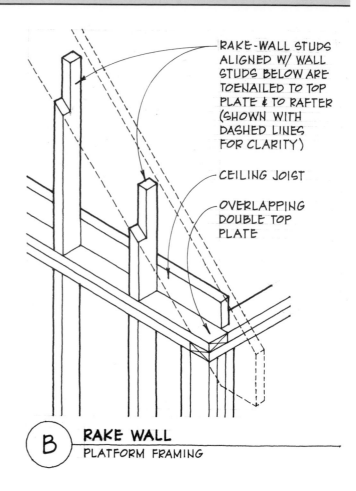

RAKE-WALL STUDS ALIGNED W/ WALL STUDS BELOW ARE TOENAILED TO TOP PLATE & TO RAFTER (SHOWN WITH DASHED LINES FOR CLARITY)

CEILING JOIST

OVERLAPPING DOUBLE TOP PLATE

A **RAKE WALL**
NOTES

B **RAKE WALL**
PLATFORM FRAMING

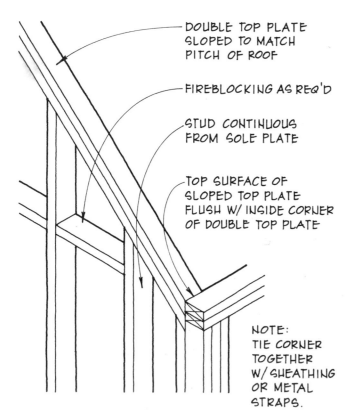

DOUBLE TOP PLATE SLOPED TO MATCH PITCH OF ROOF

FIREBLOCKING AS REQ'D

STUD CONTINUOUS FROM SOLE PLATE

TOP SURFACE OF SLOPED TOP PLATE FLUSH W/ INSIDE CORNER OF DOUBLE TOP PLATE

NOTE: TIE CORNER TOGETHER W/ SHEATHING OR METAL STRAPS.

C **RAKE WALL**
BALLOON FRAMING

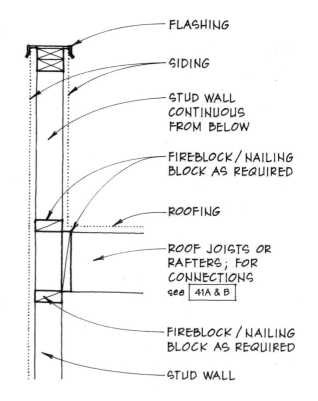

FLASHING

SIDING

STUD WALL CONTINUOUS FROM BELOW

FIREBLOCK / NAILING BLOCK AS REQUIRED

ROOFING

ROOF JOISTS OR RAFTERS; FOR CONNECTIONS see 41A & B

FIREBLOCK / NAILING BLOCK AS REQUIRED

STUD WALL

D **PARAPET WALL FRAMING**
ROOF JOISTS SHOWN ⊥ TO WALL

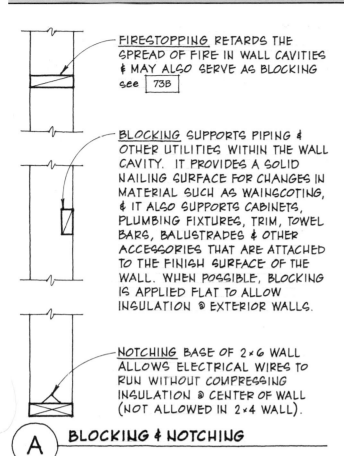

FIRESTOPPING RETARDS THE SPREAD OF FIRE IN WALL CAVITIES & MAY ALSO SERVE AS BLOCKING see 73B

BLOCKING SUPPORTS PIPING & OTHER UTILITIES WITHIN THE WALL CAVITY. IT PROVIDES A SOLID NAILING SURFACE FOR CHANGES IN MATERIAL SUCH AS WAINSCOTING, & IT ALSO SUPPORTS CABINETS, PLUMBING FIXTURES, TRIM, TOWEL BARS, BALUSTRADES & OTHER ACCESSORIES THAT ARE ATTACHED TO THE FINISH SURFACE OF THE WALL. WHEN POSSIBLE, BLOCKING IS APPLIED FLAT TO ALLOW INSULATION @ EXTERIOR WALLS.

NOTCHING BASE OF 2×6 WALL ALLOWS ELECTRICAL WIRES TO RUN WITHOUT COMPRESSING INSULATION @ CENTER OF WALL (NOT ALLOWED IN 2×4 WALL).

Ⓐ BLOCKING & NOTCHING

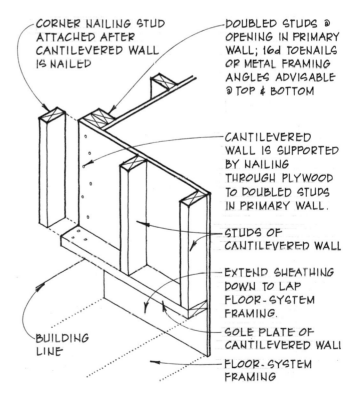

FIRESTOPPING MAY BE STAGGERED FOR EASE OF NAILING.

CONTINUOUS STUDS

NOTE:
CODES VARY, BUT FIRESTOPPING IS USUALLY REQUIRED: AT STAIRS ALONGSIDE THE STRINGERS; BETWEEN FLOORS & BETWEEN THE TOP FLOOR AND THE ATTIC IN BALLOON-FRAME BUILDINGS (THE PLATES IN PLATFORM-FRAME BUILDINGS AUTOMATICALLY PROVIDE FIREBLOCKING BETWEEN FLOORS); BETWEEN WALL CAVITIES & CONCEALED HORIZONTAL SPACES SUCH AS SOFFITS & DROP CEILINGS; IN TALL WALLS EVERY 10 FT. VERTICALLY.

FIRESTOPPING IS USUALLY 2× FRAMING LUMBER BUT CAN ALSO BE OTHER MATERIALS SUCH AS LAYERS OF PLYWOOD OR GYPSUM WALLBOARD WHEN APPROVED BY LOCAL CODES.

Ⓑ FIRESTOPPING

IT IS OCCASIONALLY DIFFICULT OR IMPOSSIBLE TO CANTILEVER THE FLOOR FRAMING TO SUPPORT A PROJECTION FROM THE BUILDING. WHERE LOADS ARE NOT GREAT, IT IS POSSIBLE TO SUPPORT THE PROJECTION WITH CANTILEVERED WALLS.

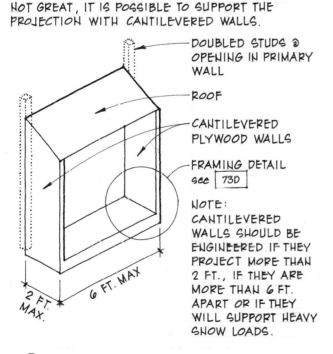

DOUBLED STUDS @ OPENING IN PRIMARY WALL

ROOF

CANTILEVERED PLYWOOD WALLS

FRAMING DETAIL see 73D

NOTE:
CANTILEVERED WALLS SHOULD BE ENGINEERED IF THEY PROJECT MORE THAN 2 FT., IF THEY ARE MORE THAN 6 FT. APART OR IF THEY WILL SUPPORT HEAVY SNOW LOADS.

6 FT. MAX

2 FT. MAX.

Ⓒ CANTILEVERED WALLS

CORNER NAILING STUD ATTACHED AFTER CANTILEVERED WALL IS NAILED

DOUBLED STUDS @ OPENING IN PRIMARY WALL; 16d TOENAILS OR METAL FRAMING ANGLES ADVISABLE @ TOP & BOTTOM

CANTILEVERED WALL IS SUPPORTED BY NAILING THROUGH PLYWOOD TO DOUBLED STUDS IN PRIMARY WALL.

STUDS OF CANTILEVERED WALL

EXTEND SHEATHING DOWN TO LAP FLOOR-SYSTEM FRAMING.

SOLE PLATE OF CANTILEVERED WALL

FLOOR-SYSTEM FRAMING

BUILDING LINE

Ⓓ CANTILEVERED-WALL FRAMING
DETAIL @ BASE

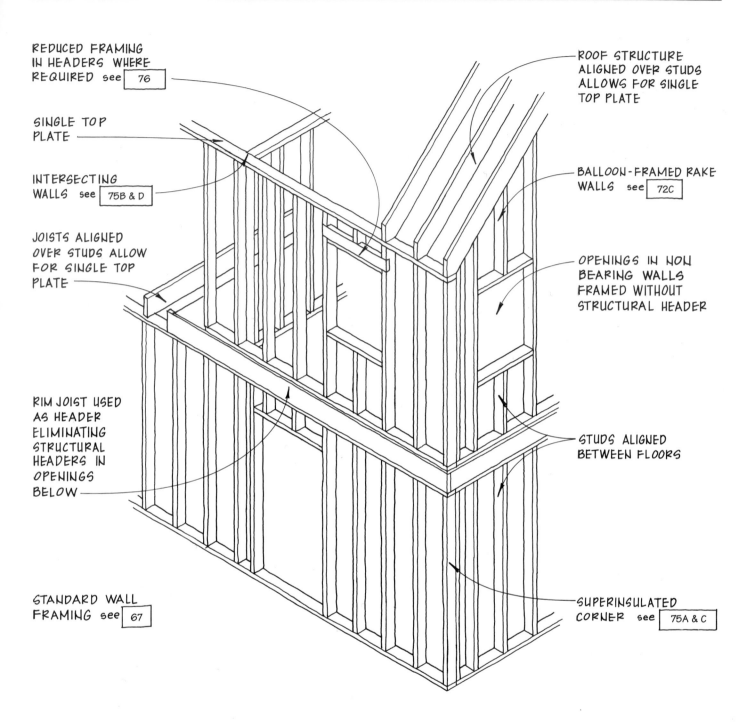

REDUCED FRAMING IN HEADERS WHERE REQUIRED see 76

SINGLE TOP PLATE

INTERSECTING WALLS see 75B & D

JOISTS ALIGNED OVER STUDS ALLOW FOR SINGLE TOP PLATE

RIM JOIST USED AS HEADER ELIMINATING STRUCTURAL HEADERS IN OPENINGS BELOW

STANDARD WALL FRAMING see 67

ROOF STRUCTURE ALIGNED OVER STUDS ALLOWS FOR SINGLE TOP PLATE

BALLOON-FRAMED RAKE WALLS see 72C

OPENINGS IN NON BEARING WALLS FRAMED WITHOUT STRUCTURAL HEADER

STUDS ALIGNED BETWEEN FLOORS

SUPERINSULATED CORNER see 75A & C

Advanced framing—Advanced framing minimizes the amount of framing that spans from the interior to the exterior of a wall, thus lowering the effect of thermal bridging. By limiting the amount of framing, more volume in the wall can be occupied by insulation, which increases thermal performance of the overall assembly. Advanced framing alone can increase the thermal performance of framed walls by only about 7%, but, given that it uses less material than standard framing and actually helps to conserve a precious resource, it should be considered for every framed building. Details of advanced framing are illustrated on 75-76.

 ADVANCED WALL FRAMING

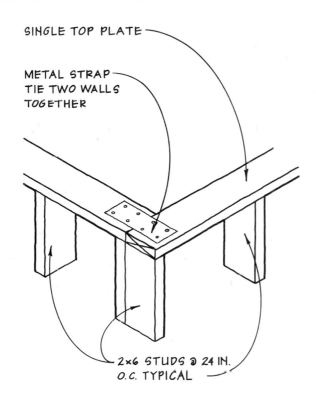

SINGLE TOP PLATE

METAL STRAP
TIE TWO WALLS
TOGETHER

2×6 STUDS @ 24 IN.
O.C. TYPICAL

A **SUPERINSULATED 2×6 CORNER**
OUTSIDE CORNER ONLY @ TOP PLATE

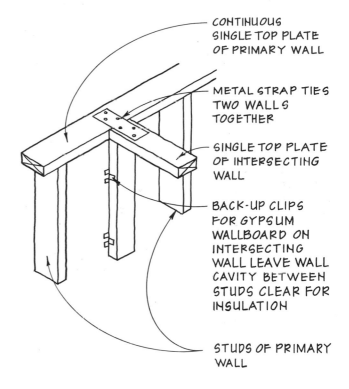

CONTINUOUS
SINGLE TOP PLATE
OF PRIMARY WALL

METAL STRAP TIES
TWO WALLS
TOGETHER

SINGLE TOP PLATE
OF INTERSECTING
WALL

BACK-UP CLIPS
FOR GYPSUM
WALLBOARD ON
INTERSECTING
WALL LEAVE WALL
CAVITY BETWEEN
STUDS CLEAR FOR
INSULATION

STUDS OF PRIMARY
WALL

B **INTERSECTING 2× WALLS**
@ TOP PLATE

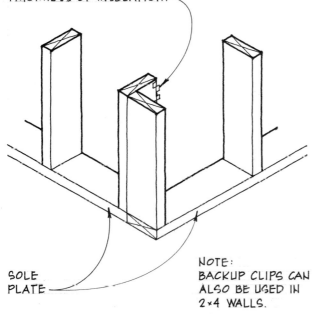

BACKUP CLIPS @ INSIDE CORNERS
OF GYPSUM WALLBOARD ELIMINATE NEED
FOR EXTRA STUD, ALLOWING FOR FULL
THICKNESS OF INSULATION.

SOLE
PLATE

NOTE:
BACKUP CLIPS CAN
ALSO BE USED IN
2×4 WALLS.

C **SUPERINSULATED 2×6 CORNER**
OUTSIDE CORNER ONLY @ SOLE PLATE

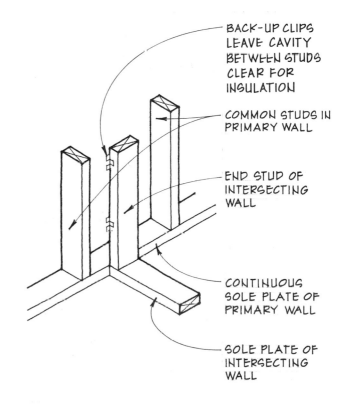

BACK-UP CLIPS
LEAVE CAVITY
BETWEEN STUDS
CLEAR FOR
INSULATION

COMMON STUDS IN
PRIMARY WALL

END STUD OF
INTERSECTING
WALL

CONTINUOUS
SOLE PLATE OF
PRIMARY WALL

SOLE PLATE OF
INTERSECTING
WALL

D **INTERSECTING 2× WALLS**
@ SOLE PLATE

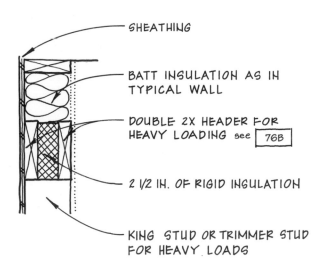

- SHEATHING
- BATT INSULATION AS IN TYPICAL WALL
- DOUBLE 2X HEADER FOR HEAVY LOADING see │76B│
- 2 1/2 IN. OF RIGID INSULATION
- KING STUD OR TRIMMER STUD FOR HEAVY LOADS

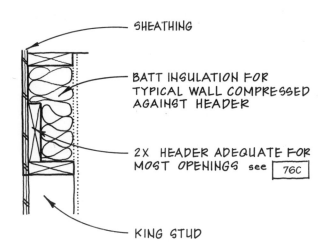

- SHEATHING
- BATT INSULATION FOR TYPICAL WALL COMPRESSED AGAINST HEADER
- 2X HEADER ADEQUATE FOR MOST OPENINGS see │76C│
- KING STUD

The goal when designing an energy-efficient header is to allow for the most insulation while providing for nailing at both the exterior and interior of the opening.

When a structural header is required over an opening in an exterior wall, the header itself occupies space that could otherwise be filled with insulation. Because a deep (tall) header is more effective structurally than a wide one, the header does not usually have to fill the entire width of the wall. In fact, the taller and thinner the header, the more space there

will be for insulation. The headers illustrated on this page provide both structure and space for insulation. The box header (see 69D) also provides space for insulation because it uses sheathing as structure.

The elimination of the trimmer studs that usually support a header at its ends also allows for more insulation in the wall. The header can usually be supported by the king stud as illustrated in the two examples below. (Backing may need to be added to the king studs when wide casings are used.)

A SUPERINSULATED HEADERS
GENERAL

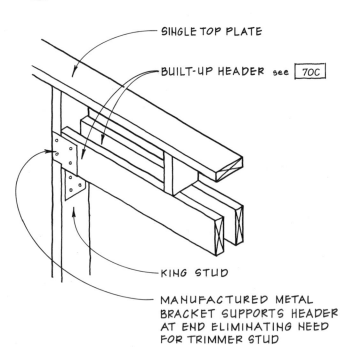

- SINGLE TOP PLATE
- BUILT-UP HEADER see │70C│
- KING STUD
- MANUFACTURED METAL BRACKET SUPPORTS HEADER AT END ELIMINATING NEED FOR TRIMMER STUD

**B** SUPERINSULATED HEADER
RELATIVELY HEAVY LOADS

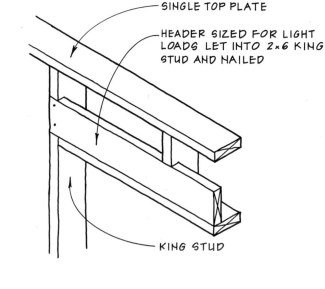

- SINGLE TOP PLATE
- HEADER SIZED FOR LIGHT LOADS LET INTO 2x6 KING STUD AND NAILED
- KING STUD

**C** SUPERINSULATED HEADER
RELATIVELY LIGHT LOADS

Most wood buildings are sheathed with plywood, OSB, or other structural panels that provide the necessary lateral stability when fastened directly to the stud frame (see 78–80). Where lateral forces on walls are extreme, such as in areas subject to hurricanes or earthquakes, specially designed shear walls are commonly required to withstand these forces (see 82–87).

When neither structural panels nor shear walls are required, there are two good methods of bracing the building for lateral stability: the let-in wood brace (see 77B) and the kerfed-in metal brace (see 77C).

The old-fashioned method of bracing with diagonal blocking between studs is not recommended because the nails may withdraw under tension and the many joints tend to open up as the blocking shrinks.

Bracing is often referred to as "corner bracing," but there is really no need to locate the braces only at corners. Braces may be located anywhere along a wall, and the bracing effect will be transferred to the rest of the wall through the continuous top and bottom plates. The methods shown here are located at a corner only for ease of illustration.

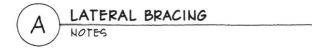

A LATERAL BRACING
NOTES

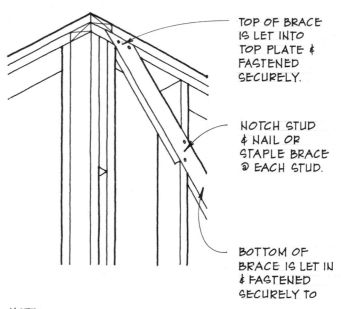

TOP OF BRACE IS LET INTO TOP PLATE & FASTENED SECURELY.

NOTCH STUD & NAIL OR STAPLE BRACE @ EACH STUD.

BOTTOM OF BRACE IS LET IN & FASTENED SECURELY TO

NOTE:
LET-IN BRACES SHOULD BE MADE OF STRUCTURALLY SOUND 1×4 OR 1×6 LUMBER. THEY SHOULD BE FROM TOP PLATE TO SOLE PLATE & @ 45° TO 60° FROM THE HORIZONTAL.

B LET-IN WOOD BRACE

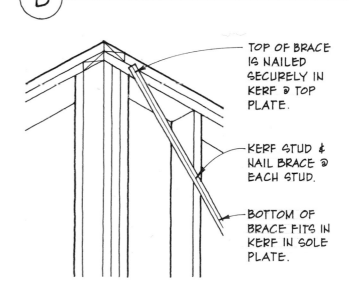

TOP OF BRACE IS NAILED SECURELY IN KERF @ TOP PLATE.

KERF STUD & NAIL BRACE @ EACH STUD.

BOTTOM OF BRACE FITS IN KERF IN SOLE PLATE.

NOTE:
METAL BRACING SET IN A SAW KERF & NAILED TO EACH STUD IS NOT AS GOOD AS LET-IN WOOD BRACING. BECAUSE OF ITS THIN PROFILE, THE METAL MAY BUCKLE UNDER EXTREME COMPRESSION. IN ADDITION, THE METAL WILL NOT SHRINK & SWELL ALONG W/ THE WOOD FRAMING, AS THE LET-IN WOOD BRACE WILL.

C KERFED-IN METAL BRACE

Plywood, OSB, and other panel materials may be used as structural sheathing or as finish siding (in single-wall construction, these functions are combined in one layer, as in 80A, B, and C). Structural-sheathing panels resist lateral loads and contribute to the overall stiffness of the building, thereby eliminating the need for let-in bracing. In earthquake or hurricane zones or where walls are very tall or penetrated by many openings, structural sheathing may require engineering, or shear walls (see 82) may be required.

Panels may be installed either vertically or horizontally. Vertically applied sheathing does not usually require blocking because all edges are aligned with framing members. Horizontally applied plywood sheathing is stronger than vertically applied sheathing because the highest-quality veneers and the most plies are oriented with the length of the plywood panel. This horizontal strength acts in concert with the vertical strength of the studs. Horizontal orientation is used when the stiffness of plywood is required for the backing of siding materials, such as shingles or stucco.

The capacity of plywood panels to span between studs is related to thickness and to the orientation and number of plies. The spanning capacity of composite panels, like OSB, is generally slightly less than plywood and is related only to panel thickness. The following chart applies as a rule of thumb:

Stud spacing	Panel thickness
16 in. o.c.	⅜ in.
24 in. o.c.	½ in.

Nails or other approved fasteners should be sized and spaced according to the following schedule. Verify with manufacturer and local codes.

Panel thickness	Nail size	Panel edge nailing	Field nailing
½ in. or less	6d	6 in. o.c.	12 in. o.c.
over ½ in.	8d		

A STRUCTURAL SHEATHING
NOTES

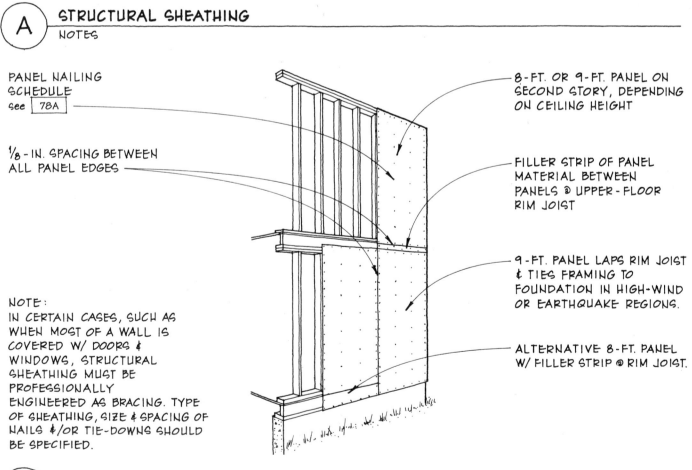

PANEL NAILING SCHEDULE
see 78A

⅛-IN. SPACING BETWEEN ALL PANEL EDGES

8-FT. OR 9-FT. PANEL ON SECOND STORY, DEPENDING ON CEILING HEIGHT

FILLER STRIP OF PANEL MATERIAL BETWEEN PANELS ⓐ UPPER-FLOOR RIM JOIST

9-FT. PANEL LAPS RIM JOIST & TIES FRAMING TO FOUNDATION IN HIGH-WIND OR EARTHQUAKE REGIONS.

ALTERNATIVE 8-FT. PANEL W/ FILLER STRIP ⓐ RIM JOIST.

NOTE:
IN CERTAIN CASES, SUCH AS WHEN MOST OF A WALL IS COVERED W/ DOORS & WINDOWS, STRUCTURAL SHEATHING MUST BE PROFESSIONALLY ENGINEERED AS BRACING. TYPE OF SHEATHING, SIZE & SPACING OF NAILS &/OR TIE-DOWNS SHOULD BE SPECIFIED.

B STRUCTURAL SHEATHING
MULTIPLE-STORY BUILDING

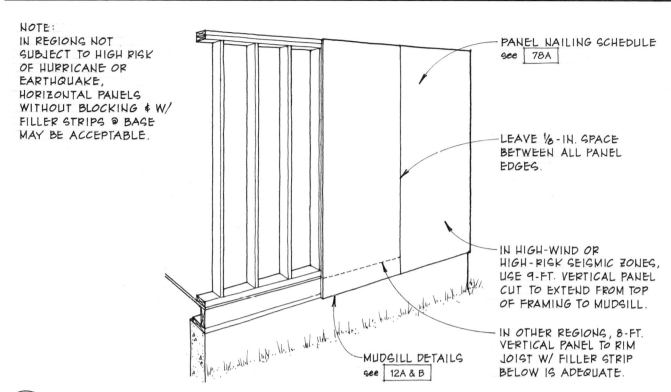

NOTE:
IN REGIONS NOT SUBJECT TO HIGH RISK OF HURRICANE OR EARTHQUAKE, HORIZONTAL PANELS WITHOUT BLOCKING & W/ FILLER STRIPS @ BASE MAY BE ACCEPTABLE.

PANEL NAILING SCHEDULE see 78A

LEAVE 1/8-IN. SPACE BETWEEN ALL PANEL EDGES.

IN HIGH-WIND OR HIGH-RISK SEISMIC ZONES, USE 9-FT. VERTICAL PANEL CUT TO EXTEND FROM TOP OF FRAMING TO MUDSILL.

IN OTHER REGIONS, 8-FT. VERTICAL PANEL TO RIM JOIST W/ FILLER STRIP BELOW IS ADEQUATE.

MUDSILL DETAILS see 12A & B

Ⓐ STRUCTURAL SHEATHING / SINGLE-STORY BUILDING
DISTANCE FROM MUDSILL TO TOP PLATE OVER 8 FT.

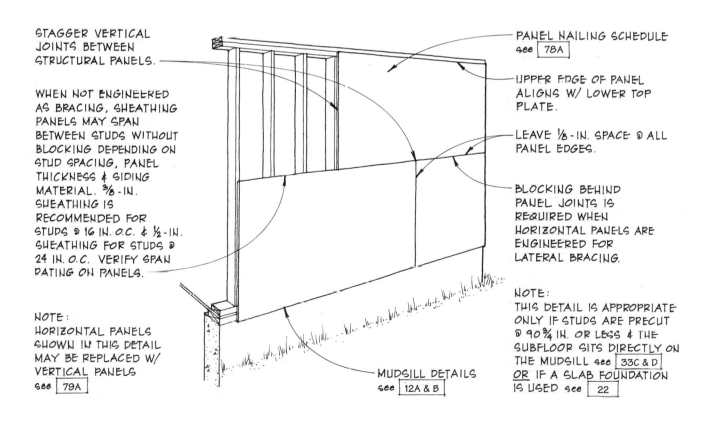

STAGGER VERTICAL JOINTS BETWEEN STRUCTURAL PANELS.

WHEN NOT ENGINEERED AS BRACING, SHEATHING PANELS MAY SPAN BETWEEN STUDS WITHOUT BLOCKING DEPENDING ON STUD SPACING, PANEL THICKNESS & SIDING MATERIAL. 3/8-IN. SHEATHING IS RECOMMENDED FOR STUDS @ 16 IN. O.C. & 1/2-IN. SHEATHING FOR STUDS @ 24 IN. O.C. VERIFY SPAN RATING ON PANELS.

NOTE:
HORIZONTAL PANELS SHOWN IN THIS DETAIL MAY BE REPLACED W/ VERTICAL PANELS see 79A

PANEL NAILING SCHEDULE see 78A

UPPER EDGE OF PANEL ALIGNS W/ LOWER TOP PLATE.

LEAVE 1/8-IN. SPACE @ ALL PANEL EDGES.

BLOCKING BEHIND PANEL JOINTS IS REQUIRED WHEN HORIZONTAL PANELS ARE ENGINEERED FOR LATERAL BRACING.

NOTE:
THIS DETAIL IS APPROPRIATE ONLY IF STUDS ARE PRECUT @ 90 3/4 IN. OR LESS & THE SUBFLOOR SITS DIRECTLY ON THE MUDSILL see 33C & D OR IF A SLAB FOUNDATION IS USED see 22

MUDSILL DETAILS see 12A & B

Ⓑ STRUCTURAL SHEATHING / SINGLE-STORY BUILDING
DISTANCE FROM MUDSILL TO TOP PLATE 8 FT. OR LESS

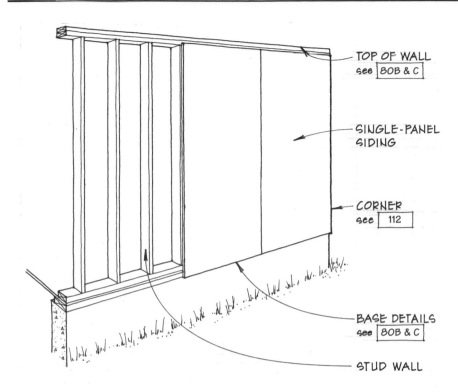

In single-wall construction, a single panel of plywood or composite board siding provides both structural and weathering functions. This is an inexpensive, low-quality type of construction most appropriate for garages and sheds, but also used for residential construction. Panels are installed vertically, usually over a moisture barrier.

Precut studs (from 88½ in. to 92⅜ in.) allow 8-ft. panels to cover the framing on the exterior if the subfloor sits directly on the mudsill (see 80B) or if there is a slab floor. Adding trim to the base allows the use of 8-ft. panels with taller studs and/or different subfloor connections (see 80C).

Taller (9-ft. and 10-ft.) plywood panels are also available.

TOP OF WALL see 80B & C

SINGLE-PANEL SIDING

CORNER see 112

BASE DETAILS see 80B & C

STUD WALL

A **SINGLE-WALL CONSTRUCTION**
STRUCTURAL SHEATHING

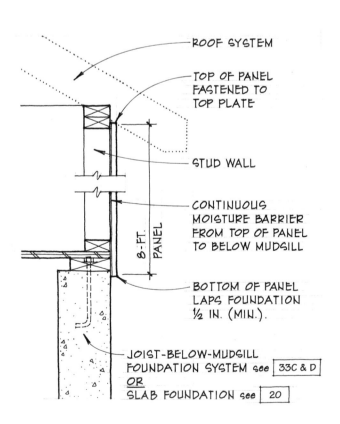

ROOF SYSTEM

TOP OF PANEL FASTENED TO TOP PLATE

STUD WALL

8-FT. PANEL

CONTINUOUS MOISTURE BARRIER FROM TOP OF PANEL TO BELOW MUDSILL

BOTTOM OF PANEL LAPS FOUNDATION ½ IN. (MIN.)

JOIST-BELOW-MUDSILL FOUNDATION SYSTEM see 33C & D
OR
SLAB FOUNDATION see 20

B **SINGLE-WALL CONSTRUCTION**
8-FT. PANEL TYPICAL

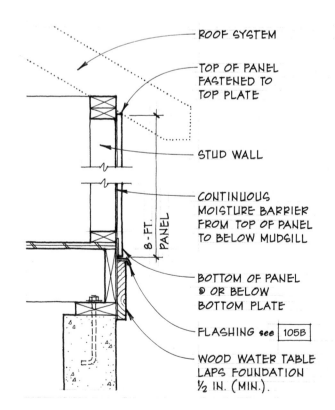

ROOF SYSTEM

TOP OF PANEL FASTENED TO TOP PLATE

STUD WALL

8-FT. PANEL

CONTINUOUS MOISTURE BARRIER FROM TOP OF PANEL TO BELOW MUDSILL

BOTTOM OF PANEL @ OR BELOW BOTTOM PLATE

FLASHING see 105B

WOOD WATER TABLE LAPS FOUNDATION ½ IN. (MIN.)

C **SINGLE-WALL CONSTRUCTION**
8-FT. PANEL W/ WATER TABLE

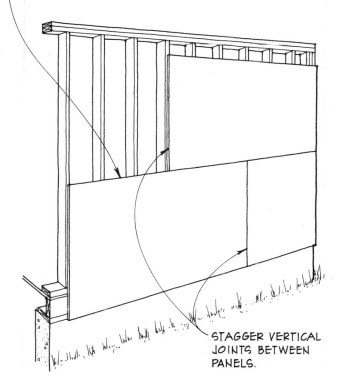

SHEATHING PANELS MAY SPAN BETWEEN STUDS WITHOUT BLOCKING SINCE SIDING MUST BE NAILED TO STUDS IN ANY CASE.

STAGGER VERTICAL JOINTS BETWEEN PANELS.

Fire-protective sheathings are often required at walls on or near property lines, between attached dwellings, and to separate garages from living space. Type-X gypsum wallboard applied directly to the studs will satisfy most codes.

Siding must be nailed through nonstructural sheathings directly into the studs beneath them. These sheathings do not produce an adequate base for shingles or brick. The need for lateral bracing is often satisfied by applying plywood or other structural panels to the corners of a building, with less-expensive nonstructural sheathing elsewhere.

Many sheet materials that can be used for sheathing do not provide adequate lateral bracing. In addition to providing a base for a moisture barrier and siding, such nonstructural sheathings may also provide insulation or fire protection.

Insulative sheathings range in thickness from ½ in. to 1½ in. They include fiberboards, foam plastic, and rigid fiberglass boards. R-values vary. Verify that the permeability of the sheathing is higher than the permeability of the vapor barrier (see 88A).

(A) NON-STRUCTURAL SHEATHING

In most cases, minimum code requirements for let-in bracing or structural sheathing will sufficiently stiffen the walls of a light wood-frame building to resist the typical lateral loads of wind or eccentric loading. The stiffened walls act like the sides of a shoe box working in concert with the lid to maintain the overall shape of the box.

In more extreme conditions such as zones with a high risk of earthquakes or severe winds, lateral bracing measures beyond standard structural sheathing or let-in bracing must be taken. For small simple buildings in these zones, codes typically require increased nailing, strapping, and anchoring, as well as extra framing members.

But it is common to have conditions where even these increased code requirements are not adequate. Such conditions generally involve a building in which numerous wall openings reduce the ability of the wall to resist the lateral forces. In these cases, more extreme measures must be taken to resist lateral loads, and these usually involve calculations by an engineer to design diaphragms coupled with shear walls.

The following diagram summarizes how diaphragms and shear walls work together to resist lateral forces. For simplicity, the diagram shows a wind acting in a single direction perpendicular to the building wall, but in reality, the direction of lateral forces cannot be predicted, so lateral resisting systems must be designed for the eventuality of forces in all directions.

The lateral force follows a continuous path through the structure: (1) the force of wind on the windward wall is transferred through studs to the top (and base) of the wall, (2) the diaphragm collects the loads from the top of the windward wall and transfers them to the top of the shear walls at either side, and (3) the shear walls at opposite ends of the diaphragm transfer the loads down to the foundation.

The diagrams on these pages use wind forces to illustrate how lateral forces follow a continuous path through diaphragm and shear walls. Although these structural elements are designed essentially the same to resist the forces of wind or earthquake, these two forces act differently on buildings. Simply stated, wind forces act on the top of a building and earthquake forces act on the bottom. The relatively light weight of wood-frame buildings works to their advantage in the case of earthquakes, but works against them in the case of high winds.

Diaphragm—A diaphragm is a horizontal structure such as a floor or roof composed of sheathing, framing members, and a structural perimeter. In the case of a floor, the framing members are joists, and the structural perimeter is composed of rim joists and/or blocking (see 32). In the case of a roof, the framing members are common rafters (or trusses), and the structural perimeter is composed of end rafters (or trusses) and frieze blocks (see 129). A diaphragm acts as a horizontal beam to collect lateral forces and transfer these forces to the shear walls.

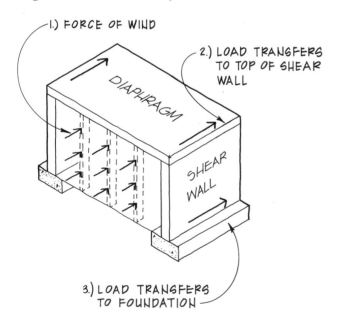

1.) FORCE OF WIND

2.) LOAD TRANSFERS TO TOP OF SHEAR WALL

DIAPHRAGM

SHEAR WALL

3.) LOAD TRANSFERS TO FOUNDATION

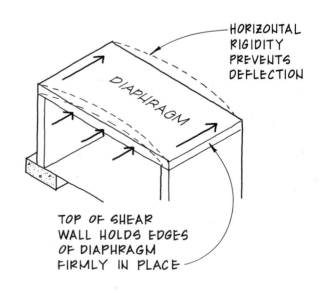

HORIZONTAL RIGIDITY PREVENTS DEFLECTION

DIAPHRAGM

TOP OF SHEAR WALL HOLDS EDGES OF DIAPHRAGM FIRMLY IN PLACE

A SHEAR WALLS

Shear walls—Shear walls are extremely strong framed walls that connect the horizontal diaphragm to the foundation. They act like regular braced or structurally sheathed walls to resist the action of lateral forces except that they are much stronger. Their greater strength comes from increased nailing, thicker sheathing, more framing members at their edges, and more substantial anchoring.

Shear walls act as beams cantilevered from the foundation (or upper floor) to resist forces parallel to them. They are connected at their base to the foundation (or to another shear wall) and at their top to a diaphragm.

At their base, shear walls must resist both sliding and overturning. Horizontal forces can slide the wall off the foundation if adequate shear connections are not provided. Sliding forces are resisted by anchor bolts, by nailing, and/or by framing anchors at upper floors (see 85).

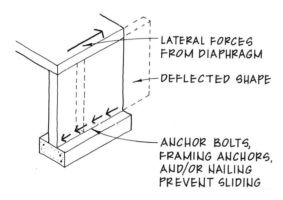

LATERAL FORCES FROM DIAPHRAGM

DEFLECTED SHAPE

ANCHOR BOLTS, FRAMING ANCHORS, AND/OR NAILING PREVENT SLIDING

Horizontal forces applied to the top of a shear wall can cause overturning unless the bottom corners are adequately tied (with hold-downs) to resist uplift (see 85 & 86A). While the force is applied, one edge of the

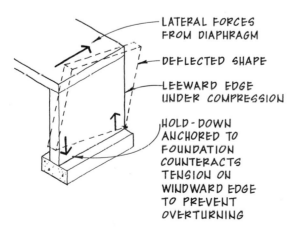

LATERAL FORCES FROM DIAPHRAGM

DEFLECTED SHAPE

LEEWARD EDGE UNDER COMPRESSION

HOLD-DOWN ANCHORED TO FOUNDATION COUNTERACTS TENSION ON WINDWARD EDGE TO PREVENT OVERTURNING

wall will be in tension while the opposite edge is in compression.

Longer shear walls are inherently better because they have a longer base to resist sliding and because the hold-downs are farther apart to resist overturning.

Connections—Because shear walls involve a large number and variety of components and connections, it is critical that each connection be designed and constructed to resist the forces that pass through it. Depending on their location, connections may be called upon to resist vertical and horizontal forces in several directions. When designing and building to resist extreme conditions, it is especially important to pay close attention to manufacturers' instructions for the installation of connectors. A shear wall is only as strong as its weakest connection.

Distribution—Shear walls are generally located within each (principal) exterior wall of a building, but may also be located strategically at interior walls. For earthquake resistance, shear walls should generally be balanced on all four sides of the building; for wind resistance, however, shear walls should be longer (or stronger, see 85B) at the short walls in order to resist the larger wind forces imposed on the long walls.

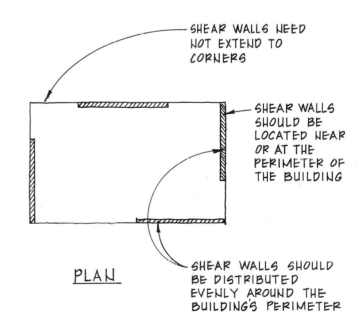

SHEAR WALLS NEED NOT EXTEND TO CORNERS

SHEAR WALLS SHOULD BE LOCATED NEAR OR AT THE PERIMETER OF THE BUILDING

PLAN

SHEAR WALLS SHOULD BE DISTRIBUTED EVENLY AROUND THE BUILDING'S PERIMETER

A SHEAR WALLS

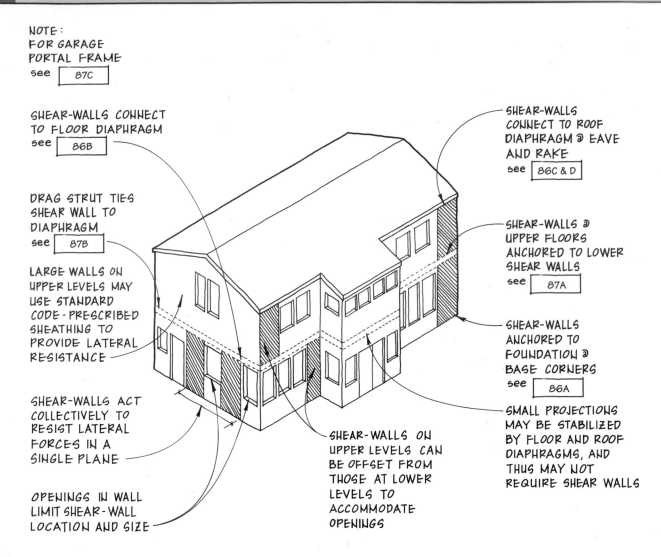

NOTE:
FOR GARAGE
PORTAL FRAME
see [87C]

SHEAR-WALLS CONNECT
TO FLOOR DIAPHRAGM
see [86B]

DRAG STRUT TIES
SHEAR WALL TO
DIAPHRAGM
see [87B]

LARGE WALLS ON
UPPER LEVELS MAY
USE STANDARD
CODE-PRESCRIBED
SHEATHING TO
PROVIDE LATERAL
RESISTANCE

SHEAR-WALLS ACT
COLLECTIVELY TO
RESIST LATERAL
FORCES IN A
SINGLE PLANE

OPENINGS IN WALL
LIMIT SHEAR-WALL
LOCATION AND SIZE

SHEAR-WALLS ON
UPPER LEVELS CAN
BE OFFSET FROM
THOSE AT LOWER
LEVELS TO
ACCOMMODATE
OPENINGS

SHEAR-WALLS
CONNECT TO ROOF
DIAPHRAGM @ EAVE
AND RAKE
see [86C & D]

SHEAR-WALLS @
UPPER FLOORS
ANCHORED TO LOWER
SHEAR WALLS
see [87A]

SHEAR-WALLS
ANCHORED TO
FOUNDATION @
BASE CORNERS
see [86A]

SMALL PROJECTIONS
MAY BE STABILIZED
BY FLOOR AND ROOF
DIAPHRAGMS, AND
THUS MAY NOT
REQUIRE SHEAR WALLS

Because lateral forces such as wind are assumed to act perpendicularly to the walls of a building, they can theoretically be resisted by shear walls in each of the four walls of a simple building. Forces acting in a north-south direction, for example, can be resisted by shear walls located in the east and west walls of the building (and vice versa). When the wind blows on a diagonal (as it usually does), shear walls in all four walls will be in play.

Because they connect diaphragm to the foundation, shear walls cannot be placed where there are openings in the wall. Therefore, in walls with many openings, there may need to be several shear wall segments in order to provide ample resistance to lateral forces.

Shear walls are most effective when they are wide relative to their height and their base anchors are far apart. For this reason, codes have specified that shear walls must have a height-to-width ratio of 3.5-to-1 or less. The practical effect of this limitation is a minimum shear wall width of approximately 2 ft. for a wall 8 ft. tall.

In a building with more than one floor, the need for shear walls is greater on floors nearest the ground. This is because the lower floors are required to resist the forces from upper floors in addition to their own. It is not unusual to have a two-story wood-frame building with engineered shear walls on the ground floor and standard code-prescribed sheathing on the upper floor.

The calculation of shear wall values is fairly complicated—involving different factors for earthquake or wind forces—and is thus usually performed by a licensed engineer.

 SHEAR WALLS IN CONTEXT

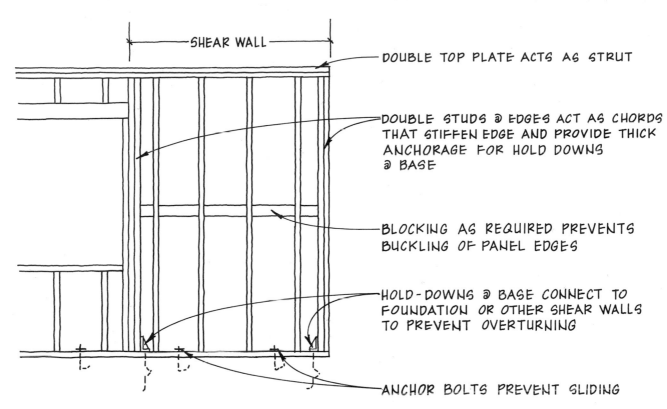

- DOUBLE TOP PLATE ACTS AS STRUT
- DOUBLE STUDS @ EDGES ACT AS CHORDS THAT STIFFEN EDGE AND PROVIDE THICK ANCHORAGE FOR HOLD DOWNS @ BASE
- BLOCKING AS REQUIRED PREVENTS BUCKLING OF PANEL EDGES
- HOLD-DOWNS @ BASE CONNECT TO FOUNDATION OR OTHER SHEAR WALLS TO PREVENT OVERTURNING
- ANCHOR BOLTS PREVENT SLIDING

 A   COMPONENTS OF A SHEAR WALL

Once the lateral forces have been determined, there are seven basic considerations that need to be taken into account when designing a shear wall:

Proportion—Most codes specify a maximum height-to-width ratio of 3.5-to-1. This generally means that shear walls cannot be less than 2 ft. wide.

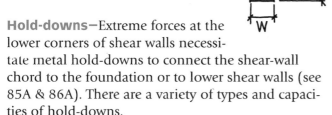

Hold-downs—Extreme forces at the lower corners of shear walls necessitate metal hold-downs to connect the shear-wall chord to the foundation or to lower shear walls (see 85A & 86A). There are a variety of types and capacities of hold-downs.

Anchor bolts—To prevent sliding, anchor bolts are used to connect the base of a shear wall to the foundation. At framed floors, framing anchors and nailing are used to prevent sliding. Hold-downs also resist sliding but are not generally considered in engineering calculations.

Sheathing strength—The strength of the rated sheathing must match the required capacity of the shear wall. Sheathing on both sides of the shear wall will double its capacity. All panel edges must be blocked to prevent buckling of the panel.

Chord strength—At the boundaries of the shear wall where stress is greatest, chords must be stronger than standard studs. A minimum of two studs is required by most codes (see 85A).

Strut strength—Like chords, struts are at the boundary of shear walls where stresses are greatest. Typical framing (i.e., single sole plate and double top plate) is usually sufficient as struts. Splices in struts should be avoided if possible.

Nailing—Size and spacing of nails must be specified. More nailing is required at the edges of panels than in the field of the panel. Increased nailing acts to increase wall strength (see 78A).

 B   SHEAR WALL DESIGN CONSIDERATIONS

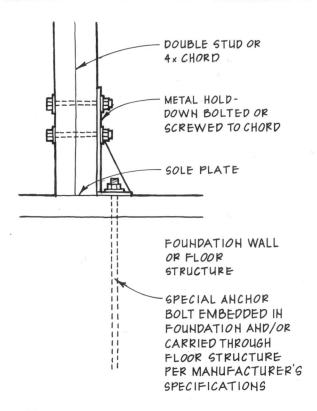

DOUBLE STUD OR
4x CHORD

METAL HOLD-
DOWN BOLTED OR
SCREWED TO CHORD

SOLE PLATE

FOUNDATION WALL
OR FLOOR
STRUCTURE

SPECIAL ANCHOR
BOLT EMBEDDED IN
FOUNDATION AND/OR
CARRIED THROUGH
FLOOR STRUCTURE
PER MANUFACTURER'S
SPECIFICATIONS

(A) SHEAR WALL HOLD-DOWNS

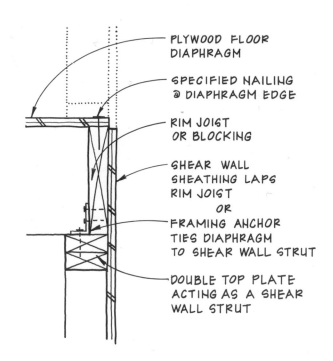

PLYWOOD FLOOR
DIAPHRAGM

SPECIFIED NAILING
@ DIAPHRAGM EDGE

RIM JOIST
OR BLOCKING

SHEAR WALL
SHEATHING LAPS
RIM JOIST
OR
FRAMING ANCHOR
TIES DIAPHRAGM
TO SHEAR WALL STRUT

DOUBLE TOP PLATE
ACTING AS A SHEAR
WALL STRUT

(B) SHEAR WALL / FLOOR DIAPHRAGM

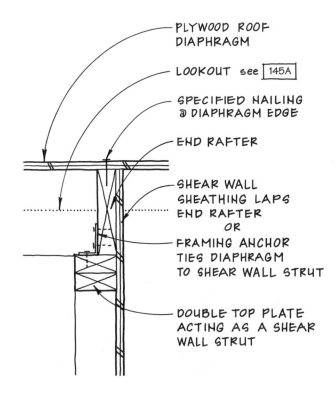

PLYWOOD ROOF
DIAPHRAGM

SPECIFIED NAILING
@ DIAPHRAGM EDGE

FRIEZE BLOCK

ALTERNATIVE FRIEZE
BLOCK LOCATION

SHEAR WALL
SHEATHING LAPS
FRIEZE BLOCK
OR
FRAMING ANCHOR
TIES DIAPHRAGM TO
SHEAR WALL STRUT

DOUBLE TOP PLATE
ACTING AS A SHEAR
WALL STRUT

(C) SHEAR WALL / ROOF DIAPHRAGM
@ EAVE

PLYWOOD ROOF
DIAPHRAGM

LOOKOUT see 145A

SPECIFIED NAILING
@ DIAPHRAGM EDGE

END RAFTER

SHEAR WALL
SHEATHING LAPS
END RAFTER
OR
FRAMING ANCHOR
TIES DIAPHRAGM
TO SHEAR WALL STRUT

DOUBLE TOP PLATE
ACTING AS A SHEAR
WALL STRUT

(D) SHEAR WALL / ROOF DIAPHRAGM
@ RAKE

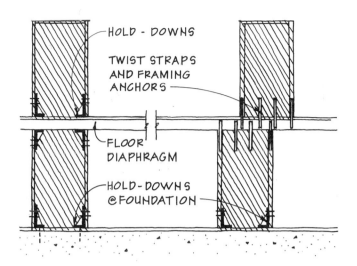

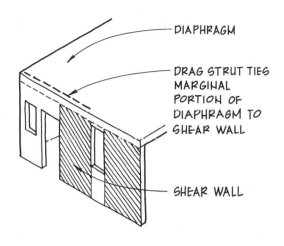

When shear walls are required on upper floors, they must be tied, through the floor diaphragm, to the shear walls below. If upper and lower shear walls align, their corners may be tied with hold-downs (see 86A) with the lower hold-downs inverted. If the shear walls do not align, their edges may be tied to the diaphragm with a combination of twist straps (for uplift) and framing anchors (for horizontal shear).

Drag struts are sometimes required to tie the diaphragm to the shear walls, especially if the diaphragm is not bounded by shear walls at each end. A drag strut consists of a long metal strap firmly attached to the diaphragm above the shear wall. The drag strut extends into the diaphragm in a line parallel to the shear wall to pull or "drag" the force from the diaphragm to the shear wall.

Ⓐ **SHEAR WALL / SHEAR WALL**
TIE BETWEEN FLOORS

Ⓑ **DRAG STRUT**

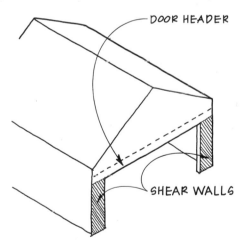

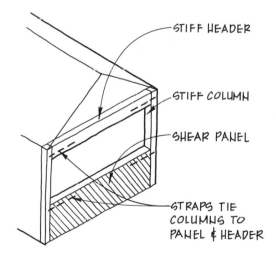

Garages with wide doors and limited walls are typical of buildings requiring shear walls. These conditions are so typical that several companies have developed proprietary premanufactured walls specifically for garages. The shear walls are strapped to the door header and work in conjunction with it. Garage shear walls are also commonly site-built.

Engineers can design reinforced windows so the window can extend virtually from wall to wall in small buildings and building extensions. A shear panel below the window opening is strapped to stiff single-piece or built-up columns at the corners. The columns effectively cantilever up from the panel, stiffening the entire wall.

Ⓒ **GARAGE PORTAL FRAME**

Ⓓ **REINFORCED WINDOW**

Once the walls are framed and sheathed, they must be protected from moisture. This involves the installation of a moisture barrier. The moisture barrier must be coordinated with an air barrier (to control air infiltration), a vapor barrier (to control water vapor), and insulation.

A moisture barrier (also called a weather barrier) is a membrane directly under the siding that prevents any water penetrating the siding from reaching the sheathing or the framing. An effective moisture barrier stops liquid water but lets water vapor through, thereby letting the wall breathe.

A vapor barrier (also known as a vapor retarder) is a membrane on the warm side of the wall (usually the interior) that retards the passage of water vapor from the warm inside air into the cooler wall, where it could condense (see 120).

An air barrier limits the infiltration of air through the wall. Either a moisture barrier or a vapor barrier may be detailed to seal the wall against air infiltration, thereby becoming an air barrier as well (see 120).

Coordinating these components is critical to avoid trapping water vapor in the wall cavity. The principle to follow is that the permeability (the degree to which water vapor will pass through a material) must be higher for materials on the cool side of the wall (usually the outside) than for materials on the warm side of the wall (usually the inside). For example, foil-faced rigid insulation, which has a very low permeability, should not be placed on the exterior of a wall in a cool climate. The following chart rates the permeability of several common materials.

Material	Permeability (perms per STM-E96)
Foil-faced insulation	0
4-mil PVC	0.08
Extruded polystyrene	0.3–1.0
½-in. CDX plywood	0.4–1.2
Kraft paper	1.8
15-lb. felt	5.6
½-in. fiberboard	50–90
Building or house wraps	88–107

A **MOISTURE, VAPOR & AIR BARRIERS**
NOTES

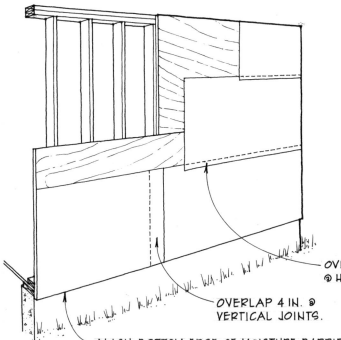

OVERLAP 2 IN. TO 4 IN. @ HORIZONTAL JOINTS.

OVERLAP 4 IN. @ VERTICAL JOINTS.

ALIGN BOTTOM EDGE OF MOISTURE BARRIER W/ BOTTOM EDGE OF SHEATHING. SEE SPECIFIC SIDING TYPE FOR DETAILS.

A moisture barrier under the siding is a sensible second line of defense to prevent water from reaching the frame of the building. Many products such as 15-lb. felt and bitumen-impregnated paper (which come in 3-ft. wide rolls, as shown here) have been used historically and are suitable for this purpose.

A moisture barrier acting also as an air infiltration barrier under the siding must retard the passage of air and be impermeable to water, but allow vapor to pass. Polyolefin membranes, commonly called building or house wraps, meet these specifications and are the most prevalent barriers. They are very lightweight and come in rolls up to 12 ft. wide, allowing a single-story building to be covered in one pass. Building wraps can provide better protection against air infiltration than felt and kraft paper because the wide rolls require fewer joints, and these joints are taped.

B **MOISTURE & AIR INFILTRATION BARRIERS**
INSTALLATION

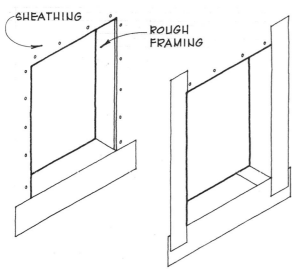
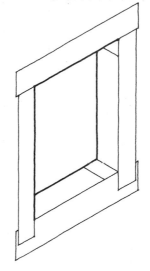

SHEATHING

ROUGH FRAMING

1. STAPLE MOISTURE BARRIER TO SILL & FOLD 6 IN. DOWN, EXTENDING 6 IN. TO EACH SIDE. DO NOT STAPLE LOWER EDGE; IT WILL LAP WALL MOISTURE BARRIER.

2. STAPLE MOISTURE BARRIER TO JAMBS OF ROUGH OPENING & FOLD 6 IN. OVER SHEATHING & 6 IN. ABOVE & BELOW ROUGH OPENING.

3. REPEAT STEP 2, BUT FOR TOP OF ROUGH OPENING. LEAVE OUTER EDGES UNSTAPLED FOR FUTURE INTEGRATION W/ WALL MOISTURE BARRIER.

NOTE:
IT IS EXTREMELY IMPORTANT TO WRAP ROUGH OPENINGS WITH A MOISTURE BARRIER BECAUSE THIS IS WHERE LEAKS ARE MOST LIKELY TO OCCUR & BECAUSE THE FRAMING IS MOST VULNERABLE AT OPENINGS. THIS PROCEDURE IS ADEQUATE FOR MOST EXPOSED SITUATIONS BECAUSE ALL LAYERS OVERLAP IN AN ORDER THAT DIRECTS WATER AWAY FROM THE STRUCTURAL FRAME OF THE BUILDING. SIMPLER METHODS MAY BE EMPLOYED WHERE EXPOSURE TO RAIN IS NOT LIKELY TO OCCUR. FOR THE METHOD SHOWN, MANY BUILDERS PREFER TO USE THIN MOISTURE BARRIERS (SUCH AS KRAFT PAPER) THAT WILL NOT BUILD UP W/ THE FOLDS & W/ SEVERAL LAYERS.

(A) WINDOW / DOOR ROUGH - OPENING WRAP

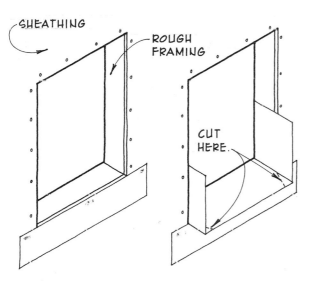

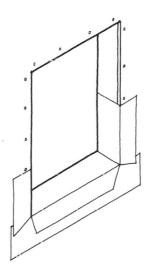
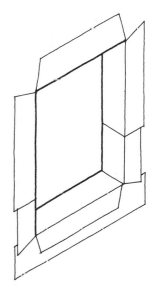

SHEATHING

ROUGH FRAMING

CUT HERE.

1. STAPLE 6-IN. MOISTURE-BARRIER PAPER @ BOTTOM EDGE OF ROUGH OPENING & EXTENDING 6 IN. TO EACH SIDE.

2. STAPLE MOISTURE BARRIER, WHICH EXTENDS 6 IN. PAST BUILDING'S FACE, AROUND FRAMING @ BOTTOM OF ROUGH OPENING. CUT AS SHOWN.

3. FOLD MOISTURE BARRIER INSTALLED IN STEP 2 AGAINST FACE OF BUILDING.

4. REPEAT STEPS 2 & 3 BUT FOR UPPER PART OF ROUGH OPENING.

(B) WINDOW / DOOR ROUGH - OPENING WRAP
ALTERNATIVE DETAIL FOR SEVERE EXPOSURE TO RAIN

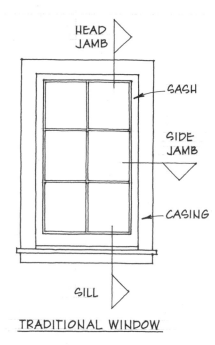

HEAD JAMB

SASH

SIDE JAMB

CASING

SILL

TRADITIONAL WINDOW

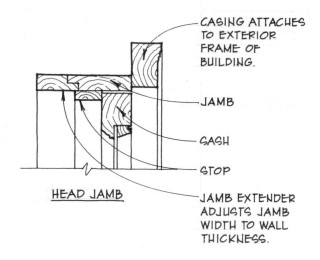

CASING ATTACHES TO EXTERIOR FRAME OF BUILDING.

JAMB

SASH

STOP

JAMB EXTENDER ADJUSTS JAMB WIDTH TO WALL THICKNESS.

HEAD JAMB

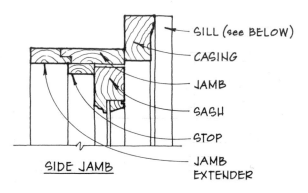

SILL (see BELOW)

CASING

JAMB

SASH

STOP

JAMB EXTENDER

SIDE JAMB

Modern windows derive from the traditional wooden window shown above. Older windows have a wooden sash that holds the glass, which is usually divided into small panes by muntin bars. This sash is hinged within a wooden frame that is fixed to an opening in the wall. At the bottom of the frame is a wood sill, sloped to shed water, and the sides and top of the frame are called jambs.

These components and their terminology have been handed down to the modern window, but modern windows are better insulated and better sealed, and usually need less maintenance than the traditional prototypes.

Today's window is made in a factory and is usually assembled there and shipped ready to install in a rough opening. Several popular types, classified by their method of operation, include casement, double-hung, sliding, hopper, awning, and fixed. Each of these types is made in wood, vinyl, metal, or a combi-nation of materials. Sizes and details vary with the manufacturer. Double-hung, sliding, and fixed win-dows are generally made in larger sizes than the hinged types. Optional trim packages are available with most.

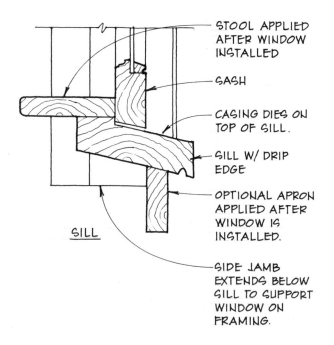

STOOL APPLIED AFTER WINDOW INSTALLED

SASH

CASING DIES ON TOP OF SILL.

SILL W/ DRIP EDGE

OPTIONAL APRON APPLIED AFTER WINDOW IS INSTALLED.

SIDE JAMB EXTENDS BELOW SILL TO SUPPORT WINDOW ON FRAMING.

SILL

A **WINDOW TERMINOLOGY**

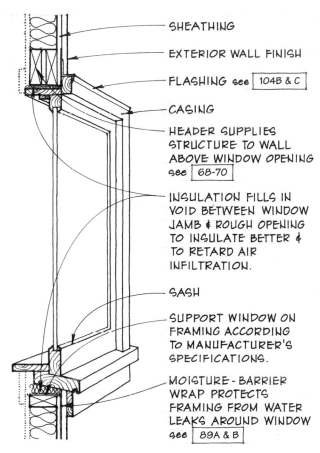

SHEATHING

EXTERIOR WALL FINISH

FLASHING see 104B & C

CASING

HEADER SUPPLIES STRUCTURE TO WALL ABOVE WINDOW OPENING see 68-70

INSULATION FILLS IN VOID BETWEEN WINDOW JAMB & ROUGH OPENING TO INSULATE BETTER & TO RETARD AIR INFILTRATION.

SASH

SUPPORT WINDOW ON FRAMING ACCORDING TO MANUFACTURER'S SPECIFICATIONS.

MOISTURE - BARRIER WRAP PROTECTS FRAMING FROM WATER LEAKS AROUND WINDOW see 89A & B

All windows require a coordinated installation in wood-frame walls, as follows:

Header—Size the header so that loads from above do not bear on the window itself, restricting operation.

Window wrap—Wrap the framing at the rough opening with a moisture barrier to protect it from any leaks around the edges of windows and doors.

Shim and support—Shim the window at the sill and affix the shims to the framing so that the window is level and rests firmly on the framing.

Insulation—Place batt or spray foam insulation around the edges of the installed window to reduce both heat loss and air infiltration.

Air barrier—An air barrier, if used, must be sealed to the window unit. The moisture/air barrier may be sealed to the window nailing flange at the wall's outside surface, or the vapor/air barrier may be sealed to the jamb's inside edge at the wall's inside surface.

Wood windows—Wood windows (see 92–95) are pleasing for their warm, natural look. Along with the

excellent thermal properties of wood, the aesthetic appeal of the wood window is its strongest asset.

The major disadvantages of wood windows are the initial high cost and the ongoing need for maintenance. Wood is susceptible to deterioration from the weather, so periodically refinishing the exterior surfaces is necessary. Every effort should be made to protect all-wood windows from rain by locating them under overhangs.

Wood windows clad with aluminum and vinyl were developed to minimize maintenance. The cladding on these windows decreases their need for maintenance yet retains the aesthetic and thermal advantages of wood on the interior. The availability of custom shapes is limited compared to non-clad windows, however.

Vinyl windows—Made of extruded PVC that is either screwed or heat-welded at mitered corners, vinyl windows (see 93B and 94B) have come to dominate the window market. Their cost and expected maintenance are low, while their insulative properties are relatively high. They are available in all typical operating types, and some manufacturers offer true-divided-lite sash.

Vinyl windows are not available with exterior casings, so their potential to act as strong visual elements on the exterior of a building is limited. Decorative casings are often added, however (see 93B).

One disadvantage of vinyl windows is the limited range of available colors. The vinyl cannot be painted and only very light colors such as white and tan are available because dark colors tend to absorb heat, causing warping. Where color is desired, newly developed fiberglass windows are a good choice. Fiberglass windows have factory-applied warranted finishes, ranging from light to very dark, that can be painted.

Metal windows—Until recently, aluminum windows were the most common low-cost window. But energy codes and the popularity of vinyl windows have virtually eliminated aluminum windows from the residential market. Aluminum is still available for commercial applications. The ubiquitous storefront windows are available in polished aluminum, anodized bronze, and a spectrum of baked-enamel colors.

Unclad wood windows are attached to the building through the casing. This is the traditional way that windows have been fastened to wood buildings. The nail holes are typically filled, and the casings painted.

It is also possible to cover the nails with a dripmold or with a backband that may be nailed from the side or the face, depending on the profile of the backband. The backband is mitered at the corners and dies on the sill.

When attaching a window through the casing, it is important to support the weight of the window unit from below. Shim the sill and/or the extensions of the side jambs below the sill.

TYPICAL BACKBAND PROFILES

Some manufacturers also recommend blocking and nailing the units through the jamb. In this case, the nails can be covered by the stops.

Where fixed windows are acceptable, a great deal of expense may be saved by custom-building the

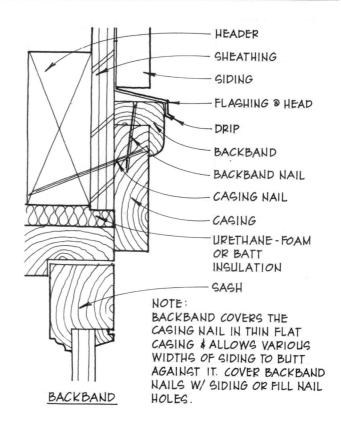

- HEADER
- SHEATHING
- SIDING
- FLASHING @ HEAD
- DRIP
- BACKBAND
- BACKBAND NAIL
- CASING NAIL
- CASING
- URETHANE-FOAM OR BATT INSULATION
- SASH

NOTE:
BACKBAND COVERS THE CASING NAIL IN THIN FLAT CASING & ALLOWS VARIOUS WIDTHS OF SIDING TO BUTT AGAINST IT. COVER BACKBAND NAILS W/ SIDING OR FILL NAIL HOLES.

BACKBAND

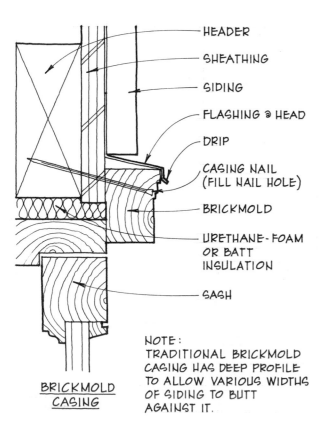

- HEADER
- SHEATHING
- SIDING
- FLASHING @ HEAD
- DRIP
- CASING NAIL (FILL NAIL HOLE)
- BRICKMOLD
- URETHANE-FOAM OR BATT INSULATION
- SASH

NOTE:
TRADITIONAL BRICKMOLD CASING HAS DEEP PROFILE TO ALLOW VARIOUS WIDTHS OF SIDING TO BUTT AGAINST IT.

BRICKMOLD CASING

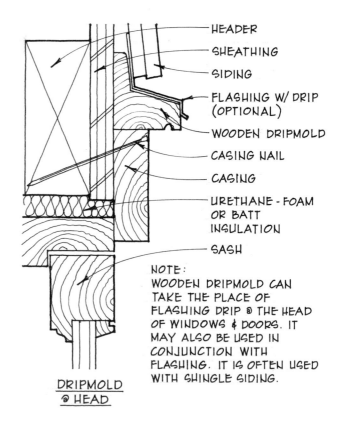

- HEADER
- SHEATHING
- SIDING
- FLASHING W/ DRIP (OPTIONAL)
- WOODEN DRIPMOLD
- CASING NAIL
- CASING
- URETHANE-FOAM OR BATT INSULATION
- SASH

NOTE:
WOODEN DRIPMOLD CAN TAKE THE PLACE OF FLASHING DRIP @ THE HEAD OF WINDOWS & DOORS. IT MAY ALSO BE USED IN CONJUNCTION WITH FLASHING. IT IS OFTEN USED WITH SHINGLE SIDING.

DRIPMOLD @ HEAD

(A) **WOOD WINDOWS**
ATTACHMENT THROUGH CASING

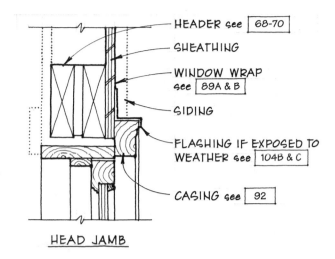

HEADER see 68-70

SHEATHING

WINDOW WRAP
see 89A & B

SIDING

FLASHING IF EXPOSED TO
WEATHER see 104B & C

CASING see 92

HEAD JAMB

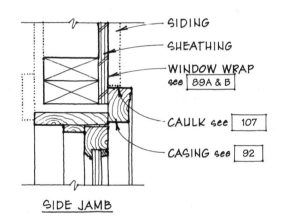

SIDING

SHEATHING

WINDOW WRAP
see 89A & B

CAULK see 107

CASING see 92

SIDE JAMB

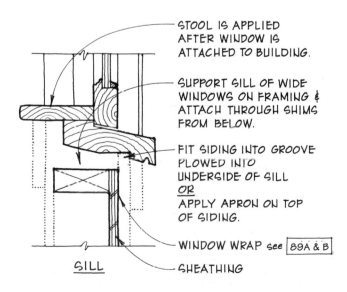

STOOL IS APPLIED
AFTER WINDOW IS
ATTACHED TO BUILDING.

SUPPORT SILL OF WIDE
WINDOWS ON FRAMING &
ATTACH THROUGH SHIMS
FROM BELOW.

FIT SIDING INTO GROOVE
PLOWED INTO
UNDERSIDE OF SILL
OR
APPLY APRON ON TOP
OF SIDING.

WINDOW WRAP see 89A & B

SHEATHING

SILL

METAL, VINYL & CLAD WOOD WINDOWS ARE USUALLY
MANUFACTURED W/ NAILING FINS THAT ACT AS
FLASHING & PROVIDE NAILING FOR ATTACHING THE
WINDOW TO THE BUILDING. CLAD UNITS W/ NAILING
FINS CAN BE USED BOTH WITH & WITHOUT CASINGS.

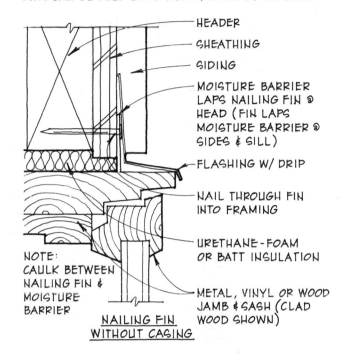

HEADER

SHEATHING

SIDING

MOISTURE BARRIER
LAPS NAILING FIN @
HEAD (FIN LAPS
MOISTURE BARRIER @
SIDES & SILL)

FLASHING W/ DRIP

NAIL THROUGH FIN
INTO FRAMING

URETHANE-FOAM
OR BATT INSULATION

METAL, VINYL OR WOOD
JAMB & SASH (CLAD
WOOD SHOWN)

NOTE:
CAULK BETWEEN
NAILING FIN &
MOISTURE
BARRIER

**NAILING FIN
WITHOUT CASING**

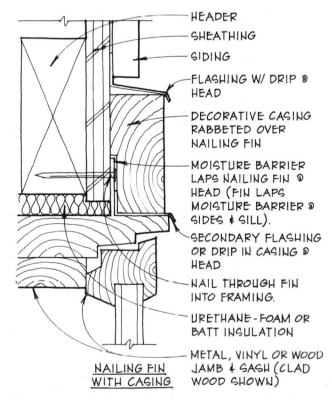

HEADER

SHEATHING

SIDING

FLASHING W/ DRIP @
HEAD

DECORATIVE CASING
RABBETED OVER
NAILING FIN

MOISTURE BARRIER
LAPS NAILING FIN @
HEAD (FIN LAPS
MOISTURE BARRIER @
SIDES & SILL).

SECONDARY FLASHING
OR DRIP IN CASING @
HEAD

NAIL THROUGH FIN
INTO FRAMING.

URETHANE-FOAM OR
BATT INSULATION

METAL, VINYL OR WOOD
JAMB & SASH (CLAD
WOOD SHOWN)

**NAILING FIN
WITH CASING**

A **UNCLAD WOOD WINDOWS**
ATTACHMENT THROUGH CASING

B **WOOD, METAL OR VINYL WINDOWS**
ATTACHMENT THROUGH NAILING FIN

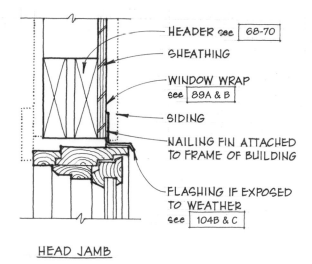

HEADER see 68-70

SHEATHING

WINDOW WRAP see 89A & B

SIDING

NAILING FIN ATTACHED TO FRAME OF BUILDING

FLASHING IF EXPOSED TO WEATHER see 104B & C

HEAD JAMB

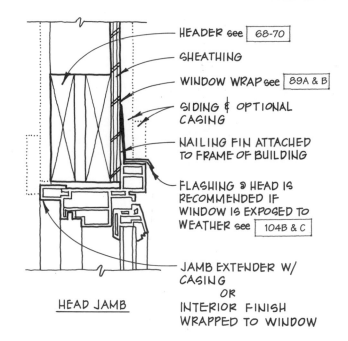

HEADER see 68-70

SHEATHING

WINDOW WRAP see 89A & B

SIDING & OPTIONAL CASING

NAILING FIN ATTACHED TO FRAME OF BUILDING

FLASHING @ HEAD IS RECOMMENDED IF WINDOW IS EXPOSED TO WEATHER see 104B & C

JAMB EXTENDER W/ CASING OR INTERIOR FINISH WRAPPED TO WINDOW

HEAD JAMB

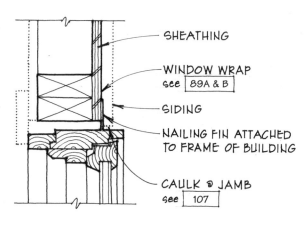

SHEATHING

WINDOW WRAP see 89A & B

SIDING

NAILING FIN ATTACHED TO FRAME OF BUILDING

CAULK @ JAMB see 107

SIDE JAMB

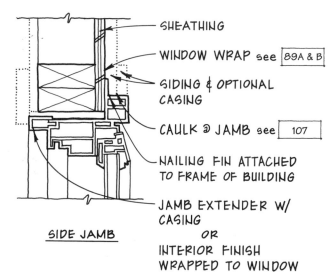

SHEATHING

WINDOW WRAP see 89A & B

SIDING & OPTIONAL CASING

CAULK @ JAMB see 107

NAILING FIN ATTACHED TO FRAME OF BUILDING

JAMB EXTENDER W/ CASING OR INTERIOR FINISH WRAPPED TO WINDOW

SIDE JAMB

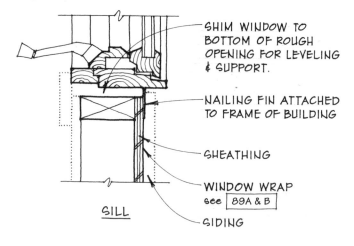

SHIM WINDOW TO BOTTOM OF ROUGH OPENING FOR LEVELING & SUPPORT.

NAILING FIN ATTACHED TO FRAME OF BUILDING

SHEATHING

WINDOW WRAP see 89A & B

SIDING

SILL

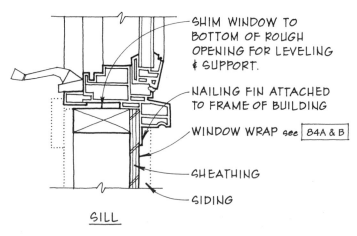

SHIM WINDOW TO BOTTOM OF ROUGH OPENING FOR LEVELING & SUPPORT.

NAILING FIN ATTACHED TO FRAME OF BUILDING

WINDOW WRAP see 84A & B

SHEATHING

SIDING

SILL

(A) **CLAD WOOD WINDOWS**
ATTACHMENT THROUGH NAILING FIN

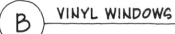

(B) VINYL WINDOWS

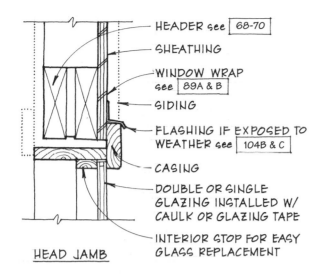

HEADER see 68-70
SHEATHING
WINDOW WRAP see 89A & B
SIDING
FLASHING IF EXPOSED TO WEATHER see 104B & C
CASING
DOUBLE OR SINGLE GLAZING INSTALLED W/ CAULK OR GLAZING TAPE
INTERIOR STOP FOR EASY GLASS REPLACEMENT

HEAD JAMB

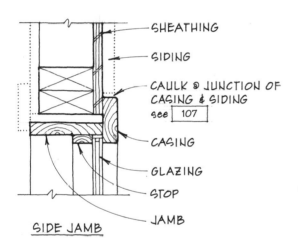

SHEATHING
SIDING
CAULK @ JUNCTION OF CASING & SIDING see 107
CASING
GLAZING
STOP
JAMB

SIDE JAMB

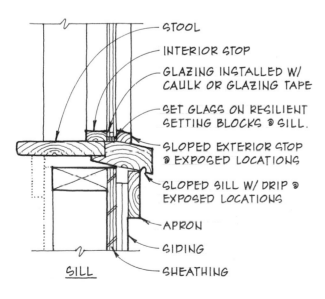

STOOL
INTERIOR STOP
GLAZING INSTALLED W/ CAULK OR GLAZING TAPE
SET GLASS ON RESILIENT SETTING BLOCKS @ SILL.
SLOPED EXTERIOR STOP @ EXPOSED LOCATIONS
SLOPED SILL W/ DRIP @ EXPOSED LOCATIONS
APRON
SIDING
SHEATHING

SILL

(A) SITE-BUILT FIXED WINDOWS

windows on the job without sash. In this case, the glass is stopped directly into the window frame, and caulk or glazing tape seals the glass to the casing just as it would to sash. Ventilation must be provided for the space by means other than operable windows.

When designing and installing site-built fixed windows, the following guidelines are useful:
1. Allow ⅛ in. minimum clearance at the top and sides of the glass.
2. Rest the base of the glass on setting blocks spaced one-quarter of the width from each end.
3. Glass can be set closer to the interior of the building than shown in 95A by using exterior stop.
4. At protected locations, stool and sill can be one single flat piece of wood.
5. Support the sill of wide or heavy windows by shimming it from the framing.

(B) SITE-BUILT FIXED WINDOWS

Storm sash made today are usually fitted to aging single-glazed windows. The storm sash protects the existing window from the weather and also improves the thermal performance of the window.

Usually made of aluminum, storm sash are custom fit to the exterior face of the existing window. Many are operable from the interior and are fitted with screens. Depending on how they are installed, storm sash can either significantly extend the useful life of old windows or actually contribute to their deterioration. A proper installation depends on numerous factors including the climate and the detailing of the original window.

New custom wood windows can be manufactured with single glazing if fitted with storm sash. This can be useful for historic work or when attempting to make simple inexpensive sash for a microclimate that requires them. The storm sash provide the thermal performance required by code at the same time they protect the most precious part of the assembly—the sash itself—from the weather. Storms located at fixed sash can be left in place year-round, while storms at operable windows can be exchanged for screens during the summer.

(C) STORM SASH

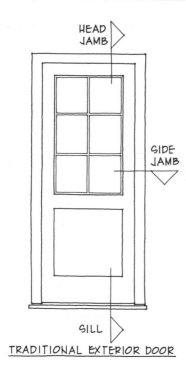

HEAD JAMB

SIDE JAMB

SILL

TRADITIONAL EXTERIOR DOOR

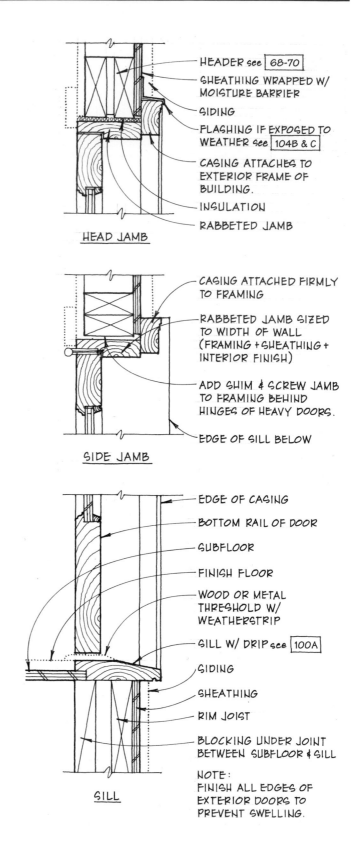

HEADER see 68-70

SHEATHING WRAPPED W/ MOISTURE BARRIER

SIDING

FLASHING IF EXPOSED TO WEATHER see 104B & C

CASING ATTACHES TO EXTERIOR FRAME OF BUILDING.

INSULATION

RABBETED JAMB

HEAD JAMB

CASING ATTACHED FIRMLY TO FRAMING

RABBETED JAMB SIZED TO WIDTH OF WALL (FRAMING + SHEATHING + INTERIOR FINISH)

ADD SHIM & SCREW JAMB TO FRAMING BEHIND HINGES OF HEAVY DOORS.

EDGE OF SILL BELOW

SIDE JAMB

EDGE OF CASING

BOTTOM RAIL OF DOOR

SUBFLOOR

FINISH FLOOR

WOOD OR METAL THRESHOLD W/ WEATHERSTRIP

SILL W/ DRIP see 100A

SIDING

SHEATHING

RIM JOIST

BLOCKING UNDER JOINT BETWEEN SUBFLOOR & SILL

NOTE:
FINISH ALL EDGES OF EXTERIOR DOORS TO PREVENT SWELLING.

SILL

Modern doors have been derived from traditional prototypes; they are better insulated and better sealed, and usually require less maintenance than their ancestors. Exterior hinged doors are made of wood (plywood, composite, or solid wood), fiberglass (fiberglass skin over a wood frame with a foam core), or insulated steel. Wood is the most beautiful, fiberglass the most durable, steel the most inexpensive.

Most exterior doors swing inward to protect them from the weather. Nearly all manufacturers sell their doors prehung (hinged to a jamb and with exterior casing attached). Sills and thresholds are the most variable elements in manufactured prehung doors. Most doors come with an extruded metal sill and integral threshold, which is installed on top of the subfloor (see 100B). Wood sills must be thicker for strength, so they are installed lower than metal sills, flush with the floor framing (see 100A).

Because of the torsional forces exerted by the hinges on the jamb when the door is open, doors that swing need to have their jambs fastened directly and securely to the building's frame. The best way to accomplish this is to nail the jamb directly to the supporting stud, using shims to make the jamb plumb. It is common practice to attach a prehung door through the casing with long screws through the hinge and jamb into the stud.

 EXTERIOR HINGED DOORS
ATTACHMENT TO WALLS

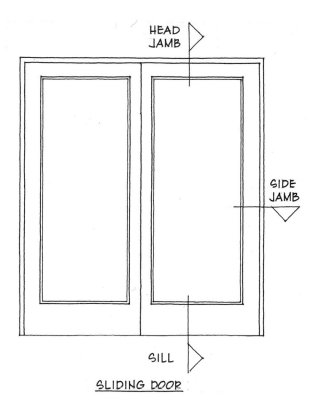

HEAD
JAMB

SIDE
JAMB

SILL

SLIDING DOOR

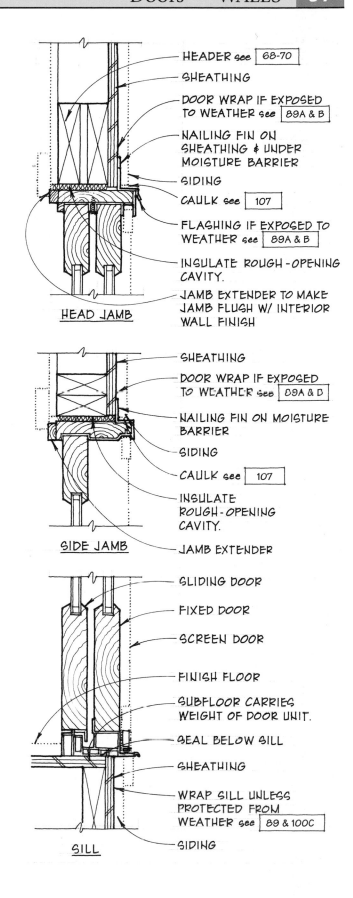

HEADER see 68-70

SHEATHING

DOOR WRAP IF EXPOSED
TO WEATHER see 89A & B

NAILING FIN ON
SHEATHING & UNDER
MOISTURE BARRIER

SIDING

CAULK see 107

FLASHING IF EXPOSED TO
WEATHER see 89A & B

INSULATE ROUGH-OPENING
CAVITY.

JAMB EXTENDER TO MAKE
JAMB FLUSH W/ INTERIOR
WALL FINISH

HEAD JAMB

SHEATHING

DOOR WRAP IF EXPOSED
TO WEATHER see 89A & B

NAILING FIN ON MOISTURE
BARRIER

SIDING

CAULK see 107

INSULATE
ROUGH-OPENING
CAVITY.

JAMB EXTENDER

SIDE JAMB

SLIDING DOOR

FIXED DOOR

SCREEN DOOR

FINISH FLOOR

SUBFLOOR CARRIES
WEIGHT OF DOOR UNIT.

SEAL BELOW SILL

SHEATHING

WRAP SILL UNLESS
PROTECTED FROM
WEATHER see 89 & 100C

SIDING

SILL

Sliding doors, whether they are wood, vinyl, fiberglass, or aluminum, fasten to a building more like a window than like a hinged door. Because the weight of a sliding door remains within the plane of the wall, there is no lateral loading on the jamb of the door unit. Sliding doors are therefore supported on the sill and can be attached to the building like windows—through the casing or with a nailing fin. As with sliding windows, most sliding-door manufacturers recommend not fastening the nailing fin at the head because header deflection can impede door operation.

Sliding doors are trimmed to the finish materials of the wall in the same way as swinging doors and windows (see 92-94).

A **SLIDING DOORS**
ATTACHMENT TO WALLS

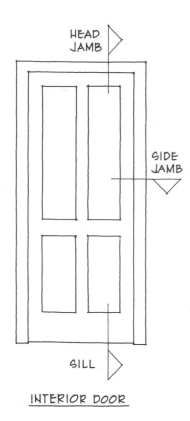

HEAD JAMB

SIDE JAMB

SILL

INTERIOR DOOR

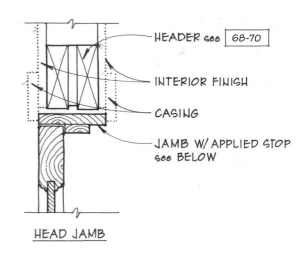

HEADER see 68-70

INTERIOR FINISH

CASING

JAMB W/ APPLIED STOP see BELOW

HEAD JAMB

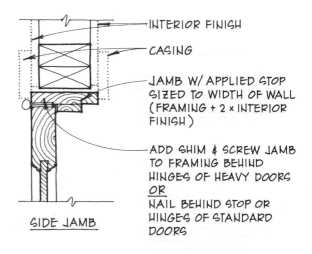

INTERIOR FINISH

CASING

JAMB W/ APPLIED STOP SIZED TO WIDTH OF WALL (FRAMING + 2 × INTERIOR FINISH)

ADD SHIM & SCREW JAMB TO FRAMING BEHIND HINGES OF HEAVY DOORS OR NAIL BEHIND STOP OR HINGES OF STANDARD DOORS

SIDE JAMB

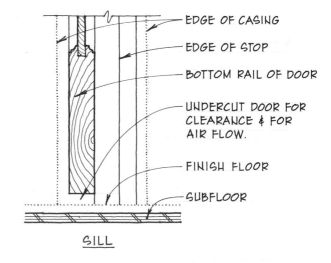

EDGE OF CASING

EDGE OF STOP

BOTTOM RAIL OF DOOR

UNDERCUT DOOR FOR CLEARANCE & FOR AIR FLOW.

FINISH FLOOR

SUBFLOOR

SILL

Because they do not have to be sealed against the weather, interior doors are much simpler than exterior doors. Interior doors are used primarily for privacy and to control air flow. The doors themselves are typically made of wood or composite wood products. They are 1⅜ in. thick, and have either panels, like the one shown above, or a flush plywood veneer over a hollow core or solid core.

Hinged interior doors are usually prehung on a jamb without casings. The jamb on the hinged side is first nailed to the frame of the building, using shims to make it plumb. The jambs at the head and opposite side are then shimmed for proper clearance and nailed.

Some doors are hinged to a split jamb that will expand to accommodate some variation in wall thickness. Interior doors do not have sills and rarely have a threshold unless the floor material changes at the door.

A INTERIOR HINGED DOORS

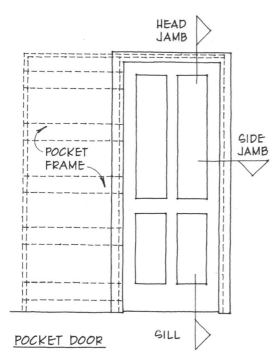

HEAD
JAMB

POCKET
FRAME

SIDE
JAMB

SILL

POCKET DOOR

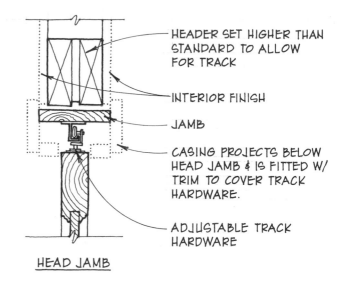

HEADER SET HIGHER THAN
STANDARD TO ALLOW
FOR TRACK

INTERIOR FINISH

JAMB

CASING PROJECTS BELOW
HEAD JAMB & IS FITTED W/
TRIM TO COVER TRACK
HARDWARE.

ADJUSTABLE TRACK
HARDWARE

HEAD JAMB

Pocket doors—Pocket doors slide on a track attached to the head jamb and are sold as a kit, with the door and pocket separate and the pocket broken-down for ease of transport. The pocket is assembled at the site, and the head jamb (which much be set higher than 6 ft. 8 in. to allow for the track) is leveled, shimmed, and attached to the frame of the building. Next the pocket itself and the opposite jamb are shimmed and nailed. The heavier and wider the door and the better the quality of the hardware, the less likely the door is to derail. Pocket doors can't be made to seal as tightly as hinged doors. The walls are flimsy at the pocket, and wiring or plumbing can't be put in this section of wall.

Bypass doors—Bypass doors, such as sliding closet doors, slide on a track, like pocket doors, but have a double track and two doors that are not concealed in a pocket in the wall. Nylon guides on the floor keep the bottom of the doors in line. As with pocket doors, the header of a bypass door should be set higher than normal, and the casing should be designed to cover the track hardware. The jambs are like those for hinged doors but without stops.

Bifold doors—Bifold doors have two hinged halves that fold to one side, with a track at the top. Installation notes for bypass doors apply, except that casing trim must be kept above the top of the doors to allow the doors to fold.

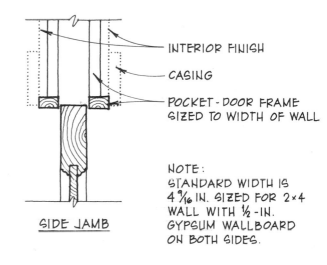

INTERIOR FINISH

CASING

POCKET-DOOR FRAME
SIZED TO WIDTH OF WALL

NOTE:
STANDARD WIDTH IS
4 9/16 IN. SIZED FOR 2×4
WALL WITH 1/2-IN.
GYPSUM WALLBOARD
ON BOTH SIDES.

SIDE JAMB

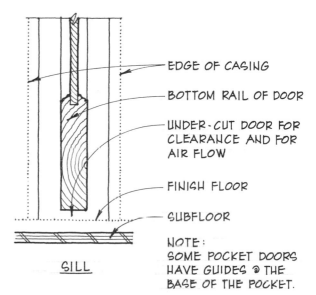

EDGE OF CASING

BOTTOM RAIL OF DOOR

UNDER-CUT DOOR FOR
CLEARANCE AND FOR
AIR FLOW

FINISH FLOOR

SUBFLOOR

NOTE:
SOME POCKET DOORS
HAVE GUIDES @ THE
BASE OF THE POCKET.

SILL

 A POCKET DOORS, BYPASS DOORS & BIFOLD DOORS

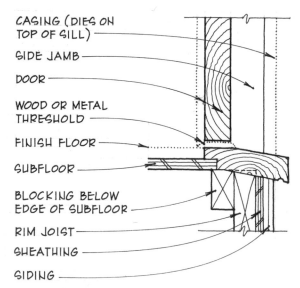

CASING (DIES ON TOP OF SILL)
SIDE JAMB
DOOR
WOOD OR METAL THRESHOLD
FINISH FLOOR
SUBFLOOR
BLOCKING BELOW EDGE OF SUBFLOOR
RIM JOIST
SHEATHING
SIDING

TRADITIONAL WOOD SILL W/ DRIP SLOPES @ 10° & REQUIRES THAT TOP OF RIM JOIST & COMMON JOISTS BE SHAVED OFF FOR INSTALLATION. SILL EXTENDS TO OUTSIDE EDGES OF DOOR CASINGS.

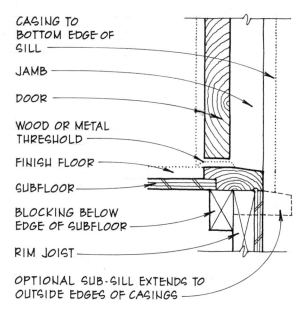

CASING TO BOTTOM EDGE OF SILL
JAMB
DOOR
WOOD OR METAL THRESHOLD
FINISH FLOOR
SUBFLOOR
BLOCKING BELOW EDGE OF SUBFLOOR
RIM JOIST
OPTIONAL SUB-SILL EXTENDS TO OUTSIDE EDGES OF CASINGS

FLATTENED WOOD SILL SLOPES @ 7° & IS INSTALLED ON TOP OF JOIST SYSTEM. OUTSIDE EDGE IS FLUSH W/ JAMB (SHOWN) OR CASING.

NOTES:
ADJUST PROFILE OF SILLS FOR OUTSWINGING DOORS.
WEATHERSTRIP BOTTOM OF DOOR.
WOOD SILLS ARE NOT COMPATIBLE W/ SLAB SUBFLOORS.

A WOOD SILLS

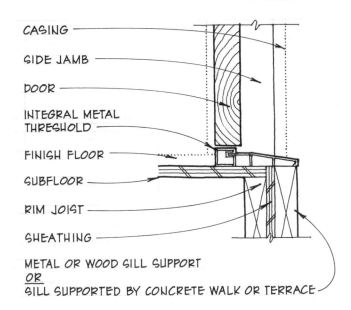

CASING
SIDE JAMB
DOOR
INTEGRAL METAL THRESHOLD
FINISH FLOOR
SUBFLOOR
RIM JOIST
SHEATHING
METAL OR WOOD SILL SUPPORT
OR
SILL SUPPORTED BY CONCRETE WALK OR TERRACE

EXTRUDED SILLS OF ALUMINUM OR POLYCARBONATE ARE THE MOST COMMON FOR ALL MODERN DOORS. THE THRESHOLD IS INTEGRAL. THE SILL MUST BE SUPPORTED @ OUTER EDGE. EXTRUDED SILLS MAY ALSO BE USED IN SLAB-ON-GRADE CONSTRUCTION.

B EXTRUDED SILLS

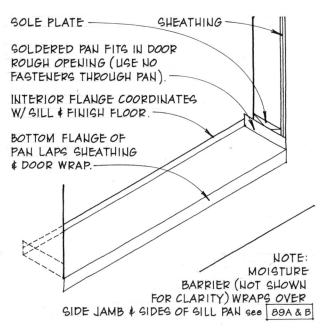

SOLE PLATE   SHEATHING
SOLDERED PAN FITS IN DOOR ROUGH OPENING (USE NO FASTENERS THROUGH PAN).
INTERIOR FLANGE COORDINATES W/ SILL & FINISH FLOOR.
BOTTOM FLANGE OF PAN LAPS SHEATHING & DOOR WRAP.

NOTE: MOISTURE BARRIER (NOT SHOWN FOR CLARITY) WRAPS OVER SIDE JAMB & SIDES OF SILL PAN see 89A & B

AT DOOR LOCATIONS EXPOSED TO THE WEATHER, A GALVANIZED METAL DOOR-SILL PAN FIT INTO THE DOOR ROUGH OPENING WILL PROTECT THE STRUCTURE OF A WOODEN FLOOR SYSTEM BELOW.

C DOOR-SILL PAN

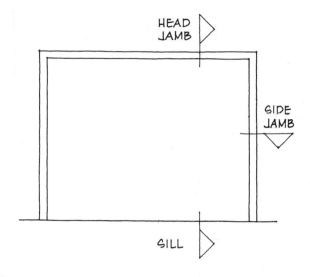

HEAD JAMB

SIDE JAMB

SILL

GARAGE DOOR

Residential garage doors have evolved from swinging and sliding types to almost exclusively the overhead variety. They are manufactured primarily with a solid-wood frame and plywood or particleboard panels. Paneled metal, fiberglass, and vinyl doors are available in some regions. There are two operating types, sectional and one-piece, both which can be manual or fitted with automatic openers.

Sectional doors—Sectional doors are the more common (see 101B). They are hinged horizontally—usually in four sections—and roll up overhead. The advantages are that a sectional door is totally protected by the structure when in the open position, and that it closes to the inside face of the jamb, making the design of the jamb opening somewhat flexible.

One-piece doors—One-piece doors pivot up (see 102A). The door usually fits within the jamb and extends to the outside of the building when in the open position. This exposes the open door to the weather. The advantage of this style is the greater flexibility of design afforded by the one-piece door.

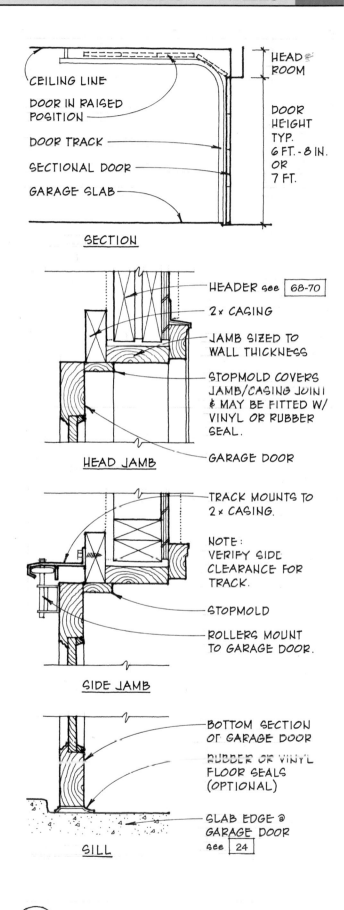

CEILING LINE
DOOR IN RAISED POSITION
DOOR TRACK
SECTIONAL DOOR
GARAGE SLAB

HEAD ROOM

DOOR HEIGHT TYP. 6 FT. - 8 IN. OR 7 FT.

SECTION

HEADER see 68-70
2 x CASING
JAMB SIZED TO WALL THICKNESS
STOPMOLD COVERS JAMB/CASING JOINT & MAY BE FITTED W/ VINYL OR RUBBER SEAL.
GARAGE DOOR

HEAD JAMB

TRACK MOUNTS TO 2 x CASING.
NOTE: VERIFY SIDE CLEARANCE FOR TRACK.
STOPMOLD
ROLLERS MOUNT TO GARAGE DOOR.

SIDE JAMB

BOTTOM SECTION OF GARAGE DOOR
RUBBER OR VINYL FLOOR SEALS (OPTIONAL)
SLAB EDGE @ GARAGE DOOR see 24

SILL

(A) GARAGE DOORS

(B) SECTIONAL GARAGE DOOR

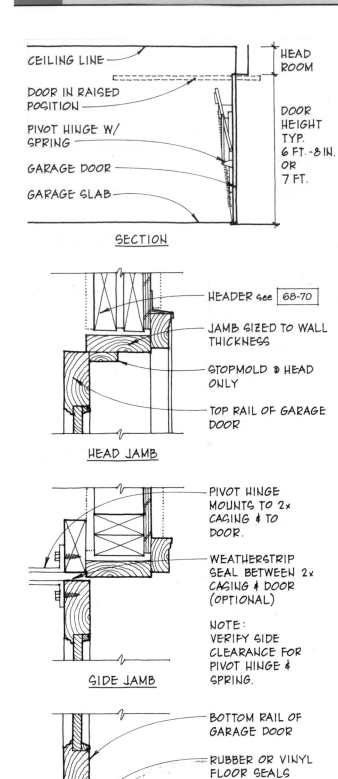

CEILING LINE

DOOR IN RAISED POSITION

PIVOT HINGE W/ SPRING

GARAGE DOOR

GARAGE SLAB

HEAD ROOM

DOOR HEIGHT TYP. 6 FT.-8 IN. OR 7 FT.

SECTION

HEADER see 68-70

JAMB SIZED TO WALL THICKNESS

STOPMOLD ⓐ HEAD ONLY

TOP RAIL OF GARAGE DOOR

HEAD JAMB

PIVOT HINGE MOUNTS TO 2x CASING & TO DOOR.

WEATHERSTRIP SEAL BETWEEN 2x CASING & DOOR (OPTIONAL)

NOTE: VERIFY SIDE CLEARANCE FOR PIVOT HINGE & SPRING.

SIDE JAMB

BOTTOM RAIL OF GARAGE DOOR

RUBBER OR VINYL FLOOR SEALS (OPTIONAL)

SLAB EDGE ⓐ GARAGE DOOR see 24

SILL

(A) ONE-PIECE GARAGE DOOR

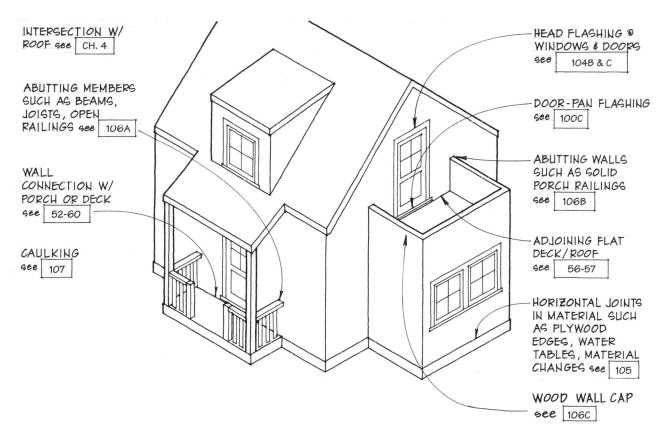

INTERSECTION W/
ROOF see CH. 4

ABUTTING MEMBERS
SUCH AS BEAMS,
JOISTS, OPEN
RAILINGS see 106A

WALL
CONNECTION W/
PORCH OR DECK
see 52-60

CAULKING
see 107

HEAD FLASHING @
WINDOWS & DOORS
see 104B & C

DOOR-PAN FLASHING
see 100C

ABUTTING WALLS
SUCH AS SOLID
PORCH RAILINGS
see 106B

ADJOINING FLAT
DECK/ROOF
see 56-57

HORIZONTAL JOINTS
IN MATERIAL SUCH
AS PLYWOOD
EDGES, WATER
TABLES, MATERIAL
CHANGES see 105

WOOD WALL CAP
see 106C

Flashing is essential to keeping water away from the structure and the interior of a building. It is used wherever there is a horizontal or sloped penetration of the outer building skin or a juncture of dissimilar materials that is likely to be exposed to the weather. Flashing provides a permanent barrier to the water and directs it to the outer surface of the building, where gravity carries the water down to the ground. Of course, the best protection against water penetration of walls is an adequate eave, but wind-driven rain may make this strategy occasionally unreliable.

Wall flashing, which provides the first line of defense against water, should be taken very seriously, especially because walls, unlike roofs, are not intended to be replaced regularly. Wall flashing is likely to be in place for the life of the building.

Two physical properties affect the flow of water on vertical surfaces. The first property, gravity, can be used to advantage in directing water down the wall of a building. The other property, surface tension, creates capillary action that results in water migrating in all directions along cracks in and between materials. In many cases, the negative effects of surface tension can be avoided by the proper use of a drip.

A drip is a thin edge or undercut at the bottom of a material placed far enough away from the building surface so that a drop of water forming on it will not touch the wall but will drop away. Drips may be made of flashing or may be cut into the building material itself.

In the case of vertical joints, a sealant may be required to counter the effects of surface tension. Caulk (sealant) should be used primarily as an air barrier, not a water barrier (see 107A). Except for vertical joints that cannot be flashed effectively, a well-designed flashing (see 104–106) is always preferable to a bead of caulk.

Common flashing materials include galvanized steel, baked enamel steel, aluminum, copper, stainless steel, and lead. Because flashing materials may be affected in different ways by different climates, air pollutants, and building materials, the selection of appropriate materials is specific to each job. It is also important to isolate different metals when flashing to prevent corrosive interaction (galvanic action) between them. Consult with local sheet-metal shops for appropriate materials for specific applications.

 WALL FLASHING

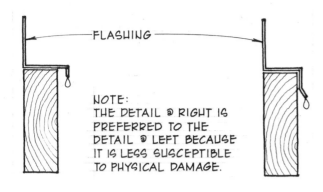

NOTE:
THE DETAIL @ RIGHT IS PREFERRED TO THE DETAIL @ LEFT BECAUSE IT IS LESS SUSCEPTIBLE TO PHYSICAL DAMAGE.

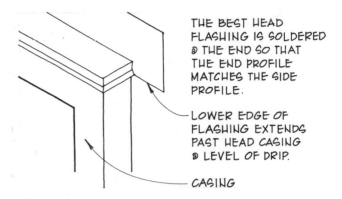

THE BEST HEAD FLASHING IS SOLDERED @ THE END SO THAT THE END PROFILE MATCHES THE SIDE PROFILE.

— LOWER EDGE OF FLASHING EXTENDS PAST HEAD CASING @ LEVEL OF DRIP.

— CASING

<u>SOLDERED HEAD FLASHING</u>

PAINT TENDS TO CLOG FLASHING DRIPS, BUT IT ALSO TENDS TO SEAL THE CRACK BETWEEN FLASHING & THE MATERIAL THE FLASHING COVERS. FLASHING OVER PAINTED WOOD, THEREFORE, IS OFTEN MADE WITHOUT A DRIP, AS SHOWN @ LEFT.

 FLASHING DRIPS

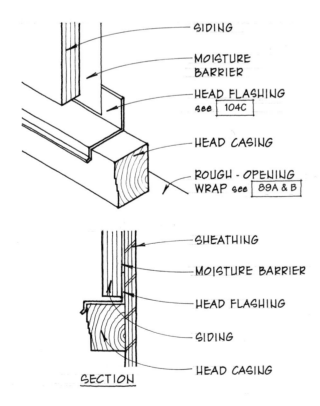

— SIDING

— MOISTURE BARRIER

— HEAD FLASHING see 104C

— HEAD CASING

— ROUGH-OPENING WRAP see 89A & B

— SHEATHING

— MOISTURE BARRIER

— HEAD FLASHING

— SIDING

— HEAD CASING

<u>SECTION</u>

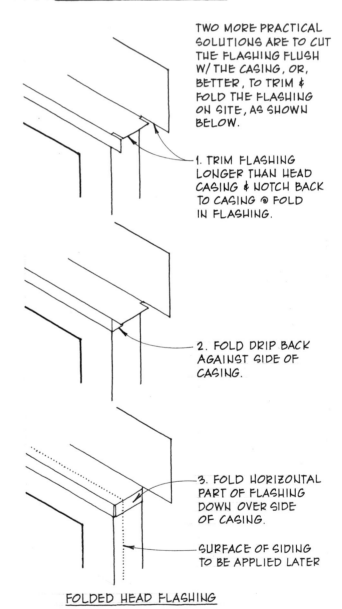

TWO MORE PRACTICAL SOLUTIONS ARE TO CUT THE FLASHING FLUSH W/ THE CASING, OR, BETTER, TO TRIM & FOLD THE FLASHING ON SITE, AS SHOWN BELOW.

1. TRIM FLASHING LONGER THAN HEAD CASING & NOTCH BACK TO CASING @ FOLD IN FLASHING.

2. FOLD DRIP BACK AGAINST SIDE OF CASING.

3. FOLD HORIZONTAL PART OF FLASHING DOWN OVER SIDE OF CASING.

— SURFACE OF SIDING TO BE APPLIED LATER

<u>FOLDED HEAD FLASHING</u>

 WINDOW/DOOR HEAD FLASHING

 WINDOW/DOOR HEAD FLASHING
@ END OF FLASHING

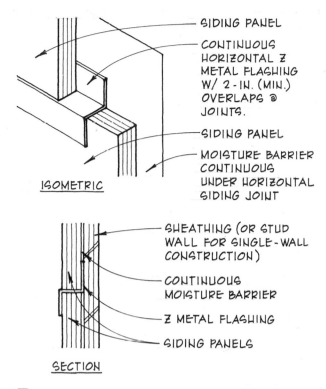

SIDING PANEL

CONTINUOUS HORIZONTAL Z METAL FLASHING W/ 2-IN. (MIN.) OVERLAPS @ JOINTS.

SIDING PANEL

MOISTURE BARRIER CONTINUOUS UNDER HORIZONTAL SIDING JOINT

ISOMETRIC

SHEATHING (OR STUD WALL FOR SINGLE-WALL CONSTRUCTION)

CONTINUOUS MOISTURE BARRIER

Z METAL FLASHING

SIDING PANELS

SECTION

(A) HORIZONTAL WALL FLASHING
Z METAL @ PANEL JOINT

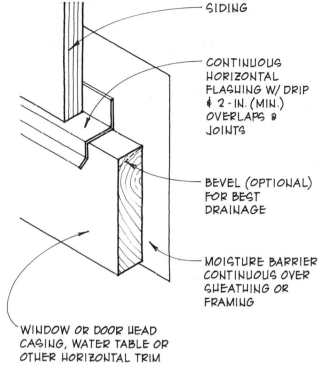

SIDING

CONTINUOUS HORIZONTAL FLASHING W/ DRIP & 2-IN. (MIN.) OVERLAPS @ JOINTS

BEVEL (OPTIONAL) FOR BEST DRAINAGE

MOISTURE BARRIER CONTINUOUS OVER SHEATHING OR FRAMING

WINDOW OR DOOR HEAD CASING, WATER TABLE OR OTHER HORIZONTAL TRIM

(B) HORIZONTAL WALL FLASHING
JOINT BETWEEN DISSIMILAR MATERIALS

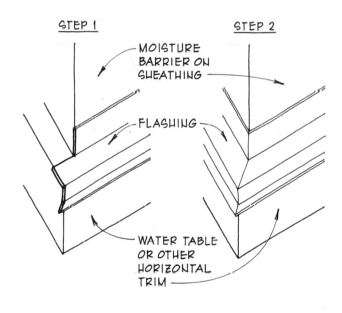

STEP 1   STEP 2

MOISTURE BARRIER ON SHEATHING

FLASHING

WATER TABLE OR OTHER HORIZONTAL TRIM

OUTSIDE CORNER

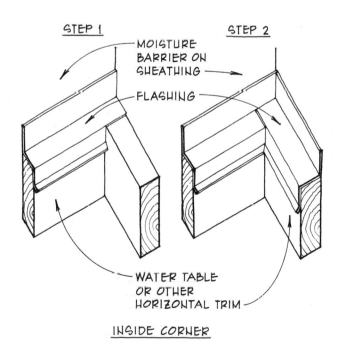

STEP 1   STEP 2

MOISTURE BARRIER ON SHEATHING

FLASHING

WATER TABLE OR OTHER HORIZONTAL TRIM

INSIDE CORNER

NOTE:
IT IS PRUDENT TO COVER THE VERTICAL END OF THE FLASHING W/ A SMALL PIECE OF MOISTURE BARRIER OR A DAB OF CAULK TO MINIMIZE THE POTENTIAL FOR LEAKS.

(C) HORIZONTAL WALL FLASHING
CORNER DETAILS

Any horizontal member such as a handrail, a trellis, or a joist that butts into an exterior wall poses an inherently difficult flashing problem at the top edge of the abutting members. Where such a connection is likely to get wet, the best approach is to avoid the problem by supporting the member independent of the wall. A handrail, for example, could be supported by a column near the wall but not touching it. A trellis could be self-supported.

If a horizontal member must be connected to a wall in a location exposed to the weather, two things can be done to protect the structure of the wall. First, do not puncture the surface of the siding with the member, and do everything possible to attach the member to the surface of the siding with a minimum number of fasteners. Second, place an adequate gasket, such as 30-lb. or 90-lb. felt, behind the siding at the location of the attachment. This will help seal nails or screws that pass through the siding to the structure of the wall.

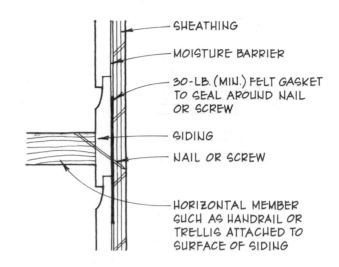

- SHEATHING
- MOISTURE BARRIER
- 30-LB. (MIN.) FELT GASKET TO SEAL AROUND NAIL OR SCREW
- SIDING
- NAIL OR SCREW
- HORIZONTAL MEMBER SUCH AS HANDRAIL OR TRELLIS ATTACHED TO SURFACE OF SIDING

A FLASHING ABUTTING MEMBERS

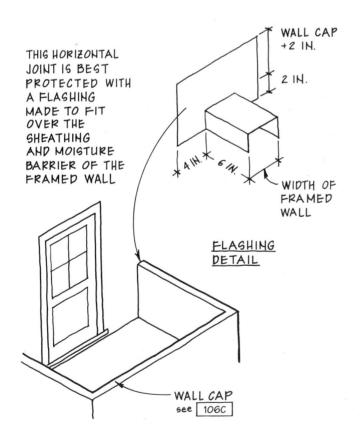

THIS HORIZONTAL JOINT IS BEST PROTECTED WITH A FLASHING MADE TO FIT OVER THE SHEATHING AND MOISTURE BARRIER OF THE FRAMED WALL

WALL CAP +2 IN.

2 IN.

4 IN.   6 IN.

WIDTH OF FRAMED WALL

FLASHING DETAIL

WALL CAP
see 106C

B FLASHING ABUTTING WALLS

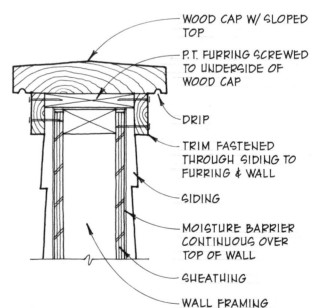

- WOOD CAP W/ SLOPED TOP
- P.T. FURRING SCREWED TO UNDERSIDE OF WOOD CAP
- DRIP
- TRIM FASTENED THROUGH SIDING TO FURRING & WALL
- SIDING
- MOISTURE BARRIER CONTINUOUS OVER TOP OF WALL
- SHEATHING
- WALL FRAMING

NOTE:
THIS DETAIL HAS A CONTINUOUS MOISTURE BARRIER OVER THE TOP OF THE WALL WITHOUT PENETRATIONS. THE MOISTURE BARRIER MAY BE REPLACED W/ METAL FLASHING.

C WOOD WALL CAP

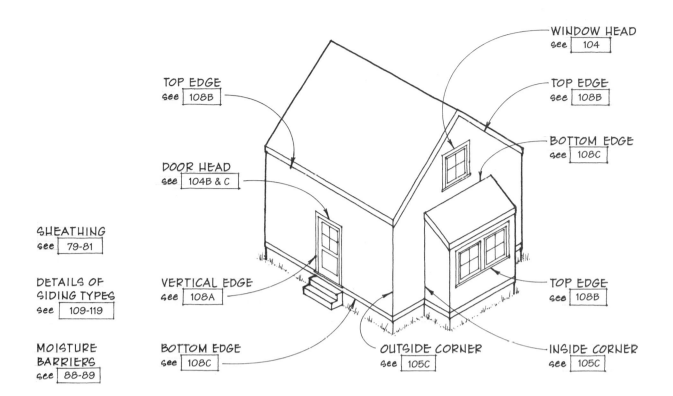

WINDOW HEAD
see 104

TOP EDGE
see 108B

TOP EDGE
see 108B

BOTTOM EDGE
see 108C

DOOR HEAD
see 104B & C

SHEATHING
see 79-81

DETAILS OF
SIDING TYPES
see 109-119

VERTICAL EDGE
see 108A

TOP EDGE
see 108B

MOISTURE
BARRIERS
see 88-89

BOTTOM EDGE
see 108C

OUTSIDE CORNER
see 105C

INSIDE CORNER
see 105C

Many of today's common exterior wall finishes have been protecting walls from the weather for hundreds of years. Others such as plywood, hardboard, and vinyl have been developed more recently. Regardless of their history, when applied properly, each is capable of protecting the building for as long as the finish material itself lasts.

If possible, the best way to protect both the exterior finish and the building from the weather is with adequate overhangs. But even then, wind-driven rain will occasionally get the building wet. It is important, therefore, to detail exterior wall finishes carefully at all but the most protected locations.

The introduction of effective moisture barriers under the siding has the potential to prolong the life of walls beyond the life of the siding alone. While the siding is still the first line of defense against weather, it is possible to view one of its primary functions as keeping sunlight from causing the deterioration of the moisture barrier, which ultimately protects the walls of the building.

Where the moisture barrier stops—at the edges and the openings through the wall—special attention must be paid to the detailing of exterior wall finishes.

Caulks—In this country alone, there are more than 200 manufacturers of 20 different types of caulks and sealants. (The term "caulk" is commonly applied to sealant, which is more resilient than caulk and more properly used in good-quality construction.) However, the appropriate use of caulks for wood-frame buildings is limited for two reasons. First, caulking is not really needed—there are 200-year-old wooden buildings still in good condition that were built without caulks. Second, the lifespan of caulk is limited—manufacturers claim only 20 to 25 years for the longest-lasting caulks and sealants.

However, some situations in wood-frame construction do call for the use of caulking. These are mostly cases where the caulk is a second or third line of defense against water intrusion or where the caulk is used to retard the infiltration of air into the building. In all instances, it is recommended that the caulk not be exposed to the sunlight.

A VERTICAL EDGE IS A LIKELY PLACE FOR WATER TO LEAK AROUND THE EXTERIOR WALL FINISH INTO THE STRUCTURE OF A BUILDING. A CONTINUOUS MOISTURE BARRIER BEHIND THE VERTICAL JOINT IS CRUCIAL. CAULKING CAN HELP DETER THE MOISTURE, BUT WILL DETERIORATE IN THE ULTRAVIOLET LIGHT UNLESS PLACED BEHIND THE WALL FINISH, WHERE IT WILL BE PROTECTED.

AT THE UPPER EDGES OF WALL FINISHES (@ EAVES & RAKES, UNDER WINDOWS & DOORS, & @ OTHER HORIZONTAL BREAKS), DIRECT MOISTURE AWAY FROM THE TOP EDGE OF THE FINISH MATERIAL TO THE FACE OF THE WALL.

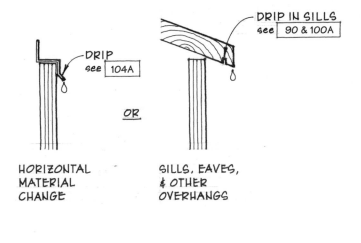

DRIP IN SILLS
see 90 & 100A

DRIP
see 104A

OR

HORIZONTAL MATERIAL CHANGE

SILLS, EAVES, & OTHER OVERHANGS

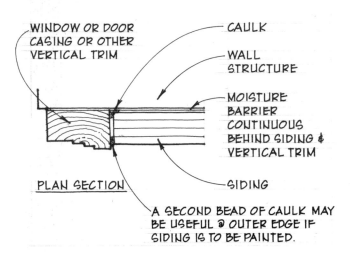

WINDOW OR DOOR CASING OR OTHER VERTICAL TRIM

CAULK

WALL STRUCTURE

MOISTURE BARRIER CONTINUOUS BEHIND SIDING & VERTICAL TRIM

PLAN SECTION

SIDING

A SECOND BEAD OF CAULK MAY BE USEFUL @ OUTER EDGE IF SIDING IS TO BE PAINTED.

A **EXTERIOR WALL FINISHES**
@ VERTICAL EDGES

B **EXTERIOR WALL FINISHES**
@ TOP EDGES

THE BOTTOM EDGE OF THE WALL FINISH IS MORE LIKELY TO GET WET THAN THE TOP. ALLOW WATER TO FALL FROM THE BOTTOM EDGE OF THE WALL FINISH IN A WAY THAT AVOIDS CAPILLARY ACTION.

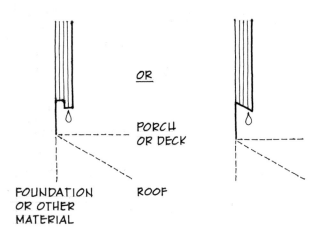

OR

PORCH OR DECK

FOUNDATION OR OTHER MATERIAL

ROOF

C **EXTERIOR WALL FINISHES**
@ BOTTOM EDGES

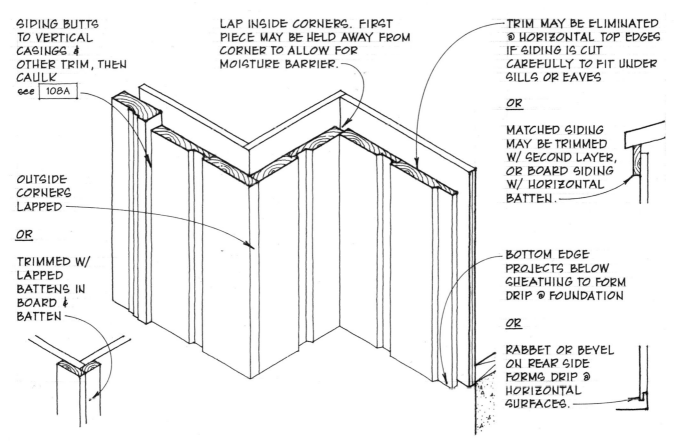

SIDING BUTTS TO VERTICAL CASINGS & OTHER TRIM, THEN CAULK
see 108A

LAP INSIDE CORNERS. FIRST PIECE MAY BE HELD AWAY FROM CORNER TO ALLOW FOR MOISTURE BARRIER.

TRIM MAY BE ELIMINATED @ HORIZONTAL TOP EDGES IF SIDING IS CUT CAREFULLY TO FIT UNDER SILLS OR EAVES

OR

MATCHED SIDING MAY BE TRIMMED W/ SECOND LAYER, OR BOARD SIDING W/ HORIZONTAL BATTEN.

OUTSIDE CORNERS LAPPED

OR

TRIMMED W/ LAPPED BATTENS IN BOARD & BATTEN

BOTTOM EDGE PROJECTS BELOW SHEATHING TO FORM DRIP @ FOUNDATION

OR

RABBET OR BEVEL ON REAR SIDE FORMS DRIP @ HORIZONTAL SURFACES.

Vertical wood siding falls into two major groups. One group, such as the tongue-and-groove and channel patterns shown below, has its side edges rabbeted or grooved and lies flat on the wall, one board thick. The other group, including board and batten, has square edges and uses a second layer to cover the edges of the first layer. The thicker patterns in the second group may require careful coordination with casings and trim. Both groups require ⅜-in. (min.) plywood sheathing or horizontal nailing strips to strengthen the wall. Where end joints occur, siding is sealed and joined with a scarf joint or a miter joint sloped to the exterior.

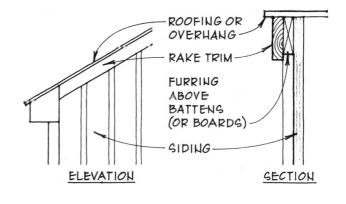

ROOFING OR OVERHANG

RAKE TRIM

FURRING ABOVE BATTENS (OR BOARDS)

SIDING

ELEVATION

SECTION

RAKE DETAILS
(BOARD & BATTEN)

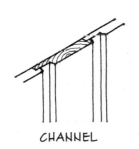

CHANNEL

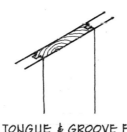

TONGUE & GROOVE FLUSH
(SHOWN) & V-GROOVE

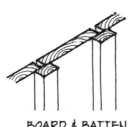

BOARD & BATTEN

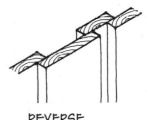

REVERSE
BOARD & BATTEN

 A **VERTICAL WOOD SIDING**

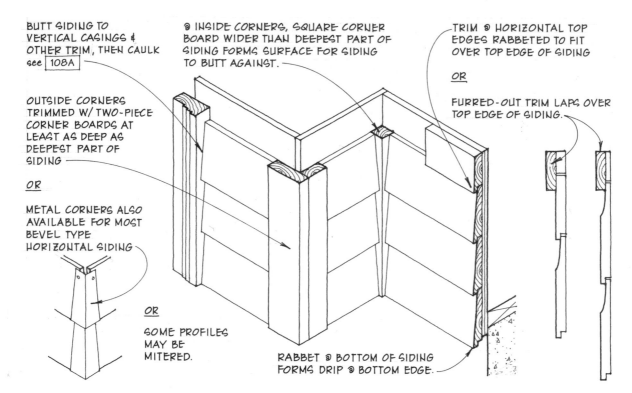

BUTT SIDING TO VERTICAL CASINGS & OTHER TRIM, THEN CAULK see 108A

OUTSIDE CORNERS TRIMMED W/ TWO-PIECE CORNER BOARDS AT LEAST AS DEEP AS DEEPEST PART OF SIDING

OR

METAL CORNERS ALSO AVAILABLE FOR MOST BEVEL TYPE HORIZONTAL SIDING

OR

SOME PROFILES MAY BE MITERED.

@ INSIDE CORNERS, SQUARE CORNER BOARD WIDER THAN DEEPEST PART OF SIDING FORMS SURFACE FOR SIDING TO BUTT AGAINST.

TRIM @ HORIZONTAL TOP EDGES RABBETED TO FIT OVER TOP EDGE OF SIDING

OR

FURRED-OUT TRIM LAPS OVER TOP EDGE OF SIDING.

RABBET @ BOTTOM OF SIDING FORMS DRIP @ BOTTOM EDGE.

Horizontal wood siding is common in both historic and modern buildings. The boards cast a horizontal shadow line unique to this type of siding.

Materials—Profiles (see below right) are commonly cut from 4-in., 6-in., and 8-in. boards. Cedar, redwood, and pine are the most typical. Clear grades are available in cedar and redwood. Many profiles are also made from composite hardboard or cementboard. This material is much less expensive than siding milled from lumber and is almost indistinguishable from it when painted.

Types—Siding joints may be tongue and groove, rabbeted, or lapped. Common profiles (names may vary regionally) are illustrated at bottom right.

Application—Boards are typically applied over a moisture barrier and sheathing, and should generally be back-primed before installation. Boards are face-nailed with a single nail near the bottom of each board but above the board below to allow movement. Siding is joined end to end with miter or scarf joints and caulk over a stud.

Finish—Horizontal wood siding is usually painted or stained. Clear lumber siding is sometimes treated with a semitransparent stain.

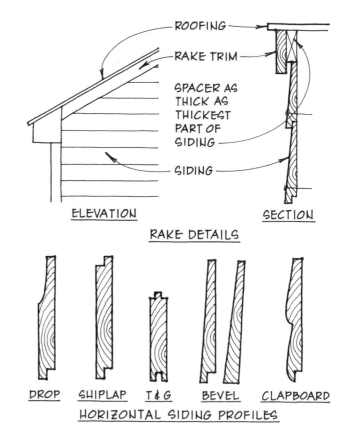

ROOFING

RAKE TRIM

SPACER AS THICK AS THICKEST PART OF SIDING

SIDING

ELEVATION

SECTION

RAKE DETAILS

DROP SHIPLAP T&G BEVEL CLAPBOARD

HORIZONTAL SIDING PROFILES

HORIZONTAL SIDING

WOOD, HARDBOARD, CEMENTBOARD

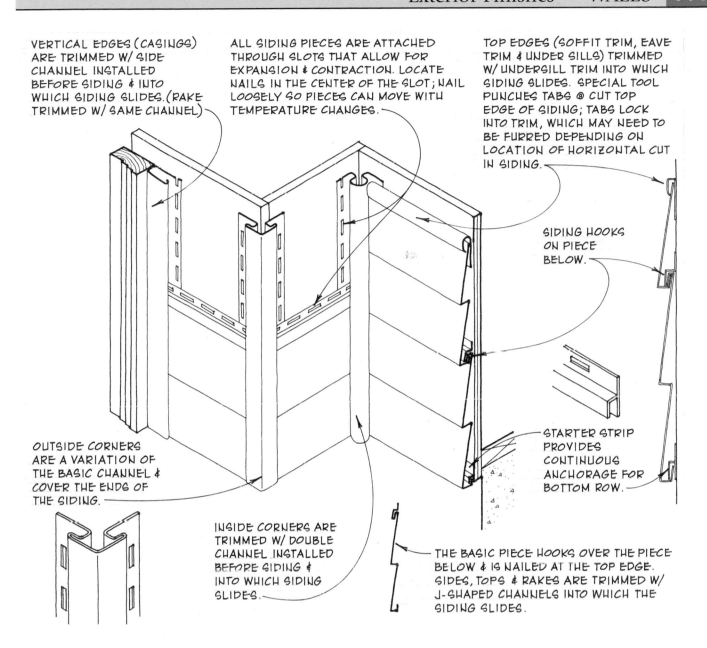

VERTICAL EDGES (CASINGS) ARE TRIMMED W/ SIDE CHANNEL INSTALLED BEFORE SIDING & INTO WHICH SIDING SLIDES.(RAKE TRIMMED W/ SAME CHANNEL)

ALL SIDING PIECES ARE ATTACHED THROUGH SLOTS THAT ALLOW FOR EXPANSION & CONTRACTION. LOCATE NAILS IN THE CENTER OF THE SLOT; NAIL LOOSELY SO PIECES CAN MOVE WITH TEMPERATURE CHANGES.

TOP EDGES (SOFFIT TRIM, EAVE TRIM & UNDER SILLS) TRIMMED W/ UNDERSILL TRIM INTO WHICH SIDING SLIDES. SPECIAL TOOL PUNCHES TABS @ CUT TOP EDGE OF SIDING; TABS LOCK INTO TRIM, WHICH MAY NEED TO BE FURRED DEPENDING ON LOCATION OF HORIZONTAL CUT IN SIDING.

SIDING HOOKS ON PIECE BELOW.

OUTSIDE CORNERS ARE A VARIATION OF THE BASIC CHANNEL & COVER THE ENDS OF THE SIDING.

INSIDE CORNERS ARE TRIMMED W/ DOUBLE CHANNEL INSTALLED BEFORE SIDING & INTO WHICH SIDING SLIDES.

STARTER STRIP PROVIDES CONTINUOUS ANCHORAGE FOR BOTTOM ROW.

THE BASIC PIECE HOOKS OVER THE PIECE BELOW & IS NAILED AT THE TOP EDGE. SIDES, TOPS & RAKES ARE TRIMMED W/ J-SHAPED CHANNELS INTO WHICH THE SIDING SLIDES.

Vinyl sidings were developed in an attempt to eliminate the maintenance required of wood sidings. Most aluminum-siding manufacturers are moving to vinyl.

Material—There are several shapes available. Most imitate horizontal wood bevel patterns, but there are some vertical patterns as well. Lengths are generally about 12 ft., and widths are 8 in. to 12 in. The ends of panels are factory-notched to allow for lapping at end joints, which accommodates expansion and contraction. Color is integral with the material and ranges mostly in the whites, grays, and imitation wood colors. The vinyl will not dent like metal, but will shatter on sharp impact, especially when cold.

Most manufacturers also make vinyl soffit material, and some also make decorative trim.

Installation—Vinyl has little structural strength, so most vinyl sidings must be installed over solid sheathing. Proper nailing with corrosion-resistant nails is essential to allow for expansion and contraction. Because vinyl trim pieces are rather narrow, many architects use vinyl siding in conjunction with wood trim, as suggested in the isometric drawing above.

(A) **VINYL SIDING**

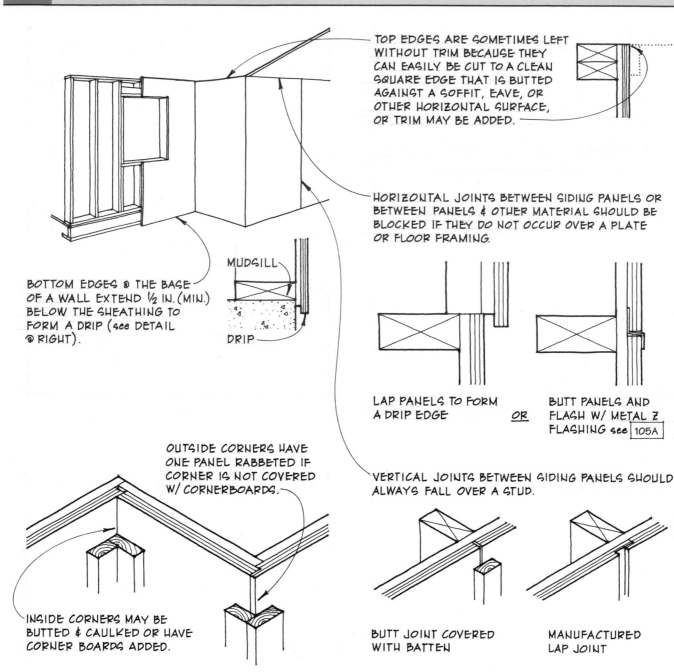

TOP EDGES ARE SOMETIMES LEFT WITHOUT TRIM BECAUSE THEY CAN EASILY BE CUT TO A CLEAN SQUARE EDGE THAT IS BUTTED AGAINST A SOFFIT, EAVE, OR OTHER HORIZONTAL SURFACE, OR TRIM MAY BE ADDED.

HORIZONTAL JOINTS BETWEEN SIDING PANELS OR BETWEEN PANELS & OTHER MATERIAL SHOULD BE BLOCKED IF THEY DO NOT OCCUR OVER A PLATE OR FLOOR FRAMING.

MUDSILL

BOTTOM EDGES @ THE BASE OF A WALL EXTEND ½ IN. (MIN.) BELOW THE SHEATHING TO FORM A DRIP (see DETAIL @ RIGHT).

DRIP

LAP PANELS TO FORM A DRIP EDGE

OR

BUTT PANELS AND FLASH W/ METAL Z FLASHING see 105A

OUTSIDE CORNERS HAVE ONE PANEL RABBETED IF CORNER IS NOT COVERED W/ CORNERBOARDS.

VERTICAL JOINTS BETWEEN SIDING PANELS SHOULD ALWAYS FALL OVER A STUD.

INSIDE CORNERS MAY BE BUTTED & CAULKED OR HAVE CORNER BOARDS ADDED.

BUTT JOINT COVERED WITH BATTEN

MANUFACTURED LAP JOINT

Materials—Plywood siding is available in 4-ft. wide panels, 8 ft., 9 ft., and 10 ft. tall. Typical thicknesses are ⅜ in., ½ in. and ⅝ in. The panels are usually installed vertically to avoid horizontal joints, which require blocking and flashing. Textures and patterns can be cut into the face of the plywood to resemble vertical wood-siding patterns.

Installation—Manufacturers suggest leaving a ⅛-in. gap at panel edges to allow for expansion. All edges should be treated with water repellent before installation. It is wise to plan to have window and door trim

because of the difficulty of cutting panels precisely around openings. Fasten panels to framing following the manufacturer's recommendation.

Single-wall construction—Since plywood, even in a vertical orientation, will provide lateral bracing for a building, it is often applied as the only surface to cover a building. This is called single-wall construction and has some unique details (see 80 and 113).

A ̲P̲L̲Y̲W̲O̲O̲D̲ ̲S̲I̲D̲I̲N̲G̲

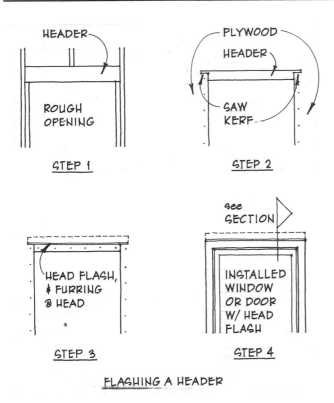

STEP 1

STEP 2

STEP 3

STEP 4

FLASHING A HEADER

Flashing—Windows and doors that are attached through the casing and need head flashing because of exposure to rain or snow are very difficult to flash. As shown in the drawings above, a saw kerf must be cut into the siding at the precise location of the flashing. The flashing and siding must be installed simultaneously before the door or window is attached.

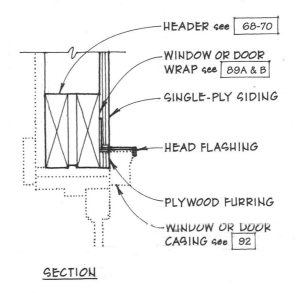

SECTION

Most of the details for double-wall plywood construction also apply to single-wall construction. But with single-wall construction, the moisture barrier is applied directly to the framing, making it more difficult to achieve a good seal. The wide-roll, polyolefin moisture/air infiltration barriers work best (see 88B). Also, the bottom edge of the plywood is flush against the foundation, so a drip detail is impossible (see below).

NO SHEATHING BENEATH PLYWOOD, SO PLYWOOD DOES NOT FORM DRIP @ BOTTOM EDGE. CAULK MAY BE BETTER THAN NOTHING IN SOME SITUATIONS.

(A) SINGLE-WALL PLYWOOD SIDING

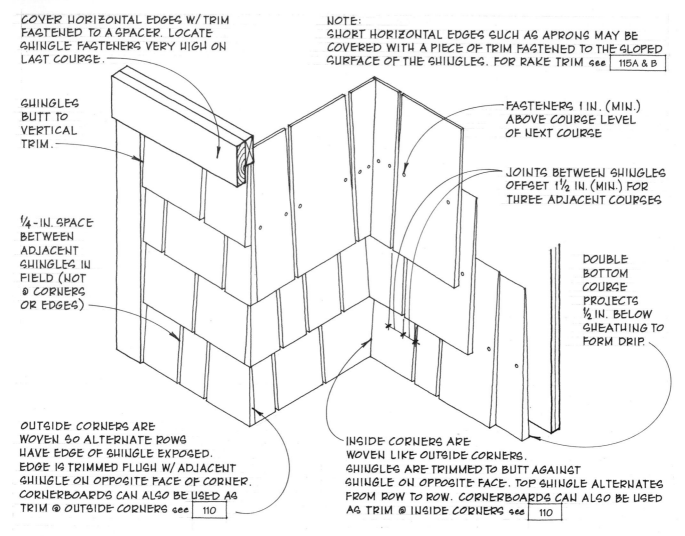

COVER HORIZONTAL EDGES W/ TRIM FASTENED TO A SPACER. LOCATE SHINGLE FASTENERS VERY HIGH ON LAST COURSE.

NOTE:
SHORT HORIZONTAL EDGES SUCH AS APRONS MAY BE COVERED WITH A PIECE OF TRIM FASTENED TO THE SLOPED SURFACE OF THE SHINGLES. FOR RAKE TRIM see 115A & B

SHINGLES BUTT TO VERTICAL TRIM.

FASTENERS 1 IN. (MIN.) ABOVE COURSE LEVEL OF NEXT COURSE

JOINTS BETWEEN SHINGLES OFFSET 1½ IN. (MIN.) FOR THREE ADJACENT COURSES

¼-IN. SPACE BETWEEN ADJACENT SHINGLES IN FIELD (NOT @ CORNERS OR EDGES)

DOUBLE BOTTOM COURSE PROJECTS ½ IN. BELOW SHEATHING TO FORM DRIP.

OUTSIDE CORNERS ARE WOVEN SO ALTERNATE ROWS HAVE EDGE OF SHINGLE EXPOSED. EDGE IS TRIMMED FLUSH W/ ADJACENT SHINGLE ON OPPOSITE FACE OF CORNER. CORNERBOARDS CAN ALSO BE USED AS TRIM @ OUTSIDE CORNERS see 110

INSIDE CORNERS ARE WOVEN LIKE OUTSIDE CORNERS. SHINGLES ARE TRIMMED TO BUTT AGAINST SHINGLE ON OPPOSITE FACE. TOP SHINGLE ALTERNATES FROM ROW TO ROW. CORNERBOARDS CAN ALSO BE USED AS TRIM @ INSIDE CORNERS see 110

Shingles are popular because they can provide a durable, low-maintenance siding with a refined natural appearance. Shadow lines are primarily horizontal but are complemented with minor verticals. Material costs are relatively moderate but installation costs may be very high.

Materials—Shingles are available in a variety of sizes, grades, and patterns. The most typical is a western red cedar shingle 16 in. long. Redwood and cypress shingles are also available. Because shingles are relatively small, they are extremely versatile, with a wide variety of coursings and patterns.

Installation—Shingles are applied over a moisture barrier to a plywood or OSB wall sheathing so at least two layers of shingles always cover the wall. Standard coursing allows nail or staple fasteners to be concealed by subsequent courses. With shingles there is less waste than with other wood sidings.

Finish—Enough moisture gets between and behind shingles that paint will not adhere to them reliably. Left unfinished, they endure extremely well, but may weather differentially, especially between those places exposed to the rain and those that are protected. Stains and bleaching stains will produce more even weathering.

Preassembled shingles—Shingles are also available mounted to boards. These shingle boards increase material cost, decrease installation cost, and are most appropriate for large, uninterrupted surfaces. Corner boards are required at corners.

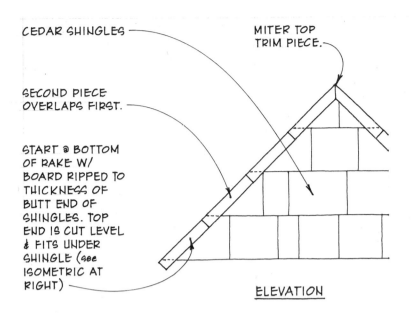

CEDAR SHINGLES

MITER TOP TRIM PIECE.

SECOND PIECE OVERLAPS FIRST.

START @ BOTTOM OF RAKE W/ BOARD RIPPED TO THICKNESS OF BUTT END OF SHINGLES. TOP END IS CUT LEVEL & FITS UNDER SHINGLE (see ISOMETRIC AT RIGHT)

ELEVATION

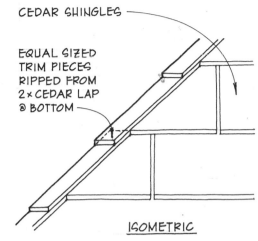

CEDAR SHINGLES

EQUAL SIZED TRIM PIECES RIPPED FROM 2× CEDAR LAP @ BOTTOM

ISOMETRIC

ONE METHOD OF FINISHING THE TOP EDGE OF A SHINGLE WALL IS TO LAP THE SHINGLE COURSES WITH TRIM PIECES RIPPED FROM A CEDAR 2×. IF THE COURSING IS EQUAL, ALL THE TRIM PIECES, EXCEPT FOR THE MITERED TOP PIECES, WILL ALSO BE EQUAL.

 A **SHINGLE SIDING @ RAKE**
LAPPED TRIM

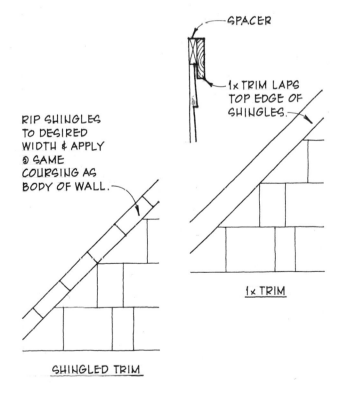

RIP SHINGLES TO DESIRED WIDTH & APPLY @ SAME COURSING AS BODY OF WALL.

SPACER

1× TRIM LAPS TOP EDGE OF SHINGLES.

SHINGLED TRIM

1× TRIM

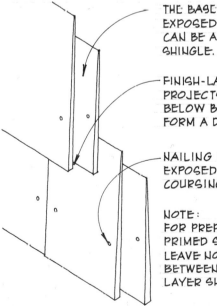

THE BASE LAYER IS NOT EXPOSED & THEREFORE CAN BE A LOWER-GRADE SHINGLE.

FINISH-LAYER SHINGLE PROJECTS ABOUT ½ IN. BELOW BASE LAYER TO FORM A DRIP.

NAILING MUST BE EXPOSED FOR THIS COURSING.

NOTE:
FOR PREPAINTED OR PRIMED SHINGLES, LEAVE NO SPACE BETWEEN FINISH LAYER SHINGLES.

DOUBLE COURSING, AN ALTERNATIVE COURSING METHOD, CALLS FOR TWO LAYERS APPLIED @ THE SAME COURSE. A PREPAINTED OR PRIMED SHINGLE CALLED "SIDEWALL SHAKE" IS COMMONLY USED.

 B **SHINGLE SIDING @ RAKE**
SHINGLED & 1× TRIM

 C **DOUBLE-COURSED SHINGLES**

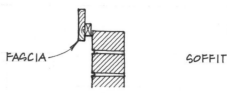

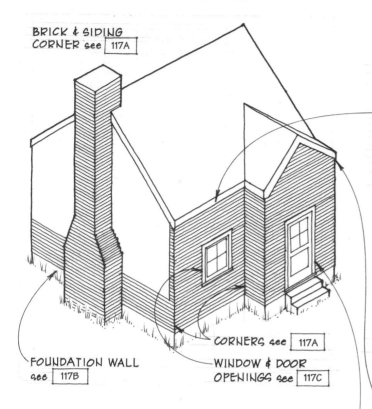

BRICK & SIDING CORNER see | 117A |

FOUNDATION WALL see | 117B |

CORNERS see | 117A |

WINDOW & DOOR OPENINGS see | 117C |

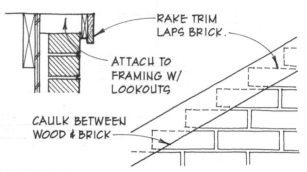

FASCIA

SOFFIT

TOP OF WALL IS DETAILED TO KEEP WATER OFF THE HORIZONTAL SURFACE OF THE TOP BRICK. THIS CAN USUALLY BE ACCOMPLISHED WITH THE DETAILING OF THE ROOF ITSELF. COVER THE JOINT BETWEEN BRICK & ROOF WITH WOOD TRIM. CAULK THE JOINT AS FOR VERTICAL JOINTS, BELOW.

RAKE TRIM LAPS BRICK.

ATTACH TO FRAMING W/ LOOKOUTS

CAULK BETWEEN WOOD & BRICK

RAKE IS USUALLY TRIMMED WITH WOOD SUFFICIENTLY WIDE TO COVER STEPPING OF BRICK CAUSED BY SLOPE. DETAIL AS FOR TOP OF WALL.

Brick veneer covers wood-frame construction across the country. Where it is not subjected to moisture and severe freezing, it is the most durable exterior finish.

Materials—Bricks come in a wide variety of sizes, with the most common (and the smallest) being the modular brick (2¼ in. by 3⅝ in. by 7⅝ in.). These bricks, when laid in mortar, can follow 8-in. modules both horizontally and vertically. Colors vary from cream and yellows to browns and reds, depending on the clay color and method of firing. Bricks should be selected for their history of durability in a given region.

Installation—Bricks are laid in mortar that should be tooled at the joints to compress it for increased resistance to the weather. Because both brick and mortar are porous (increasingly so as they weather over the years), they must be detailed to allow for ventilation and drainage of the unexposed surface. A 1-in. air space between the brick and the wood framing, with weep holes located at the base of the wall, typically suffices (see 117B). It is important to keep this space and the weep holes clean and free of mortar droppings to ensure proper drainage.

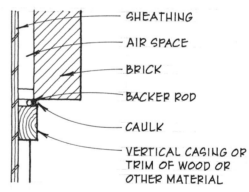

SHEATHING

AIR SPACE

BRICK

BACKER ROD

CAULK

VERTICAL CASING OR TRIM OF WOOD OR OTHER MATERIAL

VERTICAL JOINTS SUCH AS WINDOW & DOOR CASINGS AND @ TRANSITIONS TO OTHER MATERIALS MUST BE CAREFULLY CAULKED TO SEAL AGAINST THE WEATHER. BACKPRIME WOOD COVERED BY OR IN CONTACT W/ BRICK.

Finish—A number of clear sealers and masonry paints can be applied to the finished masonry to improve weather resistance, but reapplication is required every few years.

 BRICK VENEER

BOTH INSIDE & OUTSIDE CORNERS CAN BE MADE SIMPLY W/ THE BRICKS THEMSELVES.

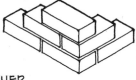

BRICK CORNER

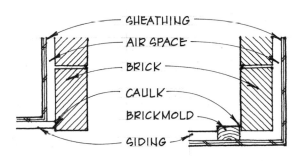

OUTSIDE CORNER   INSIDE CORNER

- SHEATHING
- AIR SPACE
- BRICK
- CAULK
- BRICKMOLD
- SIDING

BRICK AND
SIDING CORNERS

A **BRICK VENEER**
CORNERS

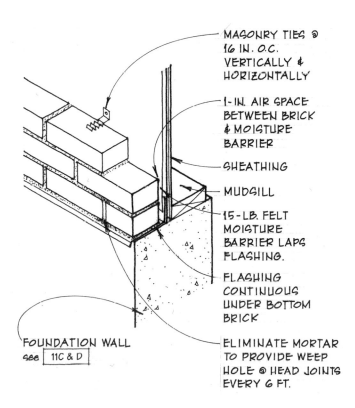

MASONRY TIES @ 16 IN. O.C. VERTICALLY & HORIZONTALLY

1-IN. AIR SPACE BETWEEN BRICK & MOISTURE BARRIER

SHEATHING

MUDSILL

15-LB. FELT MOISTURE BARRIER LAPS FLASHING.

FLASHING CONTINUOUS UNDER BOTTOM BRICK

ELIMINATE MORTAR TO PROVIDE WEEP HOLE @ HEAD JOINTS EVERY 6 FT.

FOUNDATION WALL
SEE 11C & D

B **BRICK VENEER**
WALL CONSTRUCTION

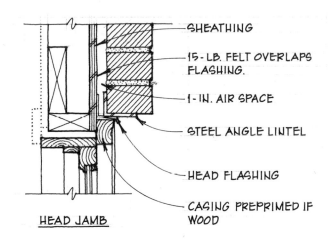

- SHEATHING
- 15-LB. FELT OVERLAPS FLASHING.
- 1-IN. AIR SPACE
- STEEL ANGLE LINTEL
- HEAD FLASHING
- CASING PREPRIMED IF WOOD

HEAD JAMB

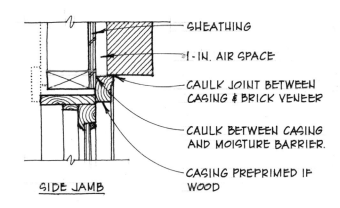

- SHEATHING
- 1-IN. AIR SPACE
- CAULK JOINT BETWEEN CASING & BRICK VENEER
- CAULK BETWEEN CASING AND MOISTURE BARRIER.
- CASING PREPRIMED IF WOOD

SIDE JAMB

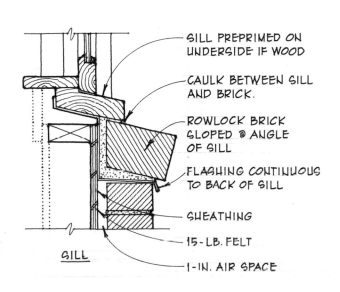

- SILL PREPRIMED ON UNDERSIDE IF WOOD
- CAULK BETWEEN SILL AND BRICK.
- ROWLOCK BRICK SLOPED @ ANGLE OF SILL
- FLASHING CONTINUOUS TO BACK OF SILL
- SHEATHING
- 15-LB. FELT
- 1-IN. AIR SPACE

SILL

C **BRICK VENEER @ WINDOW/DOOR**
ATTACHMENT TO CASING & SILL

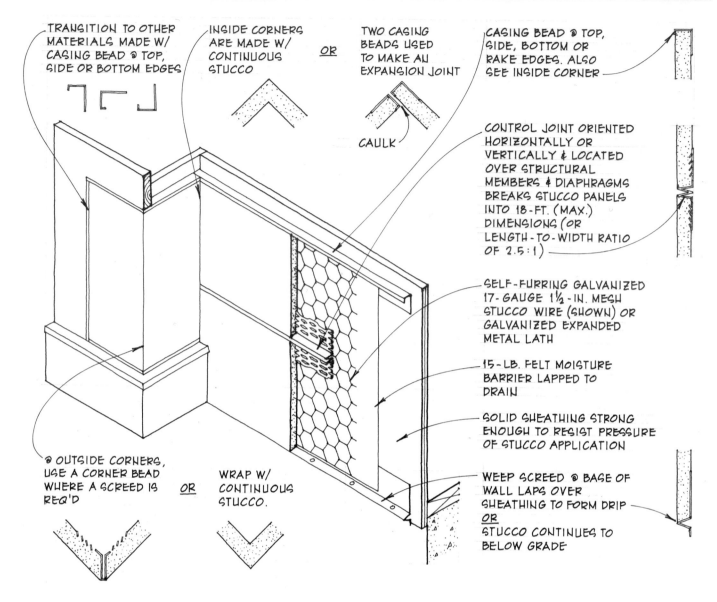

TRANSITION TO OTHER MATERIALS MADE W/ CASING BEAD @ TOP, SIDE OR BOTTOM EDGES

INSIDE CORNERS ARE MADE W/ CONTINUOUS STUCCO

OR

TWO CASING BEADS USED TO MAKE AN EXPANSION JOINT

CAULK

CASING BEAD @ TOP, SIDE, BOTTOM OR RAKE EDGES. ALSO SEE INSIDE CORNER

CONTROL JOINT ORIENTED HORIZONTALLY OR VERTICALLY & LOCATED OVER STRUCTURAL MEMBERS & DIAPHRAGMS BREAKS STUCCO PANELS INTO 18-FT. (MAX.) DIMENSIONS (OR LENGTH-TO-WIDTH RATIO OF 2.5:1)

SELF-FURRING GALVANIZED 17-GAUGE 1½-IN. MESH STUCCO WIRE (SHOWN) OR GALVANIZED EXPANDED METAL LATH

15-LB. FELT MOISTURE BARRIER LAPPED TO DRAIN

SOLID SHEATHING STRONG ENOUGH TO RESIST PRESSURE OF STUCCO APPLICATION

@ OUTSIDE CORNERS, USE A CORNER BEAD WHERE A SCREED IS REQ'D

OR

WRAP W/ CONTINUOUS STUCCO.

WEEP SCREED @ BASE OF WALL LAPS OVER SHEATHING TO FORM DRIP OR STUCCO CONTINUES TO BELOW GRADE

Stucco is made of cement, sand, and lime. It is usually applied in three coats, building to a minimum thickness of ¾ in. Cost may be moderate in areas with high use, but high where skilled workers are few.

Materials—Reinforcing materials through which the plaster is forced are either stucco wire or metal lath. This reinforcing is fastened either to the sheathing or directly to the framing (without sheathing). When sheathing is used, it must be rigid enough to remain stiff during the process of applying the stucco—⅝-in. plywood is typical.

Application—The first (scratch) coat has a raked finish, the second (brown) coat has a floated finish, and the final (color) coat may have a variety of finishes.

Applying stucco takes skill, so stucco is the least appropriate of all the exterior wall finishes for owner-builders to attempt.

Finish—Textures ranging from smooth to rustic are achieved by troweling the final coat. Color may be integral in the final coat or may be painted on the surface. Stucco is not very moisture resistant and must be sealed or painted.

Ⓐ STUCCO WALL SYSTEM

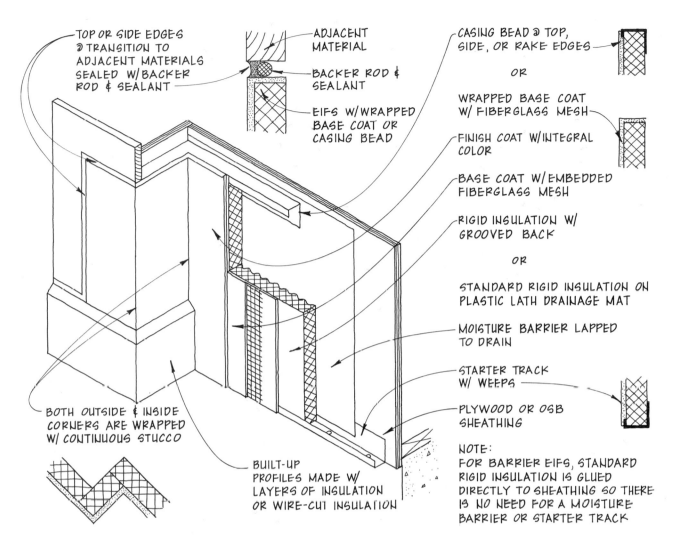

TOP OR SIDE EDGES @ TRANSITION TO ADJACENT MATERIALS SEALED W/ BACKER ROD & SEALANT

ADJACENT MATERIAL

BACKER ROD & SEALANT

EIFS W/ WRAPPED BASE COAT OR CASING BEAD

CASING BEAD @ TOP, SIDE, OR RAKE EDGES

OR

WRAPPED BASE COAT W/ FIBERGLASS MESH

FINISH COAT W/ INTEGRAL COLOR

BASE COAT W/ EMBEDDED FIBERGLASS MESH

RIGID INSULATION W/ GROOVED BACK

OR

STANDARD RIGID INSULATION ON PLASTIC LATH DRAINAGE MAT

MOISTURE BARRIER LAPPED TO DRAIN

STARTER TRACK W/ WEEPS

PLYWOOD OR OSB SHEATHING

NOTE:
FOR BARRIER EIFS, STANDARD RIGID INSULATION IS GLUED DIRECTLY TO SHEATHING SO THERE IS NO NEED FOR A MOISTURE BARRIER OR STARTER TRACK

BOTH OUTSIDE & INSIDE CORNERS ARE WRAPPED W/ CONTINUOUS STUCCO

BUILT-UP PROFILES MADE W/ LAYERS OF INSULATION OR WIRE-CUT INSULATION

Synthetic stucco looks like traditional stucco but is really a flexible acrylic coating applied over rigid insulation. Called EIFS (Exterior Insulation and Finish Systems), synthetic stucco is more flexible than standard stucco and more moisture resistant. There are two basic types: barrier EIFS and water-managed EIFS. Barrier EIFS are designed to entirely prevent moisture penetration of the wall. Water-managed EIFS assume that some moisture will penetrate the system and therefore provide a drainage path for the moisture to escape. Water-managed EIFS were developed in response to serious problems that developed when leaks in barrier EIFS trapped moisture in the framing.

Materials—There are several similar barrier EIFS and water-managed EIFS. Each starts with rigid insulation, usually ¾-in. to 1½-in. thick expanded polystyrene. The insulation is protected from impact by a stucco base made of acrylic portland cement reinforced with

fiberglass mesh. An acrylic finish coat with integral color provides moisture protection.

Application—For barrier EIFS, the insulation is glued directly to the sheathing. For water-managed EIFS, a moisture barrier is located between insulation and sheathing, and the insulation is fastened with mechanical fasteners fitted with large plastic washers. A drainage channel is provided between insulation and moisture barrier with either drainage grooves in the insulation or with a plastic lath drainage mat. From the insulation out, barrier EIFS and water-managed EIFS are essentially the same. The base coat is troweled directly onto the insulation, then reinforced with mesh and another layer of base coat. The final coat is troweled over the hardened base coat.

Finish—There are a variety of common troweled finish textures. Color is integral in the final coat.

SYNTHETIC STUCCO (EIFS)

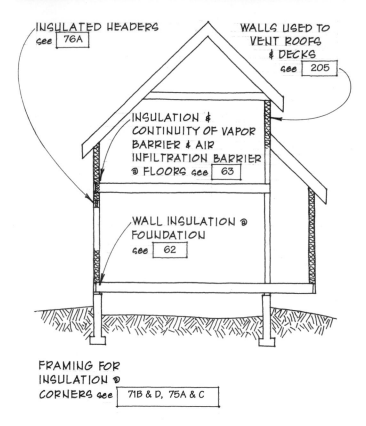

INSULATED HEADERS see 76A

WALLS USED TO VENT ROOFS & DECKS see 205

INSULATION & CONTINUITY OF VAPOR BARRIER & AIR INFILTRATION BARRIER @ FLOORS see 63

WALL INSULATION @ FOUNDATION see 62

FRAMING FOR INSULATION @ CORNERS see 71B & D, 75A & C

Wall insulation is typically provided by fiberglass batts. Building codes in most climates allow 2x4 walls with 3½ in. of insulation (R-11) or 2x6 walls with 5½ in. of insulation (R-19).

Vapor barrier—Vapor barriers are installed in conjunction with wall insulation. The purpose of a vapor barrier, a continuous membrane located on the warm side of the insulation, is to prevent vaporized (gaseous) moisture from entering the insulated wall cavity, where it can condense, causing structural or other damage.

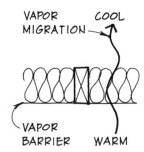

VAPOR MIGRATION

COOL

VAPOR BARRIER

WARM

Currently, the most common vapor barrier is a specially formulated paint or primer applied to drywall. Where drywall is not used or in warm climates where the barrier is located at the exterior, a 4-mil

polyethylene film applied to the wall provides an effective vapor barrier. Rigid insulation with taped joints may also be employed.

The location of the vapor barrier may be adjusted in upgraded applications provided that two-thirds or more of the insulative value of the wall remains to the cold side of the barrier. This rule of thumb is called the one-third/two-thirds rule.

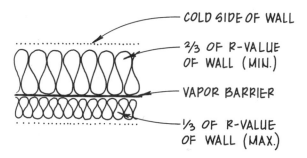

COLD SIDE OF WALL

⅔ OF R-VALUE OF WALL (MIN.)

VAPOR BARRIER

⅓ OF R-VALUE OF WALL (MAX.)

Air barrier—An air barrier is intended to control the migration of air through the insulated envelope of a building. Standard construction practices allow voids and breaks in the building envelope that can leak up to two times the total air volume of the building per hour—accounting for up to 30% of the total heat loss (or gain) of the building. Upgrading the envelope can cut this air leakage to one-third of an air change per hour and can thus have significant consequences for energy bills in most climates.

An effective air barrier combines a continuous membrane with tight seals around openings such as windows where the membrane is penetrated. It may be made of a variety of materials and may be located either inside or outside of the insulation. When inside the insulation, the barrier may be drywall, rigid insulation, or the same polyethylene film that forms a vapor barrier. Outside the insulation, poly-olefin film (housewrap), rigid insulation, or sheathing may be used. In each case, joints are taped or overlapped and caulked, and tight seals are made with floor and ceiling air barriers. Windows, doors, electrical, plumbing, and other services that penetrate the membrane are sealed with expansive foam, caulk, and/or special tape.

It is important to consider that the reduced ventilation rate due to control of air leakage can lower indoor air quality. The provision of controlled ventilation with simple energy-saving devices such as air-to-air heat exchangers can alleviate this problem.

(A) INSULATION
STANDARD PRACTICE

Unfaced batts—The most common method of insulating walls is to use unfaced batts that are fitted between studs. A vapor barrier is applied to the warm side of the wall in the form of a vapor retarding paint or primer or a 4-mil polyethylene film. Properly detailed, this vapor barrier can serve as the air barrier.

COLD SIDE

CONTINUOUS VAPOR BARRIER

WARM SIDE

Faced batts—Batt insulation is often manufactured with a paper facing that, in cold climates, serves as both vapor barrier and means of attachment. For attachment, the facing material has tabs that are stapled in place between the studs.

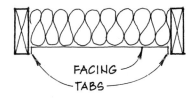

FACING

TABS

To use the facing as a vapor barrier, it is better to staple the tabs to the face of the studs to make a better seal. However, this interferes with the installation of interior finish materials because the tabs build up unevenly on the face of the studs.

Rigid insulation—In standard construction, rigid insulation is generally used only in extreme situations where wall depth is limited but a code-prescribed R-value is required. Examples of such situations include headers (see 76A & B) and locations where heat ducts, vents, or plumbing must be in exterior walls. In upgraded framing systems, however, rigid insulation is used extensively (see 122A).

In climatic zones with extremely cold or hot weather (or high utility rates), there is special incentive to insulate buildings beyond code minimums. A decision to superinsulate affects the construction of walls more than floors or roofs because walls are generally thinner (being constructed of 2x4s or 2x6s rather

than 2x10s or 2x12s). Walls are also in direct contact with the ambient air because they do not have a crawl space or attic to intervene as a buffer.

The most direct way to increase the insulative capacity of walls is to make them thicker. A 2x4 framed wall upgraded to 2x6, for example, will increase from a combined (batt plus framing) R-value of 9.0 to a value of R-15.1. But increasing wall thickness alone is only effective to a point because a significant part of the wall (about 9% of a wall framed @ 24 in. o.c.) is composed of studs, plates, etc., which conduct heat at about three times the rate of insulative batts. When headers and other extra framing are considered, walls often have as much as 20% of their area devoted to framing. The conductance of heat through this framing is called thermal bridging.

There are two strategies for decreasing the effects of thermal bridging. The first is to reduce the quantity of framing members and is called advanced framing (see 74). The second strategy is to insulate the framing members so that they do not "bridge" between the cold and warm sides of the wall. Several ways to insulate framing members are discussed on the following pages.

Rigid insulation—Rigid insulation added to the exterior or interior of a framed wall can typically add an R-value of 7 to 14 at the same time that it interrupts thermal bridging (see 122).

Strapping—Strapping consists of horizontal nailing strips attached to the inside of a stud wall. The strapping touches the studs only at the intersection between the two, so thermal bridging is virtually eliminated. Insulative values of R-25 are easily attainable with the system (see 123).

Staggered-stud framing—Staggered-stud framing is a double stud wall framed on a single wide plate with the studs offset from one another so that there is no thermal bridging. Combined insulative values of R-30 are common (see 124).

Double wall framing—Double wall framing involves building a duplicate (redundant) wall. The system is the most effective at eliminating thermal bridging. R-values of up to 40 are easily reached (see 125).

(A) **INSULATION**
STANDARD PRACTICE

(B) **UPGRADED INSULATION**

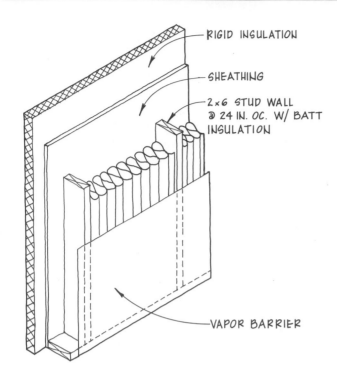

RIGID INSULATION

SHEATHING

2×6 STUD WALL @ 24 IN. OC. W/ BATT INSULATION

VAPOR BARRIER

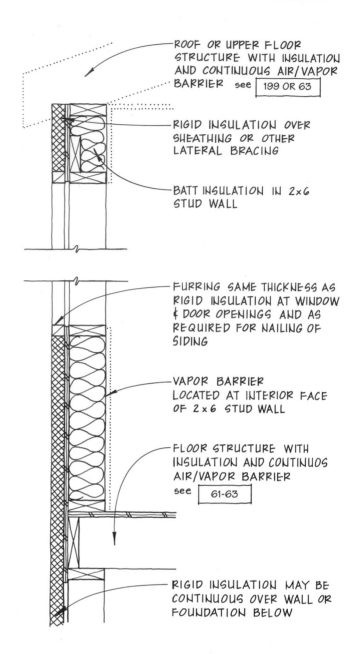

ROOF OR UPPER FLOOR STRUCTURE WITH INSULATION AND CONTINUOUS AIR/VAPOR BARRIER see 199 OR 63

RIGID INSULATION OVER SHEATHING OR OTHER LATERAL BRACING

BATT INSULATION IN 2×6 STUD WALL

FURRING SAME THICKNESS AS RIGID INSULATION AT WINDOW & DOOR OPENINGS AND AS REQUIRED FOR NAILING OF SIDING

VAPOR BARRIER LOCATED AT INTERIOR FACE OF 2×6 STUD WALL

FLOOR STRUCTURE WITH INSULATION AND CONTINUOS AIR/VAPOR BARRIER see 61-63

RIGID INSULATION MAY BE CONTINUOUS OVER WALL OR FOUNDATION BELOW

Rigid insulation, with a potential R-value approximately double that of batt insulation, is a very attractive alternative for upgrading the thermal performance of walls. The material is easy to install in large lightweight sheets, has sufficient strength to support most siding and interior finish materials, and can double as an air/vapor barrier in some cases. Its disadvantages are high cost and potential for toxic off-gassing in a fire.

Rigid insulation is most effective when used on the exterior of the building because it covers the entire skin of the building continuously without the interruption of floors or interior partitions. It can act as the backing for siding but does not provide the strength to act as structural sheathing. Alternative methods of bracing the building, such as sheathing (see 78A) or let-in bracing (see 77B & C), must therefore be used.

When applied to the exterior of buildings in cold climates, the low permeability of rigid insulation can trap vapor in the stud cavities, causing structural damage. The reverse can be true in warm climates. It is therefore advisable to carefully coordinate the use of rigid insulation with a vapor barrier and to verify the practicality of specific types of insulation with local professionals.

Used on the interior of a building in a cold climate, rigid insulation can perform three functions at once: insulation, vapor barrier, and air barrier. To accomplish this, a foil-faced insulation board carefully taped at all seams and caulked and/or gasketed at top, bottom, and openings would be used.

The use of interior rigid insulation requires deep electrical boxes and the need for extra-wide backing at corners and at the top plate.

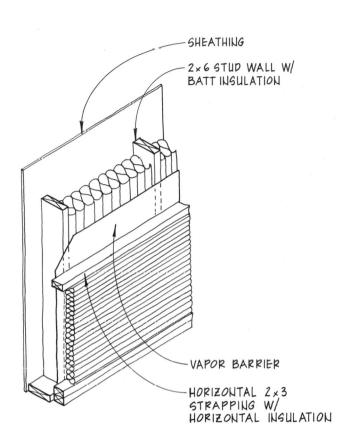

SHEATHING

2×6 STUD WALL W/ BATT INSULATION

VAPOR BARRIER

HORIZONTAL 2×3 STRAPPING W/ HORIZONTAL INSULATION

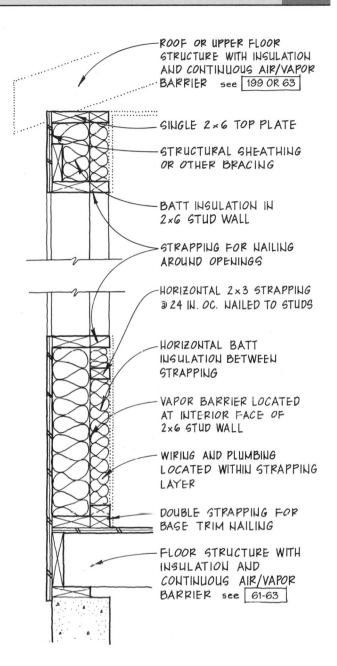

ROOF OR UPPER FLOOR STRUCTURE WITH INSULATION AND CONTINUOUS AIR/VAPOR BARRIER see 199 OR 63

SINGLE 2×6 TOP PLATE

STRUCTURAL SHEATHING OR OTHER BRACING

BATT INSULATION IN 2×6 STUD WALL

STRAPPING FOR NAILING AROUND OPENINGS

HORIZONTAL 2×3 STRAPPING @ 24 IN. OC. NAILED TO STUDS

HORIZONTAL BATT INSULATION BETWEEN STRAPPING

VAPOR BARRIER LOCATED AT INTERIOR FACE OF 2×6 STUD WALL

WIRING AND PLUMBING LOCATED WITHIN STRAPPING LAYER

DOUBLE STRAPPING FOR BASE TRIM NAILING

FLOOR STRUCTURE WITH INSULATION AND CONTINUOUS AIR/VAPOR BARRIER see 61-63

Strapping consists of horizontal nailing strips attached to the inside of a stud wall. The strapping touches the studs only at the intersection between the two, so thermal bridging is virtually eliminated. Strapping is used extensively in energy-efficient buildings. With 2x6 studs and 2x3 strapping, an R-25 value can be achieved.

The advantages of the system are that it is simple and straightforward, and uses a minimal amount of extra framing materials. With two-thirds of the insulative value in the (2x6) stud cavities, an air/vapor barrier can be located at the inside face of the framed wall, thus eliminating the need to puncture it with services. In addition, the plumbing and electrical work itself is simplified by the creation of horizontal chases on the walls.

Extra strapping is usually required for nailing at corners, at window and door openings, and at the base of the wall (see drawing above). In addition, vertical blocks are required for the attachment of electrical boxes.

Strapping may also be applied to the exterior of a building. In this case, the strapping is more easily installed, but the advantage of a horizontal chase interior of the vapor barrier is lost. Furthermore, the strapping insulation must be installed from the exterior, exposed to the weather.

 STRAPPING

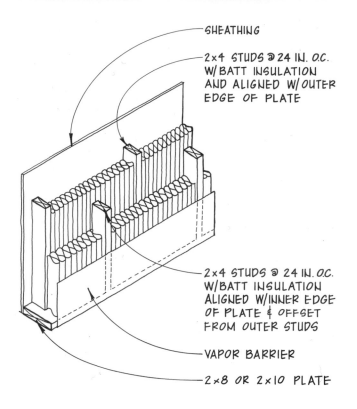

SHEATHING

2×4 STUDS @ 24 IN. O.C. W/BATT INSULATION AND ALIGNED W/OUTER EDGE OF PLATE

2×4 STUDS @ 24 IN. O.C. W/BATT INSULATION ALIGNED W/INNER EDGE OF PLATE & OFFSET FROM OUTER STUDS

VAPOR BARRIER

2×8 OR 2×10 PLATE

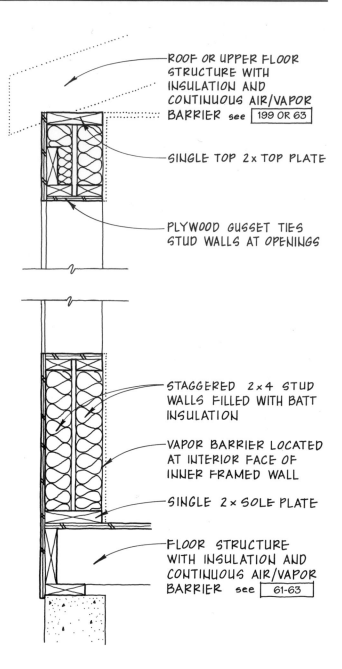

ROOF OR UPPER FLOOR STRUCTURE WITH INSULATION AND CONTINUOUS AIR/VAPOR BARRIER see 199 OR 63

SINGLE TOP 2× TOP PLATE

PLYWOOD GUSSET TIES STUD WALLS AT OPENINGS

STAGGERED 2×4 STUD WALLS FILLED WITH BATT INSULATION

VAPOR BARRIER LOCATED AT INTERIOR FACE OF INNER FRAMED WALL

SINGLE 2× SOLE PLATE

FLOOR STRUCTURE WITH INSULATION AND CONTINUOUS AIR/VAPOR BARRIER see 61-63

Staggered-stud framing is essentially a double stud wall framed on a single wide plate with the studs offset from one another so that there is no thermal bridging. The system is appreciated by builders for its minimal deviation from standard frame construction. Staggered-stud framing is substantially the same as platform framing, and subcontractors are sequenced in the same order as standard construction. With this technique, insulative values of R-30 or more can be attained while virtually eliminating thermal bridging. A 2x8 or 2x10 plate with staggered 2x4 studs @ 24 in. o.c. is most common.

Because there are effectively two separate walls, this system offers a special opportunity at windows and doors to splay the opening.

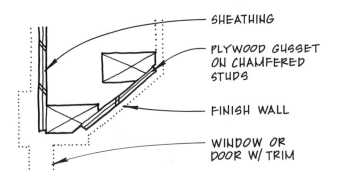

SHEATHING

PLYWOOD GUSSET ON CHAMFERED STUDS

FINISH WALL

WINDOW OR DOOR W/TRIM

By increasing the rough-opening size at the "inner wall," the opening will be more generous from the inside and reflect light better into the room.

The disadvantages of the system also stem from its similarity to standard platform frame construction. Unlike strapping systems or double wall systems, staggered-stud systems have the air/vapor barrier located on the inside (warm) face of the wall, with the attendant problems of sealing perforations of the barrier from plumbing and electrical services.

 A STAGGERED STUD FRAMING

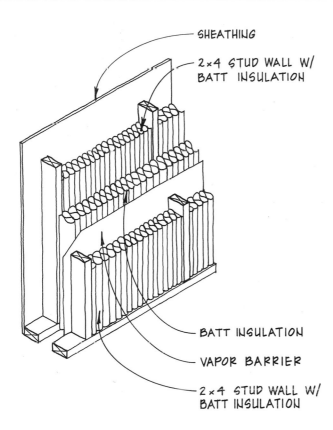

- SHEATHING
- 2×4 STUD WALL W/ BATT INSULATION
- BATT INSULATION
- VAPOR BARRIER
- 2×4 STUD WALL W/ BATT INSULATION

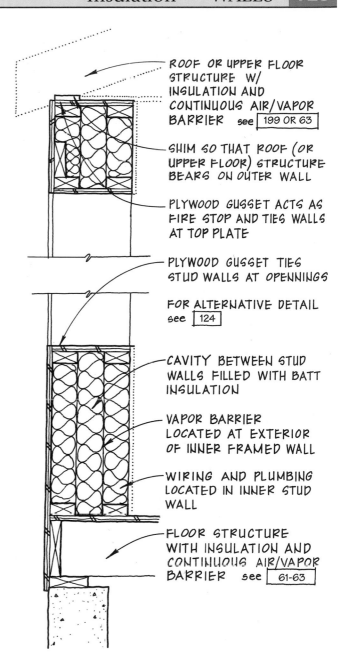

- ROOF OR UPPER FLOOR STRUCTURE W/ INSULATION AND CONTINUOUS AIR/VAPOR BARRIER see 199 OR 63
- SHIM SO THAT ROOF (OR UPPER FLOOR) STRUCTURE BEARS ON OUTER WALL
- PLYWOOD GUSSET ACTS AS FIRE STOP AND TIES WALLS AT TOP PLATE
- PLYWOOD GUSSET TIES STUD WALLS AT OPENNINGS
- FOR ALTERNATIVE DETAIL see 124
- CAVITY BETWEEN STUD WALLS FILLED WITH BATT INSULATION
- VAPOR BARRIER LOCATED AT EXTERIOR OF INNER FRAMED WALL
- WIRING AND PLUMBING LOCATED IN INNER STUD WALL
- FLOOR STRUCTURE WITH INSULATION AND CONTINUOUS AIR/VAPOR BARRIER see 61-63

Double wall framing is capable of achieving the highest insulation values of all the upgraded framing techniques. Values of R-40 are common. Slightly more framing materials and considerably more labor (than strapping or staggered stud) are required for the increased performance.

The outer framed wall is most commonly used as the bearing wall. This strategy has two advantages: The insulation and the inner wall can be installed under the roof out of the weather, and the shear walls are most easily installed in this (outer wall) location. However, finish detailing at the wall/ceiling joint is complicated if the inner wall is to be maintained as nonstructural, and the continuity of the air/vapor barrier is somewhat difficult to achieve at the wall/floor intersection.

Less common (and not illustrated) is the use of the inner wall as the bearing wall. This system avoids the minor disadvantage of the outer bearing wall system, but has two major disadvantages: it requires support of the outer wall beyond the edge of the foundation and the outer wall and the extra insulation must be installed from the outside of the building, exposed to the weather.

The ability to locate an air/vapor barrier at the outside surface of the inner wall contributes significantly to its continuity because plumbing and electrical services can be located within the inner wall without having to penetrate the barrier. To get the air/vapor barrier into this position is simple with an interior bearing wall, but somewhat involved with an exterior bearing wall. It can be accomplished, however, by fastening the avb to the (outer face of the) inner wall before it is tipped into place. The cavity can be filled with horizontal batts tied to the exterior wall before the inner wall is positioned or can be blown in afterward through holes predrilled in the top plywood gusset.

(A) DOUBLE WALL FRAMING

CHAPTER 4

ROOFS

The roof is the part of the wood-frame structure that varies most widely across the country. This is because the roof plays the most active role of all the parts of a building in protecting against the weather, and in the U.S., variations in weather are extreme. Some roofs protect primarily against the heat of the sun; others must shelter the inhabitants under tons of snow.

SELECTION OF ROOF SLOPE

One of the most obvious variations of roof form has to do with the slope or pitch of the roof. The main factors affecting the slope of a roof are stylistic considerations, the type of roofing material to be used, and the space desired beneath the roof. The climate also has a strong influence on roof slope. Areas of significant rainfall have roofs pitched to shed the rain, while warm, arid climates tend to favor flatter roofs.

The slope or pitch of a roof is measured as a proportion of rise to run. A roof that rises 4 in. in 1 ft. (12 in.) is said to have a 4-in-12 pitch (or 4:12). The second number in the roof-pitch proportion is always 12.

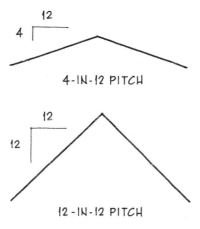

4-IN-12 PITCH

12-IN-12 PITCH

THE SHAPE OF ROOFS

Roof shapes tend to have a regional character that reflects not only climatic variation, but also historical and material influences. All roof forms are derived from four basic roof shapes shown below: the flat roof, the shed roof, the gable roof, and the hip roof.

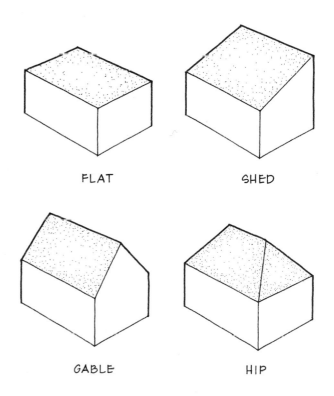

FLAT   SHED

GABLE   HIP

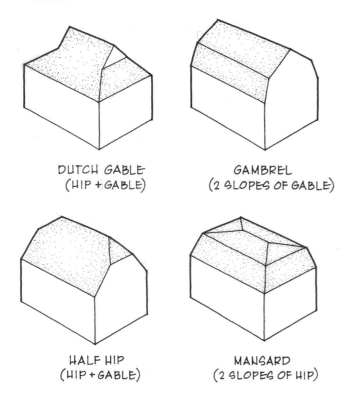

DUTCH GABLE
(HIP + GABLE)

GAMBREL
(2 SLOPES OF GABLE)

HALF HIP
(HIP + GABLE)

MANSARD
(2 SLOPES OF HIP)

Virtually any roof form may be made by combining the four basic shapes with the connections illustrated in this chapter. Some of these composite shapes are so common they have their own names. For example, the hip and gable shapes can combine to form a Dutch gable. Two different slopes of gable roof can combine to form a gambrel roof. A shed dormer may be added to a gable roof, and so forth. Four common combinations are shown above.

WHAT TYPE OF CONSTRUCTION SYSTEM?

Roofs are constructed either with rafters (stick-framed roofs) or with trusses. Stick-framed roofs are usually made with dimension lumber but may also use composite materials such as plywood I-rafters (which are simply plywood I-joists).

Stick framing originated before the development of balloon-frame construction in the 19th century. Antecedents of the modern stick-framed roof can be seen on ancient roofs around the world, and modern stick-frame roofing remains popular because it is the most flexible roof-framing system and the materials are least expensive.

Trusses are made of a number of small members (usually 2x4s) joined in a factory or shop to make one long structural assembly. Only in very simple buildings does the labor savings of a truss system compete with stick framing.

Stick framing—One advantage of stick framing is that the space within the roof structure can become living space or storage. Vaulted (cathedral) ceilings, half-story living spaces on upper floors, and true storage attics are all examples. A second advantage is that complex roofs may be stick-framed more economically than truss-framed. For owner-builders who need not include the cost of labor, stick framing is especially attractive.

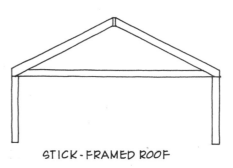

STICK-FRAMED ROOF

Truss framing—Trusses can span much farther than stick-framed roofs, leaving large open areas below them or permitting partition walls to be relocated without consideration for the roof structure above. Trusses go up quickly, usually resulting in a cost saving over stick-framed roofs on simply shaped buildings. A big disadvantage of trusses is that the truss roof is almost impossible to remodel, since trusses should never be cut.

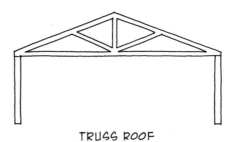

TRUSS ROOF

OTHER CONSIDERATIONS

In addition to the choices about pitch, shape, and structure discussed above, many other decisions contribute to the overall performance of the roof. These include selection of sheathing, underlayment, and roofing material; eave, rake, and flashing details; gutters and downspouts; and insulation and ventilation of the roof assembly. All of these issues are discussed in this chapter.

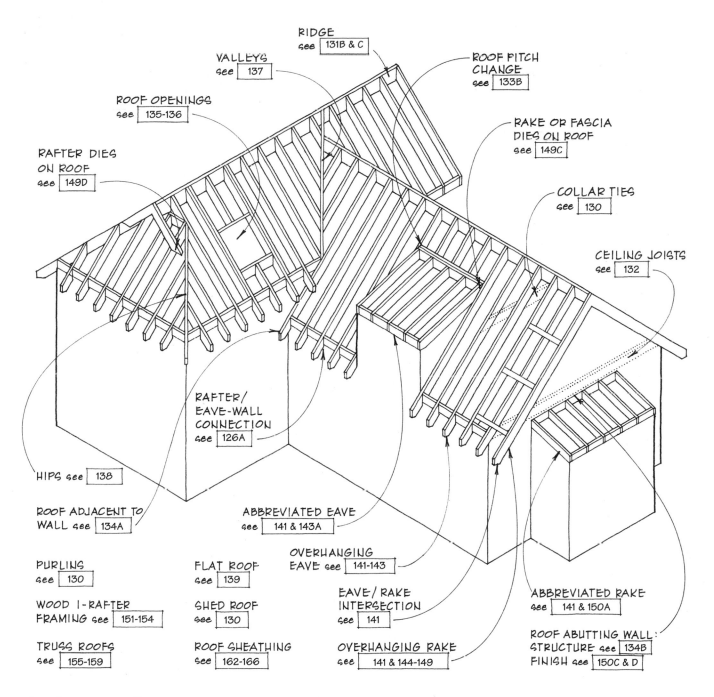

RIDGE
see 131B & C

VALLEYS
see 137

ROOF PITCH
CHANGE
see 133B

ROOF OPENINGS
see 135-136

RAKE OR FASCIA
DIES ON ROOF
see 149C

RAFTER DIES
ON ROOF
see 149D

COLLAR TIES
see 130

CEILING JOISTS
see 132

RAFTER/
EAVE-WALL
CONNECTION
see 126A

HIPS see 138

ROOF ADJACENT TO
WALL see 134A

ABBREVIATED EAVE
see 141 & 143A

PURLINS
see 130

FLAT ROOF
see 139

OVERHANGING
EAVE see 141-143

ABBREVIATED RAKE
see 141 & 150A

WOOD I-RAFTER
FRAMING see 151-154

SHED ROOF
see 130

EAVE/RAKE
INTERSECTION
see 141

ROOF ABUTTING WALL:
STRUCTURE see 134B
FINISH see 150C & D

TRUSS ROOFS
see 155-159

ROOF SHEATHING
see 162-166

OVERHANGING RAKE
see 141 & 144-149

Rafter sizes are usually 2x6, 2x8, 2x10 or 2x12, and spacing is usually 16 in. or 24 in. o.c. Species of wood vary from region to region. Rafter sizing depends primarily on span, spacing, roof loads, and sometimes on required insulation depth.

For a rafter-span table, see 131A.

 ROOF FRAMING

Stick-framed rafters may be supported by the walls of the building, by a structural ridge beam, or by purlins.

Simple-span roof—The simplest sloped roof—the shed roof—has rafters that span from one wall to another, as shown at right. These rafters must be strong enough to carry the dead-load weight of the roof itself and subsequent layers of reroofing, plus the live-load weight of snow. The rafters must usually be deep enough to contain adequate insulation.

The total roof load is transferred to the ends of the rafters, where it is supported by the walls. In the simple example at right, each wall carries part of the roof load.

Triangulated roof—Common (full-length) rafters are paired and usually joined to a ridge board, as shown in the drawing at right. Each rafter spans only half the distance between the two walls (the gable roof, shown in the drawing at right, is the simplest version). Horizontal ties—either ceiling joists or collar ties—form a triangle with the rafters. Ceiling joists are generally located on the top plate of the walls but may also be located higher to form a partially vaulted ceiling. Collar ties are usually nailed near the top of the roof between opposing rafters and spaced at 4 ft. o.c. Collar ties are not sufficient by themselves to resist the outward thrust of the rafters.

Rafters in triangulated roofs are shallower than those in shed roofs of equal width because they span only half the distance of the shed rafters and because they do not usually contain insulation.

Structural ridge beam—The horizontal ties that are required in a triangulated roof may be avoided if the rafters are attached at the ridge to a structural ridge beam (or a wall), which effectively changes the triangulated roof into two simple-span roofs, as shown in the drawing below.

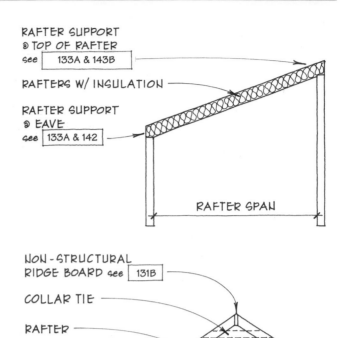

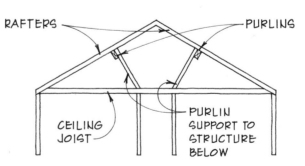

Purlin—A purlin is a horizontal member that supports several rafters—usually at midspan. Purlins were commonly used to help support the long slender rafters of pioneer houses and barns. Today they are also used occasionally to reduce the span of a set of rafters, but the purlins must themselves be supported by the frame of the structure, as shown in the drawing below.

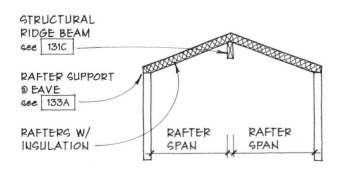

NOTE:
THE NAME "PURLIN" IS ALSO GIVEN TO A MEMBER THAT SPANS ACROSS RAFTERS TO SUPPORT ROOF DECKING see 150C

(A) **STICK FRAMING**
TERMINOLOGY

Rafter size, species and grade	Rafter span (ft.)		
	12 in. o.c.	16 in. o.c.	24 in. o.c.
2x6 hem-fir #1	11.5	10.5	9.2
2x6 south. pine #1	12.0	10.9	9.6
2x6 Douglas-fir #1	12.2	11.1	9.7
2x8 hem-fir #1	15.2	13.8	12.1
2x8 south. pine #1	15.8	14.4	12.6
2x8 Douglas-fir #1	16.2	14.7	12.8
2x10 hem-fir #1	19.4	17.7	16.4
2x10 south. pine #1	20.3	18.4	17.1
2x10 Douglas-fir #1	20.6	18.7	17.4
2x12 hem-fir #1	23.6	21.5	18.7
2x12 south. pine #1	24.6	22.4	19.5
2x12 Douglas-fir #1	25.1	22.8	19.8

This table compares three species for a roof with a 30-psf live load. The table is for estimating purposes only. For a roof-sheathing span table, see 163.

 A **RAFTER-SPAN COMPARISON TABLE**

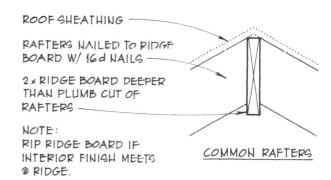

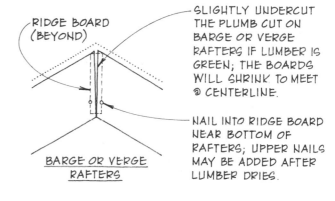

ROOF SHEATHING

RAFTERS NAILED TO RIDGE BOARD W/ 16d NAILS

2 x RIDGE BOARD DEEPER THAN PLUMB CUT OF RAFTERS

NOTE: RIP RIDGE BOARD IF INTERIOR FINISH MEETS @ RIDGE.

COMMON RAFTERS

RIDGE BOARD (BEYOND)

SLIGHTLY UNDERCUT THE PLUMB CUT ON BARGE OR VERGE RAFTERS IF LUMBER IS GREEN; THE BOARDS WILL SHRINK TO MEET @ CENTERLINE.

NAIL INTO RIDGE BOARD NEAR BOTTOM OF RAFTERS; UPPER NAILS MAY BE ADDED AFTER LUMBER DRIES.

BARGE OR VERGE RAFTERS

B **RAFTER/RIDGE** NON-STRUCTURAL RIDGE BOARD

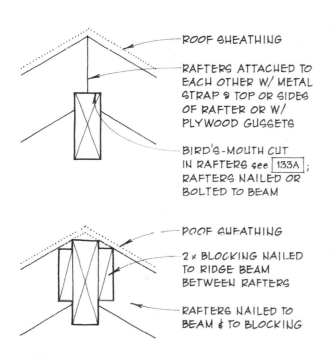

ROOF SHEATHING

RAFTERS ATTACHED TO EACH OTHER W/ METAL STRAP @ TOP OR SIDES OF RAFTER OR W/ PLYWOOD GUSSETS

BIRD'S-MOUTH CUT IN RAFTERS see 133A ; RAFTERS NAILED OR BOLTED TO BEAM

ROOF SHEATHING

2 x BLOCKING NAILED TO RIDGE BEAM BETWEEN RAFTERS

RAFTERS NAILED TO BEAM & TO BLOCKING

NOTE: AS AN ALTERNATIVE, USE METAL RIDGE HANGERS FOR SMALL RAFTERS UP TO 7-IN-12 PITCH.

 C **RAFTER/RIDGE** STRUCTURAL RIDGE BEAM: 4 ALTERNATIVES

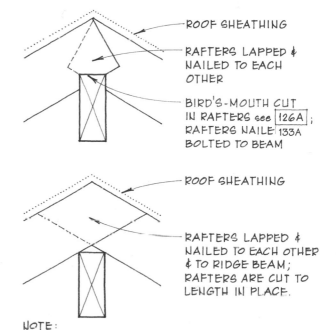

ROOF SHEATHING

RAFTERS LAPPED & NAILED TO EACH OTHER

BIRD'S-MOUTH CUT IN RAFTERS see 126A ; RAFTERS NAILE 133A BOLTED TO BEAM

ROOF SHEATHING

RAFTERS LAPPED & NAILED TO EACH OTHER & TO RIDGE BEAM; RAFTERS ARE CUT TO LENGTH IN PLACE.

NOTE: RAFTERS IN THESE DETAILS LAP @ RIDGE, SO @ THE END RAFTERS, FUR OUT INNER RAFTER TO ALIGN W/ OUTER RAFTER.

Ceiling joists are very similar to floor joists. In fact, the second-floor joists of a two-story building act as the ceiling joists for the story below. Ceiling joists are distinguished from floor joists only when there is no floor (except an attic floor) above the joists.

Ceiling joists are sized like floor joists. The span of the joists depends on spacing and whether the attic above the joists will be used for storage.

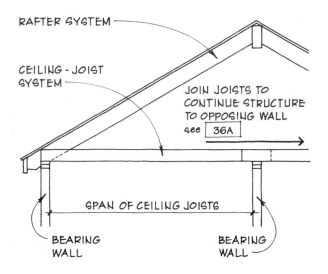

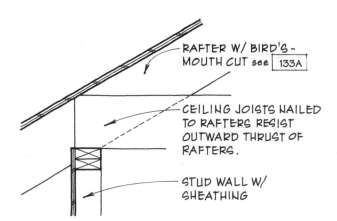

NOTE:
CHECK CODES FOR NAILING REQUIREMENTS & ANGLE NAILS THROUGH JOISTS INTO RAFTERS TOWARD CENTER OF BUILDING.

The joists can function as ties to resist the lateral forces of rafters. For this purpose, it is important to attach the joists securely to the rafters.

The underside of ceiling joists is often furred down with a layer of 1x lumber to resist plaster or drywall cracking due to movement of the joists. The drawing below illustrates furring parallel to the joists to resist cracking along a beam that interrupts the continuity of the joists. Furring perpendicular to the joists, usually called strapping, is also common.

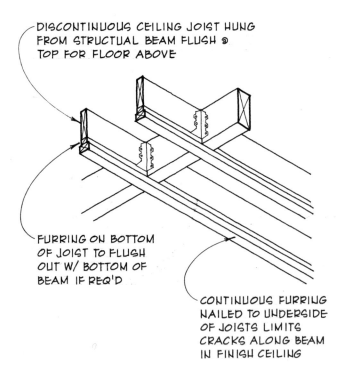

Ceiling-joist span comparison			
Joist size and species	**Ceiling joist span (ft.)**		
	12 in. o.c.	**16 in. o.c.**	**24 in. o.c.**
2x6 hem-fir #1	13.2	12.0	10.5
2x6 south. pine #1	13.7	12.5	11.0
2x6 Douglas-fir #1	14.0	12.7	11.1
2x8 hem-fir #1	17.5	15.8	13.8
2x8 south. pine #1	18.2	16.5	14.5
2x8 Douglas-fir #1	18.5	16.7	14.7
2x10 hem-fir #1	22.2	20.2	17.7
2x10 south. pine #1	23.2	21.0	18.4
2x10 Douglas-fir #1	23.6	21.5	18.7
2x12 hem-fir #1	27.0	24.5	21.5
2x12 south. pine #1	28.1	25.6	22.4
2x12 Douglas-fir #1	28.7	26.0	22.8

This table is based on a light attic load of 20 psf and a deflection of L/360. The table is for estimating purposes only.

RAFTERS/CEILING JOISTS

At walls or beams that support them at the eave, rafters are cut at the point of support with a notch called a bird's mouth.

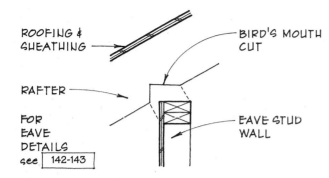

ROOFING & SHEATHING

BIRD'S MOUTH CUT

RAFTER

FOR EAVE DETAILS see 142-143

EAVE STUD WALL

The width of the bird's mouth is equal to the width of the sheathed stud wall (or unsheathed wall if sheathing is to be applied later). The underside of the rafters should meet the inside corner of the top of the wall. This is especially important if the ceiling is vaulted and a smooth transition between wall and ceiling is desired (see below).

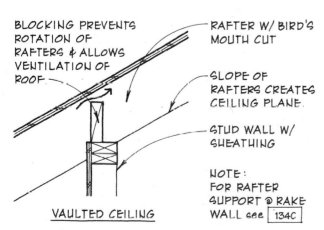

BLOCKING PREVENTS ROTATION OF RAFTERS & ALLOWS VENTILATION OF ROOF.

RAFTER W/ BIRD'S MOUTH CUT

CEILING JOISTS see 131

STUD WALL W/ SHEATHING

FLAT CEILING

BLOCKING PREVENTS ROTATION OF RAFTERS & ALLOWS VENTILATION OF ROOF.

RAFTER W/ BIRD'S MOUTH CUT

SLOPE OF RAFTERS CREATES CEILING PLANE.

STUD WALL W/ SHEATHING

NOTE: FOR RAFTER SUPPORT @ RAKE WALL see 134C

VAULTED CEILING

(A) RAFTER / EAVE WALL
BIRD'S MOUTH CUT

Wherever the pitch of a roof changes from shallow to steep (as in a gambrel roof) or from steep to shallow (as in a shed dormer) the two ends of the rafters must be supported. If the pitch change occurs over a wall, the wall itself will provide the support.

If the pitch change does not occur over a wall, the support will have to be provided by a purlin or a beam (header).

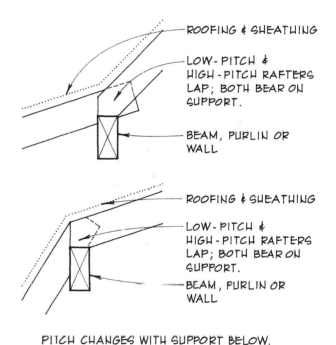

ROOFING & SHEATHING

LOW-PITCH & HIGH-PITCH RAFTERS LAP; BOTH BEAR ON SUPPORT.

BEAM, PURLIN OR WALL

ROOFING & SHEATHING

LOW-PITCH & HIGH-PITCH RAFTERS LAP; BOTH BEAR ON SUPPORT.

BEAM, PURLIN OR WALL

PITCH CHANGES WITH SUPPORT BELOW.

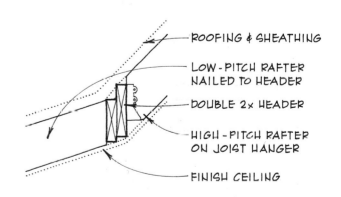

ROOFING & SHEATHING

LOW-PITCH RAFTER NAILED TO HEADER

DOUBLE 2x HEADER

HIGH-PITCH RAFTER ON JOIST HANGER

FINISH CEILING

PITCH CHANGE WITHOUT SUPPORT BELOW

(B) ROOF PITCH CHANGE

The end rafters of a gable or a shed roof are supported by the walls under them, called rake walls. The framing of the rake should be coordinated with the detailing of the rake. Of the three drawings below, the first example is the simplest method of support and is used with all types of rake, often in conjunction with an unfinished attic. The second example is best for supporting lookouts for an exposed or boxed-in rake. The third example provides nailing for a boxed-in rake or an exposed ceiling. Elements from the three examples may be combined differently for specific situations. For rake-wall framing, see 72A, B & C.

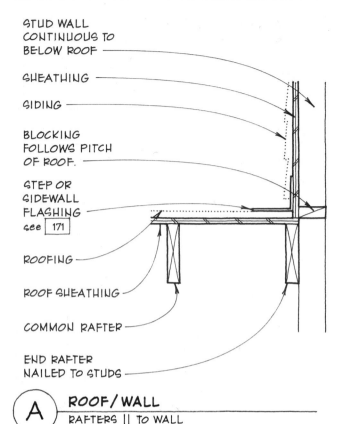

STUD WALL CONTINUOUS TO BELOW ROOF

SHEATHING

SIDING

BLOCKING FOLLOWS PITCH OF ROOF.

STEP OR SIDEWALL FLASHING see 171

ROOFING

ROOF SHEATHING

COMMON RAFTER

END RAFTER NAILED TO STUDS

Ⓐ ROOF / WALL
RAFTERS ∥ TO WALL

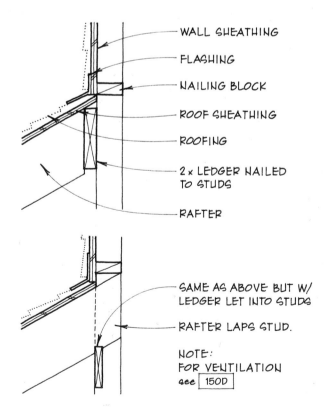

WALL SHEATHING

FLASHING

NAILING BLOCK

ROOF SHEATHING

ROOFING

2 × LEDGER NAILED TO STUDS

RAFTER

SAME AS ABOVE BUT W/ LEDGER LET INTO STUDS

RAFTER LAPS STUD.

NOTE:
FOR VENTILATION see 150D

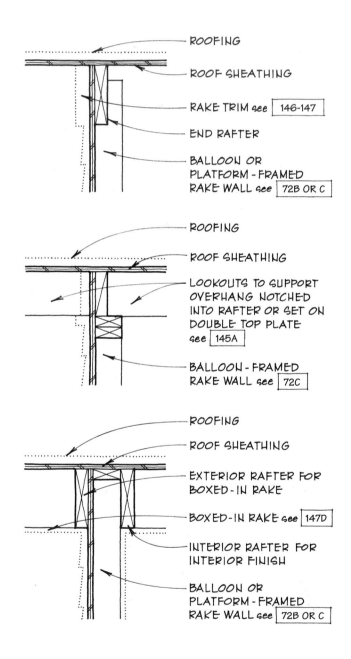

ROOFING

ROOF SHEATHING

RAKE TRIM see 146-147

END RAFTER

BALLOON OR PLATFORM - FRAMED RAKE WALL see 72B OR C

ROOFING

ROOF SHEATHING

LOOKOUTS TO SUPPORT OVERHANG NOTCHED INTO RAFTER OR SET ON DOUBLE TOP PLATE see 145A

BALLOON - FRAMED RAKE WALL see 72C

ROOFING

ROOF SHEATHING

EXTERIOR RAFTER FOR BOXED-IN RAKE

BOXED-IN RAKE see 147D

INTERIOR RAFTER FOR INTERIOR FINISH

BALLOON OR PLATFORM - FRAMED RAKE WALL see 72B OR C

Ⓑ SHED ROOF / WALL
RAFTERS ⊥ TO WALL

Ⓒ RAFTER / RAKE WALL
3 ALTERNATIVES

Framing the elements that project through the roof of a building—skylights, chimneys, and dormers—begins with a rectangular opening in the framing. For openings in a single roof plane framed entirely with common rafters, framing is relatively easy. An opening three rafter spaces wide or less can be made by heading off the interrupted rafters and doubling the side rafters, as shown below. Obviously, it is more efficient if the width and placement of the opening correspond to the rafter spacing. Larger openings should be engineered. Openings that straddle hips, valleys, or pitch changes must have special support, special framing, and special flashing.

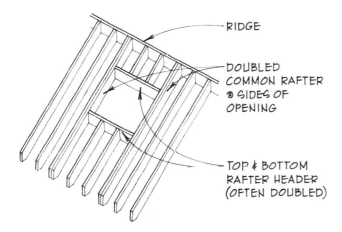

- RIDGE
- DOUBLED COMMON RAFTER @ SIDES OF OPENING
- TOP & BOTTOM RAFTER HEADER (OFTEN DOUBLED)

Headers for simple openings are, in most cases, either plumb or perpendicular to the rafters, as shown in the drawing below. Plumb openings require a header deeper than the rafters.

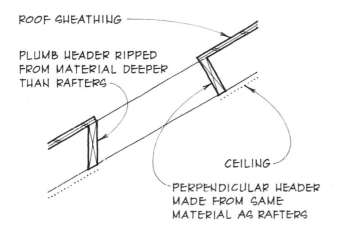

- ROOF SHEATHING
- PLUMB HEADER RIPPED FROM MATERIAL DEEPER THAN RAFTERS
- CEILING
- PERPENDICULAR HEADER MADE FROM SAME MATERIAL AS RAFTERS

FOR DORMER OPENINGS see [135B]

FOR SKYLIGHT OPENINGS see [136A & B]

FOR CHIMNEY OPENINGS see [136C]

Ⓐ ROOF OPENINGS
GENERAL

Dormers are often more than three rafter spaces wide so their structure cannot be calculated by rules of thumb. The opening in the roof may be structured to support all or part of the loads imposed by the dormer. The dormer walls and roof are framed like the walls and roof of the main building.

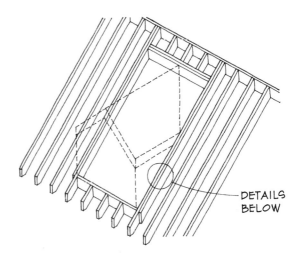

- DETAILS BELOW

If the dormer walls do not extend below ceiling level, the roof structure at the edge of the opening must support the dormer.

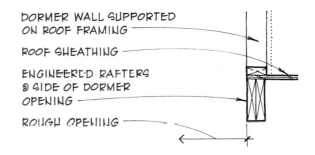

- DORMER WALL SUPPORTED ON ROOF FRAMING
- ROOF SHEATHING
- ENGINEERED RAFTERS @ SIDE OF DORMER OPENING
- ROUGH OPENING

If the dormer has side walls that extend to the floor, the floor may be used to support the dormer, and the rafters at the side of the opening may be single.

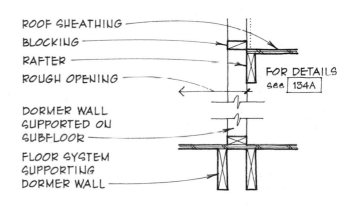

- ROOF SHEATHING
- BLOCKING
- RAFTER
- ROUGH OPENING
- FOR DETAILS see [134A]
- DORMER WALL SUPPORTED ON SUBFLOOR
- FLOOR SYSTEM SUPPORTING DORMER WALL

Ⓑ DORMER OPENING

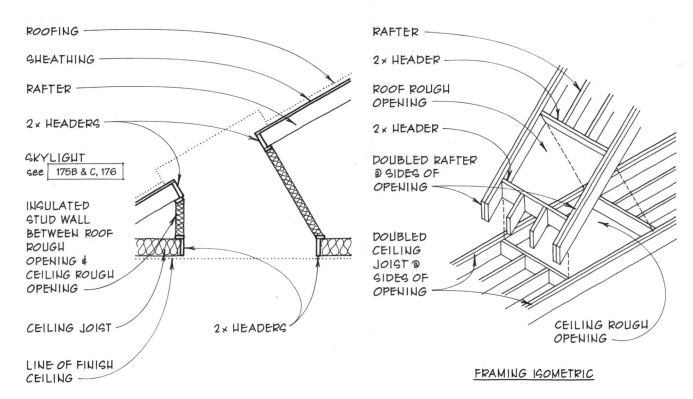

ROOFING

SHEATHING

RAFTER

2× HEADERS

SKYLIGHT
see | 175B & C, 176 |

INSULATED
STUD WALL
BETWEEN ROOF
ROUGH
OPENING &
CEILING ROUGH
OPENING

CEILING JOIST

LINE OF FINISH
CEILING

2× HEADERS

RAFTER

2× HEADER

ROOF ROUGH
OPENING

2× HEADER

DOUBLED RAFTER
@ SIDES OF
OPENING

DOUBLED
CEILING
JOIST @
SIDES OF
OPENING

CEILING ROUGH
OPENING

FRAMING ISOMETRIC

(A) SKYLIGHT OPENING
LIGHT WELL

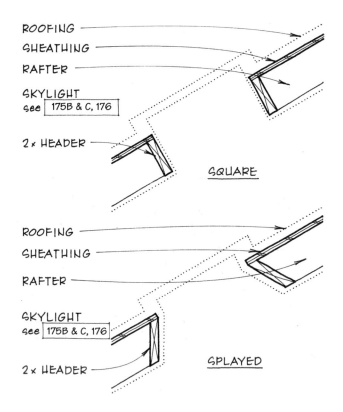

ROOFING
SHEATHING
RAFTER

SKYLIGHT
see | 175B & C, 176 |

2× HEADER

SQUARE

ROOFING
SHEATHING
RAFTER

SKYLIGHT
see | 175B & C, 176 |

2× HEADER

SPLAYED

(B) SKYLIGHT OPENINGS
VAULTED CEILING

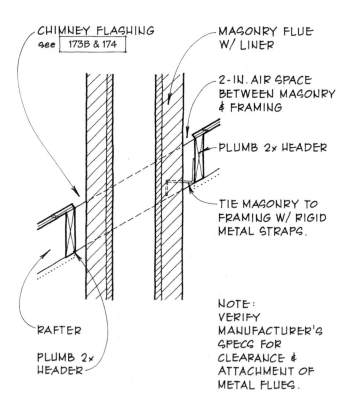

CHIMNEY FLASHING
see | 173B & 174 |

MASONRY FLUE
W/ LINER

2-IN. AIR SPACE
BETWEEN MASONRY
& FRAMING

PLUMB 2× HEADER

TIE MASONRY TO
FRAMING W/ RIGID
METAL STRAPS.

RAFTER

PLUMB 2×
HEADER

NOTE:
VERIFY
MANUFACTURER'S
SPECS FOR
CLEARANCE &
ATTACHMENT OF
METAL FLUES.

(C) CHIMNEY OPENING

The inside corner of two intersecting roof planes is called a valley. In most cases, valleys are supported by a valley rafter that extends from the outside wall of the building to the ridge or to a header. These valley rafters support large loads and should be engineered. Jack rafters support the area between the valley rafter and the ridge or header.

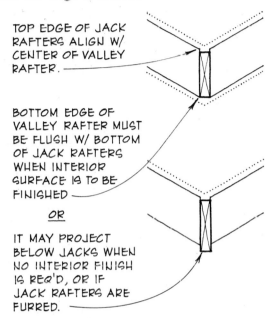

TOP EDGE OF JACK RAFTERS ALIGN W/ CENTER OF VALLEY RAFTER.

BOTTOM EDGE OF VALLEY RAFTER MUST BE FLUSH W/ BOTTOM OF JACK RAFTERS WHEN INTERIOR SURFACE IS TO BE FINISHED

OR

IT MAY PROJECT BELOW JACKS WHEN NO INTERIOR FINISH IS REQ'D, OR IF JACK RAFTERS ARE FURRED.

As shown at right, valley rafters can be supported at the top by a ridge or by a header. The ridge support system is more practical when the ridges of the intersecting roofs are close together; however, the header support system is better when the lower ridge intersects the main roof near or below the center of the rafter span.

Where headroom is not required between intersecting roofs, a simpler "farmer's valley" or "California valley" may be constructed. This valley is made without a valley rafter. One roof is first built entirely of common rafters without any special valley framing. Then 2x sleepers are installed over the rafters or over the sheathing of the first roof, and jack rafters are attached to the sleepers.

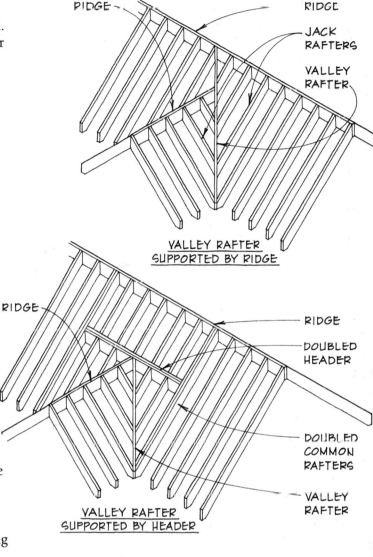

RIDGE   RIDGE
JACK RAFTERS
VALLEY RAFTER

VALLEY RAFTER
SUPPORTED BY RIDGE

RIDGE   RIDGE
DOUBLED HEADER
DOUBLED COMMON RAFTERS
VALLEY RAFTER

VALLEY RAFTER
SUPPORTED BY HEADER

COMMON RAFTER
2 x SLEEPER

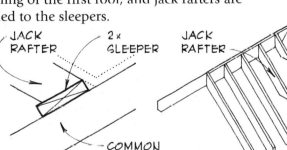

JACK RAFTER   2 x SLEEPER   JACK RAFTER

COMMON RAFTER

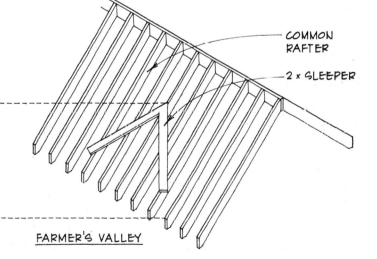

FARMER'S VALLEY

Ⓐ   VALLEY FRAMING

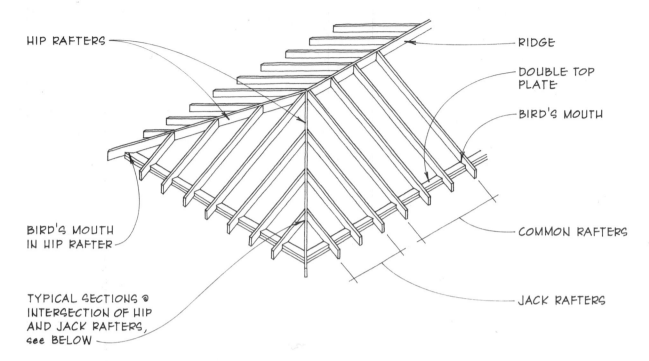

HIP RAFTERS

BIRD'S MOUTH IN HIP RAFTER

TYPICAL SECTIONS @ INTERSECTION OF HIP AND JACK RAFTERS, see BELOW

RIDGE

DOUBLE TOP PLATE

BIRD'S MOUTH

COMMON RAFTERS

JACK RAFTERS

A hip is the outside corner where two planes of a roof meet. It is composed of a hip rafter at the corner and jack rafters from the hip to the eave. The hip rafter is supported at its lower end by the wall at plate level (or by a post) and at its upper end by the ridge (or by a wall).

Most codes require that the hip rafter project below the bottom edge of the jack rafters (see the top drawing at right). This is not very logical because, unlike a valley rafter, a hip rafter does not support much roof load. The extra depth presents no problem in an attic space, but if the inside face of the roof is to be made into a finish ceiling, the hip rafter will have to be ripped to allow the planes of the finish ceiling to meet (middle drawing at right). If codes will not permit ripping the hip rafter, furring may be added to the underside of the jack and common rafters to allow the finish ceiling to clear the hip rafter.

The top ends of the jack rafters may be cut off to permit venting at the top of the hip roof (bottom drawing at right).

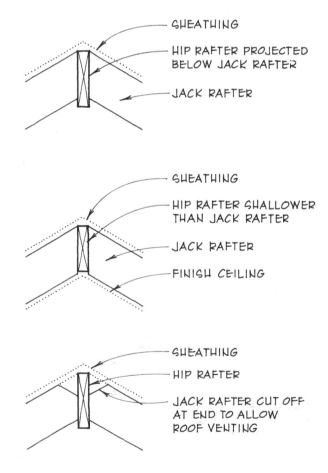

SHEATHING

HIP RAFTER PROJECTED BELOW JACK RAFTER

JACK RAFTER

SHEATHING

HIP RAFTER SHALLOWER THAN JACK RAFTER

JACK RAFTER

FINISH CEILING

SHEATHING

HIP RAFTER

JACK RAFTER CUT OFF AT END TO ALLOW ROOF VENTING

(A) HIP FRAMING

The framing of a flat roof is more like a floor than it is like a pitched roof. The joists are level or nearly level and support the ceiling below and the live loads above. Connections to walls are like those for floors (see 32), as are the framing details for openings (see 38B) and cantilevers (see 39A). As for floors, the structure of a flat roof may be a joist system (dimension lumber or I-joists), a girder system, or a truss system. Blocking and bridging (see 38A) must be considered at the appropriate locations.

Flat roofs are unlike floors, however, in that they are not really flat. They might be more properly called "low-slope" roofs because they must slope at least ¼ in. per ft. in order to eliminate standing water. This minimal slope may be achieved in several ways:

1. The joists themselves may slope if the ceiling below does not have to be level, or if the ceiling is furred to level.
2. Trusses may be manufactured with a built-in slope.
3. Shims may be added to the top of the joists.
4. Tapered rigid insulation may be added to the top of the sheathing.
5. The joists may be oversize and tapered on top.
6. Sloped rafters can be scabbed alongside level ceiling joists.

The easiest and most direct way to support an overhang at the corner of a flat roof is with a beam below the joists cantilevered from the top of a bearing wall, as shown in the drawing below.

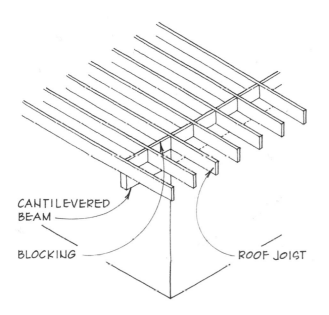

CANTILEVERED BEAM

BLOCKING

ROOF JOIST

A traditional framing method for a cantilevered corner without a beam is with joists that radiate from a doubled central diagonal joist, as shown below. A strong fascia board is advisable here, as with all framing using cantilevered joists.

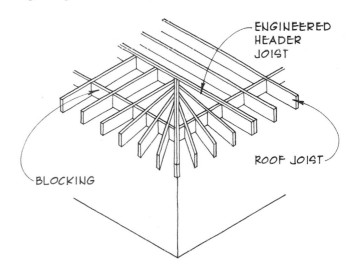

ENGINEERED HEADER JOIST

ROOF JOIST

BLOCKING

A third option for framing a cantilevered corner is shown below. All methods illustrated should be engineered by a professional.

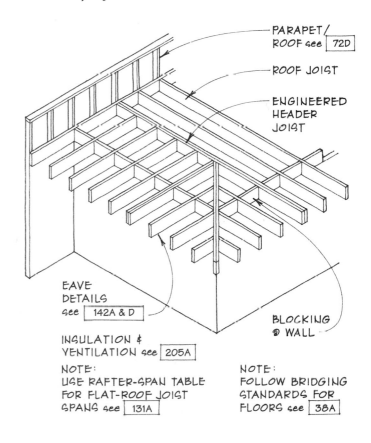

PARAPET / ROOF see 72D

ROOF JOIST

ENGINEERED HEADER JOIST

EAVE DETAILS see 142A & D

BLOCKING @ WALL

INSULATION & VENTILATION see 205A

NOTE:
USE RAFTER-SPAN TABLE FOR FLAT-ROOF JOIST SPANS see 131A

NOTE:
FOLLOW BRIDGING STANDARDS FOR FLOORS see 38A

Ⓐ FLAT-ROOF FRAMING

Designing the basic shape of the roof and designing the configuration of eaves and rakes are the most critical tasks in roof design. Stylistically, the selection of eave and rake types should complement both the roof form and the roofing material.

Functionally, the eave and rake should help protect the building from the elements. The shape of the roof will suggest certain eave and/or rake shapes (see 140B), and certain eave types work best with particular rake types (see 141).

Eave—The eave is the level connection between the roof and the wall. Eaves are common to all sloped roofs and often to flat roofs. There are four basic types of eave (see 141). For eave details, see 142 and 143A & B.

Rake—The rake is the sloped connection between the roof and the wall. Only shed and gable roof types and their derivatives have a rake. There are three basic types of rake (see 141). For rake support and rake details, see 144–147.

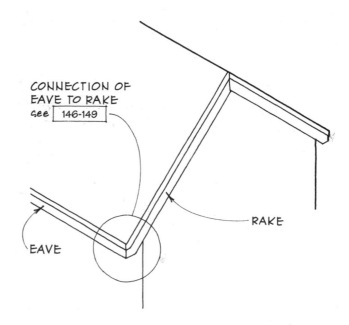

CONNECTION OF EAVE TO RAKE see 146-149

RAKE

EAVE

(A) EAVES & RAKES
INTRODUCTION

The basic shape and structure of a roof system need to be coordinated with the finish of the roof at the edges. The shape of the roof affects the treatment of the edges, and vice versa. A hip roof, for example, is easier to finish with a soffited eave than is a gable roof. The basic roof shapes are best suited for the following finish treatment at the edges:

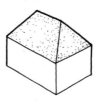

HIP ROOF

HIP ROOFS HAVE ONLY EAVES, WHICH MAY BE ABBREVIATED, BOXED, SOFFITED OR EXPOSED W/ ALMOST EQUAL EASE.

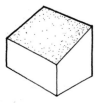

SHED ROOF

SHED ROOFS HAVE BOTH A RAKE & AN EAVE. ALL EAVE TYPES EXCEPT FOR SOFFITS CAN BE COMBINED W/ ALL RAKE TYPES. A SPECIAL EAVE DETAIL IS REQ'D FOR THE TOP EDGE see 143B

FLAT ROOF

FLAT ROOFS HAVE NO RAKES. OVERHANGING EAVES CAN BE DETAILED W/ A SOFFIT OR W/ EXPOSED RAFTERS. WHEN THERE ARE NO OVERHANGS, THERE IS AN ABBREVIATED EAVE OR A PARAPET see 72D

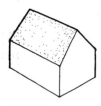

GABLE ROOF

GABLE ROOFS, LIKE SHED ROOFS, HAVE BOTH EAVES & RAKES. EXCEPT FOR SOFFITED EAVES, ALL EAVE & RAKE TYPES CAN BE COMBINED. A SPECIAL DETAIL IS REQ'D @ THE RIDGE, WHERE THE TWO RAKES MEET see 131B & 144C

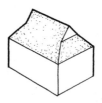

COMBINATION TYPES

COMBINATION ROOF TYPES USUALLY HAVE BOTH RAKES & EAVES. THEY FOLLOW THE GUIDELINES OF THE INDIVIDUAL ROOF TYPES.

(B) ROOF SHAPE & EAVE/RAKE SELECTION

The way in which one edge of a roof is finished affects the detailing of the other edges. For example, a soffited eave on a gable-roofed building is easier to build with an abbreviated rake than with an expos-ed rake. The designer should attempt to match the level edge of the roof (the eave) to the sloped edge (the rake).

In examining the details of the eave and rake, there-fore, the two must be considered as a set. It is logical to start with the eave, because all sloped roof types have eaves, but not all have rakes.

There are four basic sloped-roof eave types. All four types are appropriate for hip roofs, and all but the soffited type can make a simple and elegant transition from eave to rake on gable and shed roofs. The eave types and their most appropriate companion rakes are diagrammed below.

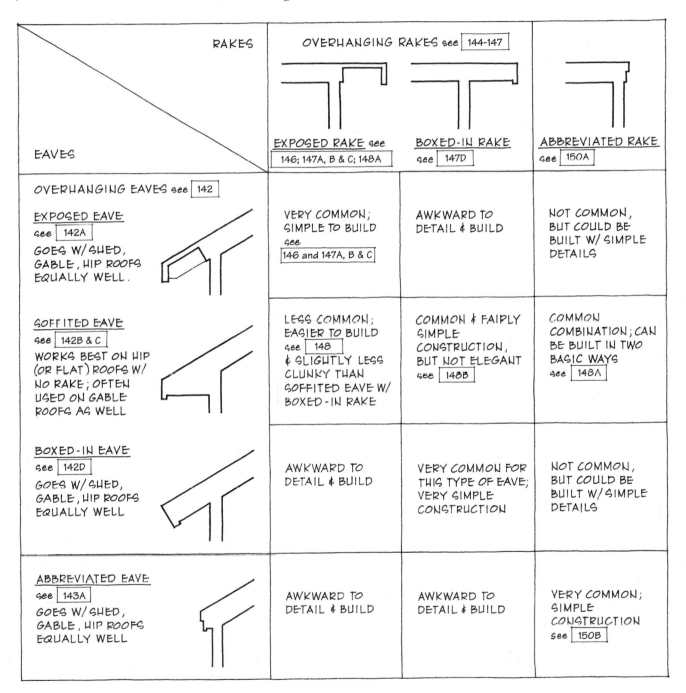

EAVES \ RAKES	OVERHANGING RAKES see 144-147		
	EXPOSED RAKE see 146; 147A, B & C; 148A	BOXED-IN RAKE see 147D	ABBREVIATED RAKE see 150A
OVERHANGING EAVES see 142			
EXPOSED EAVE see 142A GOES W/ SHED, GABLE, HIP ROOFS EQUALLY WELL.	VERY COMMON; SIMPLE TO BUILD see 146 and 147A, B & C	AWKWARD TO DETAIL & BUILD	NOT COMMON, BUT COULD BE BUILT W/ SIMPLE DETAILS
SOFFITED EAVE see 142B & C WORKS BEST ON HIP (OR FLAT) ROOFS W/ NO RAKE; OFTEN USED ON GABLE ROOFS AS WELL	LESS COMMON; EASIER TO BUILD see 148 & SLIGHTLY LESS CLUNKY THAN SOFFITED EAVE W/ BOXED-IN RAKE	COMMON & FAIRLY SIMPLE CONSTRUCTION, BUT NOT ELEGANT see 148B	COMMON COMBINATION; CAN BE BUILT IN TWO BASIC WAYS see 148A
BOXED-IN EAVE see 142D GOES W/ SHED, GABLE, HIP ROOFS EQUALLY WELL	AWKWARD TO DETAIL & BUILD	VERY COMMON FOR THIS TYPE OF EAVE; VERY SIMPLE CONSTRUCTION	NOT COMMON, BUT COULD BE BUILT W/ SIMPLE DETAILS
ABBREVIATED EAVE see 143A GOES W/ SHED, GABLE, HIP ROOFS EQUALLY WELL	AWKWARD TO DETAIL & BUILD	AWKWARD TO DETAIL & BUILD	VERY COMMON; SIMPLE CONSTRUCTION see 150B

(A) EAVE / RAKE COMBINATIONS

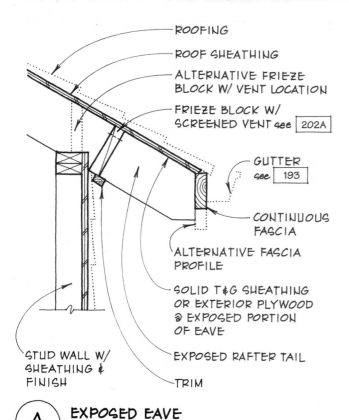

ROOFING
ROOF SHEATHING
ALTERNATIVE FRIEZE BLOCK W/ VENT LOCATION
FRIEZE BLOCK W/ SCREENED VENT see 202A
GUTTER see 193
CONTINUOUS FASCIA
ALTERNATIVE FASCIA PROFILE
SOLID T&G SHEATHING OR EXTERIOR PLYWOOD @ EXPOSED PORTION OF EAVE
EXPOSED RAFTER TAIL
TRIM
STUD WALL W/ SHEATHING & FINISH

(A) EXPOSED EAVE

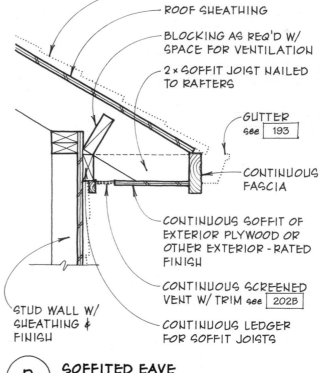

ROOFING
ROOF SHEATHING
BLOCKING AS REQ'D W/ SPACE FOR VENTILATION
2 × SOFFIT JOIST NAILED TO RAFTERS
GUTTER see 193
CONTINUOUS FASCIA
CONTINUOUS SOFFIT OF EXTERIOR PLYWOOD OR OTHER EXTERIOR-RATED FINISH
CONTINUOUS SCREENED VENT W/ TRIM see 202B
CONTINUOUS LEDGER FOR SOFFIT JOISTS
STUD WALL W/ SHEATHING & FINISH

(B) SOFFITED EAVE

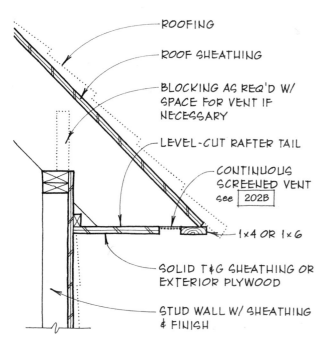

ROOFING
ROOF SHEATHING
BLOCKING AS REQ'D W/ SPACE FOR VENT IF NECESSARY
LEVEL-CUT RAFTER TAIL
CONTINUOUS SCREENED VENT see 202B
1×4 OR 1×6
SOLID T&G SHEATHING OR EXTERIOR PLYWOOD
STUD WALL W/ SHEATHING & FINISH

NOTE:
THIS DETAIL WORKS WELL ON STEEP ROOFS, WHERE A FASCIA MAY APPEAR TOO BULKY.

(C) SOFFITED EAVE
ALTERNATIVE DETAIL

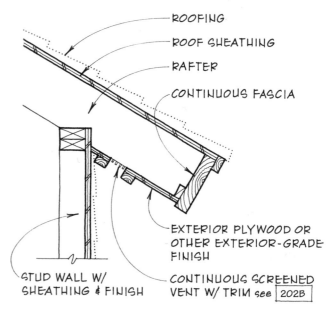

ROOFING
ROOF SHEATHING
RAFTER
CONTINUOUS FASCIA
EXTERIOR PLYWOOD OR OTHER EXTERIOR-GRADE FINISH
CONTINUOUS SCREENED VENT W/ TRIM see 202B
STUD WALL W/ SHEATHING & FINISH

NOTE:
NO GUTTER SHOWN. HANG GUTTER FROM STRAP see 195C
OR USE VERTICAL FASCIA ON PLUMB-CUT RAFTERS TO ACCOMMODATE STANDARD GUTTERS.

(D) BOXED-IN EAVE

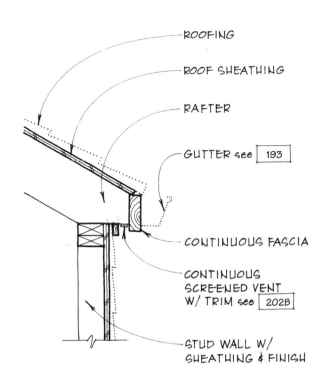

— ROOFING

— ROOF SHEATHING

— RAFTER

— GUTTER see 193

— CONTINUOUS FASCIA

— CONTINUOUS SCREENED VENT W/ TRIM see 202B

— STUD WALL W/ SHEATHING & FINISH

A **ABBREVIATED EAVE**

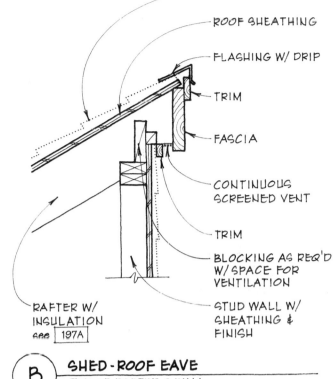

— ROOFING

— ROOF SHEATHING

— FLASHING W/ DRIP

— TRIM

— FASCIA

— CONTINUOUS SCREENED VENT

— TRIM

— BLOCKING AS REQ'D W/ SPACE FOR VENTILATION

— STUD WALL W/ SHEATHING & FINISH

RAFTER W/ INSULATION see 197A

B **SHED-ROOF EAVE**
TOP OF RAFTER @ WALL

NOTES:
DUMMY RAFTERS ARE RELATIVELY SHORT, SO A HIGH GRADE OF MATERIAL MAY BE USED. CONSIDER USING THEM IF THE EXPOSED PART OF THE RAFTER IS TO BE A DIFFERENT SIZE THAN THE UNEXPOSED PART OF THE RAFTER OR TRUSS; OR IF EXPOSED RAFTERS ARE DESIRED WHEN PLYWOOD I-RAFTERS ARE USED FOR THE ROOF STRUCTURE see 151-154
FOR ABBREVIATED EAVES, THE ENTIRE EAVE ASSEMBLY MAY BE SHOP-BUILT IN LENGTHS UP TO ABOUT 16 FT.

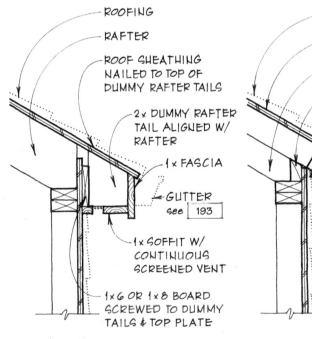

— ROOFING

— RAFTER

— ROOF SHEATHING NAILED TO TOP OF DUMMY RAFTER TAILS

— 2x DUMMY RAFTER TAIL ALIGNED W/ RAFTER

— 1x FASCIA

— GUTTER see 193

— 1x SOFFIT W/ CONTINUOUS SCREENED VENT

— 1x6 OR 1x8 BOARD SCREWED TO DUMMY TAILS & TOP PLATE

ABBREVIATED EAVE

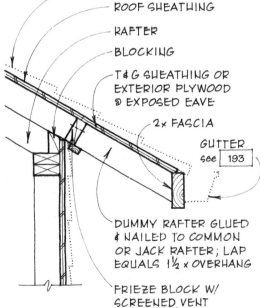

— ROOFING

— ROOF SHEATHING

— RAFTER

— BLOCKING

— T&G SHEATHING OR EXTERIOR PLYWOOD @ EXPOSED EAVE

— 2x FASCIA

— GUTTER see 193

— DUMMY RAFTER GLUED & NAILED TO COMMON OR JACK RAFTER; LAP EQUALS 1½ x OVERHANG

— FRIEZE BLOCK W/ SCREENED VENT see 202A

EXPOSED EAVE

C **DUMMY RAFTER TAIL**

When an overhang is required at the rake, the overhang is made with barge rafters, which stand away from the building and need support. There are several ways to support barge rafters. The roof sheathing alone may be strong enough to support the barge rafters (see 144B), or the ridge board or beam can be designed to support the barge rafters at their upper ends (see 144C), and the fascia may be extended to support the barge rafters at their lower ends (see below). Lookouts or brackets may be also used to support an overhanging rake (see 145A & B).

The roof sheathing can assist in supporting the barge rafter along its length, as shown below.

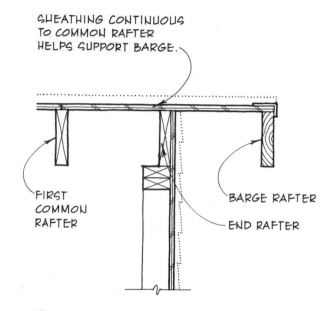

SHEATHING CONTINUOUS TO COMMON RAFTER HELPS SUPPORT BARGE.

FIRST COMMON RAFTER

BARGE RAFTER

END RAFTER

B **OVERHANGING RAKE**
SUPPORTED BY SHEATHING

END RAFTER (LAST INTERIOR RAFTER)

EXTENDED RIDGE BOARD OR BEAM
see [144C]

BARGE RAFTER

SHEATHING PROVIDES SUPPORT FOR BARGE RAFTER
see [144B]

FASCIA HELPS TO SUPPORT BARGE RAFTER @ ITS LOWER END.

NOTE: VERGE RAFTER NOT SHOWN; FOR DETAILS
see [146]

A **OVERHANGING RAKE**
METHODS OF SUPPORT

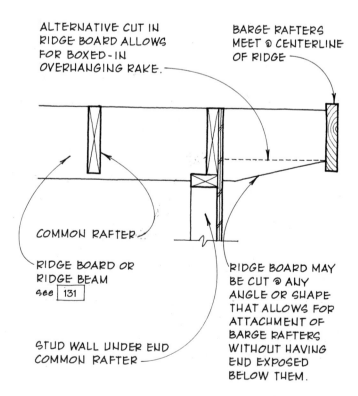

ALTERNATIVE CUT IN RIDGE BOARD ALLOWS FOR BOXED-IN OVERHANGING RAKE.

BARGE RAFTERS MEET @ CENTERLINE OF RIDGE

COMMON RAFTER

RIDGE BOARD OR RIDGE BEAM
see [131]

RIDGE BOARD MAY BE CUT @ ANY ANGLE OR SHAPE THAT ALLOWS FOR ATTACHMENT OF BARGE RAFTERS WITHOUT HAVING END EXPOSED BELOW THEM.

STUD WALL UNDER END COMMON RAFTER

C **OVERHANGING RAKE**
SUPPORTED BY RIDGE BOARD OR BEAM

If the ridge, the fascia and the sheathing together do not provide sufficient support for the barge, lookouts may be added. Lookouts extend from the barge rafter to the first common rafter (or truss) inside the wall. The lookouts are notched through the end rafter at the top of the wall. The size and spacing of lookouts depend on rafter spacing and live loading.

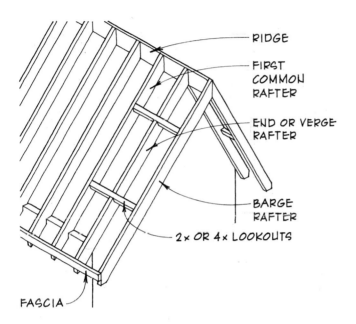

RIDGE

FIRST COMMON RAFTER

END OR VERGE RAFTER

BARGE RAFTER

2× OR 4× LOOKOUTS

FASCIA

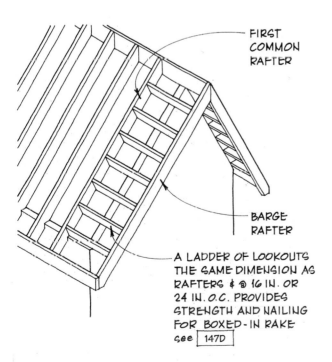

FIRST COMMON RAFTER

BARGE RAFTER

A LADDER OF LOOKOUTS THE SAME DIMENSION AS RAFTERS & @ 16 IN. OR 24 IN. O.C. PROVIDES STRENGTH AND NAILING FOR BOXED-IN RAKE see | 147D |

(A) OVERHANGING RAKE
SUPPORTED BY LOOKOUTS

Brackets attached to the face of the wall framing can support the barge rafter by means of triangulation.

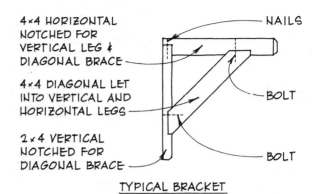

4×4 HORIZONTAL NOTCHED FOR VERTICAL LEG & DIAGONAL BRACE

NAILS

4×4 DIAGONAL LET INTO VERTICAL AND HORIZONTAL LEGS

BOLT

2×4 VERTICAL NOTCHED FOR DIAGONAL BRACE

BOLT

TYPICAL BRACKET

Attaching the bracket to the inside of the barge rafter avoids problems of weathering.

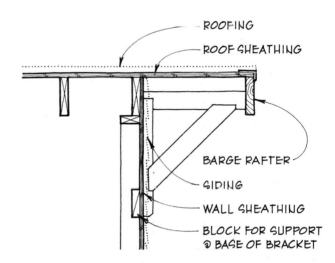

ROOFING

ROOF SHEATHING

BARGE RAFTER

SIDING

WALL SHEATHING

BLOCK FOR SUPPORT @ BASE OF BRACKET

The alternative bracket connection to the barge rafter shown below is common on Craftsman-style buildings. With this detail, moisture collects on top of the bracket, and this contributes to the decay of the bracket and the barge rafter.

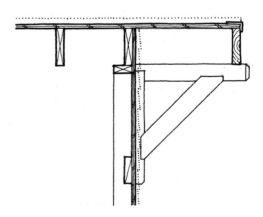

(B) OVERHANGING RAKE
SUPPORTED BY BRACKETS

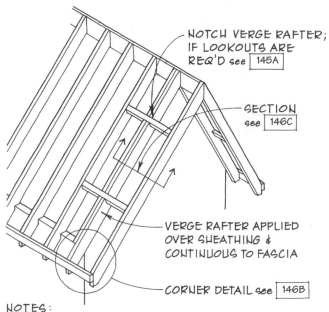

NOTCH VERGE RAFTER; IF LOOKOUTS ARE REQ'D see 145A

SECTION see 146C

VERGE RAFTER APPLIED OVER SHEATHING & CONTINUOUS TO FASCIA

CORNER DETAIL see 146B

NOTES:
ROOF SHEATHING MUST BE EXTERIOR-RATED PANEL OR SOLID (T&G) MATERIAL.
FOR ALTERNATIVE DETAIL W/ TRIM BOARD see 147A, B & C

(A) **EXPOSED RAKE W/ VERGE RAFTER**
FRAMING

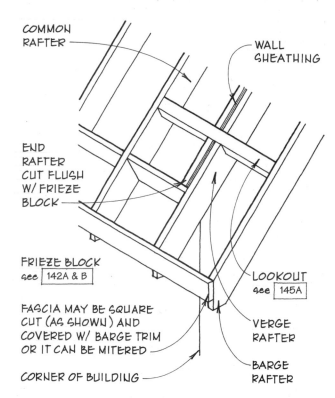

COMMON RAFTER

WALL SHEATHING

END RAFTER CUT FLUSH W/ FRIEZE BLOCK

FRIEZE BLOCK see 142A & B

FASCIA MAY BE SQUARE CUT (AS SHOWN) AND COVERED W/ BARGE TRIM OR IT CAN BE MITERED

CORNER OF BUILDING

LOOKOUT see 145A

VERGE RAFTER

BARGE RAFTER

(B) **EXPOSED RAKE W/ VERGE RAFTER**
CORNER FRAMING

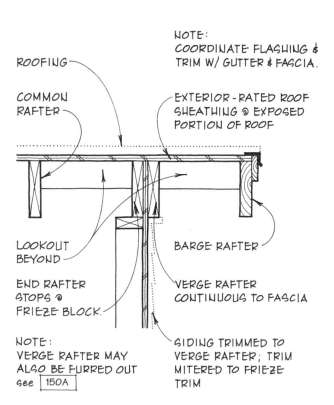

ROOFING

COMMON RAFTER

NOTE:
COORDINATE FLASHING & TRIM W/ GUTTER & FASCIA.

EXTERIOR-RATED ROOF SHEATHING @ EXPOSED PORTION OF ROOF

LOOKOUT BEYOND

END RAFTER STOPS @ FRIEZE BLOCK.

BARGE RAFTER

VERGE RAFTER CONTINUOUS TO FASCIA

SIDING TRIMMED TO VERGE RAFTER; TRIM MITERED TO FRIEZE TRIM

NOTE:
VERGE RAFTER MAY ALSO BE FURRED OUT see 150A

(C) **EXPOSED RAKE W/ VERGE RAFTER**
SECTION

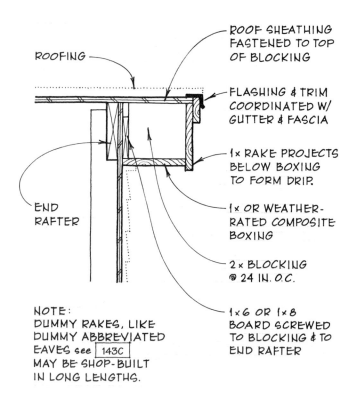

ROOFING

ROOF SHEATHING FASTENED TO TOP OF BLOCKING

FLASHING & TRIM COORDINATED W/ GUTTER & FASCIA

END RAFTER

1x RAKE PROJECTS BELOW BOXING TO FORM DRIP.

1x OR WEATHER-RATED COMPOSITE BOXING

2x BLOCKING @ 24 IN. O.C.

NOTE:
DUMMY RAKES, LIKE DUMMY ABBREVIATED EAVES see 143C MAY BE SHOP-BUILT IN LONG LENGTHS.

1x6 OR 1x8 BOARD SCREWED TO BLOCKING & TO END RAFTER

(D) **DUMMY RAKE**

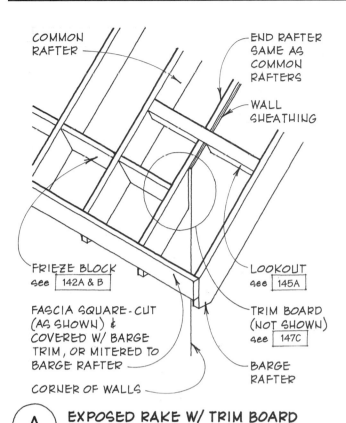

COMMON RAFTER

END RAFTER SAME AS COMMON RAFTERS

WALL SHEATHING

FRIEZE BLOCK
see 142A & B

LOOKOUT
see 145A

FASCIA SQUARE-CUT (AS SHOWN) & COVERED W/ BARGE TRIM, OR MITERED TO BARGE RAFTER

TRIM BOARD (NOT SHOWN)
see 147C

CORNER OF WALLS

BARGE RAFTER

A **EXPOSED RAKE W/ TRIM BOARD**
CORNER FRAMING

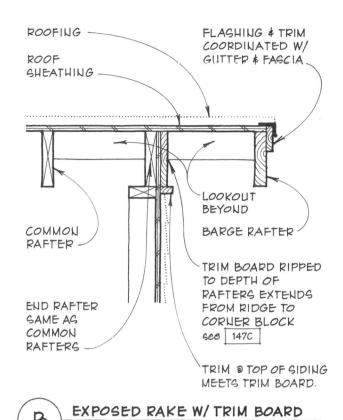

ROOFING

ROOF SHEATHING

FLASHING & TRIM COORDINATED W/ GUTTER & FASCIA

COMMON RAFTER

LOOKOUT BEYOND

BARGE RAFTER

END RAFTER SAME AS COMMON RAFTERS

TRIM BOARD RIPPED TO DEPTH OF RAFTERS EXTENDS FROM RIDGE TO CORNER BLOCK
see 147C

TRIM @ TOP OF SIDING MEETS TRIM BOARD.

B **EXPOSED RAKE W/ TRIM BOARD**
SECTION

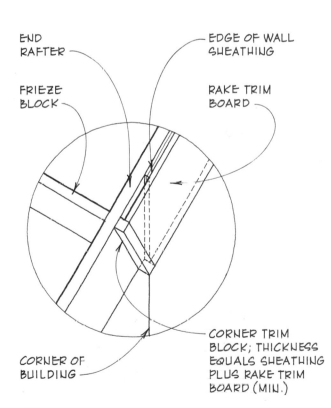

END RAFTER

FRIEZE BLOCK

EDGE OF WALL SHEATHING

RAKE TRIM BOARD

CORNER OF BUILDING

CORNER TRIM BLOCK; THICKNESS EQUALS SHEATHING PLUS RAKE TRIM BOARD (MIN.)

C **EXPOSED RAKE W/ TRIM BOARD**
DETAIL @ EAVE

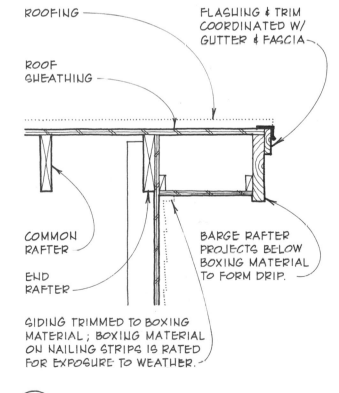

ROOFING

ROOF SHEATHING

FLASHING & TRIM COORDINATED W/ GUTTER & FASCIA

COMMON RAFTER

END RAFTER

BARGE RAFTER PROJECTS BELOW BOXING MATERIAL TO FORM DRIP.

SIDING TRIMMED TO BOXING MATERIAL; BOXING MATERIAL ON NAILING STRIPS IS RATED FOR EXPOSURE TO WEATHER.

D **BOXED-IN RAKE**

The transition from soffited eave to rake can demand some carpentry heroics. Only when the soffit is terminated at the plane of the end wall is the detailing reasonably direct, requiring only that the end of the soffit space be finished. This situation may occur with an abbreviated rake (see below) or with an overhanging rake (see below and 148B). As shown below, the end of the soffit space may be finished with a pork chop or with a layered gable—a continuation of the gable-wall finish over the end of the soffit.

When the soffit extends beyond the plane of the end wall, the rear side of the soffited space (opposite the fascia) must be finished as well as the end. As shown in the drawings below, this may be accomplished most elegantly with a Greek return, or with a simpler soffit return.

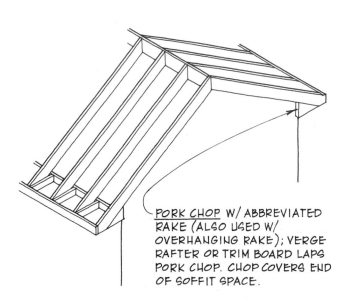

PORK CHOP W/ ABBREVIATED RAKE (ALSO USED W/ OVERHANGING RAKE); VERGE RAFTER OR TRIM BOARD LAPS PORK CHOP. CHOP COVERS END OF SOFFIT SPACE.

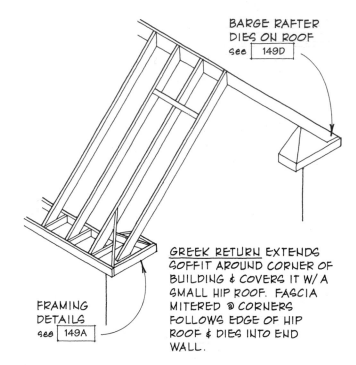

BARGE RAFTER DIES ON ROOF
see 149D

FRAMING DETAILS
see 149A

GREEK RETURN EXTENDS SOFFIT AROUND CORNER OF BUILDING & COVERS IT W/ A SMALL HIP ROOF. FASCIA MITERED @ CORNERS FOLLOWS EDGE OF HIP ROOF & DIES INTO END WALL.

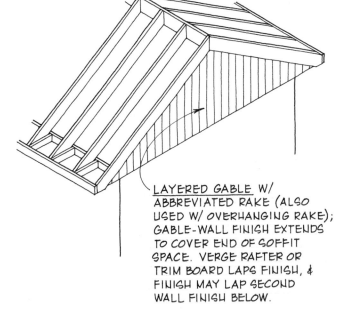

LAYERED GABLE W/ ABBREVIATED RAKE (ALSO USED W/ OVERHANGING RAKE); GABLE-WALL FINISH EXTENDS TO COVER END OF SOFFIT SPACE. VERGE RAFTER OR TRIM BOARD LAPS FINISH, & FINISH MAY LAP SECOND WALL FINISH BELOW.

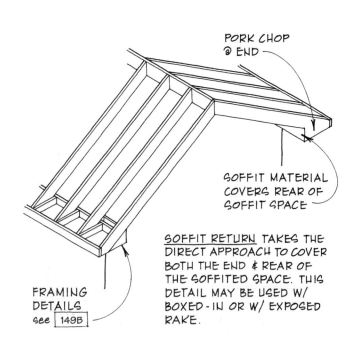

PORK CHOP @ END

SOFFIT MATERIAL COVERS REAR OF SOFFIT SPACE

SOFFIT RETURN TAKES THE DIRECT APPROACH TO COVER BOTH THE END & REAR OF THE SOFFITED SPACE. THIS DETAIL MAY BE USED W/ BOXED-IN OR W/ EXPOSED RAKE.

FRAMING DETAILS
see 149B

(A) SOFFITED EAVE/RAKE TRANSITION
ABBREVIATED OR OVERHANGING RAKE

(B) SOFFITED EAVE/RAKE TRANSITION
OVERHANGING RAKE

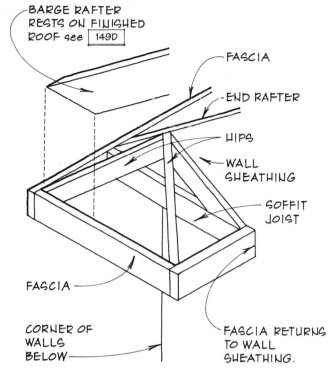

BARGE RAFTER RESTS ON FINISHED ROOF see 149D

FASCIA

END RAFTER

HIPS

WALL SHEATHING

SOFFIT JOIST

FASCIA

CORNER OF WALLS BELOW

FASCIA RETURNS TO WALL SHEATHING.

A GREEK RETURN
FRAMING

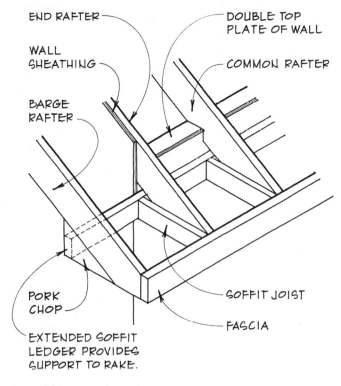

END RAFTER

DOUBLE TOP PLATE OF WALL

WALL SHEATHING

COMMON RAFTER

BARGE RAFTER

PORK CHOP

EXTENDED SOFFIT LEDGER PROVIDES SUPPORT TO RAKE.

SOFFIT JOIST

FASCIA

B SOFFIT RETURN
FRAMING

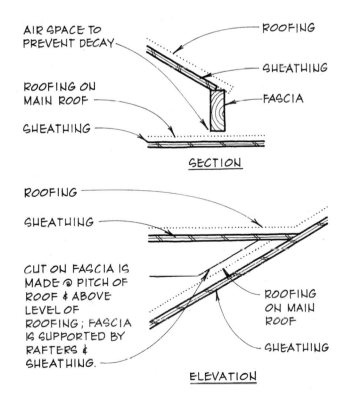

AIR SPACE TO PREVENT DECAY

ROOFING

SHEATHING

FASCIA

ROOFING ON MAIN ROOF

SHEATHING

SECTION

ROOFING

SHEATHING

CUT ON FASCIA IS MADE @ PITCH OF ROOF & ABOVE LEVEL OF ROOFING; FASCIA IS SUPPORTED BY RAFTERS & SHEATHING.

ROOFING ON MAIN ROOF

SHEATHING

ELEVATION

C FASCIA DIES ON ROOF

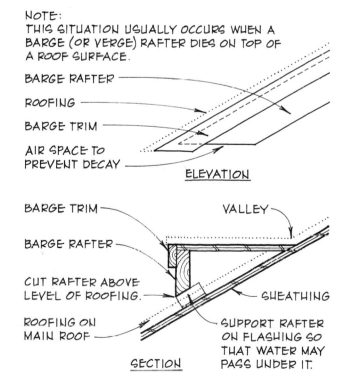

NOTE:
THIS SITUATION USUALLY OCCURS WHEN A BARGE (OR VERGE) RAFTER DIES ON TOP OF A ROOF SURFACE.

BARGE RAFTER

ROOFING

BARGE TRIM

AIR SPACE TO PREVENT DECAY

ELEVATION

BARGE TRIM

VALLEY

BARGE RAFTER

CUT RAFTER ABOVE LEVEL OF ROOFING.

SHEATHING

ROOFING ON MAIN ROOF

SECTION

SUPPORT RAFTER ON FLASHING SO THAT WATER MAY PASS UNDER IT.

D RAFTER DIES ON ROOF

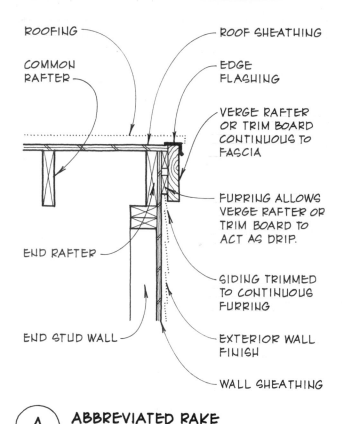

ROOFING

COMMON RAFTER

ROOF SHEATHING

EDGE FLASHING

VERGE RAFTER OR TRIM BOARD CONTINUOUS TO FASCIA

FURRING ALLOWS VERGE RAFTER OR TRIM BOARD TO ACT AS DRIP.

END RAFTER

SIDING TRIMMED TO CONTINUOUS FURRING

END STUD WALL

EXTERIOR WALL FINISH

WALL SHEATHING

A **ABBREVIATED RAKE**

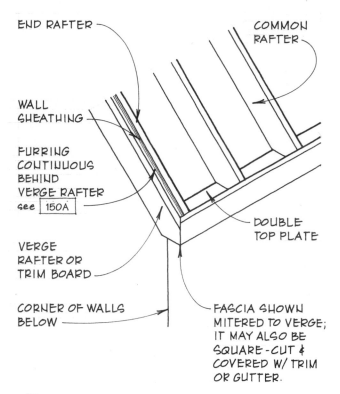

END RAFTER

COMMON RAFTER

WALL SHEATHING

FURRING CONTINUOUS BEHIND VERGE RAFTER
see | 150A |

VERGE RAFTER OR TRIM BOARD

CORNER OF WALLS BELOW

DOUBLE TOP PLATE

FASCIA SHOWN MITERED TO VERGE; IT MAY ALSO BE SQUARE-CUT & COVERED W/ TRIM OR GUTTER.

B **ABBREVIATED RAKE/EAVE**
CORNER FRAMING

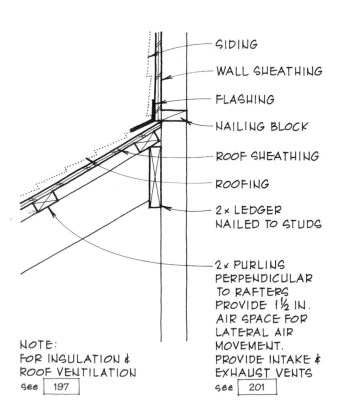

SIDING

WALL SHEATHING

FLASHING

NAILING BLOCK

ROOF SHEATHING

ROOFING

2× LEDGER NAILED TO STUDS

2× PURLINS PERPENDICULAR TO RAFTERS PROVIDE 1½ IN. AIR SPACE FOR LATERAL AIR MOVEMENT. PROVIDE INTAKE & EXHAUST VENTS
see | 201 |

NOTE:
FOR INSULATION & ROOF VENTILATION
see | 197 |

C **TOP OF RAFTER/WALL**
SHED ROOF W/ PURLINS

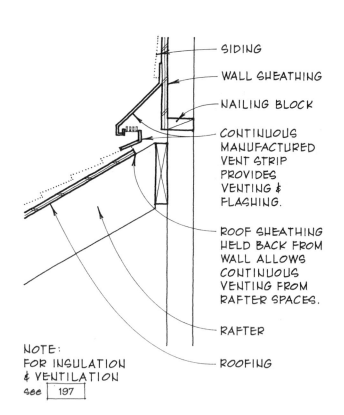

SIDING

WALL SHEATHING

NAILING BLOCK

CONTINUOUS MANUFACTURED VENT STRIP PROVIDES VENTING & FLASHING.

ROOF SHEATHING HELD BACK FROM WALL ALLOWS CONTINUOUS VENTING FROM RAFTER SPACES.

RAFTER

ROOFING

NOTE:
FOR INSULATION & VENTILATION
see | 197 |

D **TOP OF RAFTER/WALL**
SHED ROOF W/ CONTINUOUS VENT STRIP

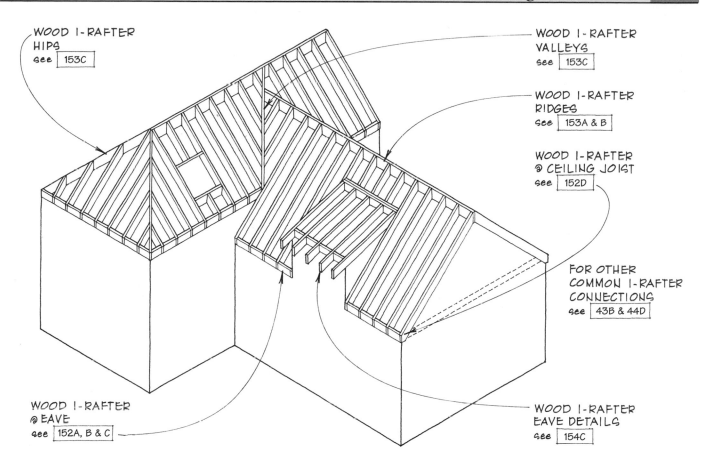

WOOD I-RAFTER
HIPS
see [153C]

WOOD I-RAFTER
VALLEYS
see [153C]

WOOD I-RAFTER
RIDGES
see [153A & B]

WOOD I-RAFTER
@ CEILING JOIST
see [152D]

FOR OTHER
COMMON I-RAFTER
CONNECTIONS
see [43B & 44D]

WOOD I-RAFTER
@ EAVE
see [152A, B & C]

WOOD I-RAFTER
EAVE DETAILS
see [154C]

The light weight, strength, precision manufacturing, and the long lengths that make wood I-joists appropriate for floors (see 43A) also indicate their use for rafters. Called I-rafters when used on the roof, these materials are generally stiffer and stronger and can span farther than dimension-lumber rafters of the same size, but they can also cost more, and their appearance is not satisfactory if exposed.

Wood I-rafters can be attached to each other and to other members with metal straps and hangers, and can be cut on site. They do not have as much strength perpendicular to their length as lumber rafters and must therefore be stiffened at joints and at other conditions required by manufacturers' specifications and local codes. Many builders find the details required of I-rafter connections at hips, valleys, and other locations with compound angles to be more complicated than stick building, so in these locations they are likely to substitute dimension lumber, while using wood I-rafters for simple framing.

Wood I-rafters are manufactured items. To perform as designed, they must be installed completely in accordance with the individual manufacturer's instructions. The general framing principles that apply to dimension-lumber roof framing also hold true for plywood I rafters. The drawings in this section, therefore, emphasize conditions where I-rafters require different detailing from dimension-lumber rafters.

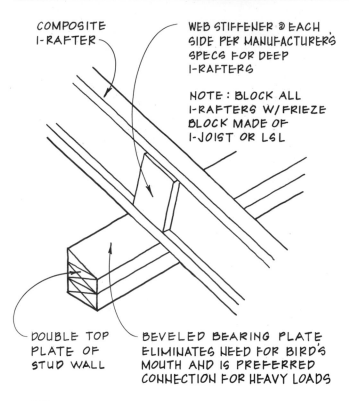

COMPOSITE I-RAFTER

WEB STIFFENER @ EACH SIDE PER MANUFACTURER'S SPECS FOR DEEP I-RAFTERS

NOTE: BLOCK ALL I-RAFTERS W/ FRIEZE BLOCK MADE OF I-JOIST OR LSL

DOUBLE TOP PLATE OF STUD WALL

BEVELED BEARING PLATE ELIMINATES NEED FOR BIRD'S MOUTH AND IS PREFERRED CONNECTION FOR HEAVY LOADS

(A) WOOD I-RAFTER @ EAVE
W/ BEVELED BEARING PLATE

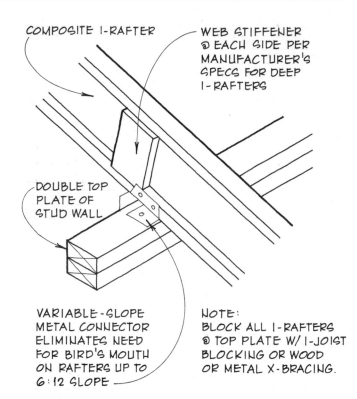

COMPOSITE I-RAFTER

WEB STIFFENER @ EACH SIDE PER MANUFACTURER'S SPECS FOR DEEP I-RAFTERS

DOUBLE TOP PLATE OF STUD WALL

VARIABLE-SLOPE METAL CONNECTOR ELIMINATES NEED FOR BIRD'S MOUTH ON RAFTERS UP TO 6:12 SLOPE

NOTE: BLOCK ALL I-RAFTERS @ TOP PLATE W/ I-JOIST BLOCKING OR WOOD OR METAL X-BRACING.

(B) WOOD I-RAFTER @ EAVE
W/ METAL CONNECTOR

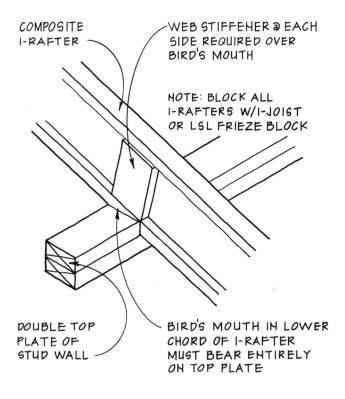

COMPOSITE I-RAFTER

WEB STIFFENER @ EACH SIDE REQUIRED OVER BIRD'S MOUTH

NOTE: BLOCK ALL I-RAFTERS W/ I-JOIST OR LSL FRIEZE BLOCK

DOUBLE TOP PLATE OF STUD WALL

BIRD'S MOUTH IN LOWER CHORD OF I-RAFTER MUST BEAR ENTIRELY ON TOP PLATE

(C) WOOD I-RAFTER @ EAVE
W/ BIRD'S MOUTH

NOTE:
COLLAR TIES, LOCATED HIGHER ON THE RAFTER, ARE CONNECTED IN THE SAME FASHION AS THIS DETAIL.

CEILING JOIST RESISTS OUTWARD THRUST OF RAFTERS
see [130]

WEB STIFFENER @ I-RAFTER PROVIDES NAILING SURFACE FOR CEILING JOISTS.

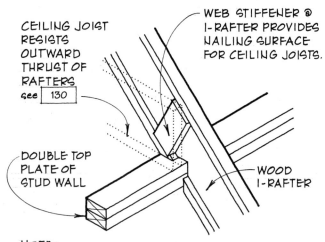

DOUBLE TOP PLATE OF STUD WALL

WOOD I-RAFTER

NOTE:
BLOCK ALL I-RAFTERS @ TOP PLATE W/ I-JOIST BLOCKING OR WOOD OR METAL X-BRACING.

(D) WOOD I-RAFTER/CEILING JOIST

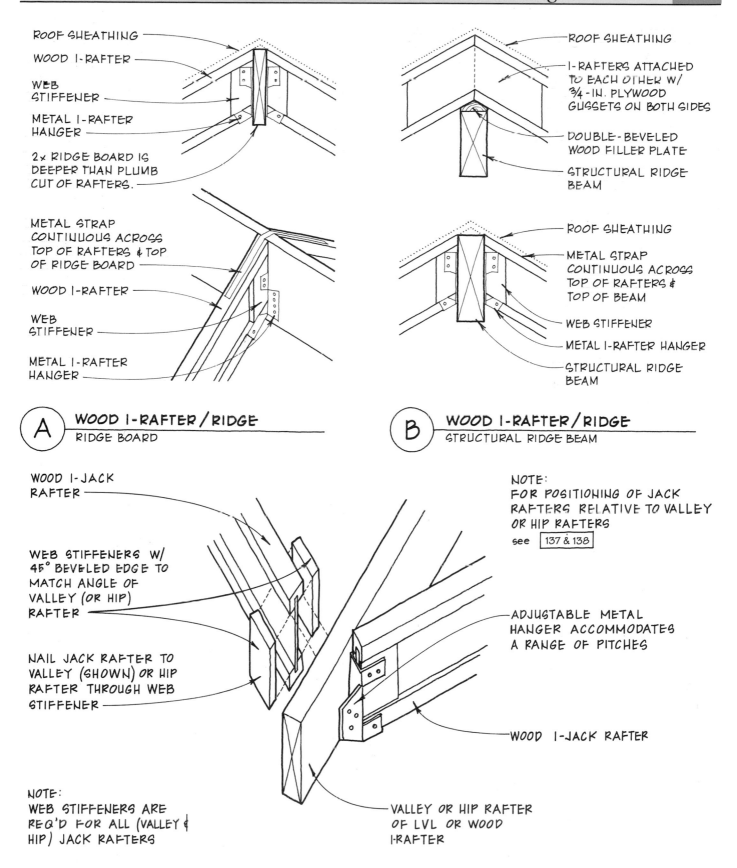

ROOF SHEATHING

WOOD I-RAFTER

WEB STIFFENER

METAL I-RAFTER HANGER

2x RIDGE BOARD IS DEEPER THAN PLUMB CUT OF RAFTERS.

METAL STRAP CONTINUOUS ACROSS TOP OF RAFTERS & TOP OF RIDGE BOARD

WOOD I-RAFTER

WEB STIFFENER

METAL I-RAFTER HANGER

ROOF SHEATHING

I-RAFTERS ATTACHED TO EACH OTHER W/ 3/4-IN. PLYWOOD GUSSETS ON BOTH SIDES

DOUBLE-BEVELED WOOD FILLER PLATE

STRUCTURAL RIDGE BEAM

ROOF SHEATHING

METAL STRAP CONTINUOUS ACROSS TOP OF RAFTERS & TOP OF BEAM

WEB STIFFENER

METAL I-RAFTER HANGER

STRUCTURAL RIDGE BEAM

A WOOD I-RAFTER/RIDGE
RIDGE BOARD

B WOOD I-RAFTER/RIDGE
STRUCTURAL RIDGE BEAM

WOOD I-JACK RAFTER

WEB STIFFENERS W/ 45° BEVELED EDGE TO MATCH ANGLE OF VALLEY (OR HIP) RAFTER

NAIL JACK RAFTER TO VALLEY (SHOWN) OR HIP RAFTER THROUGH WEB STIFFENER

NOTE:
WEB STIFFENERS ARE REQ'D FOR ALL (VALLEY & HIP) JACK RAFTERS

NOTE:
FOR POSITIONING OF JACK RAFTERS RELATIVE TO VALLEY OR HIP RAFTERS

see 137 & 138

ADJUSTABLE METAL HANGER ACCOMMODATES A RANGE OF PITCHES

WOOD I-JACK RAFTER

VALLEY OR HIP RAFTER OF LVL OR WOOD I-RAFTER

C WOOD I-RAFTER/VALLEY OR HIP
CONNECTION OF JACK RAFTERS WITH NAILS OR HANGERS

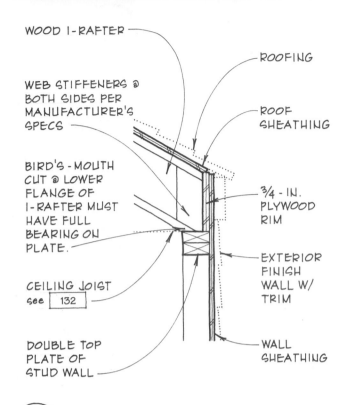

WOOD I-RAFTER

WEB STIFFENERS @ BOTH SIDES PER MANUFACTURER'S SPECS

BIRD'S-MOUTH CUT @ LOWER FLANGE OF I-RAFTER MUST HAVE FULL BEARING ON PLATE.

CEILING JOIST see 132

DOUBLE TOP PLATE OF STUD WALL

ROOFING

ROOF SHEATHING

¾-IN. PLYWOOD RIM

EXTERIOR FINISH WALL W/ TRIM

WALL SHEATHING

(A) WOOD I-RAFTER
ABBREVIATED EAVE

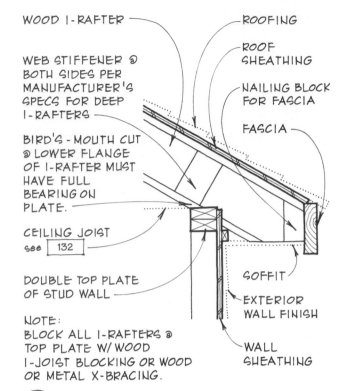

WOOD I-RAFTER

WEB STIFFENER @ BOTH SIDES PER MANUFACTURER'S SPECS FOR DEEP I-RAFTERS

BIRD'S-MOUTH CUT @ LOWER FLANGE OF I-RAFTER MUST HAVE FULL BEARING ON PLATE.

CEILING JOIST see 132

DOUBLE TOP PLATE OF STUD WALL

NOTE:
BLOCK ALL I-RAFTERS @ TOP PLATE W/ WOOD I-JOIST BLOCKING OR WOOD OR METAL X-BRACING.

ROOFING

ROOF SHEATHING

NAILING BLOCK FOR FASCIA

FASCIA

SOFFIT

EXTERIOR WALL FINISH

WALL SHEATHING

(B) WOOD I-RAFTER
SOFFITED EAVE

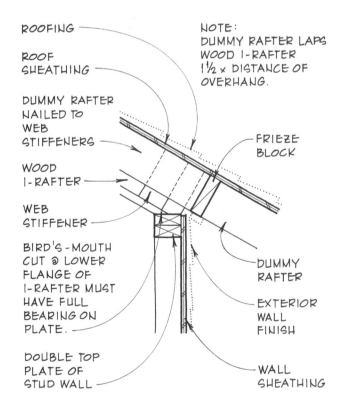

ROOFING

ROOF SHEATHING

DUMMY RAFTER NAILED TO WEB STIFFENERS

WOOD I-RAFTER

WEB STIFFENER

BIRD'S-MOUTH CUT @ LOWER FLANGE OF I-RAFTER MUST HAVE FULL BEARING ON PLATE.

DOUBLE TOP PLATE OF STUD WALL

NOTE:
DUMMY RAFTER LAPS WOOD I-RAFTER 1½ × DISTANCE OF OVERHANG.

FRIEZE BLOCK

DUMMY RAFTER

EXTERIOR WALL FINISH

WALL SHEATHING

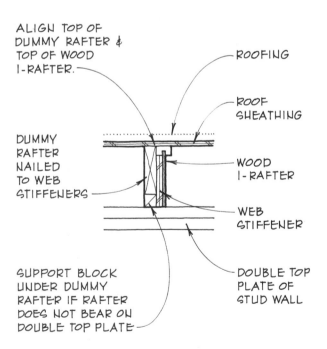

ALIGN TOP OF DUMMY RAFTER & TOP OF WOOD I-RAFTER.

DUMMY RAFTER NAILED TO WEB STIFFENERS

SUPPORT BLOCK UNDER DUMMY RAFTER IF RAFTER DOES NOT BEAR ON DOUBLE TOP PLATE

ROOFING

ROOF SHEATHING

WOOD I-RAFTER

WEB STIFFENER

DOUBLE TOP PLATE OF STUD WALL

SECTION PARALLEL TO EAVE

(C) WOOD I-RAFTER @ EXPOSED EAVE
EXPOSED DUMMY RAFTER

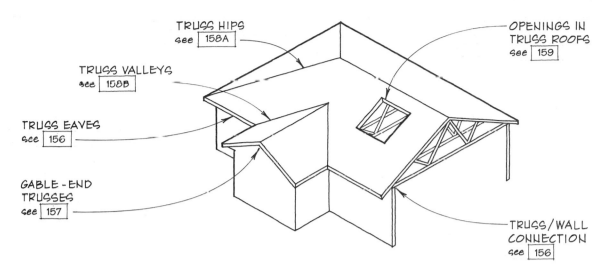

TRUSS HIPS
see 158A

OPENINGS IN
TRUSS ROOFS
see 159

TRUSS VALLEYS
see 158B

TRUSS EAVES
see 156

GABLE - END
TRUSSES
see 157

TRUSS / WALL
CONNECTION
see 156

Roof trusses, like floor trusses, are a framework of small members (usually 2x4s) that are connected so that they act like a single large member. They are always engineered by the manufacturer.

Engineered roof trusses can span much greater distances than the stick-framed rafter-and-tie system. Long spans (over 40 ft.) are possible with simple trusses so that large open rooms may be designed with roof loads bearing only on the perimeter walls. Interior walls may simply be partition walls and may be repositioned without compromising the roof structure.

A second advantage of roof trusses is the reduction in roof framing labor. Trusses are typically set in place by the delivery truck and may be positioned and

fastened in a fraction of the time it would take to frame with rafters and ties.

One major disadvantage of roof trusses is the difficulty of adapting them to complex roof forms. Roofs with numerous hips, valleys, or dormers are usually less expensive to build if they are framed with rafters.

Another disadvantage of roof trusses is that the webs of the truss occupy space that could be available for storage or as a full-size attic. Furthermore, these webs cannot be cut for any future remodeling purposes.

Five common roof truss types are shown in the drawings below.

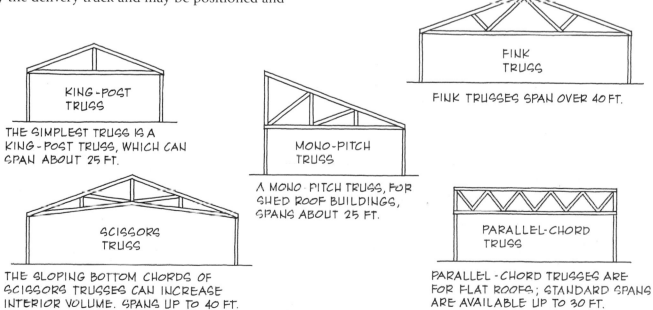

KING-POST
TRUSS

THE SIMPLEST TRUSS IS A KING-POST TRUSS, WHICH CAN SPAN ABOUT 25 FT.

SCISSORS
TRUSS

THE SLOPING BOTTOM CHORDS OF SCISSORS TRUSSES CAN INCREASE INTERIOR VOLUME. SPANS UP TO 40 FT. ARE POSSIBLE.

MONO-PITCH
TRUSS

A MONO-PITCH TRUSS, FOR SHED ROOF BUILDINGS, SPANS ABOUT 25 FT.

FINK
TRUSS

FINK TRUSSES SPAN OVER 40 FT.

PARALLEL-CHORD
TRUSS

PARALLEL-CHORD TRUSSES ARE FOR FLAT ROOFS; STANDARD SPANS ARE AVAILABLE UP TO 30 FT.

(A) **ROOF TRUSSES**
INTRODUCTION

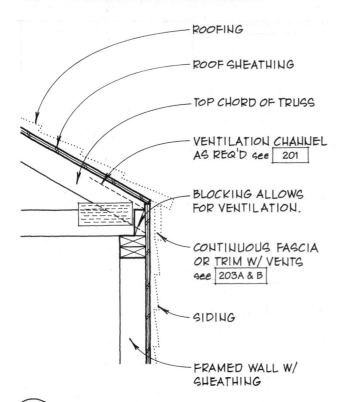

ROOFING
ROOF SHEATHING
TOP CHORD OF TRUSS
VENTILATION CHANNEL AS REQ'D see [201]
BLOCKING ALLOWS FOR VENTILATION.
CONTINUOUS FASCIA OR TRIM W/ VENTS see [203A & B]
SIDING
FRAMED WALL W/ SHEATHING

A   TRUSS W/ ABBREVIATED EAVE

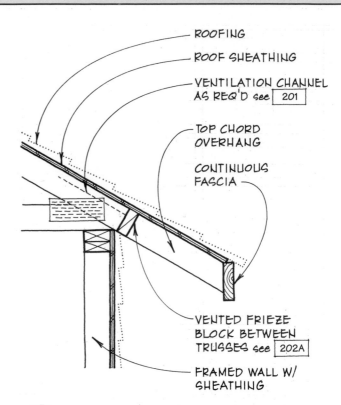

ROOFING
ROOF SHEATHING
VENTILATION CHANNEL AS REQ'D see [201]
TOP CHORD OVERHANG
CONTINUOUS FASCIA
VENTED FRIEZE BLOCK BETWEEN TRUSSES see [202A]
FRAMED WALL W/ SHEATHING

B   TRUSS W/ OVERHANGING EAVE
EXPOSED OR BOXED-IN EAVE

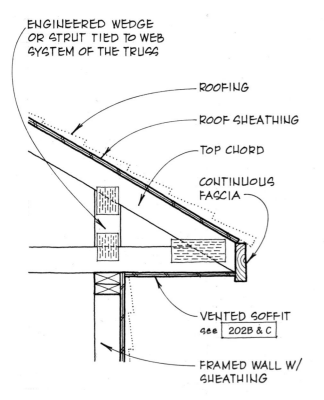

ENGINEERED WEDGE OR STRUT TIED TO WEB SYSTEM OF THE TRUSS
ROOFING
ROOF SHEATHING
TOP CHORD
CONTINUOUS FASCIA
VENTED SOFFIT see [202B & C]
FRAMED WALL W/ SHEATHING

C   TRUSS W/ SOFFITED EAVE
CANTILEVERED TRUSS

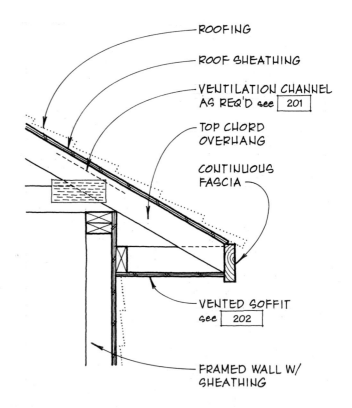

ROOFING
ROOF SHEATHING
VENTILATION CHANNEL AS REQ'D see [201]
TOP CHORD OVERHANG
CONTINUOUS FASCIA
VENTED SOFFIT see [202]
FRAMED WALL W/ SHEATHING

D   TRUSS W/ SOFFITED EAVE
OVERHANGING TRUSS

A gable-end truss transfers the load of the roof to the wall on which it bears through 2x4 struts at 24 in. o.c. The standard gable-end truss is the same size as a standard truss. A gable-end truss can be used with a rake overhang of 12 in. or less when the barge rafter is supported by the roof sheathing. It can also be used with flat 2x4 lookouts let into the truss above the struts. A dropped gable-end truss (see 157B) is shorter than a standard truss by the depth of the lookouts.

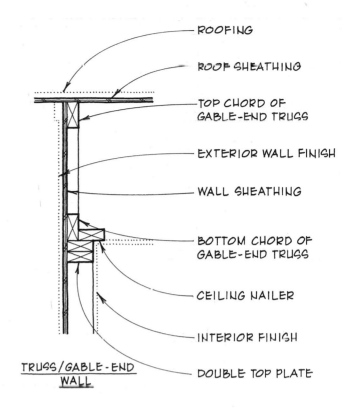

ROOFING

ROOF SHEATHING

TOP CHORD OF GABLE-END TRUSS

EXTERIOR WALL FINISH

WALL SHEATHING

BOTTOM CHORD OF GABLE-END TRUSS

CEILING NAILER

INTERIOR FINISH

DOUBLE TOP PLATE

TRUSS/GABLE-END WALL

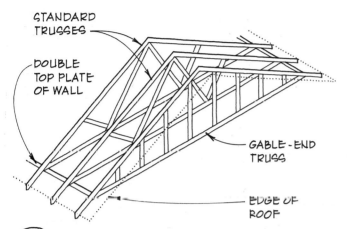

STANDARD TRUSSES

DOUBLE TOP PLATE OF WALL

GABLE-END TRUSS

EDGE OF ROOF

(A) STANDARD GABLE-END TRUSS

NOTE:
A DROPPED GABLE-END TRUSS IS SHORTER THAN A STANDARD TRUSS BY THE DEPTH OF THE LOOKOUTS.

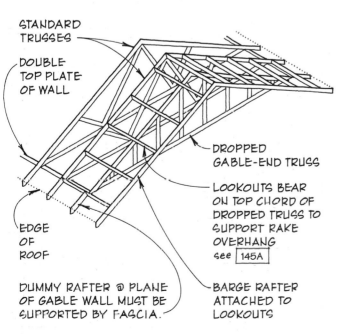

STANDARD TRUSSES

DOUBLE TOP PLATE OF WALL

EDGE OF ROOF

DUMMY RAFTER @ PLANE OF GABLE WALL MUST BE SUPPORTED BY FASCIA.

DROPPED GABLE-END TRUSS

LOOKOUTS BEAR ON TOP CHORD OF DROPPED TRUSS TO SUPPORT RAKE OVERHANG
see 145A

BARGE RAFTER ATTACHED TO LOOKOUTS

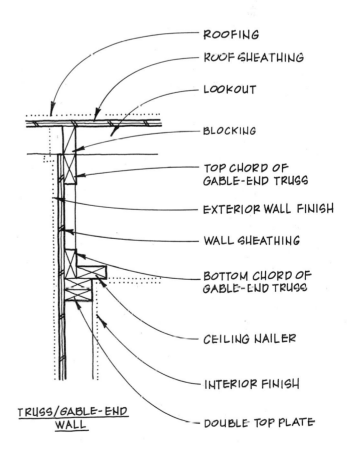

ROOFING

ROOF SHEATHING

LOOKOUT

BLOCKING

TOP CHORD OF GABLE-END TRUSS

EXTERIOR WALL FINISH

WALL SHEATHING

BOTTOM CHORD OF GABLE-END TRUSS

CEILING NAILER

INTERIOR FINISH

DOUBLE TOP PLATE

TRUSS/GABLE-END WALL

(B) DROPPED GABLE-END TRUSS

There are several ways to frame a hip roof using trusses. None is simple, so many builders elect to frame hips (even on a truss roof) with rafters (see 138).

The most common method of framing a hip with trusses is called the step-down system. A series of progressively shallower trusses with flat tops is used to create the end roof pitch of the hip roof. The last of these trusses is the girder truss, which carries the weight of short jack trusses or rafters that complete the roof.

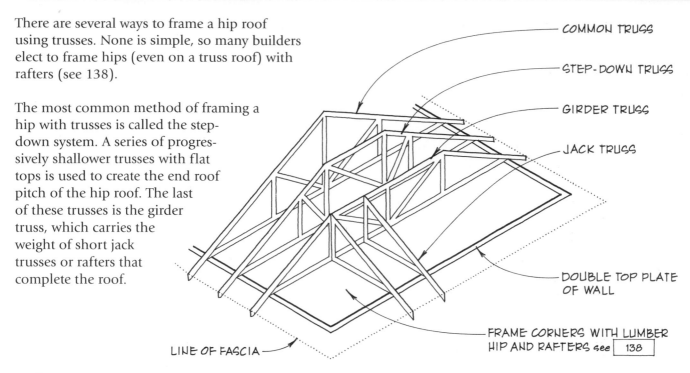

COMMON TRUSS

STEP-DOWN TRUSS

GIRDER TRUSS

JACK TRUSS

DOUBLE TOP PLATE OF WALL

FRAME CORNERS WITH LUMBER HIP AND RAFTERS see | 138 |

LINE OF FASCIA

 A **HIP FRAMING WITH TRUSSES**
STEP-DOWN SYSTEM

Framing a valley with trusses is a simple matter of attaching a series of progressively smaller trusses to the top chords of the trusses of the main roof. The main-roof trusses do not have to be oversize since the only extra weight they will carry is the dead weight of the jack trusses themselves. Simple as this system is, many builders still prefer to frame these roof intersections as a farmer's valley (see 137) with dimension lumber.

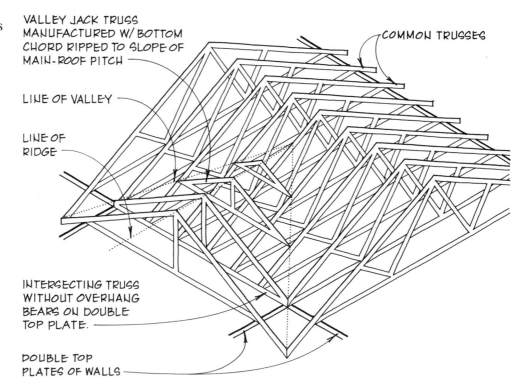

VALLEY JACK TRUSS MANUFACTURED W/ BOTTOM CHORD RIPPED TO SLOPE OF MAIN-ROOF PITCH

LINE OF VALLEY

LINE OF RIDGE

COMMON TRUSSES

INTERSECTING TRUSS WITHOUT OVERHANG BEARS ON DOUBLE TOP PLATE.

DOUBLE TOP PLATES OF WALLS

B **VALLEY FRAMING WITH TRUSSES**
VALLEY JACK TRUSSES

Rectangular openings for skylights or chimneys may be constructed in a truss roof. Small openings less than one truss space wide may be simply framed between trusses as they would be in a rafter-framed roof (see 135 136). Openings up to three truss spaces wide are made by doubling the trusses to either side of the opening and attaching header and mono or other special trusses to the doubled trusses. Larger openings (more than three truss spaces wide) require specially engineered trusses in place of the doubled trusses. Obviously, it is most efficient if the width and placement of the opening correspond to truss spacing.

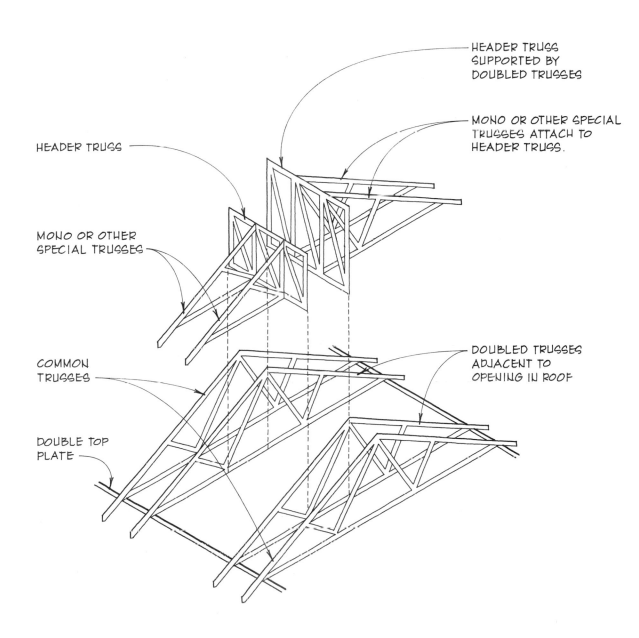

HEADER TRUSS SUPPORTED BY DOUBLED TRUSSES

MONO OR OTHER SPECIAL TRUSSES ATTACH TO HEADER TRUSS.

HEADER TRUSS

MONO OR OTHER SPECIAL TRUSSES

COMMON TRUSSES

DOUBLE TOP PLATE

DOUBLED TRUSSES ADJACENT TO OPENING IN ROOF

A OPENINGS IN TRUSS ROOF
HEADERS BETWEEN DOUBLE TRUSSES

Because roofs are the highest part of a building and are the least weighted down by other parts of the building, they are the most vulnerable to the effects of wind. In areas prone to high winds, the design and detailing of roofs is one of the most critical concerns for the longevity of a building. The bracing of buildings to resist lateral wind forces is discussed in Chapter 3 (see 77 & 82).

Wind generally moves horizontally to impose lateral forces on buildings, much as earthquakes do. But wind flows in complex shifting patterns around a building, creating pressures on some surfaces and suction on others. Thus it can create vertical forces that actually lift the roof off a building.

These vertical forces can be created in three ways. First, they may be produced as a negative pressure (suction) if developed on the leeward side of a building. In the case of a pitched roof, this condition theoretically occurs whenever the pitch of the roof is 7-in-12 or more.

A second way for wind to exert a vertical force on a roof is for the wind to catch a protrusion such as an eave or rake over-

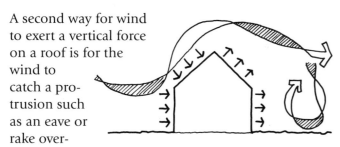

hang. In this case, the force of the wind is localized at the edge of the roof.

Finally, wind can lift the roof structure from the inside of the building. This generally occurs as a weak point in the shell of the building such as a window or garage door giving way to the pressure of the wind. The wind suddenly enters the structure, pressurizing it and forcing the roof up.

To resist the force of high winds on roofs, several strategies may be employed. Some involve design decisions to minimize the impact of high winds in the first place, others involve strengthening what is built to minimize damage.

Design strategies—One basic strategy to increase a roof's chance of survival in high winds is to keep the roof pitch low. High-pitch roofs extend higher into the sky, where wind velocity is greater, and present a greater surface area than do low-pitched roofs. Pitches between 2:12 and 7:12 are recommended for high-wind areas.

The shape of the roof also has a large impact on its durability in a windstorm. Generally, hip roofs fare the best because their geometry makes them self-bracing, and they have low eaves with no tall walls. Gable roofs present a weak point at the gable end itself, which is a tall vertical surface.

The width of overhangs at both eave and rake are important considerations for high-wind zones. Many buildings have been destroyed by winds that catch the underside of the eave and lift it off the building. Eaves of 8 in. or less are recommended for high-wind areas unless special measures are taken to anchor them.

Anchoring strategies—Assuming the building is shaped appropriately to withstand the force of high wind, it is still necessary to reinforce it beyond typical code standards. Framing members must be anchored to resist uplift and overturning, sheathing must be stronger, and fasteners must be increased. These measures are illustrated on the following page.

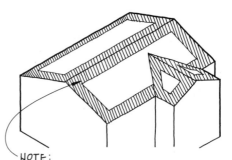

NOTE:
AREAS WITHIN 4 FT. OF ROOF EDGES
REQUIRE MORE NAILS IN HIGH WIND ZONES

 ROOF FRAMING FOR HIGH WIND

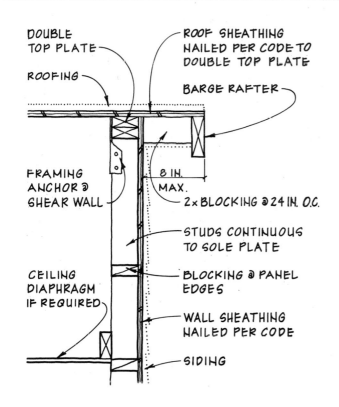

DOUBLE TOP PLATE

ROOFING

ROOF SHEATHING NAILED PER CODE TO DOUBLE TOP PLATE

BARGE RAFTER

FRAMING ANCHOR @ SHEAR WALL

8 IN. MAX.

2× BLOCKING @ 24 IN. O.C.

STUDS CONTINUOUS TO SOLE PLATE

CEILING DIAPHRAGM IF REQUIRED

BLOCKING @ PANEL EDGES

WALL SHEATHING NAILED PER CODE

SIDING

A HIGH WIND RAKE
BALLOON FRAME

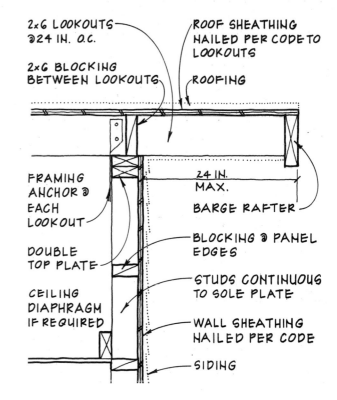

2×6 LOOKOUTS @ 24 IN. O.C.

2×6 BLOCKING BETWEEN LOOKOUTS

ROOF SHEATHING NAILED PER CODE TO LOOKOUTS

ROOFING

FRAMING ANCHOR @ EACH LOOKOUT

24 IN. MAX.

BARGE RAFTER

DOUBLE TOP PLATE

BLOCKING @ PANEL EDGES

STUDS CONTINUOUS TO SOLE PLATE

CEILING DIAPHRAGM IF REQUIRED

WALL SHEATHING NAILED PER CODE

SIDING

B HIGH WIND RAKE
BALLOON FRAME W/ LOOKOUTS

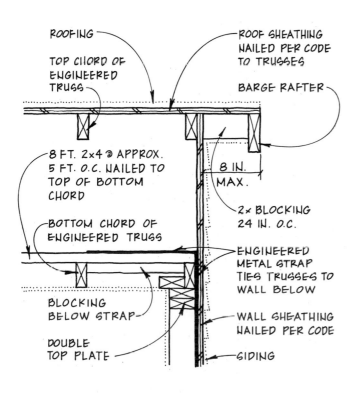

ROOFING

TOP CHORD OF ENGINEERED TRUSS

ROOF SHEATHING NAILED PER CODE TO TRUSSES

BARGE RAFTER

8 FT. 2×4 @ APPROX. 5 FT. O.C. NAILED TO TOP OF BOTTOM CHORD

8 IN. MAX.

2× BLOCKING 24 IN. O.C.

BOTTOM CHORD OF ENGINEERED TRUSS

ENGINEERED METAL STRAP TIES TRUSSES TO WALL BELOW

BLOCKING BELOW STRAP

WALL SHEATHING NAILED PER CODE

DOUBLE TOP PLATE

SIDING

C HIGH WIND RAKE
PLATFORM FRAME

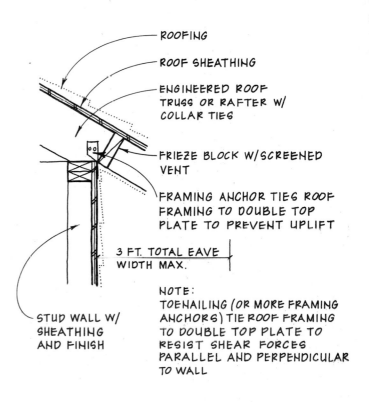

ROOFING

ROOF SHEATHING

ENGINEERED ROOF TRUSS OR RAFTER W/ COLLAR TIES

FRIEZE BLOCK W/ SCREENED VENT

FRAMING ANCHOR TIES ROOF FRAMING TO DOUBLE TOP PLATE TO PREVENT UPLIFT

3 FT. TOTAL EAVE WIDTH MAX.

NOTE:
TOENAILING (OR MORE FRAMING ANCHORS) TIE ROOF FRAMING TO DOUBLE TOP PLATE TO RESIST SHEAR FORCES PARALLEL AND PERPENDICULAR TO WALL

STUD WALL W/ SHEATHING AND FINISH

D HIGH WIND EAVE

Roof sheathing attaches to the surface of the rafters or trusses to form the structural skin of the roof. It spans the rafters to support the roofing and, in the case of panel sheathing such as plywood, it acts with the walls to resist horizontal loads. Roof-sheathing material must be coordinated with the roofing itself, since each type of roofing has special requirements.

The two basic types of sheathing are solid sheathing and open sheathing.

Solid sheathing—Solid sheathing provides a continuous surface at the plane of the roof. This type of sheathing is necessary for composition roofing and built-up roofing, which have no structural capacity themselves. Metal, tile, and shingle roofing may also be applied to solid sheathing. For economic and structural (lateral-load) reasons, solid sheathing is almost always plywood, OSB, or other structural panels (see 163). The structural panels act as a diaphragm to transfer lateral loads at the plane of the roof to the walls. When an exposed ceiling or roof overhang is desired, solid sheathing may also be constructed of solid-wood tongue-and-groove boards (see 164). Tongue-and-groove sheathing, however, does not act as a diaphragm, so other methods of providing lateral-load stability, such as diagonal bracing, must be employed (see 164).

Open sheathing—Open sheathing, also called skip sheathing, is composed of boards spaced apart (see 166). This type of roof sheathing is used under wood shingles and shakes, which usually require ventilation on both sides of the roofing material. Open sheathing may also be chosen for economic reasons, but only if used with roofing systems such as metal or tile, which have the structural capacity to span between sheathing boards. Alternative methods of providing a roof diaphragm, such as diagonal bracing (see 77), must be used with open sheathing.

Combinations, of course, are also possible and often appropriate. For example, solid sheathing at exposed overhangs is often combined with open sheathing on the rest of the roof.

Recommendations—Sheathing recommendations for roofs by roofing types are as follows:

Composition and built-up roofing must be applied to solid sheathing because these roofing materials do not have the structural capacity to span between the boards of open sheathing.

Wood shingle and shake roofing is best applied over open sheathing because the spacing between the open sheathing allows the roofing to breathe from both sides, prolonging its life. Shingle and shake roofs may also be applied to solid sheathing at exposed eaves and rakes and similar locations. In some regions, the common practice is to place an air barrier over open sheathing to keep out wind-driven rain. Consult with local codes and builders for the accepted practice.

Metal and tile roofing may be applied to either solid or open sheathing. Both materials have the structural strength to span across open sheathing, but there is no advantage for either in having them breathe from both sides.

A ROOF SHEATHING
INTRODUCTION

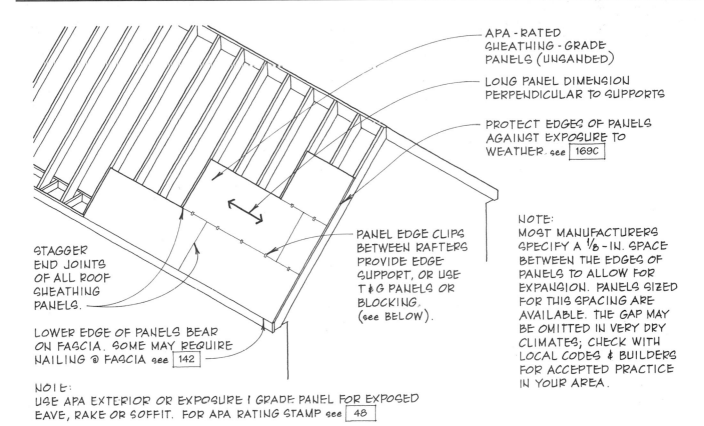

APA - RATED
SHEATHING - GRADE
PANELS (UNSANDED)

LONG PANEL DIMENSION
PERPENDICULAR TO SUPPORTS

PROTECT EDGES OF PANELS
AGAINST EXPOSURE TO
WEATHER. see 169C

NOTE:
MOST MANUFACTURERS
SPECIFY A 1/8-IN. SPACE
BETWEEN THE EDGES OF
PANELS TO ALLOW FOR
EXPANSION. PANELS SIZED
FOR THIS SPACING ARE
AVAILABLE. THE GAP MAY
BE OMITTED IN VERY DRY
CLIMATES; CHECK WITH
LOCAL CODES & BUILDERS
FOR ACCEPTED PRACTICE
IN YOUR AREA.

PANEL EDGE CLIPS
BETWEEN RAFTERS
PROVIDE EDGE
SUPPORT, OR USE
T & G PANELS OR
BLOCKING.
(see BELOW).

STAGGER
END JOINTS
OF ALL ROOF
SHEATHING
PANELS.

LOWER EDGE OF PANELS BEAR
ON FASCIA. SOME MAY REQUIRE
NAILING @ FASCIA see 142

NOTE:
USE APA EXTERIOR OR EXPOSURE I GRADE PANEL FOR EXPOSED
EAVE, RAKE OR SOFFIT. FOR APA RATING STAMP see 48

Panel installation—Low cost and ease of installation make plywood or OSB panels the sheathing of choice for most modern roofs. The system provides a structural diaphragm and is appropriate for all but wood shingle or shake roofing, which requires ventilation. The standard panel size is 4 ft. by 8 ft., so rafter or truss spacing that falls on these modules is most practical. Care must be taken to protect panel edges from the weather by the use of trim or edge flashing (see 169C). Sheathing at exposed overhangs must be exterior or exposure 1–rated panels and must be thick enough to hold a nail or other roof fastener without penetration of the exposed underside.

Recommended fastening—Recommended fastening is 6 in. o.c. at edges and 12 in. o.c. in the field (6 in. in the field for supports at 48 in. o.c.). For sheathing spans greater than 24 in., tongue-and-groove edges, lumber blocking, or panel edge clips are required at edges between supports; use two clips for supports at 48 in. o.c.

Roof-sheathing spans		
APA rating	Thickness	Maximum span
12 / 0	5/16 in.	12 in.
16 / 0	5/16 in. to 3/8 in.	16 in.
24 / 0	3/8 in. to 1/2 in.	24 in.
32 / 16	15/32 in. to 5/8 in.	32 in.
48 / 24	23/32 in. to 7/8 in.	48 in.

Notes—Values in the table above are based on APA-rated panels continuous over two or more spans with the long dimension of the panel perpendicular to supports. Verify span with panel rating. (For the APA rating stamp, see 48.)

Spans are based on a 30-lb. live load and 10-lb. dead load, the minimum rated by the APA-The Engineered Wood Association. Check local codes and with design professionals for higher loading such as greater snow loads or higher dead loads of concrete tiles or other heavy roofing. These ratings are minimum. For a more solid roof, reduce spans or increase thickness.

(A) SOLID ROOF SHEATHING
PLYWOOD & NON-VENEERED PANELS

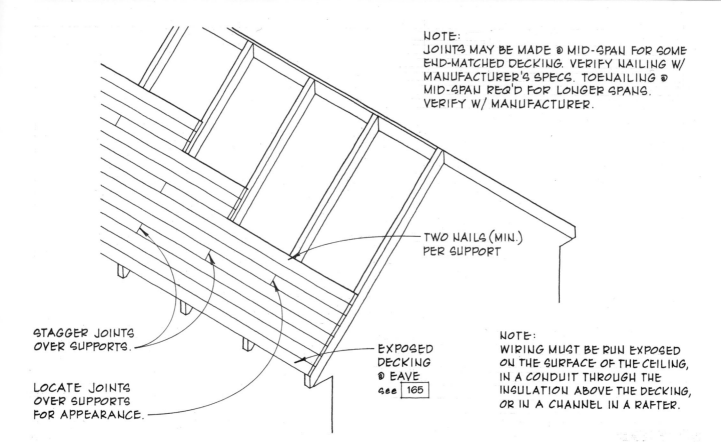

NOTE:
JOINTS MAY BE MADE @ MID-SPAN FOR SOME END-MATCHED DECKING. VERIFY NAILING W/ MANUFACTURER'S SPECS. TOENAILING @ MID-SPAN REQ'D FOR LONGER SPANS. VERIFY W/ MANUFACTURER.

TWO NAILS (MIN.) PER SUPPORT

STAGGER JOINTS OVER SUPPORTS.

LOCATE JOINTS OVER SUPPORTS FOR APPEARANCE.

EXPOSED DECKING @ EAVE see [165]

NOTE:
WIRING MUST BE RUN EXPOSED ON THE SURFACE OF THE CEILING, IN A CONDUIT THROUGH THE INSULATION ABOVE THE DECKING, OR IN A CHANNEL IN A RAFTER.

T&G sheathing (decking) is most often used for exposed ceiling applications. It can also be used selectively at exposed eaves or overhanging rakes. Rafters are spaced at wide centers since the decking will span more than 24 in. in most cases (see the table at right). Since this sheathing material does not provide a diaphragm at the plane of the roof, other means of bracing the roof against horizontal loads must usually be employed. For example, the roof may be braced with metal straps applied to the top of the sheathing or with a thin layer of plywood.

Insulation for an exposed ceiling must be located above the sheathing. Insulation will vary with climate and with roofing material. Rigid insulation is usually the most practical because of its thin profile, but is more expensive than batt insulation. Batts are often chosen for colder climates, where the thickness of either type of insulation (rigid or batts) requires adding a second level of structure above the decking to support the roof.

Exposed T&G decking spans	
Nominal thickness	**Approximate span**
2 in.	6.0 ft.
3 in.	10.5 ft.
4 in.	13.5 ft.
5 in.	17.0 ft.

This table assumes a 30-lb. live load for Douglas-fir or southern pine species. The table is for comparison and approximating purposes only. The actual span capacity depends on roof pitch, species, live-load values, and end-joint pattern.

Ⓐ **SOLID ROOF SHEATHING**
EXPOSED T&G DECKING

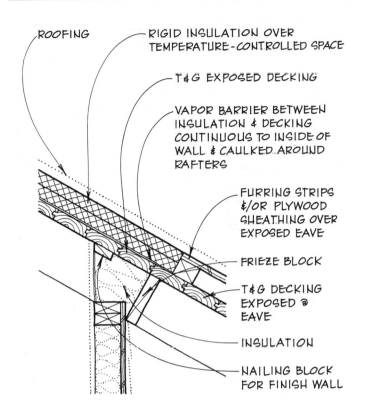

ROOFING
RIGID INSULATION OVER TEMPERATURE-CONTROLLED SPACE
T&G EXPOSED DECKING
VAPOR BARRIER BETWEEN INSULATION & DECKING CONTINUOUS TO INSIDE OF WALL & CAULKED AROUND RAFTERS
FURRING STRIPS &/OR PLYWOOD SHEATHING OVER EXPOSED EAVE
FRIEZE BLOCK
T&G DECKING EXPOSED @ EAVE
INSULATION
NAILING BLOCK FOR FINISH WALL

ROOFING
FURRING OVER RIGID INSULATION NAILED TO DECKING
RIGID INSULATION OVER TEMPERATURE-CONTROLLED SPACE
T&G EXPOSED DECKING
VAPOR BARRIER BETWEEN INSULATION & DECKING CONTINUOUS TO INSIDE OF WALL & CAULKED AROUND RAFTERS
FURRING STRIPS OVER EAVE @ SAME SPACING AS FURRING OVER INSULATION
T&G DECKING EXPOSED @ EAVE
INSULATION
FRIEZE BLOCK
NAILING BLOCK FOR FINISH WALL

Metal or composition roofing may be applied directly over rigid insulation on T&G sheathing. For this construction, fasteners must be sized to penetrate through the insulation but not through the decking.

Preformed metal roofing—Preformed metal roofing may be applied directly to the insulation over a layer of 15-lb. or 30-lb. felt. If the insulation is more than 3½ in. thick, wooden nailers equal to the thickness of the insulation and parallel to the decking are recommended to provide a stable surface for roof fasteners. Nailers should be located 3 ft. to 5 ft. o.c., depending on the profile of the metal roofing.

Composition roofing—Composition roofing may also be applied directly if the insulation board is strong enough to withstand the rigors of the roofing process. Most asphalt-shingle manufacturers, however, will not honor their warranty unless the shingles are applied to a ventilated roof. Unventilated shingles can get too hot and deteriorate prematurely. The addition of vertical furring strips and sheathing over the insulation with vents at the top and bottom of the assembly will satisfy the requirement for ventilation.

Wood or tile roofing requires another layer of material over the insulation. In some cases, it may be more economical to substitute nonrigid insulation.

Wood shingles or shakes—Wood shingles and shakes last longer it they are allowed to breathe from both sides, so they should be raised on furring strips above the level of the insulation. The furring strips may be nailed through the rigid insulation to the decking, or they may be attached directly to the decking between rows of insulation. The spaces and cracks between the shakes or shingles will usually provide adequate ventilation.

Ceramic or concrete tiles—Ceramic and concrete tiles, like shingles, commonly require furring strips. The furring strips should be spaced according to the length of the tiles (see 187B, 188, and 189).

A EXPOSED T&G DECKING @ EAVE
METAL OR COMPOSITION ROOF

B EXPOSED T&G DECKING @ EAVE
WOOD OR TILE ROOF

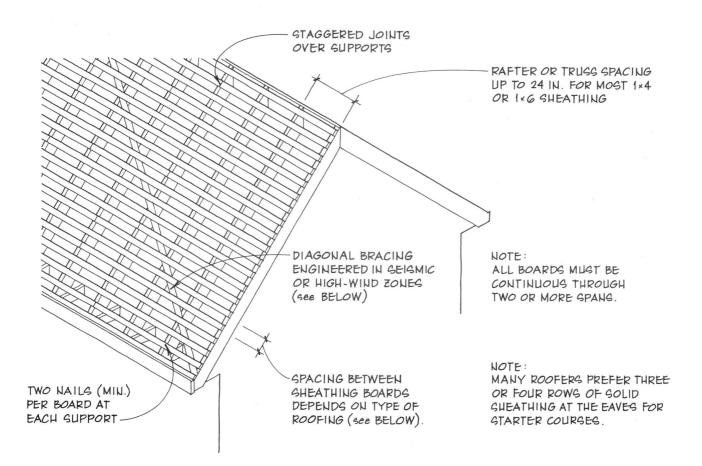

STAGGERED JOINTS OVER SUPPORTS

RAFTER OR TRUSS SPACING UP TO 24 IN. FOR MOST 1×4 OR 1×6 SHEATHING

DIAGONAL BRACING ENGINEERED IN SEISMIC OR HIGH-WIND ZONES (see BELOW)

NOTE: ALL BOARDS MUST BE CONTINUOUS THROUGH TWO OR MORE SPANS.

TWO NAILS (MIN.) PER BOARD AT EACH SUPPORT

SPACING BETWEEN SHEATHING BOARDS DEPENDS ON TYPE OF ROOFING (see BELOW).

NOTE: MANY ROOFERS PREFER THREE OR FOUR ROWS OF SOLID SHEATHING AT THE EAVES FOR STARTER COURSES.

Open, or skip, sheathing is usually made with 1x4 or 1x6 boards nailed horizontally to the rafters with a space between the boards. Since this sheathing material does not provide a diaphragm at the plane of the roof, other means of bracing the roof against horizontal loads must be employed. Let-in wooden bracing or metal strap bracing applied to the top or bottom surface of the rafters will suffice in most cases. This bracing must be engineered in seismic or high-wind zones or for very large roofs. Bracing may sometimes be omitted on hip roofs because the shape of the roof provides the bracing.

Spacing for open sheathing depends on the type of roofing. The ability of the sheathing to span between supports depends on the spacing and on the type of roofing applied over it. Check with local codes and with roofers for accepted local practices.

Wood shingles or shakes require spacing equal to the exposure of the shingles or shakes—usually about 5 in. for shingles to 10 in. for shakes. The sheathing is usually 1x4.

Concrete tiles, depending on the type, may be installed on open sheathing spaced in the 12-in. to 14-in. range. The roofing material is heavy, so 1x6 or 1x8 or 2x4 sheathing is practical.

Preformed metal roofing is lightweight and runs continuously in the direction of the rafters. In most cases, 1x6 sheathing @ 24 in. o.c. is adequate.

A **OPEN ROOF SHEATHING**

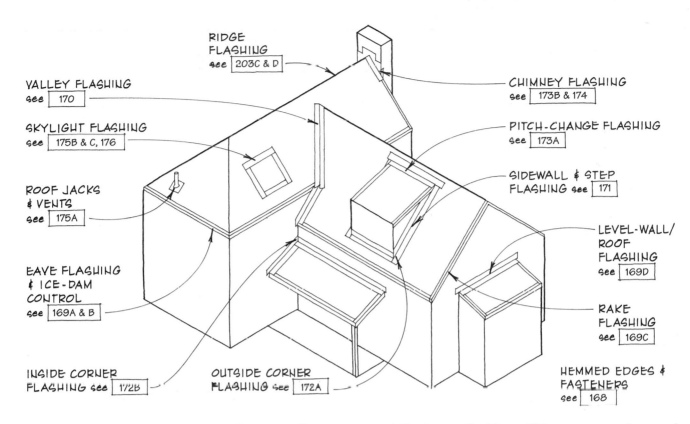

RIDGE FLASHING
see [203C & D]

VALLEY FLASHING
see [170]

SKYLIGHT FLASHING
see [175B & C, 176]

ROOF JACKS & VENTS
see [175A]

EAVE FLASHING & ICE-DAM CONTROL
see [169A & B]

INSIDE CORNER FLASHING see [172B]

OUTSIDE CORNER FLASHING see [172A]

CHIMNEY FLASHING
see [173B & 174]

PITCH-CHANGE FLASHING
see [173A]

SIDEWALL & STEP FLASHING see [171]

LEVEL-WALL/ ROOF FLASHING
see [169D]

RAKE FLASHING
see [169C]

HEMMED EDGES & FASTENERS
see [168]

Flashing is a necessary component of most roofing systems. Flashing makes the roof watertight at edges, openings, and bends in the roof where the roofing material cannot perform the job alone.

Flashing materials and details must be coordinated with the roofing material to make a durable and waterproof roof. Although design principles are transferable from one type of roofing to another, proportions of materials may vary. For example, the details drawn in this section show a thin-profile roofing material such as asphalt or wood shingles, but flashing for thicker roofing materials such as tile or shake will have different proportions. Some of these special flashings can be found with the details for the particular roofing type. (For a discussion of flashing materials, see 103.)

You may want to use different flashing materials for roofs than for walls, because roofs are constantly exposed to the weather and, in most cases, are replaced much more frequently than walls. Moreover, roof flashing itself is not always replaced at the same time as the roof. Chimney or wall flashing may not be easily changed when the building is reroofed, so it should be made of materials like copper or stainless steel, which can last as long as the building. Valley or

pitch-change flashing will be easy to replace at the time of reroofing if the original roof is removed. This flashing may be made of material with a life span equivalent to the roof itself.

The flashing and its fasteners must be compatible with each other and with the roofing material itself. For example, flashing and fasteners for metal roofs must be compatible with the roofing metal to avoid galvanic corrosion. Flashing may be isolated from other materials with 30-lb. felt or bituminous paint.

The basic principle of roof flashing is to have the roofing, the flashing and other materials overlap each other like shingles. Water running down the surface of the roof should always be directed by the flashing across the surface of the roof. Gravity will then work to direct water down the roof, away from the gaps covered by the flashing. This way, only wind-driven rain can force water through the roofing to the waterproof underlayment (see 177), which acts as a second line of defense. Each detail may have local variations to account for such weather-related factors. All flashing materials, therefore, should be discussed with local sheet-metal contractors or roofers.

ROOF FLASHING
INTRODUCTION

Hemmed edges—One very important detail for roof flashing is the hemmed edge, which folds back on itself about ½ in.

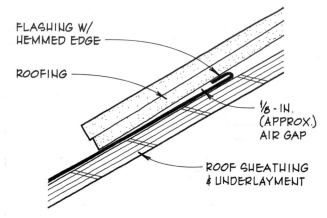

This fold makes the flashing thicker at the edge, which, aside from forming a stronger and neater edge when exposed, helps control the flow of water on roofs, as shown in the drawings on this page. Tucked under roofing, the turned-up hemmed edge creates an air gap that prevents moisture from migrating between the roofing and flashing by capillary action.

FLASHING W/ HEMMED EDGE

ROOFING

⅛-IN. (APPROX.) AIR GAP

ROOF SHEATHING & UNDERLAYMENT

A hemmed edge also works when it is horizontal, as in sidewall flashing (see 171A & B), where the hemmed edge not only resists capillary action but also forms a barrier to water running down the flashing and thus keeps it from running onto the roof sheathing.

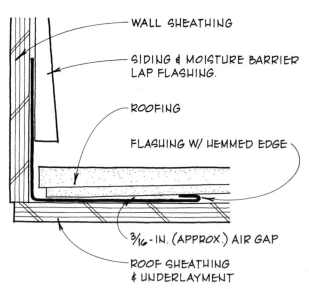

WALL SHEATHING

SIDING & MOISTURE BARRIER LAP FLASHING.

ROOFING

FLASHING W/ HEMMED EDGE

³⁄₁₆-IN. (APPROX.) AIR GAP

ROOF SHEATHING & UNDERLAYMENT

Turned down and lapped over roofing, the hemmed edge creates an air gap under the flashing that discourages capillary action. The hemmed edge can also form a seal on smooth surfaces such as skylight glass, which is only made more complete by the presence of water adhering by surface tension to the two surfaces.

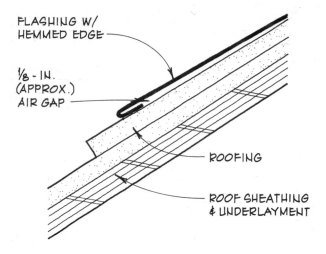

FLASHING W/ HEMMED EDGE

⅛-IN. (APPROX.) AIR GAP

ROOFING

ROOF SHEATHING & UNDERLAYMENT

Fasteners—Flashing is usually nailed to the structure. Nails are located at the edge of the flashing to avoid punctures in the flashing where it is designed to keep moisture from entering. Care must be taken to select nails that will not cause galvanic corrosion.

Another method of attaching flashing is the cleat, a small metal clip usually made of the same material as the flashing itself. Cleats fasten flashing to the roof without puncturing the flashing and allow for expansion and contraction of flashing metal without dislodging of fasteners. Cleats may also be used to make concealed connections of flashing.

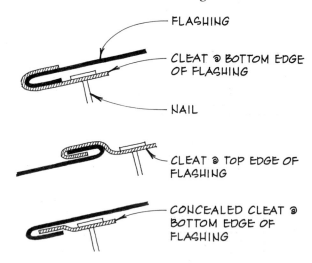

FLASHING

CLEAT @ BOTTOM EDGE OF FLASHING

NAIL

CLEAT @ TOP EDGE OF FLASHING

CONCEALED CLEAT @ BOTTOM EDGE OF FLASHING

(A) ROOF FLASHING
HEMMED EDGES & FASTENERS

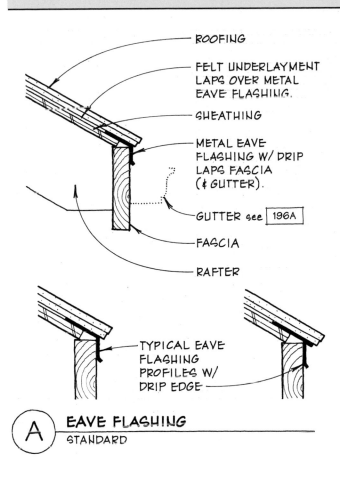

ROOFING

FELT UNDERLAYMENT LAPS OVER METAL EAVE FLASHING.

SHEATHING

METAL EAVE FLASHING W/ DRIP LAPS FASCIA (& GUTTER).

GUTTER see 196A

FASCIA

RAFTER

TYPICAL EAVE FLASHING PROFILES W/ DRIP EDGE

A EAVE FLASHING
STANDARD

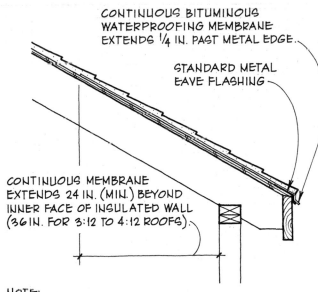

CONTINUOUS BITUMINOUS WATERPROOFING MEMBRANE EXTENDS 1/4 IN. PAST METAL EDGE.

STANDARD METAL EAVE FLASHING

CONTINUOUS MEMBRANE EXTENDS 24 IN. (MIN.) BEYOND INNER FACE OF INSULATED WALL (36 IN. FOR 3:12 TO 4:12 ROOFS).

NOTE:
THIS EAVE FLASHING IS REQ'D BY CODE IN MANY AREAS WITH COLD WINTERS, BUT SHOULD BE CONSIDERED A BACKUP STRATEGY BECAUSE ICE DAMS CAN BE PREVENTED W/ ADEQUATE INSULATION AND VENTILATION see 197 & 200

B EAVE FLASHING
COLD CLIMATE

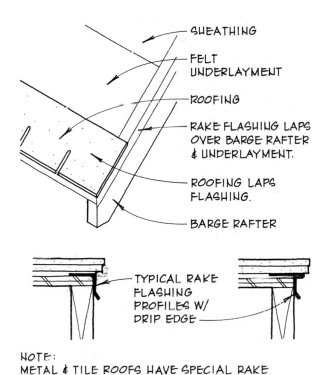

SHEATHING

FELT UNDERLAYMENT

ROOFING

RAKE FLASHING LAPS OVER BARGE RAFTER & UNDERLAYMENT.

ROOFING LAPS FLASHING.

BARGE RAFTER

TYPICAL RAKE FLASHING PROFILES W/ DRIP EDGE

NOTE:
METAL & TILE ROOFS HAVE SPECIAL RAKE FLASHINGS see 191C OR 189B & C

C RAKE FLASHING

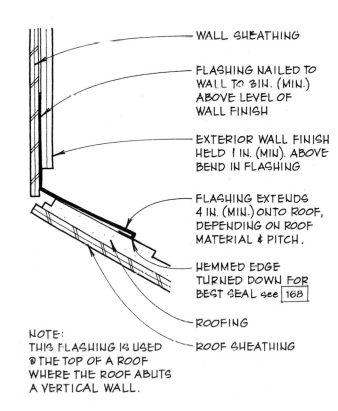

WALL SHEATHING

FLASHING NAILED TO WALL TO 3 IN. (MIN.) ABOVE LEVEL OF WALL FINISH

EXTERIOR WALL FINISH HELD 1 IN. (MIN.) ABOVE BEND IN FLASHING

FLASHING EXTENDS 4 IN. (MIN.) ONTO ROOF, DEPENDING ON ROOF MATERIAL & PITCH.

HEMMED EDGE TURNED DOWN FOR BEST SEAL see 168

ROOFING

ROOF SHEATHING

NOTE:
THIS FLASHING IS USED @ THE TOP OF A ROOF WHERE THE ROOF ABUTS A VERTICAL WALL.

D LEVEL WALL FLASHING

Valleys on roofs, like valleys in the landscape, collect the runoff of all the slopes above them. To handle such a concentration of water, valleys must be carefully flashed. Except when using roofing materials that can bend, such as asphalt shingles or roll roofing, valleys are usually flashed with metal flashing.

Open valley flashing is the most common and may be used with virtually all roofing materials. An open valley allows the runoff water to flow within the confines of the exposed metal flashing rather than over the roofing material itself.

Cleats at 2 ft. o.c. fasten valley flashing to the roof without puncturing the flashing and allow for expansion and contraction of flashing metal without dislodging fasteners (see 168). Without cleats, flashing is wider and is nailed at the outer edges.

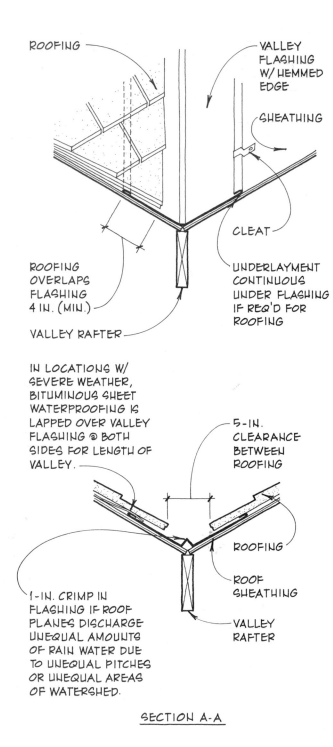

NOTE:
BITUMINOUS SHEET WATERPROOFING LAPS VALLEY FLASHING IN LOCATIONS W/ SEVERE WEATHER see SECTION A-A @ LOWER RIGHT

VALLEY FLASHING EXTENDS FULL LENGTH OF VALLEY.

UNDERLAYMENT

ROOFING

VALLEY BETWEEN ROOFING IS WIDER AT EAVE THAN AT TOP, ESPECIALLY IN AREAS OF EXTREME COLD. TYPICAL VALLEY IS 5 IN. TO 6 IN. WIDE @ TOP & INCREASES @ 1/8 IN. PER LINEAR FOOT OF VALLEY.

NOTES:
FOR VALLEY FLASHING OF ASPHALT SHINGLES see 183B & C
FOR ROLL ROOFING WITHOUT FLASHING see 181B

ROOFING

VALLEY FLASHING W/ HEMMED EDGE

SHEATHING

CLEAT

UNDERLAYMENT CONTINUOUS UNDER FLASHING IF REQ'D FOR ROOFING

ROOFING OVERLAPS FLASHING 4 IN. (MIN.)

VALLEY RAFTER

IN LOCATIONS W/ SEVERE WEATHER, BITUMINOUS SHEET WATERPROOFING IS LAPPED OVER VALLEY FLASHING @ BOTH SIDES FOR LENGTH OF VALLEY.

5-IN. CLEARANCE BETWEEN ROOFING

ROOFING

ROOF SHEATHING

VALLEY RAFTER

1-IN. CRIMP IN FLASHING IF ROOF PLANES DISCHARGE UNEQUAL AMOUNTS OF RAIN WATER DUE TO UNEQUAL PITCHES OR UNEQUAL AREAS OF WATERSHED.

SECTION A-A

Ⓐ VALLEY FLASHING

Sidewall flashing is a single-piece flashing installed before the roofing to create a flashing channel against the wall (see 171B). This type of flashing is adequate for most situations and allows easy reroofing.

Step flashing is a multiple-piece flashing that is woven in with the courses of roofing material (see 171C). This flashing is best for severe weather conditions. It may present some reroofing difficulties, especially if the type of roofing material is changed.

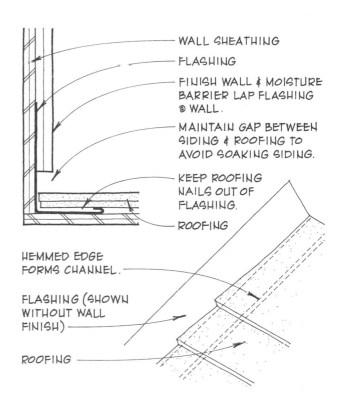

- WALL SHEATHING
- FLASHING
- FINISH WALL & MOISTURE BARRIER LAP FLASHING @ WALL.
- MAINTAIN GAP BETWEEN SIDING & ROOFING TO AVOID SOAKING SIDING.
- KEEP ROOFING NAILS OUT OF FLASHING.
- ROOFING

- HEMMED EDGE FORMS CHANNEL.
- FLASHING (SHOWN WITHOUT WALL FINISH)
- ROOFING

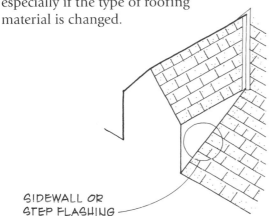

(A) SIDEWALL & STEP FLASHING
INTRODUCTION

SIDEWALL OR STEP FLASHING

(B) SIDEWALL FLASHING

- WALL SHEATHING
- FLASHING
- FINISH WALL & MOISTURE BARRIER LAP FLASHING @ WALL.
- KEEP SIDING NAILS OUT OF FLASHING TO ALLOW VERTICAL ADJUSTMENT WHEN RE-ROOFING.
- ROOFING

FLASHING —
ROOFING —
SHEATHING —

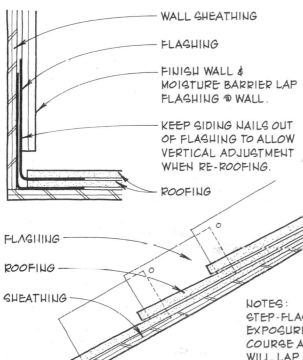

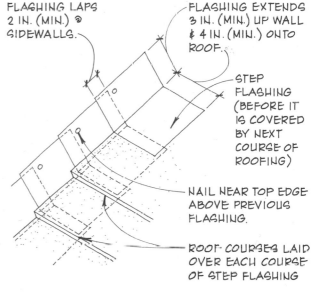

FLASHING LAPS 2 IN. (MIN.) @ SIDEWALLS.

FLASHING EXTENDS 3 IN. (MIN.) UP WALL & 4 IN. (MIN.) ONTO ROOF.

- STEP FLASHING (BEFORE IT IS COVERED BY NEXT COURSE OF ROOFING)
- NAIL NEAR TOP EDGE ABOVE PREVIOUS FLASHING.
- ROOF COURSES LAID OVER EACH COURSE OF STEP FLASHING

NOTES:
STEP-FLASHING PIECES ARE 2 IN. LONGER THAN ROOF COURSING EXPOSURE & ARE INSTALLED WITH THE ROOFING MATERIAL, ONE COURSE AT A TIME. EXTERIOR WALL FINISH & MOISTURE BARRIER WILL LAP STEP FLASHING. FLASHING DIMENSIONS DEPEND ON ROOFING MATERIAL AND PITCH.

(C) STEP FLASHING

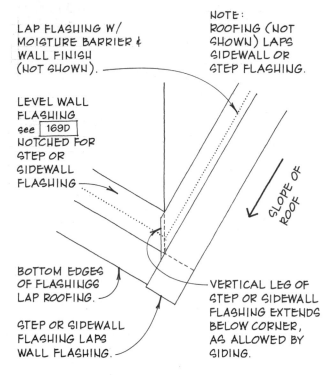

LAP FLASHING W/ MOISTURE BARRIER & WALL FINISH (NOT SHOWN).

NOTE: ROOFING (NOT SHOWN) LAPS SIDEWALL OR STEP FLASHING.

LEVEL WALL FLASHING see 169D NOTCHED FOR STEP OR SIDEWALL FLASHING

BOTTOM EDGES OF FLASHINGS LAP ROOFING.

STEP OR SIDEWALL FLASHING LAPS WALL FLASHING.

VERTICAL LEG OF STEP OR SIDEWALL FLASHING EXTENDS BELOW CORNER, AS ALLOWED BY SIDING.

SLOPE OF ROOF

LAPPED FLASHING FOR MODERATE WEATHER

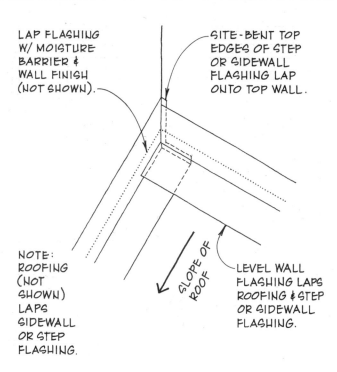

LAP FLASHING W/ MOISTURE BARRIER & WALL FINISH (NOT SHOWN).

SITE-BENT TOP EDGES OF STEP OR SIDEWALL FLASHING LAP ONTO TOP WALL.

NOTE: ROOFING (NOT SHOWN) LAPS SIDEWALL OR STEP FLASHING.

LEVEL WALL FLASHING LAPS ROOFING & STEP OR SIDEWALL FLASHING.

SLOPE OF ROOF

LAPPED FLASHING FOR MODERATE WEATHER

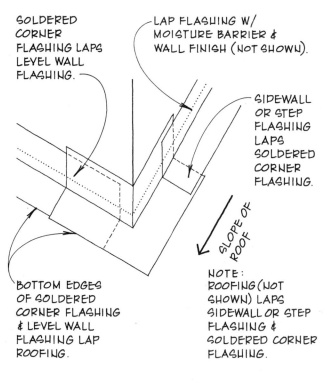

SOLDERED CORNER FLASHING LAPS LEVEL WALL FLASHING.

LAP FLASHING W/ MOISTURE BARRIER & WALL FINISH (NOT SHOWN).

SIDEWALL OR STEP FLASHING LAPS SOLDERED CORNER FLASHING.

BOTTOM EDGES OF SOLDERED CORNER FLASHING & LEVEL WALL FLASHING LAP ROOFING.

NOTE: ROOFING (NOT SHOWN) LAPS SIDEWALL OR STEP FLASHING & SOLDERED CORNER FLASHING.

SLOPE OF ROOF

SOLDERED FLASHING FOR EXTREME WEATHER

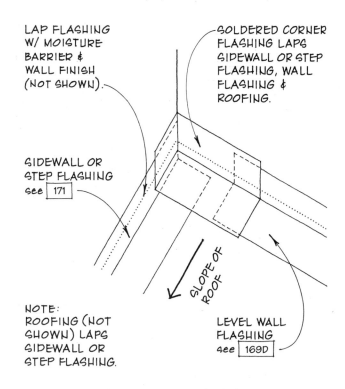

LAP FLASHING W/ MOISTURE BARRIER & WALL FINISH (NOT SHOWN).

SOLDERED CORNER FLASHING LAPS SIDEWALL OR STEP FLASHING, WALL FLASHING & ROOFING.

SIDEWALL OR STEP FLASHING see 171

NOTE: ROOFING (NOT SHOWN) LAPS SIDEWALL OR STEP FLASHING.

LEVEL WALL FLASHING see 169D

SLOPE OF ROOF

SOLDERED FLASHING FOR EXTREME WEATHER

 A OUTSIDE CORNER FLASHING

 B INSIDE CORNER FLASHING

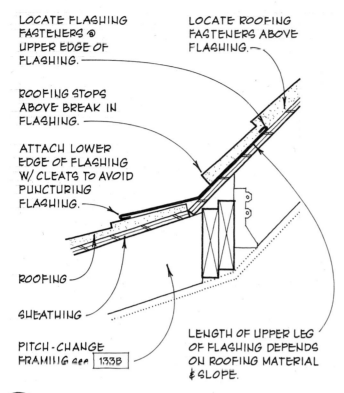

LOCATE FLASHING FASTENERS @ UPPER EDGE OF FLASHING.

LOCATE ROOFING FASTENERS ABOVE FLASHING.

ROOFING STOPS ABOVE BREAK IN FLASHING.

ATTACH LOWER EDGE OF FLASHING W/ CLEATS TO AVOID PUNCTURING FLASHING.

ROOFING

SHEATHING

PITCH-CHANGE FRAMING see [133B]

LENGTH OF UPPER LEG OF FLASHING DEPENDS ON ROOFING MATERIAL & SLOPE.

The flashing detail at left applies to both reduced pitch (shown) and increased pitch. Reduced pitch-change flashing can be avoided in favor of a cleaner detail by bending asphalt shingles or by soaking or steaming and bending wood shingles. The pitch change can also be made gradual by adding a strip of sheathing at the bend in the roof (see below) so that stiffer roofing materials such as wood shingles and shakes, tiles and slates can make the transition without flashing.

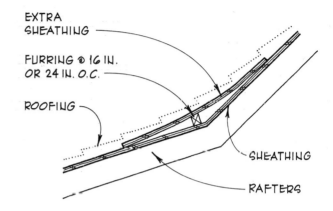

EXTRA SHEATHING

FURRING @ 16 IN. OR 24 IN. O.C.

ROOFING

SHEATHING

RAFTERS

A PITCH-CHANGE FLASHING

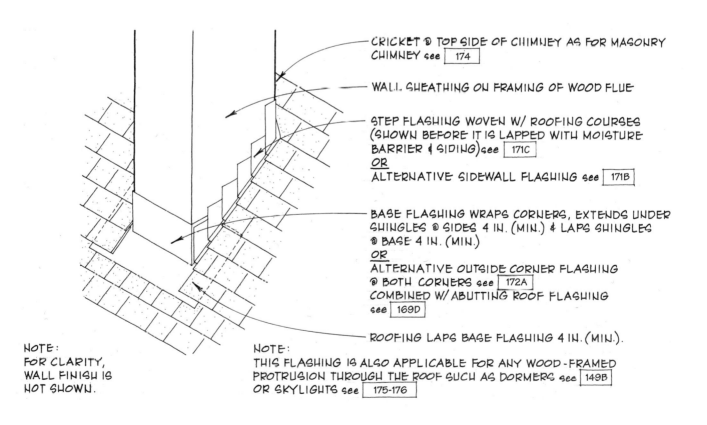

CRICKET @ TOP SIDE OF CHIMNEY AS FOR MASONRY CHIMNEY see [174]

WALL SHEATHING ON FRAMING OF WOOD FLUE

STEP FLASHING WOVEN W/ ROOFING COURSES (SHOWN BEFORE IT IS LAPPED WITH MOISTURE BARRIER & SIDING) see [171C]
OR
ALTERNATIVE SIDEWALL FLASHING see [171B]

BASE FLASHING WRAPS CORNERS, EXTENDS UNDER SHINGLES @ SIDES 4 IN. (MIN.) & LAPS SHINGLES @ BASE 4 IN. (MIN.)
OR
ALTERNATIVE OUTSIDE CORNER FLASHING @ BOTH CORNERS see [172A]
COMBINED W/ ABUTTING ROOF FLASHING see [169D]

ROOFING LAPS BASE FLASHING 4 IN. (MIN.).

NOTE:
FOR CLARITY, WALL FINISH IS NOT SHOWN.

NOTE:
THIS FLASHING IS ALSO APPLICABLE FOR ANY WOOD-FRAMED PROTRUSION THROUGH THE ROOF SUCH AS DORMERS see [149B] OR SKYLIGHTS see [175-176]

B CHIMNEY FLASHING
WOOD-FRAMED FLUE

The flashing for a masonry chimney is best made of permanent materials such as copper or stainless steel. The flashing fits to the roof using the same principles as flashing for wood-framed flues (see 173B). The top edge of this flashing is then lapped with a counterflashing that is set into the mortar joints between masonry units. Because of the complex shapes, many of the pieces in chimney flashing cannot be folded but must be soldered or welded.

A chimney located in the slope of the roof will require a cricket (also called a saddle), a ridged connection between chimney and roof that directs water away from the chimney. Most crickets may be formed with exterior-grade plywood; larger crickets may need to be framed like a typical roof. The entire surface of the cricket is flashed, as shown in the drawing below.

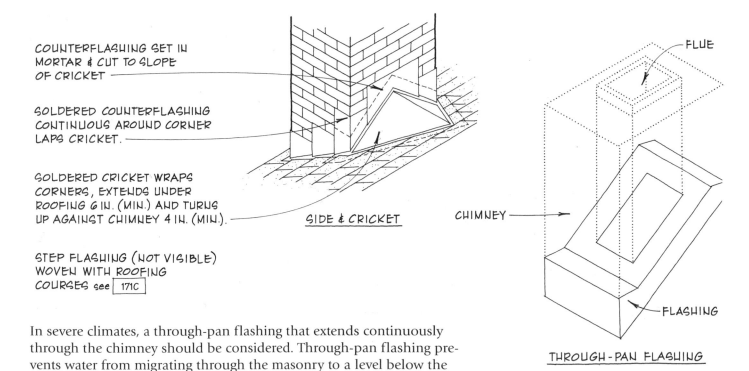

STEP FLASHING WOVEN WITH ROOFING COURSES see 171C

COUNTERFLASHING SET IN MORTAR 1 IN. (MIN.) @ TOP EDGE, LAPS ITSELF 2 IN. (MIN.) & LAPS STEP OR OTHER SIDE FLASHING 4 IN. (MIN.)

SOLDERED BASE FLASHING WRAPS CORNERS, IS SET IN MORTAR 2 IN. (MIN.) @ TOP EDGE, EXTENDS UNDER SHINGLES @ SIDES 4 IN. (MIN.) AND LAPS SHINGLES @ BASE 4 IN. (MIN.). THIS CAN ALSO BE MADE WITH TWO PIECES — A BASE FLASHING WITH COUNTERFLASHING SET IN MORTAR

ROOFING LAPS BASE FLASHING 4 IN. (MIN.).

SIDE & BASE

COUNTERFLASHING SET IN MORTAR & CUT TO SLOPE OF CRICKET

SOLDERED COUNTERFLASHING CONTINUOUS AROUND CORNER LAPS CRICKET.

SOLDERED CRICKET WRAPS CORNERS, EXTENDS UNDER ROOFING 6 IN. (MIN.) AND TURNS UP AGAINST CHIMNEY 4 IN. (MIN.).

STEP FLASHING (NOT VISIBLE) WOVEN WITH ROOFING COURSES see 171C

SIDE & CRICKET

FLUE

CHIMNEY

FLASHING

THROUGH-PAN FLASHING

In severe climates, a through-pan flashing that extends continuously through the chimney should be considered. Through-pan flashing prevents water from migrating through the masonry to a level below the flashing. It is made of lead or copper and is penetrated only by the flue. It is wrapped down at the edges, where it acts as counterflashing. The continuous flashing through the chimney does weaken the masonry bond, so this flashing should not be used in earthquake or hurricane zones.

A CHIMNEY FLASHING
MASONRY

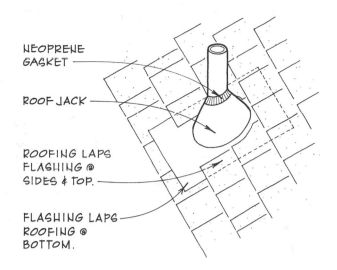

NEOPRENE GASKET

ROOF JACK

ROOFING LAPS FLASHING @ SIDES & TOP.

FLASHING LAPS ROOFING @ BOTTOM.

Modern roof jacks are typically fitted with neoprene gaskets sized to seal plumbing vents and other roof penetrations. Jacks are woven in with roofing materials where possible. Jacks for metal roofs pose special problems.

Most skylights are manufactured with a complete flashing package and instructions for installation in a rough opening in the roof framing. Some are available with a kit to adapt the flashing to unusual roofing materials or pitches. Skylights are available in fixed or operable types with screens and/or sunshade devices. Rough-opening sizes are specified and usually correspond with standard rafter spacing.

Many fixed skylights require a flashed curb to which the manufactured skylight is attached. With these skylights, the curb must be flashed like any other large penetration of the roofing surface, such as a dormer or a chimney (see 174 and 175C). Site-built curbless skylights are fixed and appear flush with the roof (see 176). Some codes prohibit these skylights because of the requirement for a curb.

For skylight framing, see 136A & B.

 A ROOF JACKS AND VENTS

 **B** SKYLIGHT FLASHING
NOTES

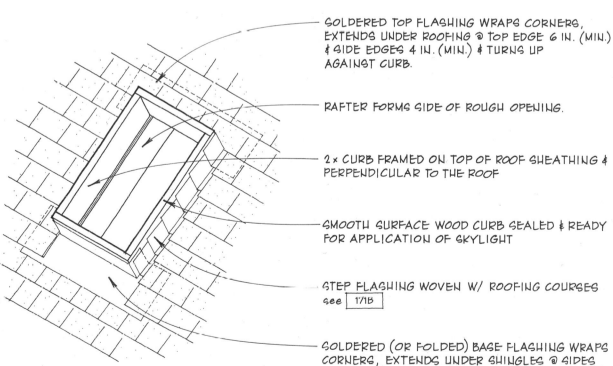

SOLDERED TOP FLASHING WRAPS CORNERS, EXTENDS UNDER ROOFING @ TOP EDGE 6 IN. (MIN.) & SIDE EDGES 4 IN. (MIN.) & TURNS UP AGAINST CURB.

RAFTER FORMS SIDE OF ROUGH OPENING.

2 × CURB FRAMED ON TOP OF ROOF SHEATHING & PERPENDICULAR TO THE ROOF

SMOOTH SURFACE WOOD CURB SEALED & READY FOR APPLICATION OF SKYLIGHT

STEP FLASHING WOVEN W/ ROOFING COURSES see 171B

SOLDERED (OR FOLDED) BASE FLASHING WRAPS CORNERS, EXTENDS UNDER SHINGLES @ SIDES 4 IN. (MIN.) & LAPS SHINGLES @ BASE 4 IN. (MIN.).

C SKYLIGHT CURB FLASHING
FOR USE W/ MANUFACTURED SKYLIGHT

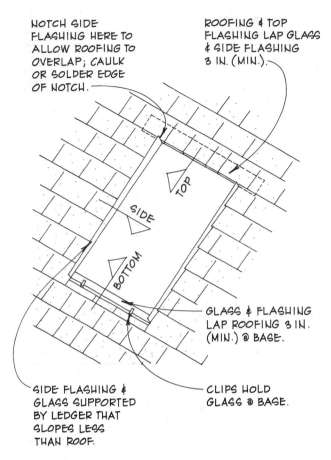

NOTCH SIDE FLASHING HERE TO ALLOW ROOFING TO OVERLAP; CAULK OR SOLDER EDGE OF NOTCH.

ROOFING & TOP FLASHING LAP GLASS & SIDE FLASHING 3 IN. (MIN.)

TOP

SIDE

BOTTOM

GLASS & FLASHING LAP ROOFING 3 IN. (MIN.) @ BASE.

SIDE FLASHING & GLASS SUPPORTED BY LEDGER THAT SLOPES LESS THAN ROOF.

CLIPS HOLD GLASS @ BASE.

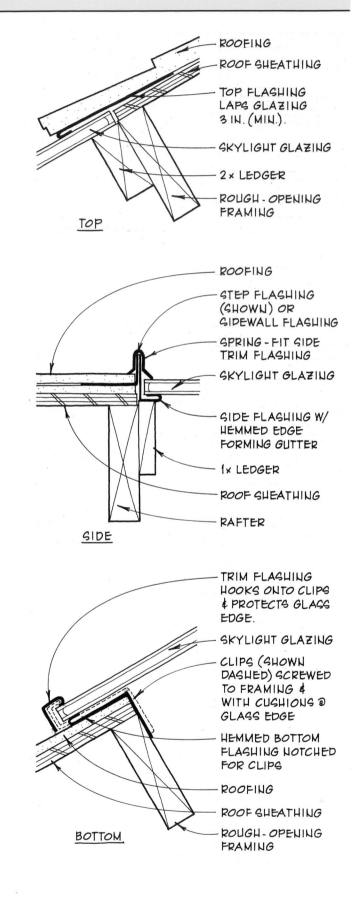

ROOFING

ROOF SHEATHING

TOP FLASHING LAPS GLAZING 3 IN. (MIN.)

SKYLIGHT GLAZING

2 × LEDGER

ROUGH - OPENING FRAMING

TOP

ROOFING

STEP FLASHING (SHOWN) OR SIDEWALL FLASHING

SPRING - FIT SIDE TRIM FLASHING

SKYLIGHT GLAZING

SIDE FLASHING W/ HEMMED EDGE FORMING GUTTER

1× LEDGER

ROOF SHEATHING

RAFTER

SIDE

TRIM FLASHING HOOKS ONTO CLIPS & PROTECTS GLASS EDGE.

SKYLIGHT GLAZING

CLIPS (SHOWN DASHED) SCREWED TO FRAMING & WITH CUSHIONS @ GLASS EDGE

HEMMED BOTTOM FLASHING NOTCHED FOR CLIPS

ROOFING

ROOF SHEATHING

ROUGH - OPENING FRAMING

BOTTOM

A site-built curbless skylight is woven in with the roofing. Its bottom edge laps the roofing, and its top edge is lapped by roofing. This means that the skylight itself must be at a slightly lower pitch than the roof. Ledgers at the sides of the rough opening provide the support at this lower pitch. If built properly, there is no need for any caulking of these skylights except at the notch at the top of the side flashing. Insulated glass should limit condensation on the glazing, but any condensation that does form can weep out through the clip notches in the bottom flashing. In extremely cold climates, the side flashing should be thermally isolated from the other flashing to prevent condensation on the flashing itself.

Curbless skylights are especially practical at the eave edge of a roof, where the lower edge of the skylight does not have to lap the roofing. This condition, often found in attached greenhouses, will simplify the details on this page because the slope of the skylight can be the same as the roof. The top and side details above right are suitable in such a case. Codes that require curbs preclude the use of these skylights.

 CURBLESS SKYLIGHT

With the exception of wood roofs, which are now made with lower-grade material than in the past, today's roofing materials will last longer than ever before, and can be installed with less labor. Composite materials now take the place of most natural roofing materials, including wood shingle and slate.

The selection of a roofing material must be carefully coordinated with the design and construction of the roof itself. Some factors to consider are the type of roof sheathing (see 162–166), insulation (see 197–205), and flashing (see 167–176). For example, some roofing materials perform best on open sheathing, but others require solid sheathing. Some roofing materials may be applied over rigid insulation; others may not.

Many roofing materials require a waterproof underlayment to be installed over solid sheathing before roofing is applied. Underlayment, usually 15-lb. felt, which can be applied quickly, is often used to keep the building dry until the permanent roofing is applied. In the case of wood shakes, the underlayment layer is woven in with the roofing courses and is called interlayment (see 186).

Other considerations for selecting a roofing material include cost, durability, fire resistance, and slope (the pitch of the roof).

Cost—Considering both labor and materials, the least expensive roofing is roll roofing (see 180–181). Next in the order of expense are asphalt shingles (see 182–183), followed by preformed metal (see 190), wood shingles (see 184–185), shakes (see 186–187), and tile (see 188–189). Extremely expensive roofs such as slate and standing-seam metal are not discussed in depth in this book.

Durability—As would be expected, the materials that cost the most also last the longest. Concrete-tile roofs are typically warranted for 50 years. Shake and shingle roofs can last as long under proper conditions but are never warranted. Preformed metal and asphalt shingles are warranted in the 15-year to 30-year range.

Fire resistance—Tile and metal are the most resistant to fire, but fiberglass-based asphalt shingles and roll roofing can also be rated in the highest class for fire resistance. Wood shakes and shingles can be chemically treated to resist fire, but are not as resistant as other types of roofing.

Slope—The slope of a roof is measured as a proportion of rise to run of the roof. A 4-in-12 roof slope, for example, rises 4 in. for every 12 in. of run.

There are wide variations among roofing manufacturers, but in general, the slope of a roof can be matched to the type of roofing. Flat roofs (⅛-in-12 to ¼-in-12) are roofed with a built-up coating or with a single ply membrane (see 178–179). Shallow-slope roofs (1-in-12 to 4-in-12) are often roofed with roll roofing. Special measures may be taken to allow asphalt shingles on a 2-in-12 slope and wood shingles or shakes on a 3-in-12 slope, and some metal roofs may be applied to 1-in-12 slopes. Normal-slope roofs (4-in-12 to 12-in-12) are the slopes required for most roofing materials. Some materials such as built-up roofing are designed for lower slopes and may not be applied to normal slopes.

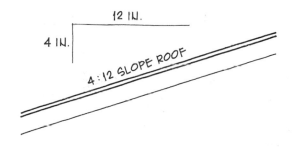

12 IN.

4 IN.

4:12 SLOPE ROOF

(A) **ROOFING**
INTRODUCTION

Flat roofs aren't actually flat, but must slope to drain water or manufacturers will not guarantee their products. The actual slope depends on the application, but most manufacturers recommend ¼ in. per ft. The slope may be achieved with the framing of the roof (see 139) or with tapered insulation. Water is usually contained at the edges of a flat roof with a curb or a wall and directed to a central drain (see 179B) or scupper at the edge of the roof (see 57D). A continuous gutter at the edge of a flat roof can also collect the water.

The selection of an appropriate roofing system for a flat roof can be complicated. As with all roofs, climate is one factor. But the fact that a flat roof is covered with a large continuous waterproof membrane presents some special technical problems, such as expansion and contraction. If the roof is going to be used for a terrace or walkway, the effects of foot traffic must also be considered. For these reasons, a flat roof is best selected by a design professional and constructed by a reputable roofing contractor.

There are several application methods for flat roofs:

Built-up roof—A built-up roof is composed of several layers of asphalt-impregnated felt interspersed with coats of hot tar (bitumen) and capped with gravel. This traditional and effective method is in widespread use. The application is technical and should be performed by professional roofers. Warranties range from one to five years.

Single-ply roof—A more recent development in roofing, the single-ply roof is less labor intensive and more elastic than the built-up roof. The single-ply roof is applied as a membrane and glued, weighted with gravel ballast, or mechanically fastened to the roof. Seams are glued with adhesive or heat sealed. Single-ply roofs are usually applied to large areas, but, like the built-up roof, can also cover small areas. Application is technical; warranties start at five years.

Liquid-applied roof—Liquid-applied roofing polymerizes from chemicals suspended in volatile solvents to form a watertight elastomeric membrane that adheres to the sheathing. Application is usually in several coats, using brush, roller, or spray. Liquid-applied roofs are practical for small areas, where they may be applied by an untrained person without specialized tools; their flexibility allows them to be applied without the cant strips required of built-up roofs (see 178B & C).

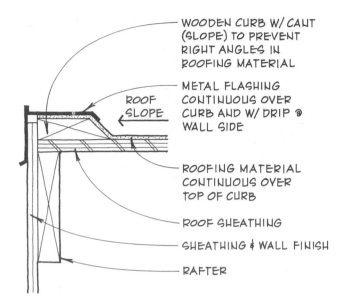

WOODEN CURB W/ CANT (SLOPE) TO PREVENT RIGHT ANGLES IN ROOFING MATERIAL

ROOF SLOPE

METAL FLASHING CONTINUOUS OVER CURB AND W/ DRIP @ WALL SIDE

ROOFING MATERIAL CONTINUOUS OVER TOP OF CURB

ROOF SHEATHING

SHEATHING & WALL FINISH

RAFTER

NOTE:
THIS CURB IS GENERALLY USED IN CONJUNCTION W/ A SCUPPER WHEN THE ROOF SLOPES TOWARD THE OUTSIDE EDGE OF THE BUILDING. FOR SCUPPER see 57D

B FLAT ROOF EDGE W/ CURB

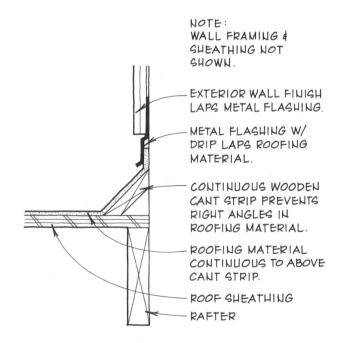

NOTE:
WALL FRAMING & SHEATHING NOT SHOWN.

EXTERIOR WALL FINISH LAPS METAL FLASHING.

METAL FLASHING W/ DRIP LAPS ROOFING MATERIAL.

CONTINUOUS WOODEN CANT STRIP PREVENTS RIGHT ANGLES IN ROOFING MATERIAL.

ROOFING MATERIAL CONTINUOUS TO ABOVE CANT STRIP.

ROOF SHEATHING

RAFTER

A FLAT ROOFING
INTRODUCTION

C FLAT ROOF EDGE @ WALL

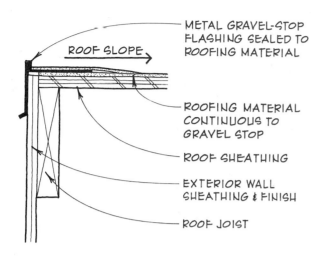

ROOF SLOPE →

METAL GRAVEL-STOP FLASHING SEALED TO ROOFING MATERIAL

ROOFING MATERIAL CONTINUOUS TO GRAVEL STOP

ROOF SHEATHING

EXTERIOR WALL SHEATHING & FINISH

ROOF JOIST

NOTE:
THIS DETAIL IS GENERALLY USED WHEN THE ROOF SLOPES AWAY FROM THE EDGE TOWARD A CENTRAL DRAIN see 179B

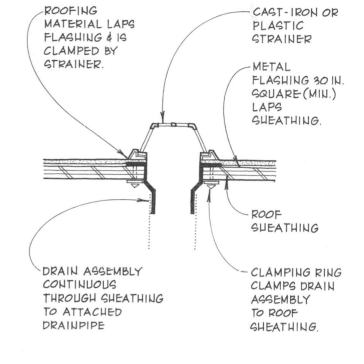

ROOFING MATERIAL LAPS FLASHING & IS CLAMPED BY STRAINER.

CAST-IRON OR PLASTIC STRAINER

METAL FLASHING 30 IN. SQUARE (MIN.) LAPS SHEATHING.

ROOF SHEATHING

DRAIN ASSEMBLY CONTINUOUS THROUGH SHEATHING TO ATTACHED DRAINPIPE

CLAMPING RING CLAMPS DRAIN ASSEMBLY TO ROOF SHEATHING.

(A) FLAT ROOF EDGE W/ GRAVEL STOP

(B) FLAT ROOF DRAIN

Roll roofing is an inexpensive roofing for shallow-pitch roofs (1-in-12 to 4-in-12). The 36-in. wide by 36-ft. long rolls are made with a fiberglass or organic felt base that is impregnated with asphalt and covered on the surface with mineral granules similar to asphalt shingles. Several colors are available. Roll roofing weighs 55 lb. to 90 lb. per square (100 sq. ft.). (The 90-lb. felt used for roll roofing is three times heavier than the 30-lb. felt used for underlayment.) The average life expectancy for roll roofing ranges from 10 to 15 years; fiberglass-base roofing is the longest lasting. Fiberglass-base rolls are also more resistant to fire.

Roll roofing must be applied over solid sheathing and does not require underlayment. It is easily nailed in place without using any specialized equipment.

There are two basic types of roll roofing, single coverage and double coverage.

Single coverage—Single-coverage roofing rolls are uniformly surfaced with mineral granules and are applied directly to the roof sheathing with only a 2-in. to 4-in. lap, which is sealed with roofing adhesive. The rolls may be parallel to the eaves or to the rake. The roofing may be applied using the concealed-nail method (see 180B) or the exposed-nail method (not shown). A minimum pitch of 2-in-12 is required for the exposed-nail method. Single coverage is the least expensive and the least durable of the roll-roofing methods.

Double coverage—Double-coverage rolls are half surfaced with mineral granules and half smooth. The smooth part of the roll is called the selvage. The rolls are lapped over each other so that the surfaced portion of each roll laps over the smooth portion of the previous course. Each course of roofing is sealed to the previous course with either cold asphalt adhesive or hot asphalt. In this fashion, the roof is covered with a double layer of felt. The double layer of felt weighs 110 lb. to 140 lb. per square. Double-coverage roofing is more expensive than single-coverage roofing, but it makes a more durable roof. Double-coverage roll roofing may be applied with the courses parallel to the eave or to the rake (see 181A).

A   ROLL ROOFING
INTRODUCTION

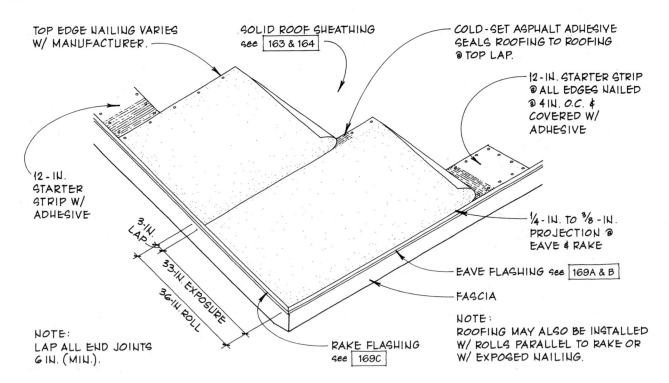

TOP EDGE NAILING VARIES W/ MANUFACTURER.

SOLID ROOF SHEATHING see [163 & 164]

COLD-SET ASPHALT ADHESIVE SEALS ROOFING TO ROOFING @ TOP LAP.

12-IN. STARTER STRIP @ ALL EDGES NAILED @ 4 IN. O.C. & COVERED W/ ADHESIVE

12-IN. STARTER STRIP W/ ADHESIVE

3-IN. LAP

33-IN. EXPOSURE

36-IN. ROLL

¼-IN. TO ⅜-IN. PROJECTION @ EAVE & RAKE

EAVE FLASHING see [169A & B]

FASCIA

RAKE FLASHING see [169C]

NOTE: LAP ALL END JOINTS 6 IN. (MIN.).

NOTE: ROOFING MAY ALSO BE INSTALLED W/ ROLLS PARALLEL TO RAKE OR W/ EXPOSED NAILING.

B   SINGLE-COVERAGE ROLL ROOFING
CONCEALED-NAIL METHOD

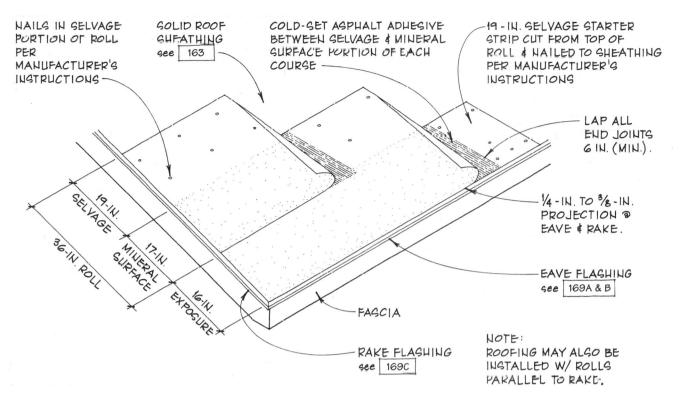

NAILS IN SELVAGE PORTION OF ROLL PER MANUFACTURER'S INSTRUCTIONS

SOLID ROOF SHEATHING see 163

COLD-SET ASPHALT ADHESIVE BETWEEN SELVAGE & MINERAL SURFACE PORTION OF EACH COURSE

19-IN. SELVAGE STARTER STRIP CUT FROM TOP OF ROLL & NAILED TO SHEATHING PER MANUFACTURER'S INSTRUCTIONS

LAP ALL END JOINTS 6 IN. (MIN.).

1/4-IN. TO 3/8-IN. PROJECTION @ EAVE & RAKE.

EAVE FLASHING see 169A & B

19-IN. SELVAGE

17-IN. MINERAL SURFACE

36-IN. ROLL

16-IN. EXPOSURE

FASCIA

RAKE FLASHING see 169C

NOTE: ROOFING MAY ALSO BE INSTALLED W/ ROLLS PARALLEL TO RAKE.

A DOUBLE-COVERAGE ROLL ROOFING

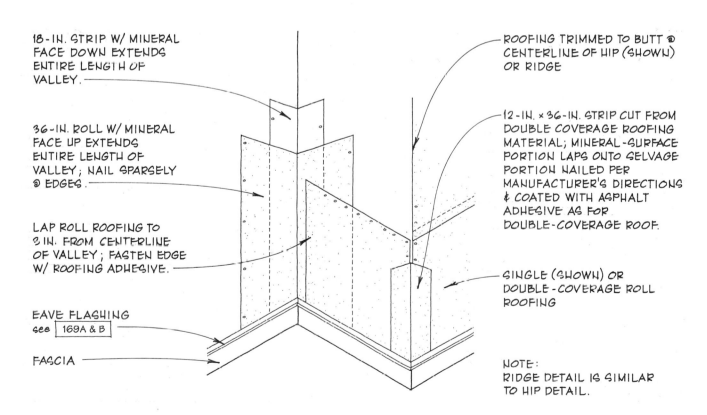

18-IN. STRIP W/ MINERAL FACE DOWN EXTENDS ENTIRE LENGTH OF VALLEY.

36-IN. ROLL W/ MINERAL FACE UP EXTENDS ENTIRE LENGTH OF VALLEY; NAIL SPARSELY @ EDGES.

LAP ROLL ROOFING TO 3 IN. FROM CENTERLINE OF VALLEY; FASTEN EDGE W/ ROOFING ADHESIVE.

EAVE FLASHING see 169A & B

FASCIA

ROOFING TRIMMED TO BUTT @ CENTERLINE OF HIP (SHOWN) OR RIDGE

12-IN. × 36-IN. STRIP CUT FROM DOUBLE COVERAGE ROOFING MATERIAL; MINERAL-SURFACE PORTION LAPS ONTO SELVAGE PORTION NAILED PER MANUFACTURER'S DIRECTIONS & COATED WITH ASPHALT ADHESIVE AS FOR DOUBLE-COVERAGE ROOF.

SINGLE (SHOWN) OR DOUBLE-COVERAGE ROLL ROOFING

NOTE: RIDGE DETAIL IS SIMILAR TO HIP DETAIL.

B ROLL-ROOFING VALLEY & HIP (OR RIDGE)
DOUBLE OR SINGLE COVERAGE

Composite asphalt shingles are almost the perfect roofing material. They are inexpensive, waterproof, lightweight, and easily cut and bent. That is why asphalt shingles are so popular nationwide. They are available in a wide range of colors and textures, some with extra thickness to imitate shakes, slate, or other uneven materials. There is also a range of quality, with warranties from 15 to 30 years.

Asphalt shingles have a fiberglass or organic-felt base that is impregnated with asphalt and covered on the surface with granulated stone or ceramic material, which gives them color. Shingles made with fiberglass are more durable and more resistant to fire than those of organic felt.

Asphalt shingles must be applied over a solid sheathing covered with 15-lb. felt underlayment. They are easily nailed in place, using no specialized equipment. Many roofing contractors, however, use air-driven staples.

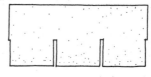

STANDARD FIELD SHINGLES HAVE 3 TABS & WEIGH 235 LB. PER SQUARE (100 SQ. FT.).

STANDARD FIELD SHINGLES MAY BE CUT INTO 3 PIECES TO MAKE HIP OR RIDGE SHINGLES.

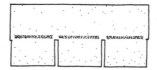

SELF-SEALING ADHESIVE AVAILABLE ON TOP SIDE OF SHINGLES TO PROTECT AGAINST WIND.

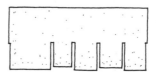

ALTERNATIVE PATTERNS AVAILABLE W/ SOME THICKER TABS TO RESEMBLE MORE NATURAL ROOFS.

COMMON SHINGLE
PATTERNS

OTHER LESS COMMON PATTERNS ARE ALSO AVAILABLE.

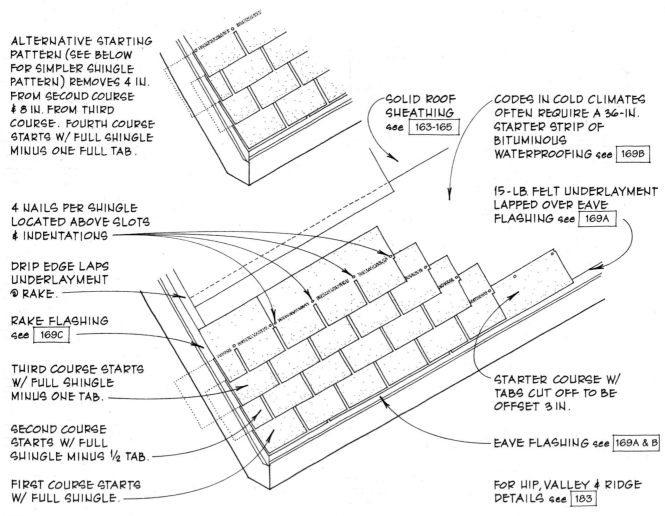

ALTERNATIVE STARTING PATTERN (SEE BELOW FOR SIMPLER SHINGLE PATTERN) REMOVES 4 IN. FROM SECOND COURSE & 8 IN. FROM THIRD COURSE. FOURTH COURSE STARTS W/ FULL SHINGLE MINUS ONE FULL TAB.

4 NAILS PER SHINGLE LOCATED ABOVE SLOTS & INDENTATIONS

DRIP EDGE LAPS UNDERLAYMENT @ RAKE.

RAKE FLASHING see 169C

THIRD COURSE STARTS W/ FULL SHINGLE MINUS ONE TAB.

SECOND COURSE STARTS W/ FULL SHINGLE MINUS ½ TAB.

FIRST COURSE STARTS W/ FULL SHINGLE.

SOLID ROOF SHEATHING see 163-165

CODES IN COLD CLIMATES OFTEN REQUIRE A 36-IN. STARTER STRIP OF BITUMINOUS WATERPROOFING see 169B

15-LB. FELT UNDERLAYMENT LAPPED OVER EAVE FLASHING see 169A

STARTER COURSE W/ TABS CUT OFF TO BE OFFSET 3 IN.

EAVE FLASHING see 169A & B

FOR HIP, VALLEY & RIDGE DETAILS see 183

(A) ASPHALT-SHINGLE ROOFING

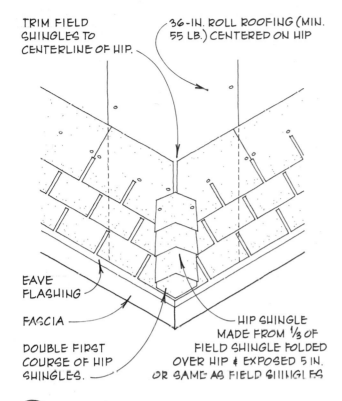

TRIM FIELD SHINGLES TO CENTERLINE OF HIP.

36-IN. ROLL ROOFING (MIN. 55 LB.) CENTERED ON HIP

EAVE FLASHING

FASCIA

DOUBLE FIRST COURSE OF HIP SHINGLES.

HIP SHINGLE MADE FROM 1/3 OF FIELD SHINGLE FOLDED OVER HIP & EXPOSED 5 IN. OR SAME AS FIELD SHINGLES

A ASPHALT-SHINGLE HIP

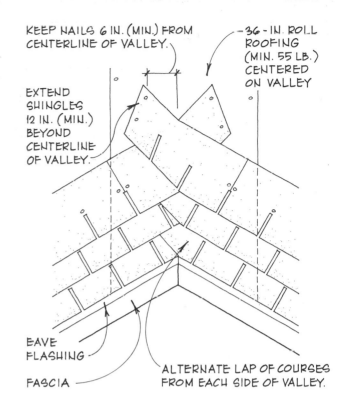

KEEP NAILS 6 IN. (MIN.) FROM CENTERLINE OF VALLEY.

36-IN. ROLL ROOFING (MIN. 55 LB.) CENTERED ON VALLEY

EXTEND SHINGLES 12 IN. (MIN.) BEYOND CENTERLINE OF VALLEY.

EAVE FLASHING

FASCIA

ALTERNATE LAP OF COURSES FROM EACH SIDE OF VALLEY.

B ASPHALT-SHINGLE VALLEY

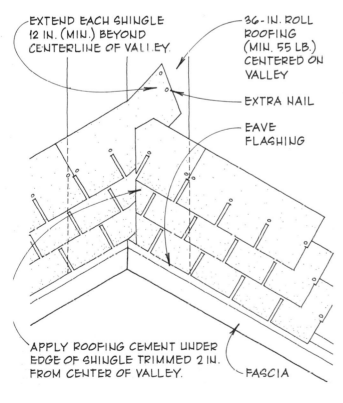

EXTEND EACH SHINGLE 12 IN. (MIN.) BEYOND CENTERLINE OF VALLEY.

36-IN. ROLL ROOFING (MIN. 55 LB.) CENTERED ON VALLEY

EXTRA NAIL

EAVE FLASHING

APPLY ROOFING CEMENT UNDER EDGE OF SHINGLE TRIMMED 2 IN. FROM CENTER OF VALLEY.

FASCIA

C CLOSED-CUT VALLEY

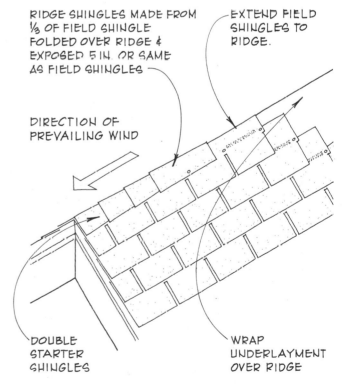

RIDGE SHINGLES MADE FROM 1/3 OF FIELD SHINGLE FOLDED OVER RIDGE & EXPOSED 5 IN. OR SAME AS FIELD SHINGLES

EXTEND FIELD SHINGLES TO RIDGE.

DIRECTION OF PREVAILING WIND

DOUBLE STARTER SHINGLES

WRAP UNDERLAYMENT OVER RIDGE

D ASPHALT-SHINGLE RIDGE

For centuries, wood shingles have been used extensively for roofing, and they continue to be very popular. However, with the advent of the asphalt shingle, they have recently lost their dominance as a roofing material. Furthermore, their use continues to decline because of cost increases and a drop in the quality of the raw materials.

Roof shingles are made predominantly from clear western red cedar, but are also available in redwood and cypress. They are sawn on both sides to a taper, and have a uniform butt thickness. Standard shingles are 16 in. long; 18-in. and 24-in. lengths are also available. Widths are random, usually in the 3-in. to 10-in. range. There are several grades of wood shingles; only the highest grade should be used for roofing.

In most cases, wood shingles will last longer if applied over open sheathing (see 166) because they will be able to breathe and dry out from both sides and therefore be less susceptible to rot and other moisture-related damage. Use solid sheathing and underlayment, however, for low pitch (3-in-12 and 3½-in-12) and in areas of severe wind-driven snow.

Chemically treated fire-rated shingles are available. They must be installed over solid sheathing that is covered with a plastic-coated steel foil.

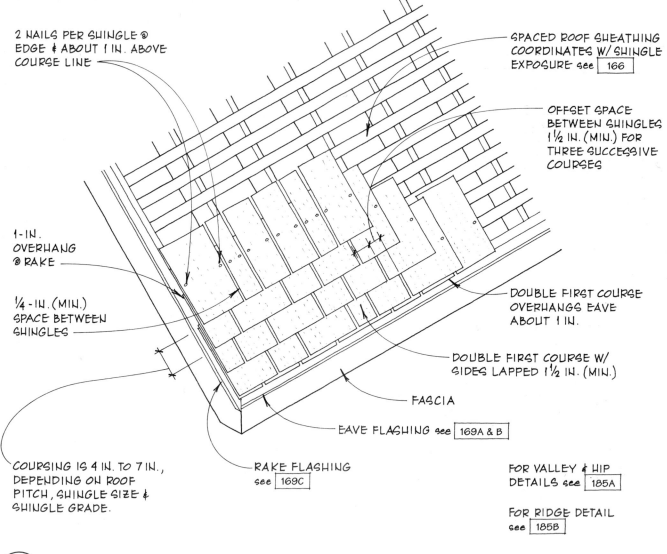

2 NAILS PER SHINGLE @ EDGE & ABOUT 1 IN. ABOVE COURSE LINE

1-IN. OVERHANG @ RAKE

¼-IN. (MIN.) SPACE BETWEEN SHINGLES

COURSING IS 4 IN. TO 7 IN., DEPENDING ON ROOF PITCH, SHINGLE SIZE & SHINGLE GRADE.

SPACED ROOF SHEATHING COORDINATES W/ SHINGLE EXPOSURE see 166

OFFSET SPACE BETWEEN SHINGLES 1½ IN. (MIN.) FOR THREE SUCCESSIVE COURSES

DOUBLE FIRST COURSE OVERHANGS EAVE ABOUT 1 IN.

DOUBLE FIRST COURSE W/ SIDES LAPPED 1½ IN. (MIN.)

FASCIA

EAVE FLASHING see 169A & B

RAKE FLASHING see 169C

FOR VALLEY & HIP DETAILS see 185A

FOR RIDGE DETAIL see 185B

 A WOOD-SHINGLE ROOFING

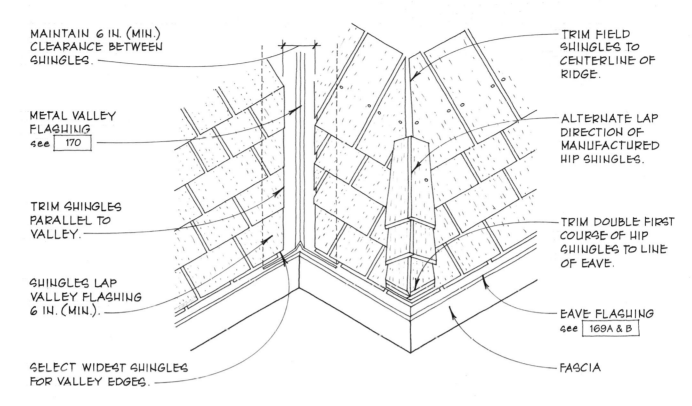

MAINTAIN 6 IN. (MIN.) CLEARANCE BETWEEN SHINGLES.

METAL VALLEY FLASHING see 170

TRIM SHINGLES PARALLEL TO VALLEY.

SHINGLES LAP VALLEY FLASHING 6 IN. (MIN.).

SELECT WIDEST SHINGLES FOR VALLEY EDGES.

TRIM FIELD SHINGLES TO CENTERLINE OF RIDGE.

ALTERNATE LAP DIRECTION OF MANUFACTURED HIP SHINGLES.

TRIM DOUBLE FIRST COURSE OF HIP SHINGLES TO LINE OF EAVE.

EAVE FLASHING see 169A & B

FASCIA

A WOOD-SHINGLE VALLEY & HIP

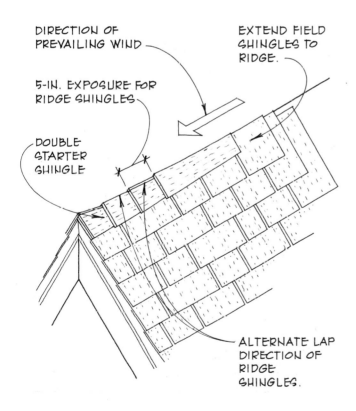

DIRECTION OF PREVAILING WIND

5-IN. EXPOSURE FOR RIDGE SHINGLES

DOUBLE STARTER SHINGLE

EXTEND FIELD SHINGLES TO RIDGE.

ALTERNATE LAP DIRECTION OF RIDGE SHINGLES.

B WOOD-SHINGLE RIDGE

Wood shakes are popular for their rustic look and their durability. They are made from the same materials as wood shingles, but they are split to achieve a taper instead of being sawn. Shakes may have split faces and sawn backs or be taper-split with both sides having a split surface. In either case, the split side is exposed to the weather because it has small smooth grooves parallel to the grain that channel rainwater down the surface of the shake. Standard shakes are 18 in. or 24 in. long and come in heavy or medium thickness.

Wood shakes may be applied over open sheathing (see 166) or solid sheathing (see 163). The courses of shakes are usually alternated with an interlayment of 30-lb. felt that retards the penetration of moisture through the relatively large gaps between shakes. Solid sheathing and cold-climate eave flashing (see 169B) are recommended in areas that have wind-driven snow.

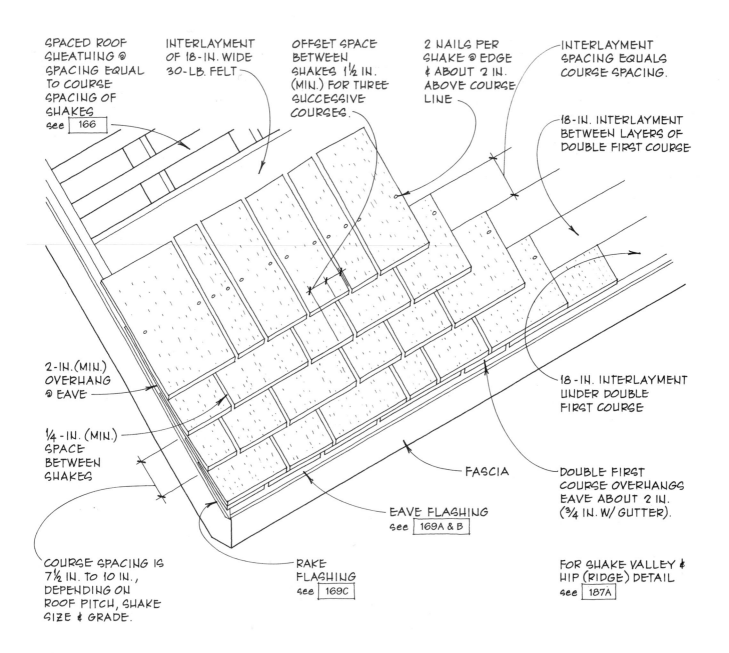

SPACED ROOF SHEATHING @ SPACING EQUAL TO COURSE SPACING OF SHAKES see 166

INTERLAYMENT OF 18-IN. WIDE 30-LB. FELT

OFFSET SPACE BETWEEN SHAKES 1½ IN. (MIN.) FOR THREE SUCCESSIVE COURSES.

2 NAILS PER SHAKE @ EDGE & ABOUT 2 IN. ABOVE COURSE LINE

INTERLAYMENT SPACING EQUALS COURSE SPACING.

18-IN. INTERLAYMENT BETWEEN LAYERS OF DOUBLE FIRST COURSE

2-IN. (MIN.) OVERHANG @ EAVE

¼-IN. (MIN.) SPACE BETWEEN SHAKES

18-IN. INTERLAYMENT UNDER DOUBLE FIRST COURSE

FASCIA

EAVE FLASHING see 169A & B

DOUBLE FIRST COURSE OVERHANGS EAVE ABOUT 2 IN. (¾ IN. W/ GUTTER).

COURSE SPACING IS 7½ IN. TO 10 IN., DEPENDING ON ROOF PITCH, SHAKE SIZE & GRADE.

RAKE FLASHING see 169C

FOR SHAKE VALLEY & HIP (RIDGE) DETAIL see 187A

(A) WOOD-SHAKE ROOFING

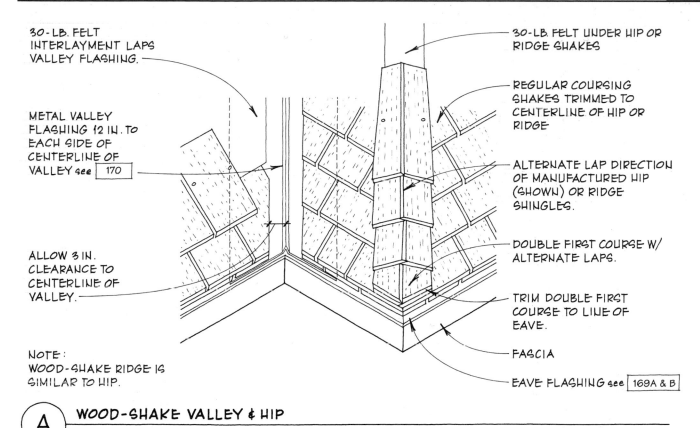

30-LB. FELT INTERLAYMENT LAPS VALLEY FLASHING.

METAL VALLEY FLASHING 12 IN. TO EACH SIDE OF CENTERLINE OF VALLEY see 170

ALLOW 3 IN. CLEARANCE TO CENTERLINE OF VALLEY.

NOTE: WOOD-SHAKE RIDGE IS SIMILAR TO HIP.

30-LB. FELT UNDER HIP OR RIDGE SHAKES

REGULAR COURSING SHAKES TRIMMED TO CENTERLINE OF HIP OR RIDGE

ALTERNATE LAP DIRECTION OF MANUFACTURED HIP (SHOWN) OR RIDGE SHINGLES.

DOUBLE FIRST COURSE W/ ALTERNATE LAPS.

TRIM DOUBLE FIRST COURSE TO LINE OF EAVE.

FASCIA

EAVE FLASHING see 169A & B

(A) WOOD-SHAKE VALLEY & HIP

Clay tiles have been used in warm climates for centuries. Their use is still common in the southern extremes of this country, but they have recently been superseded by concrete tiles, which cost less and have better quality control.

Concrete tiles are made from high-density concrete coated with a waterproof resin. They are available in a variety of shapes and colors. Most tile patterns fall in the range of 16 in. to 18 in. long and 9 in. to 13 in. wide. Tiles weigh from 6 lb. to 10½ lb. per square foot (psf), which is about 2½ to 5 times the weight of asphalt shingles. This extra weight may require that the roof structure be bolstered in some situations.

The cost of concrete tiles themselves is high compared to other common roofing materials, but most concrete tile roof systems are warranted for 50 years.

Most manufacturers recommend installing the tiles on solid sheathing with 30-lb. felt underlayment and pressure-treated nailing battens under each course. Course spacing is usually about 13 in., and can be adjusted to make courses equal on each slope of roof.

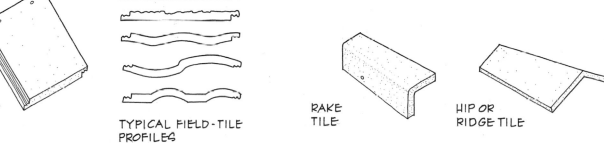

FIELD TILE

TYPICAL FIELD-TILE PROFILES

RAKE TILE

HIP OR RIDGE TILE

(B) CONCRETE TILE ROOFING
INTRODUCTION & TYPES OF TILE

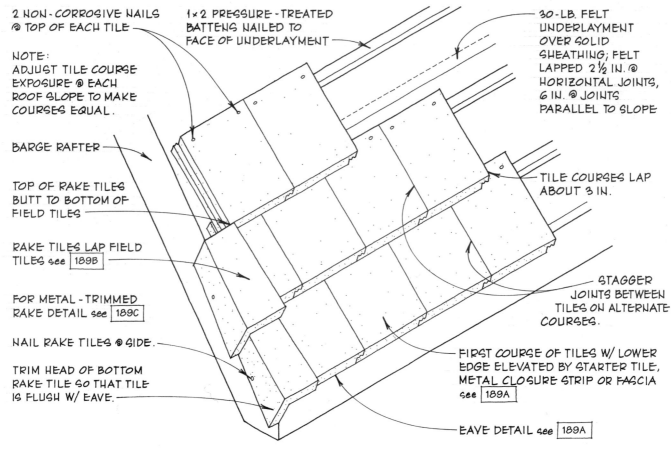

2 NON-CORROSIVE NAILS @ TOP OF EACH TILE

1×2 PRESSURE-TREATED BATTENS NAILED TO FACE OF UNDERLAYMENT

30-LB. FELT UNDERLAYMENT OVER SOLID SHEATHING; FELT LAPPED 2½ IN. @ HORIZONTAL JOINTS, 6 IN. @ JOINTS PARALLEL TO SLOPE

NOTE: ADJUST TILE COURSE EXPOSURE @ EACH ROOF SLOPE TO MAKE COURSES EQUAL.

BARGE RAFTER

TOP OF RAKE TILES BUTT TO BOTTOM OF FIELD TILES

RAKE TILES LAP FIELD TILES see 189B

FOR METAL-TRIMMED RAKE DETAIL see 189C

NAIL RAKE TILES @ SIDE.

TRIM HEAD OF BOTTOM RAKE TILE SO THAT TILE IS FLUSH W/ EAVE.

TILE COURSES LAP ABOUT 3 IN.

STAGGER JOINTS BETWEEN TILES ON ALTERNATE COURSES.

FIRST COURSE OF TILES W/ LOWER EDGE ELEVATED BY STARTER TILE, METAL CLOSURE STRIP OR FASCIA see 189A

EAVE DETAIL see 189A

Ⓐ CONCRETE-TILE ROOFING

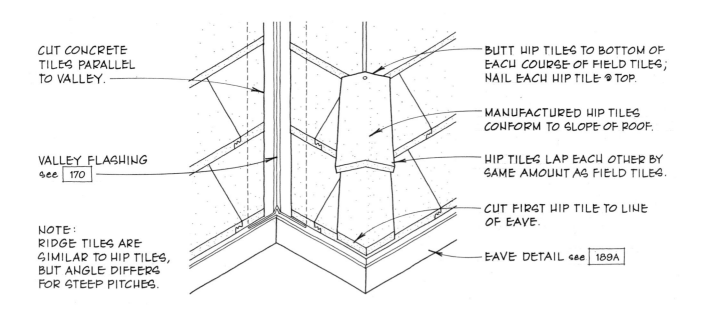

CUT CONCRETE TILES PARALLEL TO VALLEY.

VALLEY FLASHING see 170

NOTE: RIDGE TILES ARE SIMILAR TO HIP TILES, BUT ANGLE DIFFERS FOR STEEP PITCHES.

BUTT HIP TILES TO BOTTOM OF EACH COURSE OF FIELD TILES; NAIL EACH HIP TILE @ TOP.

MANUFACTURED HIP TILES CONFORM TO SLOPE OF ROOF.

HIP TILES LAP EACH OTHER BY SAME AMOUNT AS FIELD TILES.

CUT FIRST HIP TILE TO LINE OF EAVE.

EAVE DETAIL see 189A

Ⓑ CONCRETE-TILE VALLEY & HIP

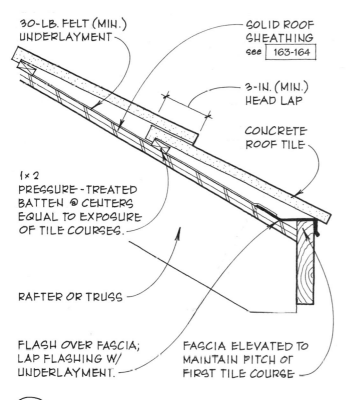

30-LB. FELT (MIN.) UNDERLAYMENT

SOLID ROOF SHEATHING
see 163-164

3-IN. (MIN.) HEAD LAP

CONCRETE ROOF TILE

1×2 PRESSURE-TREATED BATTEN @ CENTERS EQUAL TO EXPOSURE OF TILE COURSES.

RAFTER OR TRUSS

FLASH OVER FASCIA; LAP FLASHING W/ UNDERLAYMENT.

FASCIA ELEVATED TO MAINTAIN PITCH OF FIRST TILE COURSE

(A) CONCRETE-TILE EAVE

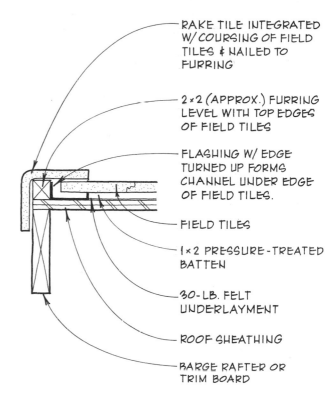

RAKE TILE INTEGRATED W/ COURSING OF FIELD TILES & NAILED TO FURRING

2×2 (APPROX.) FURRING LEVEL WITH TOP EDGES OF FIELD TILES

FLASHING W/ EDGE TURNED UP FORMS CHANNEL UNDER EDGE OF FIELD TILES.

FIELD TILES

1×2 PRESSURE-TREATED BATTEN

30-LB. FELT UNDERLAYMENT

ROOF SHEATHING

BARGE RAFTER OR TRIM BOARD

(B) CONCRETE-TILE RAKE
TILE RAKE

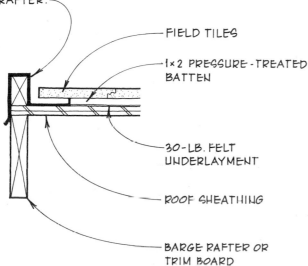

FLASHING W/ EDGE TURNED UP FORMS CHANNEL UNDER EDGE OF FIELD TILES & W/ DRIP @ BARGE RAFTER.

FIELD TILES

1×2 PRESSURE-TREATED BATTEN

30-LB. FELT UNDERLAYMENT

ROOF SHEATHING

BARGE RAFTER OR TRIM BOARD

(C) CONCRETE-TILE RAKE
METAL RAKE

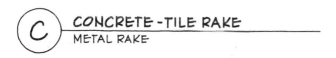

Low-cost metal roofs of aluminum or galvanized steel have been used for some time on agricultural and industrial buildings. The rolled metal panels are lightweight, long-lasting, and extremely simple to install. New panel patterns and new finishes have made metal roofing popular for residential and commercial buildings. A baked-on or porcelain enamel finish is often guaranteed for 20 years, and the galvanized steel or aluminum over which it is applied will last for another 20 years in most climates.

Rolled-metal sheets are typically 2 ft. to 3 ft. wide and are factory-cut to the full length of the roof from eave to ridge. Because of the difficulty of field cutting at angles, metal roofs are best suited to simple shed or gable roofs without extensive valleys and hips. Small openings such as vents should be kept to a minimum and collected wherever possible into single openings. (Vents are best located at the ridge, where they are most easily flashed with the ridge flashing.)

The width of the roof itself should be carefully coordinated with the width of roofing panels so that rake trim, dormers, skylights, and other interruptions of the simple system will be located at an uncut factory edge.

Because the metal roofing has structural capacity, it is possible to install the roofing over purlins, which are 2xs spaced 2 ft. to 4 ft. apart. Most metal roofing panels will span 4 ft. or more, so the load on each purlin is great, and the design of the purlins that support the roofing is a critical factor.

A wide range of finish colors is available with coordinated flashing and trim metal. Translucent fiberglass or plastic panels that match the profile of some metal roofing patterns are also available as skylights.

Choose fasteners and flashing that are compatible with the roofing in order to avoid corrosive galvanic action. Care must also be taken to avoid condensation, which can occur on metal roofs. In cold climates, where proper ventilation of the roofing system does not suffice, a fiberboard backing covered with 30-lb. felt (installed parallel to the roofing panels) will insulate the roofing from moisture-laden air and also provide protection from what little condensation does occur.

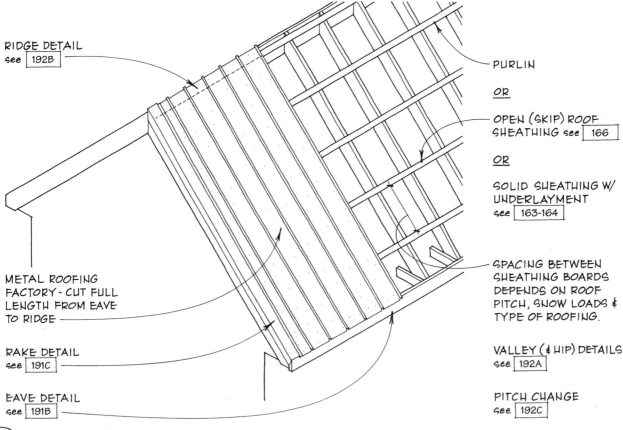

RIDGE DETAIL
see 192B

PURLIN

OR

OPEN (SKIP) ROOF
SHEATHING see 166

OR

SOLID SHEATHING W/
UNDERLAYMENT
see 163-164

METAL ROOFING
FACTORY - CUT FULL
LENGTH FROM EAVE
TO RIDGE

SPACING BETWEEN
SHEATHING BOARDS
DEPENDS ON ROOF
PITCH, SNOW LOADS &
TYPE OF ROOFING.

RAKE DETAIL
see 191C

VALLEY (& HIP) DETAILS
see 192A

EAVE DETAIL
see 191B

PITCH CHANGE
see 192C

(A)   PREFORMED METAL ROOFING

RIBBED ROOFING
SCREW (OR NAIL) W/ NEOPRENE
WASHER LOCATED IN FLAT (VALLEY)
PART OF ROOFING PROMOTES TIGHT
SEAL OF WASHER.

SNAP-TOGETHER ROOFING
SUBSEQUENT PIECE SNAP-FASTENS
TO EDGE OF PIECE PREVIOUSLY NAILED.
FLAT-HEAD NAIL IS COVERED SO
NEOPRENE WASHER IS UNNECESSARY.
SECTIONS ARE NARROWER FOR
THIS TYPE.

CORRUGATED ROOFING
SCREW (OR NAIL) W/ NEOPRENE
WASHER IS LOCATED ON RIDGE OF
CORRUGATION BECAUSE VALLEYS
ARE NOT WIDE OR FLAT ENOUGH.
IT'S DIFFICULT TO ADJUST
TENSION OF NAIL OR SCREW.

NOTE:
SOME MANUFACTURERS RECOMMEND
NEOPRENE TAPE @ JOINTS.

 A **METAL ROOFING TYPES**
PROFILES

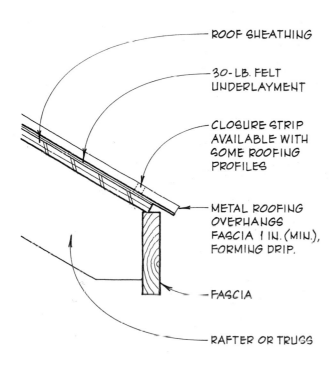

- ROOF SHEATHING
- 30-LB. FELT UNDERLAYMENT
- CLOSURE STRIP AVAILABLE WITH SOME ROOFING PROFILES
- METAL ROOFING OVERHANGS FASCIA 1 IN. (MIN.), FORMING DRIP.
- FASCIA
- RAFTER OR TRUSS

 B **METAL-ROOF EAVE**

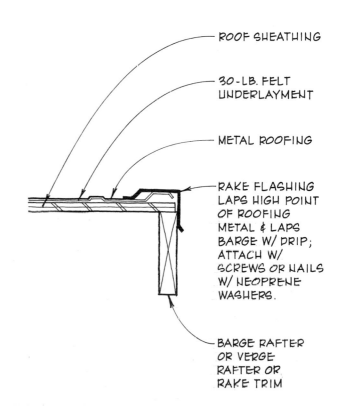

- ROOF SHEATHING
- 30-LB. FELT UNDERLAYMENT
- METAL ROOFING
- RAKE FLASHING LAPS HIGH POINT OF ROOFING METAL & LAPS BARGE W/ DRIP; ATTACH W/ SCREWS OR NAILS W/ NEOPRENE WASHERS.
- BARGE RAFTER OR VERGE RAFTER OR RAKE TRIM

 C **METAL-ROOF RAKE**

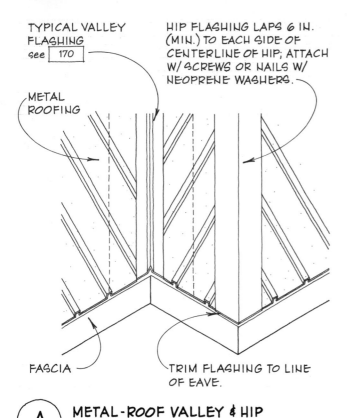

TYPICAL VALLEY FLASHING
see ⌐170¬

HIP FLASHING LAPS 6 IN. (MIN.) TO EACH SIDE OF CENTERLINE OF HIP; ATTACH W/ SCREWS OR NAILS W/ NEOPRENE WASHERS.

METAL ROOFING

FASCIA

TRIM FLASHING TO LINE OF EAVE.

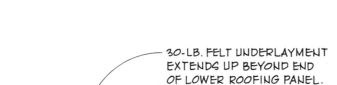

Ⓐ **METAL-ROOF VALLEY & HIP**

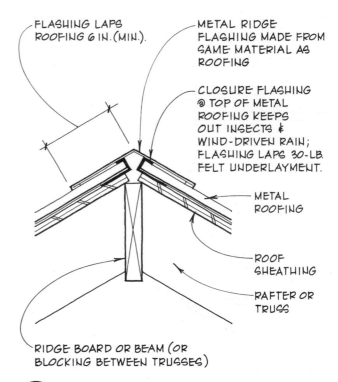

FLASHING LAPS ROOFING 6 IN. (MIN.).

METAL RIDGE FLASHING MADE FROM SAME MATERIAL AS ROOFING

CLOSURE FLASHING @ TOP OF METAL ROOFING KEEPS OUT INSECTS & WIND-DRIVEN RAIN; FLASHING LAPS 30-LB. FELT UNDERLAYMENT.

METAL ROOFING

ROOF SHEATHING

RAFTER OR TRUSS

RIDGE BOARD OR BEAM (OR BLOCKING BETWEEN TRUSSES)

Ⓑ **METAL-ROOF RIDGE FLASHING**

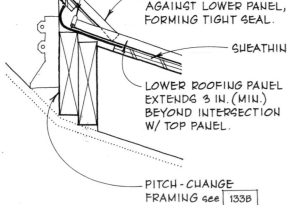

30-LB. FELT UNDERLAYMENT EXTENDS UP BEYOND END OF LOWER ROOFING PANEL.

BEAD OF CAULKING OR SEALANT @ TOP EDGE OF LOWER ROOFING PANEL FORMS A DAM AGAINST WIND-DRIVEN RAIN.

TOP ROOFING PANEL NESTS AGAINST LOWER PANEL, FORMING TIGHT SEAL.

SHEATHING

LOWER ROOFING PANEL EXTENDS 3 IN. (MIN.) BEYOND INTERSECTION W/ TOP PANEL.

PITCH-CHANGE FRAMING see ⌐133B¬

Ⓒ **METAL-ROOF PITCH CHANGE**

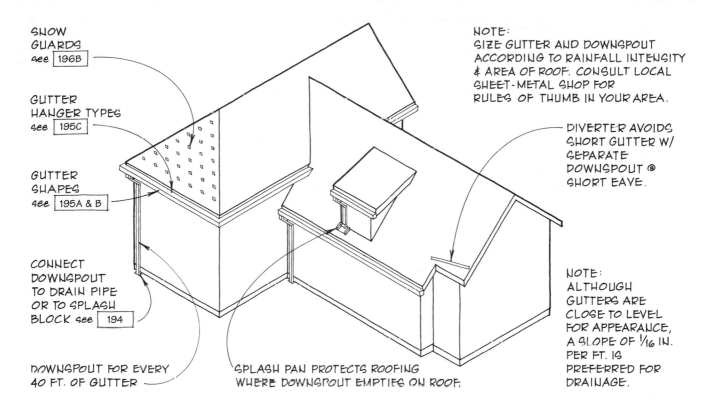

SNOW GUARDS see [196B]

GUTTER HANGER TYPES see [195C]

GUTTER SHAPES see [195A & B]

CONNECT DOWNSPOUT TO DRAIN PIPE OR TO SPLASH BLOCK see [194]

DOWNSPOUT FOR EVERY 40 FT. OF GUTTER

SPLASH PAN PROTECTS ROOFING WHERE DOWNSPOUT EMPTIES ON ROOF.

NOTE: SIZE GUTTER AND DOWNSPOUT ACCORDING TO RAINFALL INTENSITY & AREA OF ROOF. CONSULT LOCAL SHEET-METAL SHOP FOR RULES OF THUMB IN YOUR AREA.

DIVERTER AVOIDS SHORT GUTTER W/ SEPARATE DOWNSPOUT @ SHORT EAVE.

NOTE: ALTHOUGH GUTTERS ARE CLOSE TO LEVEL FOR APPEARANCE, A SLOPE OF 1/16 IN. PER FT. IS PREFERRED FOR DRAINAGE.

The collection of rainwater by gutters at the eave of a roof prevents it from falling to the ground, where it can splash back onto the building and cause discoloration and decay, or where it can seep into the ground, causing settling or undermining of the foundation. Gutters also protect people passing under the eaves from a cascade of rainwater. In areas of light rainfall, gutters may be eliminated if adequate overhangs are designed and a rock bed is placed below the eaves to control the water and prevent splashback.

Most wood-framed buildings are fitted with site-formed aluminum or galvanized steel gutters with a baked-enamel finish. Continuous straight sections of site-formed gutters are limited only by the need for expansion joints (see 194) and by the ability of workers to carry the sections without buckling them. Very long sections can be manufactured without joints, the most common location of gutter failures.

Vinyl gutters, although more expensive, are popular with owner-builders because they are more durable and can be installed without specialized equipment.

Downspouts conduct the water from the gutter to the ground, where it should be collected in a storm drain and carried away from the building to be dispersed on the surface, deposited in a dry well, or directed to a storm sewer system.

The problem of water freezing in gutters and downspouts may be solved with heat tapes.

Snow sliding off a roof can cause real problems—especially over porches, decks, and garages. The problem of sliding snow may be solved by keeping the snow on the roof with a low-pitched roof or with snow guards that project from the roofing surface to hold the snow mechanically in place (see 196B).

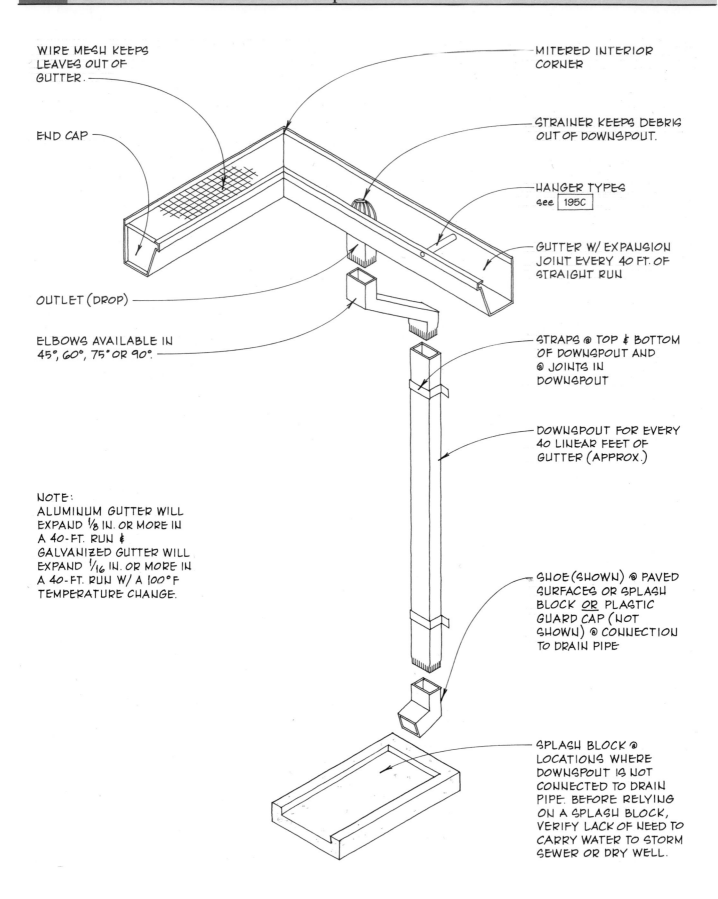

WIRE MESH KEEPS LEAVES OUT OF GUTTER.

END CAP

OUTLET (DROP)

ELBOWS AVAILABLE IN 45°, 60°, 75° OR 90°.

NOTE:
ALUMINUM GUTTER WILL EXPAND 1/8 IN. OR MORE IN A 40-FT. RUN & GALVANIZED GUTTER WILL EXPAND 1/16 IN. OR MORE IN A 40-FT. RUN W/ A 100°F TEMPERATURE CHANGE.

MITERED INTERIOR CORNER

STRAINER KEEPS DEBRIS OUT OF DOWNSPOUT.

HANGER TYPES
see 195C

GUTTER W/ EXPANSION JOINT EVERY 40 FT. OF STRAIGHT RUN

STRAPS @ TOP & BOTTOM OF DOWNSPOUT AND @ JOINTS IN DOWNSPOUT

DOWNSPOUT FOR EVERY 40 LINEAR FEET OF GUTTER (APPROX.)

SHOE (SHOWN) @ PAVED SURFACES OR SPLASH BLOCK OR PLASTIC GUARD CAP (NOT SHOWN) @ CONNECTION TO DRAIN PIPE

SPLASH BLOCK @ LOCATIONS WHERE DOWNSPOUT IS NOT CONNECTED TO DRAIN PIPE. BEFORE RELYING ON A SPLASH BLOCK, VERIFY LACK OF NEED TO CARRY WATER TO STORM SEWER OR DRY WELL.

A   PARTS OF A GUTTER SYSTEM

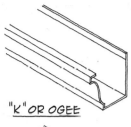

"K" OR OGEE

OGEE IS THE MOST COMMON GUTTER SHAPE. AVAILABLE IN SITE-FORMED ALUMINUM OR GALVANIZED IN A VARIETY OF SIZES, IT IS ALSO MADE IN UNPAINTED GALVANIZED STEEL OR COPPER.

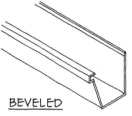

BEVELED

SAME AS OGEE, EXCEPT NOT SO COMMON

HALF-ROUND

HALF-ROUND GUTTER CANNOT BE SITE-FORMED; IT IS AVAILABLE IN VINYL OR UNPAINTED GALVANIZED STEEL OR COPPER.

WOODEN GUTTER

WOODEN GUTTERS ARE USED EXTENSIVELY IN THE NORTHEAST. THEY ARE DIFFICULT TO JOIN @ CORNERS OR FOR LONG LENGTHS & ARE PRONE TO DECAY.

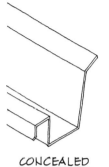

CONCEALED GUTTER

CONCEALED GUTTERS OF VARIABLE SHAPES & SIZES MAY BE DESIGNED TO FIT BEHIND THE FASCIA OR WITHIN THE SLOPE OF A ROOF. THESE ARE ALWAYS CUSTOM MADE & ARE THEREFORE EXPENSIVE. UPPER EDGE OF GUTTER IS TYPICALLY LAPPED BY ROOFING; LOWER EDGE CAPS FASCIA.

 A GUTTER SHAPES

 B SPECIAL GUTTERS

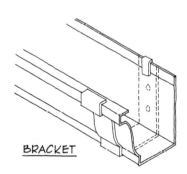

BRACKET

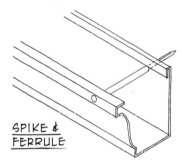

SPIKE & FERRULE

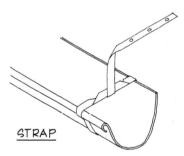

STRAP

BRACKET HANGERS ARE AVAILABLE FOR ALL TYPES OF GUTTER; SCREW TO FASCIA OR (WITH LONGER SCREWS) TO RAFTER TAILS.

SPIKE & FERRULE HANGERS ARE USED W/ BEVELED OR OGEE GUTTERS; SPIKE TO FASCIA OR TO RAFTER TAILS. THE NEED FOR EXPANSION JOINTS IS GREATEST WITH THIS TYPE OF CONNECTOR (MAXIMUM RUN WITHOUT JOINT IS 40 FT.).

STRAP HANGERS ARE USED W/ METAL HALF-ROUND GUTTERS; NAIL OR SCREW TO ROOF SHEATHING OR THROUGH SHEATHING TO TOP OF RAFTER. UNCOMMON, ARCHAIC.

 C GUTTER HANGERS

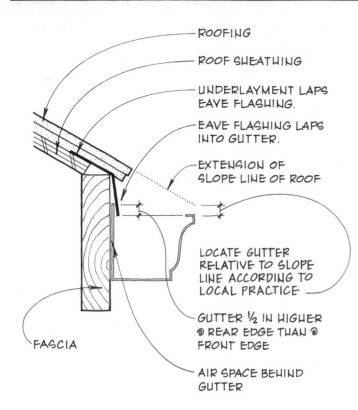

ROOFING

ROOF SHEATHING

UNDERLAYMENT LAPS
EAVE FLASHING.

EAVE FLASHING LAPS
INTO GUTTER.

EXTENSION OF
SLOPE LINE OF ROOF

LOCATE GUTTER
RELATIVE TO SLOPE
LINE ACCORDING TO
LOCAL PRACTICE

GUTTER ½ IN HIGHER
@ REAR EDGE THAN @
FRONT EDGE

AIR SPACE BEHIND
GUTTER

FASCIA

NOTES:
FASCIA IS SHOWN PLUMB FOR EASE OF
INSTALLATION OF COMMON GUTTERS.
SQUARE-CUT RAFTER TAILS WORK WHERE THERE
ARE NO GUTTERS OR WHERE HALF-ROUND
GUTTERS ARE HUNG FROM STRAP HANGERS
see 195C

FASCIA IS GENERALLY 2× MATERIAL FOR EASE OF
INSTALLATION OF COMMON GUTTERS. IN SOME AREAS,
THE 2× IS USED AS A SUB-FASCIA AND COVERED
WITH A HIGHER GRADE 1× FASCIA. GUTTERS MAY BE
HUNG FROM A SINGLE 1× FASCIA, BUT SPIKES MUST
BE LOCATED AT RAFTERS & FASCIA PRE-DRILLED TO
PREVENT SPLITTING. BRACKETS SHOULD BE
LOCATED NEAR RAFTERS.

(A) GUTTER/EAVE

Snow guards, or snow clips, are metal protrusions
that are integrated with the roofing to prevent snow
from sliding off the roof. They are either clipped to
the top edge of the roofing material (tiles and slate)
or are nailed integral with it (shakes and shingles).
Snow guards are used at the rate of 10 to 30 guards
per square, depending on roof steepness.

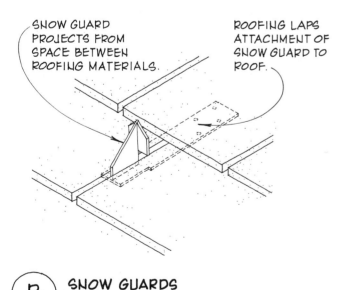

SNOW GUARD
PROJECTS FROM
SPACE BETWEEN
ROOFING MATERIALS.

ROOFING LAPS
ATTACHMENT OF
SNOW GUARD TO
ROOF.

(B) SNOW GUARDS

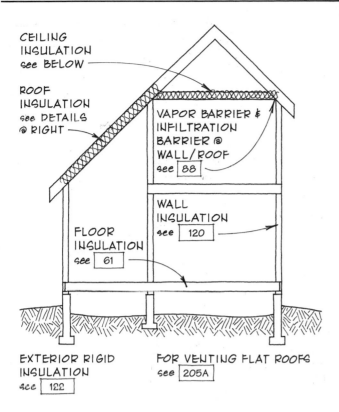

CEILING INSULATION
see BELOW

ROOF INSULATION
see DETAILS @ RIGHT

VAPOR BARRIER & INFILTRATION BARRIER @ WALL/ROOF
see [88]

WALL INSULATION
see [120]

FLOOR INSULATION
see [61]

EXTERIOR RIGID INSULATION
see [122]

FOR VENTING FLAT ROOFS
see [205A]

Roof insulation—Roof insulation may be fiberglass batts or rigid insulation. If the rafters are deep enough, batts are the most economical. When the rafters do not have adequate depth for batts, rigid insulation must be fit between the rafters. In both cases, a 1-in. air space must be provided above the insulation for ventilating the roof.

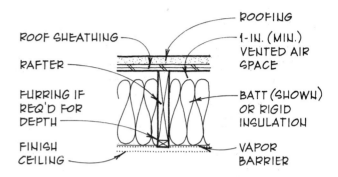

ROOF SHEATHING

RAFTER

FURRING IF REQ'D FOR DEPTH

FINISH CEILING

ROOFING

1-IN. (MIN.) VENTED AIR SPACE

BATT (SHOWN) OR RIGID INSULATION

VAPOR BARRIER

When the rafters are exposed to the living space below, the roof must be insulated from above. Rigid insulation is typically used because of its compactness and/or its structural value. Some roofing materials may be applied directly to the rigid insulation (e.g., membrane roofing on flat roofs); others require additional structure and/or an air space for ventilation.

Most heat is potentially lost or gained through the roof, so ceilings and roofs are generally more heavily insulated than floors or walls. Building codes in most climates require R-30 in roofs. The temperature difference between the two sides of a roof or ceiling can cause condensation when warm, moist interior air hits cold surfaces in the roof assembly. It is therefore important to place a vapor barrier on the warm side of the insulation (see the drawing at above right) and, in most cases, to ventilate the roof (see 200).

Ceiling insulation—Ceiling insulation consists typically of either fiberglass batts placed between ceiling joists before the ceiling is applied or loose-fill insulation blown (or poured) into place in the completed attic space. The loose-fill type has the advantage of filling tightly around trusses and other interruptions of the attic space and of being able to fill to any depth. With either type, the vapor barrier should be located on the warm side of the insulation.

When trusses or shallow rafters restrict the depth of insulation at the edges of the ceiling, ventilation channels may be needed (see 201). Baffles may also be required to keep insulation from obstructing roof intake vents or from being blown out of place.

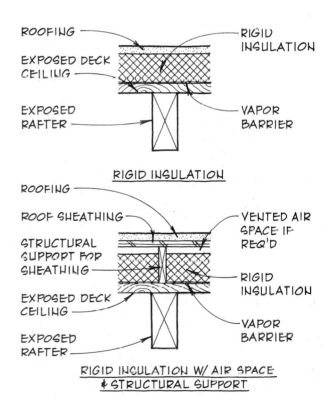

ROOFING

EXPOSED DECK CEILING

EXPOSED RAFTER

RIGID INSULATION

VAPOR BARRIER

RIGID INSULATION

ROOFING

ROOF SHEATHING

STRUCTURAL SUPPORT FOR SHEATHING

EXPOSED DECK CEILING

EXPOSED RAFTER

VENTED AIR SPACE IF REQ'D

RIGID INSULATION

VAPOR BARRIER

RIGID INSULATION W/ AIR SPACE & STRUCTURAL SUPPORT

Ⓐ   CEILING & ROOF INSULATION

Compared to walls and floors, it is usually relatively simple to add insulation to the ceiling of a building. Insulation thickness can generally be increased without adding structure or other complications. Gravity holds the insulation in place, and the only disadvantage is a loss of attic space. In addition, the ceiling is where most of the heat is gained or lost from an insulated space, so the addition of insulation is especially effective.

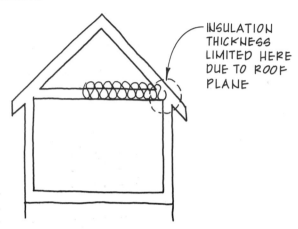

INSULATION THICKNESS LIMITED HERE DUE TO ROOF PLANE

The only complication occurs at the edge of the building where roof structure typically restricts the potential for insulation thickness. In standard construction, it is common to compress the insulation in this area and allow for ventilation using vent channels made especially for this purpose (see 201). But for superinsulated buildings, the compression of insulation in this area is not acceptable. To overcome the problem, several strategies have been developed.

Rigid insulation—Because rigid insulation can have R-values approximately double that of batt insulation, it may provide thermal protection at the edge of the ceiling without any adjustments to the framing (see 199A). This strategy may not be feasible when the roof pitch is very low, when rafter depth is shallow, or when the ceiling insulation value is very high.

Raised-heel truss—It is quite common when ordering trusses to specify a truss that has extra depth at the ends to accommodate extra insulation. This is called a raised-heel truss. Raised-heel trusses require blocking to prevent rotation, but otherwise are installed just the same as standard trusses (see 199B).

Dropped ceiling—Full insulation thickness at the edge of the building can also be accommodated by dropping the ceiling below the top plate. To maintain a given ceiling height, this strategy would require extra-length studs, extra siding, extra framing material for the ceiling, and extra labor. When using rafters (not trusses), a balloon-framed ceiling/wall connection (see 41A &, B) would allow ceiling joists to act as ties and not be redundant (see 199C).

Raised plate—Raising the rafters to the top of the ceiling joists can increase the insulation thickness by the depth of the joists. The depth of the joists and rafters combined can be sufficient for super insulation.

The extra cost of this strategy would include an extra rim joist, an extra plate, extra siding, and labor. The rafters need to be tied directly to the joists to counteract the thrust of the rafters (see 199D).

Vaulted ceilings—Vaulted ceilings do not restrict insulation thickness at the edge of the building because the insulation follows the pitch of the roof. The insulation value of vaulted roofs is limited only by the thickness of the roof itself (see 204A & B).

(A) SUPERINSULATED CEILINGS

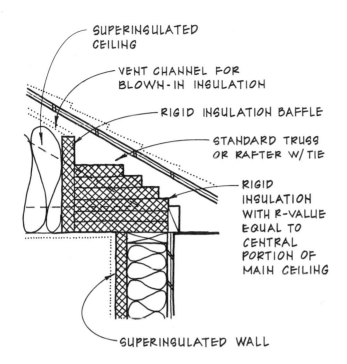

SUPERINSULATED CEILING

VENT CHANNEL FOR BLOWN-IN INSULATION

RIGID INSULATION BAFFLE

STANDARD TRUSS OR RAFTER W/ TIE

RIGID INSULATION WITH R-VALUE EQUAL TO CENTRAL PORTION OF MAIN CEILING

SUPERINSULATED WALL

A SUPERINSULATED CEILING
RIGID INSULATION

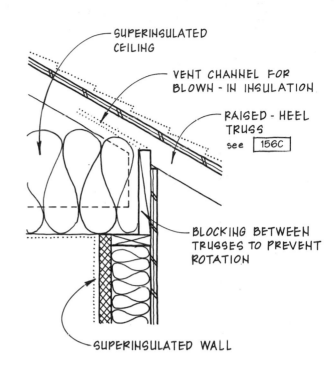

SUPERINSULATED CEILING

VENT CHANNEL FOR BLOWN-IN INSULATION

RAISED-HEEL TRUSS
see 156C

BLOCKING BETWEEN TRUSSES TO PREVENT ROTATION

SUPERINSULATED WALL

B SUPERINSULATED CEILING
RAISED HEEL TRUSS

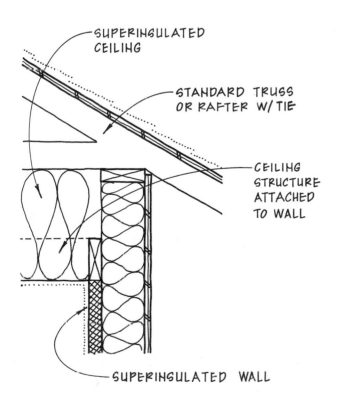

SUPERINSULATED CEILING

STANDARD TRUSS OR RAFTER W/ TIE

CEILING STRUCTURE ATTACHED TO WALL

SUPERINSULATED WALL

C SUPERINSULATED CEILING
DROPPED CEILING

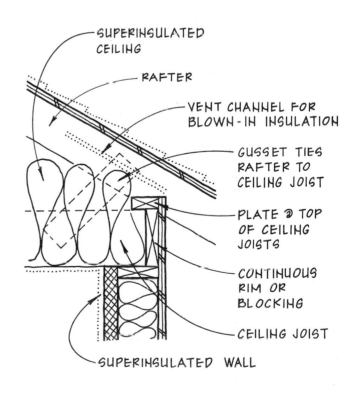

SUPERINSULATED CEILING

RAFTER

VENT CHANNEL FOR BLOWN-IN INSULATION

GUSSET TIES RAFTER TO CEILING JOIST

PLATE @ TOP OF CEILING JOISTS

CONTINUOUS RIM OR BLOCKING

CEILING JOIST

SUPERINSULATED WALL

D SUPERINSULATED CEILING
RAISED PLATE

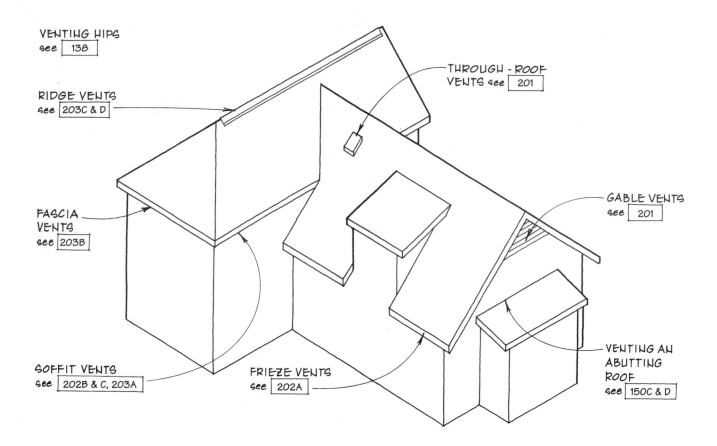

VENTING HIPS
see [138]

RIDGE VENTS
see [203C & D]

THROUGH - ROOF
VENTS see [201]

FASCIA
VENTS
see [203B]

GABLE VENTS
see [201]

SOFFIT VENTS
see [202B & C, 203A]

FRIEZE VENTS
see [202A]

VENTING AN
ABUTTING
ROOF
see [150C & D]

Roofs and attics must be vented to prevent heat buildup in summer and to help minimize condensation in winter. (Condensation is reduced primarily by the installation of a vapor barrier, see 197.) In addition, winter ventilation is necessary in cold climates to prevent escaping heat from melting snow that can refreeze and cause structural or moisture damage.

The best way to ventilate a roof or attic is with both low (intake) and high (exhaust) vents, which together create convection currents. Codes recognize this by allowing the ventilation area to be cut in half if vents are placed both high and low. Most codes allow the net free-ventilating area to be reduced from $\frac{1}{150}$ to $\frac{1}{300}$ of the area vented if half of the vents are 3 ft. above the eave line, with the other half located at the eave line.

Passive ventilation using convection will suffice for almost every winter venting need, but active ventilation is preferred in some areas for the warm season. Electric-powered fan ventilators improve summer cooling by moving more air through the attic space to remove the heat that has entered the attic space through the roof. The use of fans should be carefully coordinated with the intake and exhaust venting discussed in this section so that the flow of air through the attic is maximized.

Some roofing materials (e.g., shakes, shingles, and tile), are self-venting if applied over open sheathing. These roof assemblies can provide significant ventilation directly through voids in the roof itself. Check with local building officials to verify the acceptance of this type of ventilation.

A special roof, called a cold roof (see 204A), is designed to ventilate vaulted ceilings in extremely cold climates. The cold roof prevents the formation of ice dams—formed when snow thawed by escaping heat refreezes at the eave. When an ice dam forms, thawed snow can pond behind it and eventually find its way into the structure. The cold roof prevents ice dams by using ventilation to isolate the snow from the heated space.

A ROOF & ATTIC VENTING

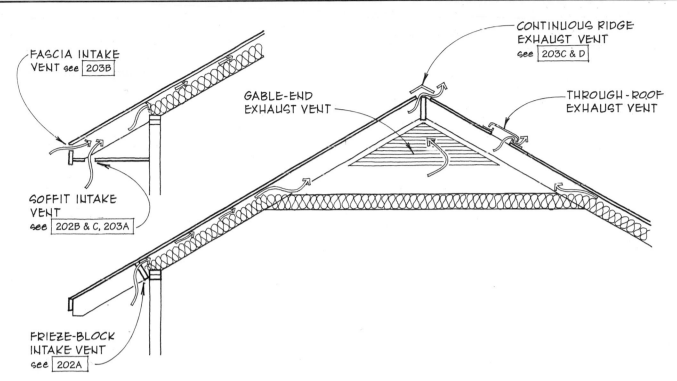

FASCIA INTAKE VENT see [203B]

GABLE-END EXHAUST VENT

CONTINUOUS RIDGE EXHAUST VENT see [203C & D]

THROUGH-ROOF EXHAUST VENT

SOFFIT INTAKE VENT see [202B & C, 203A]

FRIEZE-BLOCK INTAKE VENT see [202A]

Intake vents—Intake vents are commonly located either in a frieze block or in a soffit or fascia. They are usually screened to keep out birds and insects. The screening itself impedes the flow of air, so the vent area should be increased to allow for the screen (by a factor of 1.25 for ⅛-in. mesh screen, 2.0 for 1⁄16-in. screen). The net venting area of all intake vents together should equal about half of the total area of vents.

Vent channels may be applied to the underside of the roof sheathing in locations where the free flow of air from intake vents may be restricted by insulation. The vent channels provide an air space by holding the insulation away from the sheathing. These channels should be used only for short distances, such as at the edge of an insulated ceiling.

Exhaust vents—If appropriately sized and balanced with intake vents, exhaust vents should remove excess moisture in winter. There are three types of exhaust vents: the continuous ridge vent, the gable-end vent, and the through-roof exhaust vent.

The continuous ridge vent is best for preventing summer heat buildup because it is located highest on the roof and theoretically draws ventilation air evenly across the entire underside of the roof surface. Ridge vents can be awkward looking, but they can also be fairly unobtrusive if detailed carefully (see 203C & D). (Another type of ridge vent, the cupola, is also an effective ventilator, but is difficult to waterproof against wind-driven rain.)

The gable-end vent is a reasonably economical exhaust vent. Gable-end vents should be located across the attic space from one another. They are readily available in metal, vinyl, or wood, and in round, rectangular or triangular shapes. Because the shape of gable-end vents can be visually dominant, they may be emphasized as a design feature of the building.

The through-roof exhaust vent is available as the "cake pan" type illustrated above or the larger rotating turbine type, available in many sizes. Through-roof vents are usually shingled into the roof and are useful for areas difficult to vent with a continuous ridge vent or a gable-end vent.

THICK CEILING INSULATION

VENT CHANNEL COMPRESSES INSULATION FOR SHORT DISTANCE TO ALLOW FREE PASSAGE OF VENTILATION AIR.

ROOF SHEATHING

RAFTER

 A INTAKE & EXHAUST ROOF VENTS

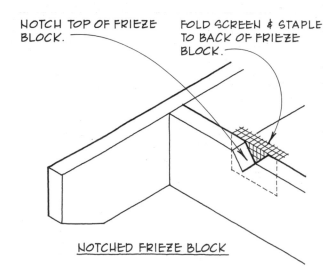

NOTCH TOP OF FRIEZE BLOCK.

FOLD SCREEN & STAPLE TO BACK OF FRIEZE BLOCK.

NOTCHED FRIEZE BLOCK

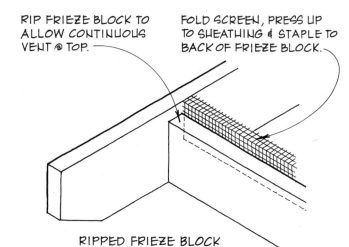

RIP FRIEZE BLOCK TO ALLOW CONTINUOUS VENT @ TOP.

FOLD SCREEN, PRESS UP TO SHEATHING & STAPLE TO BACK OF FRIEZE BLOCK.

RIPPED FRIEZE BLOCK

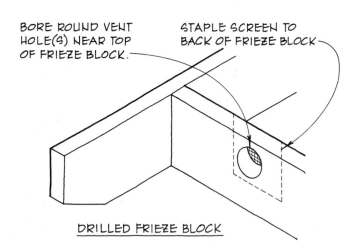

BORE ROUND VENT HOLE(S) NEAR TOP OF FRIEZE BLOCK.

STAPLE SCREEN TO BACK OF FRIEZE BLOCK

DRILLED FRIEZE BLOCK

A **FRIEZE-BLOCK INTAKE VENTS**
THREE TYPES

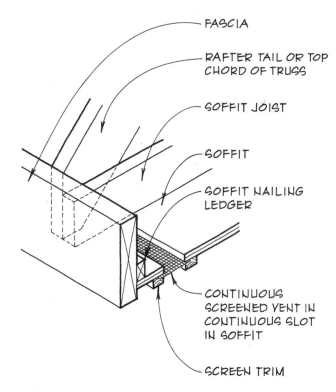

FASCIA

RAFTER TAIL OR TOP CHORD OF TRUSS

SOFFIT JOIST

SOFFIT

SOFFIT NAILING LEDGER

CONTINUOUS SCREENED VENT IN CONTINUOUS SLOT IN SOFFIT

SCREEN TRIM

B **SOFFIT INTAKE VENT**
SCREENED

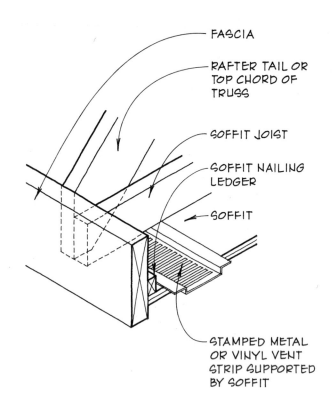

FASCIA

RAFTER TAIL OR TOP CHORD OF TRUSS

SOFFIT JOIST

SOFFIT NAILING LEDGER

SOFFIT

STAMPED METAL OR VINYL VENT STRIP SUPPORTED BY SOFFIT

C **SOFFIT INTAKE VENT**
STAMPED

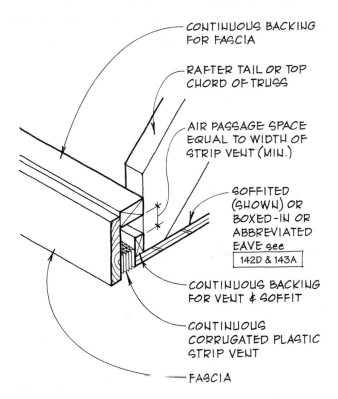

CONTINUOUS BACKING FOR FASCIA

RAFTER TAIL OR TOP CHORD OF TRUSS

AIR PASSAGE SPACE EQUAL TO WIDTH OF STRIP VENT (MIN.)

SOFFITED (SHOWN) OR BOXED-IN OR ABBREVIATED EAVE see 142D & 143A

CONTINUOUS BACKING FOR VENT & SOFFIT

CONTINUOUS CORRUGATED PLASTIC STRIP VENT

FASCIA

A SOFFIT INTAKE VENT
CORRUGATED STRIP

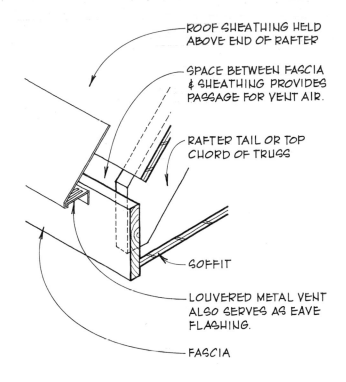

ROOF SHEATHING HELD ABOVE END OF RAFTER

SPACE BETWEEN FASCIA & SHEATHING PROVIDES PASSAGE FOR VENT AIR.

RAFTER TAIL OR TOP CHORD OF TRUSS

SOFFIT

LOUVERED METAL VENT ALSO SERVES AS EAVE FLASHING.

FASCIA

B FASCIA INTAKE VENT
STARTER

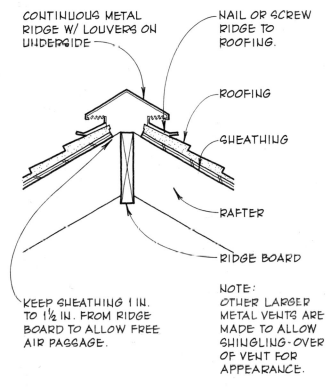

CONTINUOUS METAL RIDGE W/ LOUVERS ON UNDERSIDE

NAIL OR SCREW RIDGE TO ROOFING.

ROOFING

SHEATHING

RAFTER

RIDGE BOARD

KEEP SHEATHING 1 IN. TO 1½ IN. FROM RIDGE BOARD TO ALLOW FREE AIR PASSAGE.

NOTE: OTHER LARGER METAL VENTS ARE MADE TO ALLOW SHINGLING-OVER OF VENT FOR APPEARANCE.

C RIDGE EXHAUST VENT
METAL

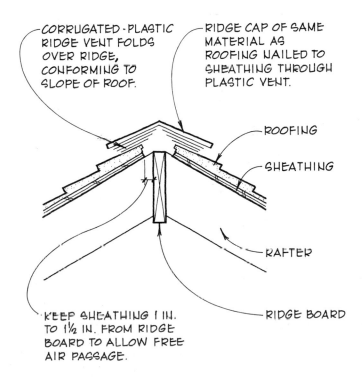

CORRUGATED-PLASTIC RIDGE VENT FOLDS OVER RIDGE, CONFORMING TO SLOPE OF ROOF.

RIDGE CAP OF SAME MATERIAL AS ROOFING NAILED TO SHEATHING THROUGH PLASTIC VENT.

ROOFING

SHEATHING

RAFTER

RIDGE BOARD

KEEP SHEATHING 1 IN. TO 1½ IN. FROM RIDGE BOARD TO ALLOW FREE AIR PASSAGE.

D RIDGE EXHAUST VENT
CORRUGATED PLASTIC

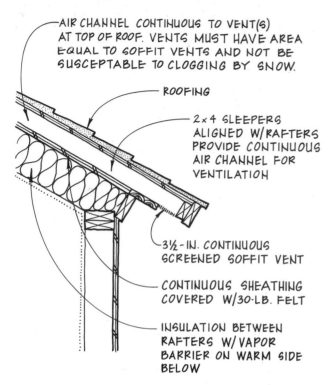

AIR CHANNEL CONTINUOUS TO VENT(S) AT TOP OF ROOF. VENTS MUST HAVE AREA EQUAL TO SOFFIT VENTS AND NOT BE SUSCEPTABLE TO CLOGGING BY SNOW.

ROOFING

2 x 4 SLEEPERS ALIGNED W/RAFTERS PROVIDE CONTINUOUS AIR CHANNEL FOR VENTILATION

3½-IN. CONTINUOUS SCREENED SOFFIT VENT

CONTINUOUS SHEATHING COVERED W/30-LB. FELT

INSULATION BETWEEN RAFTERS W/ VAPOR BARRIER ON WARM SIDE BELOW

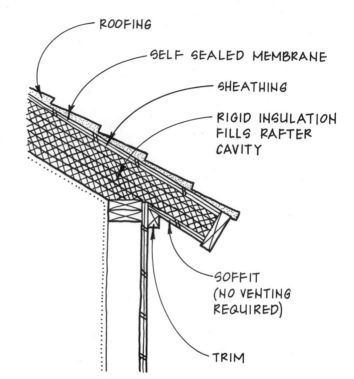

ROOFING

SELF SEALED MEMBRANE

SHEATHING

RIGID INSULATION FILLS RAFTER CAVITY

SOFFIT (NO VENTING REQUIRED)

TRIM

The cold roof is a way to protect vaulted ceilings in cold climates from the formation of ice dams. A cold roof is a double-layer roof with the upper layer vented and the lower layer insulated. The vented layer promotes continuous unrestricted air flow from eave to ridge across the entire area of the roof. This flow of cold air removes any heat that escapes through the insulated layer below. The entire outer roof surface is thus maintained at the temperature of the ambient air, thereby preventing the freeze-thaw cycle caused by heat escaping through the insulation of conventional roofs.

The typical cold roof is built with sleepers aligned over rafters and with continuous eave vents and complementary ridge or gable vents. A 3½-in. air space has been found to provide adequate ventilation, but a 1½-in. air space does not. The sleepers must be held away from obstructions such as skylights, vents, hips, and valleys to allow air to flow continuously around them.

A modified cold roof with extra-deep rafters to provide deeper than normal ventilation space but without the double-layer ventilation system can work, but it does not provide protection against condensation, which can form above the insulation in the ventilation space.

The warm roof also protects vaulted ceilings in cold climates from the formation of ice dams. Instead of isolating the snow from the insulation like a cold roof, however, the warm roof prevents escaping heat from melting the snow by increasing insulation thickness. When the ceiling R-value is sufficient (approximately R-50 is recommended), the temperature on the surface of the roof can be maintained at the temperature of the snow. The snow will therefore not melt while the ambient temperature remains below freezing.

By using rigid insulation, the warm roof eliminates the ventilation space because there are no voids within which condensation can form, so there is no need to ventilate between the insulation and the roof surface. With snow effectively adjacent to the insulation, the insulative value of the snow itself will contribute to the insulation of the building. In this respect, the warm roof is superior to the cold roof because the cold roof exposes the outer surface of the insulation to ambient air (which can be significantly colder than snow).

When compared to the cold roof, the warm roof is less complicated to build and will insulate better. It is made with expensive materials, however, so may have a higher first cost—especially for owner-builders.

 COLD ROOF

 WARM ROOF

Flat roofs, like sloped roofs, require ventilation to prevent heat buildup and to minimize condensation. The principles of ventilation are the same for flat roofs as for sloped roofs, but flat roofs have some particular ventilation requirements due to their shape. On a flat roof, a low intake vent can rarely be balanced by a high exhaust vent (3 ft. min. above the intake vent).

The net free-ventilating area therefore cannot usually be reduced from $\frac{1}{150}$ of the area of the roof.

Flat-roof ventilators are commonly of the continuous strip type, located at a soffit, or a series of small vents scattered across the roof. Parapet walls can also provide effective ventilation for flat roofs (see 205B).

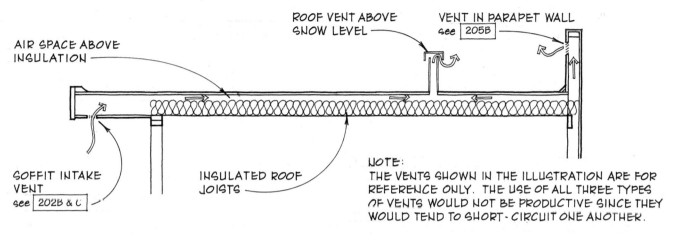

AIR SPACE ABOVE INSULATION

ROOF VENT ABOVE SNOW LEVEL

VENT IN PARAPET WALL see 205B

SOFFIT INTAKE VENT see 202B & C

INSULATED ROOF JOISTS

NOTE:
THE VENTS SHOWN IN THE ILLUSTRATION ARE FOR REFERENCE ONLY. THE USE OF ALL THREE TYPES OF VENTS WOULD NOT BE PRODUCTIVE SINCE THEY WOULD TEND TO SHORT-CIRCUIT ONE ANOTHER.

 A FLAT-ROOF VENTING

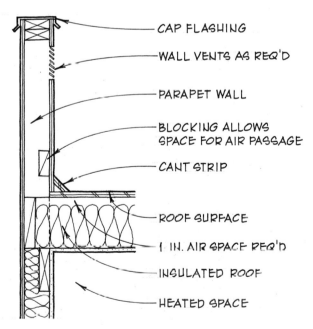

CAP FLASHING

WALL VENTS AS REQ'D

PARAPET WALL

BLOCKING ALLOWS SPACE FOR AIR PASSAGE

CANT STRIP

ROOF SURFACE

I IN. AIR SPACE REQ'D

INSULATED ROOF

HEATED SPACE

NOTE:
IT MAY BE USEFUL TO BE ABLE TO VENT AN INSULATED ROOF (OR DECK) THROUGH A PARAPET WALL IN ORDER TO GET CROSS VENTILATION.

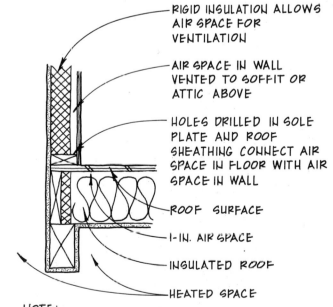

RIGID INSULATION ALLOWS AIR SPACE FOR VENTILATION

AIR SPACE IN WALL VENTED TO SOFFIT OR ATTIC ABOVE

HOLES DRILLED IN SOLE PLATE AND ROOF SHEATHING CONNECT AIR SPACE IN FLOOR WITH AIR SPACE IN WALL

ROOF SURFACE

I-IN. AIR SPACE

INSULATED ROOF

HEATED SPACE

NOTE:
SEAL CAREFULLY BETWEEN FRAMING MEMBERS AND RIGID INSULATION TO PREVENT AIR INFILTRATION

 **B** VENTED PARAPET WALL
2×4 OR 2×6 WALL

 **C** INSULATED WALL AS VENT
2×4 OR 2×6 WALL

CHAPTER 5

STAIRS

Stairs do not really support or protect a building in the same way as foundations, floors, walls, and roofs, but this book would be incomplete without them. Stairs are the vertical connectors of the parts of the building. Most buildings require a few steps just to enter the main floor, and stairs connect any internal levels. A well-designed and well-built staircase can contribute immeasurably to the function and beauty of a building.

STAIR DIMENSIONS

More than most other parts of a building, stairs need to be proportioned to the human body for safety. The height (rise) and depth (run) of the individual step must be in a comfortable relationship for the average person and must be manageable for people who are infirm or disabled. Building codes prescribe a range of dimensions for rise and run, a minimum width for stairways, the location of handrails, and minimum head clearance over stairs. The numbers vary depending on the location of the stair, the building type, and the specific code; the typical requirements are outlined as follows:

Rise and run—Rise and run of stairs are governed by building codes, which may vary. Minimum unit rise is typically 4 in. and maximum is 7 in., except for residential stairs, which can have a unit rise of 8 in. For residential stairs, however, a comfortable rise is about 7 in. Minimum unit run is 11 in., except for residential stairs, which can have 9-in. treads.

Generally, deeper treads have shallower risers. Here are two useful rules of thumb for the rise/run relationship:

$$\text{rise} + \text{run} = 17 \text{ in. to } 18 \text{ in.}$$
$$\text{run} + \text{twice the rise} = 24 \text{ in. to } 26 \text{ in.}$$

Both for safety and for code compliance, it is important to make each riser of a stair the same height. Most codes allow only ⅜-in. variance between the tallest and shortest riser in a flight of stairs. The maximum total rise between floors or landings is typically 12 ft. Landings must be as deep as the width of the stairway but need not exceed 44 in. if the stair has a straight run.

Stair width—The width of stairways is also defined by building codes. Minimum width is usually 36 in., except for residential stairs, which may sometimes be as narrow as 30 in. Minimum widths are measured inside finished stairwells, so rough openings must allow for finished wall surfaces.

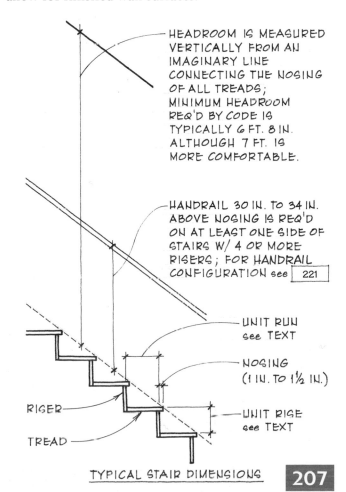

HEADROOM IS MEASURED VERTICALLY FROM AN IMAGINARY LINE CONNECTING THE NOSING OF ALL TREADS; MINIMUM HEADROOM REQ'D BY CODE IS TYPICALLY 6 FT. 8 IN. ALTHOUGH 7 FT. IS MORE COMFORTABLE.

HANDRAIL 30 IN. TO 34 IN. ABOVE NOSING IS REQ'D ON AT LEAST ONE SIDE OF STAIRS W/ 4 OR MORE RISERS; FOR HANDRAIL CONFIGURATION see | 221 |

UNIT RUN see TEXT

NOSING (1 IN. TO 1½ IN.)

UNIT RISE see TEXT

RISER

TREAD

TYPICAL STAIR DIMENSIONS

207

STAIR CONFIGURATION

The shape or configuration of a stairway is determined primarily by the circulation patterns of a building and by available space. Virtually any configuration of stairway may be constructed using the standard details of this chapter by merely breaking the stairway into smaller pieces and reassembling them. Several typical configurations that are worthy of note are shown in the drawings that follow; for clarity, these drawings do not show railings.

Straight-run stair—The straight-run stair is the most economical standard stairway from the standpoint of efficiency of floor space taken up by the stairway itself. The straight-run stair works best in two-story buildings.

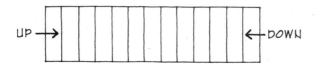

The bottom and top steps are separated horizontally from each other by the entire length of the stairway, so that a multi-story building with stacked stairways requires circulation space on each floor to get from the top step of one flight to the bottom step of the next.

U-shaped stair—The U-shaped stair, also called a switchback stair, has a landing about half a flight up, and the flights run in opposite directions. The area of the stairway is increased over a straight-run stair by the area of the landing (less one step), but the top

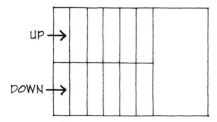

step of one flight is adjacent to the bottom step of the next. This arrangement saves circulation space at each floor level and makes this stair more efficient overall for multi-story buildings than the straight-run stair.

L-shaped stair—The L-shaped stair is not so common as the straight or U-shaped stair because it lacks the simplicity of the straight-run stair and the efficiency of the U-shaped stair. It can, however, be useful in tight spots, as it takes up less floor space than a U-shaped stair and requires less length than a straight-run stair. The framing of the opening in the floor for this stairway can be atypical because of its L-shape. A framed wall under one side of the floor projecting into the L or a column under the floor at the bend in the L is the most common way to support this floor.

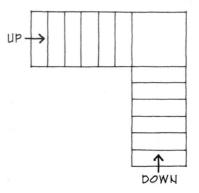

Winder stairs at the bend in the L (or at the bend in a U-shaped stair) are common, but for reasons of safety, should not be allowed to be less than 6 in. deep at the narrow end (verify with local codes).

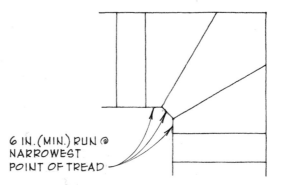

Spiral stair—A spiral stair saves space. It is most appropriate for accessing mezzanines and lofts where furniture and other large items may actually be hoisted from floor to floor by means other than the stairway. Spiral stairs usually have special code requirements that are somewhat less restrictive than standard stairs. They are usually prefabricated, often of metal or wood kits. Their details are idiosyncratic and not included in this book.

STRUCTURE

Stairs may be classified into two basic structural types: continuously supported and freespanning.

Continuously supported stairs—Continuously supported stairs are commonly used as interior stairs. Both sides of the stairway are supported by wall framing, so calculations of spanning capacities are not necessary. These stairs are site-built in some regions, but are predominantly prefabricated in others.

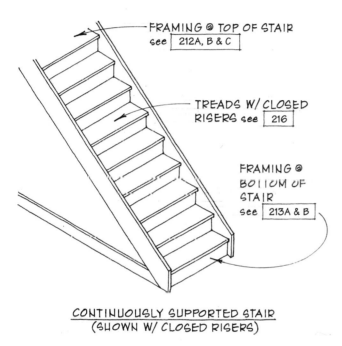

CONTINUOUSLY SUPPORTED STAIR
(SHOWN W/ CLOSED RISERS)

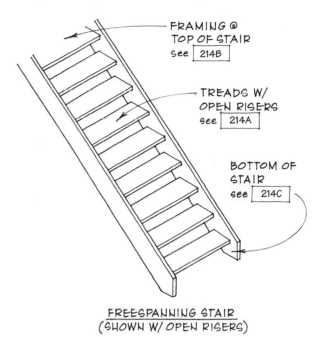

FREESPANNING STAIR
(SHOWN W/ OPEN RISERS)

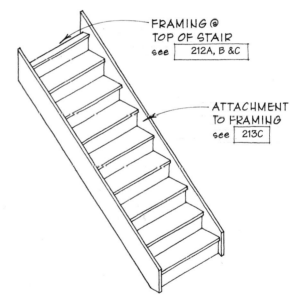

PREFABRICATED CUSTOM STAIR
(MAY BE FREESPANNING OR
CONTINUOUSLY SUPPORTED)

Freespanning stairs—Freespanning stairs have the structural capacity to span from the bottom stair to the top stair without intermediate support. The freespanning stair is commonly used as an exterior stair between floors or landing levels or in conjunction with porches and decks. It is often also seen as an access stair to basements and attics. The strength of a freespanning stair is usually in the carriages (stringers) that support the treads, although the handrail may also contribute to the strength of the stair. Freespanning stairs, like continuously supported stairs, may be site-built or prefabricated. Some freespanning stairs have only a single central support.

INTERIOR AND EXTERIOR STAIRS

The basic structure of the stair depends primarily on whether the stairway is to be located inside or outside and whether it is to be protected from the weather or not. The wood-stair details discussed in this chapter can be employed for either interior or exterior stairways, although the location will suggest basic detailing differences due to the fact that one is protected from the weather and the other isn't.

Interior stairs—Interior stairs are usually more refined than exterior stairs. Interior stairways may be the showcase of a building and so are often located near the entry and used as a major circulation route. They may also provide the opportunity to connect more than one floor with natural light.

Exterior stairs—Exterior stairs (see 222) have the same minimum proportional requirements as interior stairs, but they are generally built less steep. The treads need to be deeper and risers shallower outdoors to make the stairs safer when wet or covered with snow or ice. Materials on exterior stairs must also be chosen with the weather in mind. Weather-resistant materials such as concrete, masonry, and metal are sound choices for stairs exposed to the elements. Heavy timber or pressure-treated wood is often chosen for a wood stair out of doors. Special attention should be paid to nonskid surfaces for treads exposed to the weather.

Some exterior stairs are supported directly on the ground, in which case they are usually called steps (see 223–225). Ground-supported steps follow the contours of sloping sites to provide easy access to porches or entrances or as connections between terraces and other landscape elements.

SITE-BUILT VS. PREFABRICATED STAIRS

Most stairs are site-built because it is economical and because the process provides a temporary stair for construction. But in some cases, stairs prefabricated in a shop are more practical. Prefabricated stairs (see 213C), whether simple or complex, can be made more solidly and precisely than site-built stairs because they are made in the controlled environment of a shop.

ADDITIONAL DECISIONS

There are several other design decisions to make regarding both interior and exterior stairs. The primary decisions concern whether the risers are open (see 214A) or closed (see 216) and the design of the balustrade (see 218–220) and the handrail (see 221).

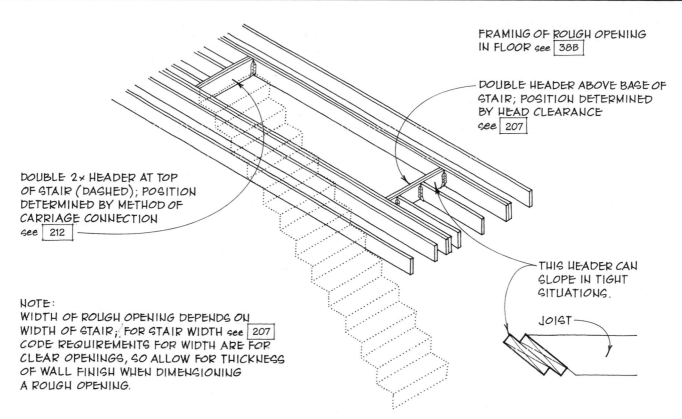

FRAMING OF ROUGH OPENING
IN FLOOR see 38B

DOUBLE HEADER ABOVE BASE OF
STAIR; POSITION DETERMINED
BY HEAD CLEARANCE
see 207

DOUBLE 2x HEADER AT TOP
OF STAIR (DASHED); POSITION
DETERMINED BY METHOD OF
CARRIAGE CONNECTION
see 212

THIS HEADER CAN
SLOPE IN TIGHT
SITUATIONS.

JOIST

NOTE:
WIDTH OF ROUGH OPENING DEPENDS ON
WIDTH OF STAIR; FOR STAIR WIDTH see 207
CODE REQUIREMENTS FOR WIDTH ARE FOR
CLEAR OPENINGS, SO ALLOW FOR THICKNESS
OF WALL FINISH WHEN DIMENSIONING
A ROUGH OPENING.

A STAIR ROUGH OPENING

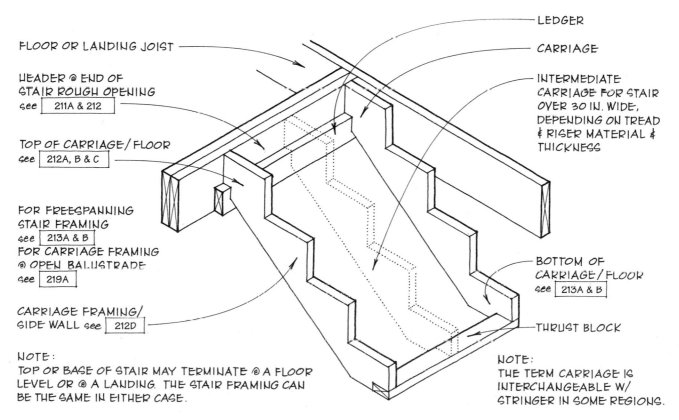

LEDGER

CARRIAGE

FLOOR OR LANDING JOIST

HEADER @ END OF
STAIR ROUGH OPENING
see 211A & 212

INTERMEDIATE
CARRIAGE FOR STAIR
OVER 30 IN. WIDE,
DEPENDING ON TREAD
& RISER MATERIAL &
THICKNESS

TOP OF CARRIAGE/FLOOR
see 212A, B & C

FOR FREESPANNING
STAIR FRAMING
see 213A & B
FOR CARRIAGE FRAMING
@ OPEN BALUSTRADE
see 219A

BOTTOM OF
CARRIAGE/FLOOR
see 213A & B

CARRIAGE FRAMING/
SIDE WALL see 212D

THRUST BLOCK

NOTE:
TOP OR BASE OF STAIR MAY TERMINATE @ A FLOOR
LEVEL OR @ A LANDING. THE STAIR FRAMING CAN
BE THE SAME IN EITHER CASE.

NOTE:
THE TERM CARRIAGE IS
INTERCHANGEABLE W/
STRINGER IN SOME REGIONS.

B CARRIAGE FRAMING
CONTINUOUSLY SUPPORTED STAIR

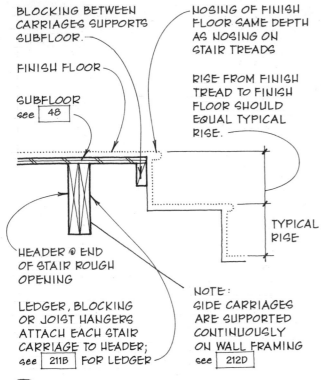

BLOCKING BETWEEN CARRIAGES SUPPORTS SUBFLOOR.

FINISH FLOOR

SUBFLOOR see [48]

NOSING OF FINISH FLOOR SAME DEPTH AS NOSING ON STAIR TREADS

RISE FROM FINISH TREAD TO FINISH FLOOR SHOULD EQUAL TYPICAL RISE.

TYPICAL RISE

HEADER @ END OF STAIR ROUGH OPENING

LEDGER, BLOCKING OR JOIST HANGERS ATTACH EACH STAIR CARRIAGE TO HEADER; see [211B] FOR LEDGER

NOTE: SIDE CARRIAGES ARE SUPPORTED CONTINUOUSLY ON WALL FRAMING see [212D]

(A) TOP OF CARRIAGE / FLOOR
FLOOR SUPPORTS TOP OF STAIR

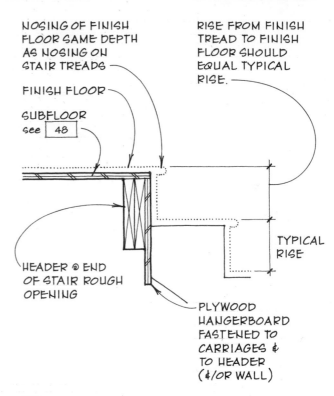

NOSING OF FINISH FLOOR SAME DEPTH AS NOSING ON STAIR TREADS

FINISH FLOOR

SUBFLOOR see [48]

RISE FROM FINISH TREAD TO FINISH FLOOR SHOULD EQUAL TYPICAL RISE.

TYPICAL RISE

HEADER @ END OF STAIR ROUGH OPENING

PLYWOOD HANGERBOARD FASTENED TO CARRIAGES & TO HEADER (&/OR WALL)

(B) TOP OF CARRIAGE / FLOOR
HANGERBOARD SUPPORTS TOP OF STAIR

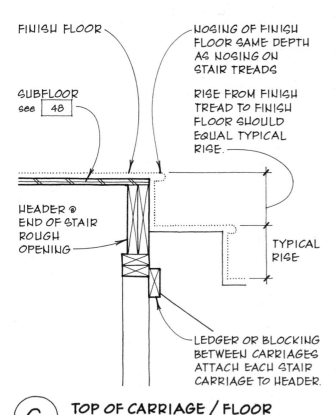

FINISH FLOOR

SUBFLOOR see [48]

NOSING OF FINISH FLOOR SAME DEPTH AS NOSING ON STAIR TREADS

RISE FROM FINISH TREAD TO FINISH FLOOR SHOULD EQUAL TYPICAL RISE.

HEADER @ END OF STAIR ROUGH OPENING

TYPICAL RISE

LEDGER OR BLOCKING BETWEEN CARRIAGES ATTACH EACH STAIR CARRIAGE TO HEADER.

(C) TOP OF CARRIAGE / FLOOR
WALL SUPPORTS TOP OF STAIR

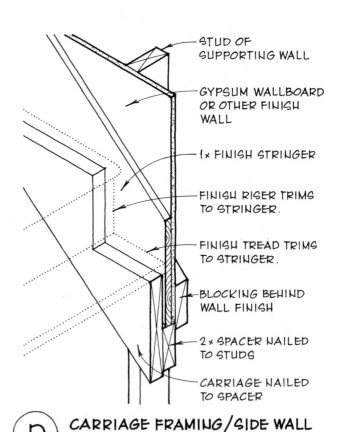

STUD OF SUPPORTING WALL

GYPSUM WALLBOARD OR OTHER FINISH WALL

1x FINISH STRINGER

FINISH RISER TRIMS TO STRINGER.

FINISH TREAD TRIMS TO STRINGER.

BLOCKING BEHIND WALL FINISH

2x SPACER NAILED TO STUDS

CARRIAGE NAILED TO SPACER

(D) CARRIAGE FRAMING / SIDE WALL
CONTINUOUSLY SUPPORTED STAIR

2× THRUST BLOCK NAILED TO SUBFLOOR & NOTCHED INTO CARRIAGES

RISE FROM FINISH FLOOR TO FIRST TREAD EQUALS TYPICAL RISE.

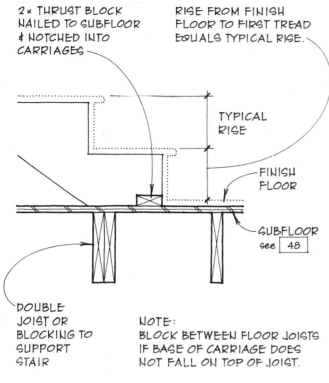

TYPICAL RISE

FINISH FLOOR

SUBFLOOR see [48]

DOUBLE JOIST OR BLOCKING TO SUPPORT STAIR

NOTE: BLOCK BETWEEN FLOOR JOISTS IF BASE OF CARRIAGE DOES NOT FALL ON TOP OF JOIST.

(A) BOTTOM OF CARRIAGE / FLOOR
SINGLE FLIGHT

NOTE: SIDE CARRIAGES MAY BE HUNG FROM HEADER OR ATTACHED TO WALL FRAMING.

RISE FROM FINISH FLOOR TO FIRST TREAD EQUALS TYPICAL RISE.

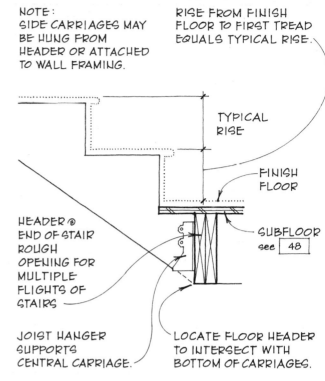

TYPICAL RISE

FINISH FLOOR

SUBFLOOR see [48]

HEADER @ END OF STAIR ROUGH OPENING FOR MULTIPLE FLIGHTS OF STAIRS

JOIST HANGER SUPPORTS CENTRAL CARRIAGE.

LOCATE FLOOR HEADER TO INTERSECT WITH BOTTOM OF CARRIAGES.

(B) BOTTOM OF CARRIAGE / FLOOR
INTERMEDIATE FLIGHT

EXTEND HOUSED STRINGER see [217B] TO MEET BASE MOLDING.

TOP NOSING OF PREFABRICATED STAIR TYPICALLY HAS RABBET ON UNDERSIDE TO ADJUST THICKNESS TO THAT OF FINISH FLOOR.

FINISH FLOOR

SUBFLOOR

HEADER @ TOP OF STAIR ROUGH OPENING

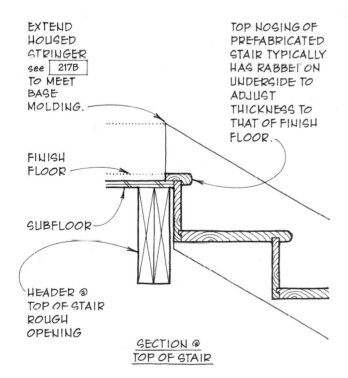

SECTION @ TOP OF STAIR

NOTES: ALIGN TOP NOSING FLUSH W/ FINISH FLOOR OR ALIGN TOP NOSING FLUSH W/ SUBFLOOR FOR WALL-TO-WALL CARPETING; BOTTOM RISER BEARS ON SUBFLOOR.

INTERIOR FINISH WALL

HOUSED STRINGER OF PREFABRICATED STAIR

5/8-IN. TO 1-IN. SHIM ACCOMMODATES THICKNESS OF FINISH WALL

ATTACH STRINGER W/ 16d NAILS THROUGH SHIMS INTO FRAMING.

WALL FRAMING

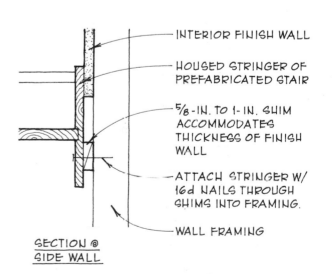

SECTION @ SIDE WALL

(C) PREFABRICATED STAIR

NOTE:
TREADS FOR OPEN-RISER
STAIRS MUST BE ABLE TO SPAN
FULL WIDTH OF STAIRWAY.

ATTACHMENT OF TREADS
TO CARRIAGE MAY BE WITH:

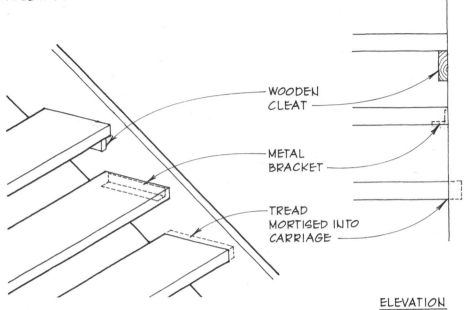

WOODEN
CLEAT

METAL
BRACKET

TREAD
MORTISED INTO
CARRIAGE

WOODEN CLEATS
SCREWED TO
STRUCTURAL CARRIAGE;

OR

METAL BRACKET LET INTO
END OF TREAD SO THAT
BRACKET IS CONCEALED
FROM ABOVE (& DOES NOT
PROJECT BELOW);

OR

MORTISED TREAD, WHICH
PROVIDES CONCEALED
CONNECTION FOR
APPEARANCE; SCREW
TREADS THROUGH
CARRIAGE OR GLUE &
TOENAIL FROM
UNDERSIDE INTO
CARRIAGE.

ELEVATION

(A) TREADS W/ OPEN RISERS

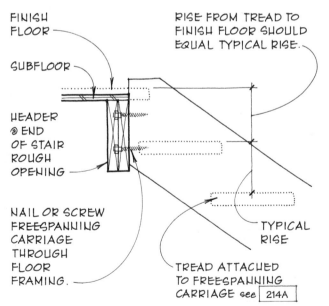

FINISH
FLOOR

SUBFLOOR

HEADER
@ END
OF STAIR
ROUGH
OPENING

NAIL OR SCREW
FREESPANNING
CARRIAGE
THROUGH
FLOOR
FRAMING.

RISE FROM TREAD TO
FINISH FLOOR SHOULD
EQUAL TYPICAL RISE.

TYPICAL
RISE

TREAD ATTACHED
TO FREESPANNING
CARRIAGE see 214A

NOTE:
A FREESTANDING CARRIAGE LEFT EXPOSED
REQUIRES A CONCEALED OR CLEAN BOLTED
CONNECTION TO THE FLOOR (OR LANDING)
@ THE TOP & BOTTOM OF THE CARRIAGE.

(B) TOP OF CARRIAGE/FLOOR
FREESPANNING STAIR

TREAD ATTACHED TO
FREESPANNING
CARRIAGE see 214A

FREESPANNING
WOODEN STAIR
CARRIAGE

TYPICAL RISE

RISE FROM
FINISH FLOOR
TO FIRST TREAD
SHOULD EQUAL
TYPICAL RISE.

FINISH FLOOR
OR SLAB; FOR
ATTACHMENT
TO SLAB
see 222D

SUBFLOOR

JOIST OR
BLOCKING
UNDER
CARRIAGE

NAIL OR SCREW
FREESPANNING
CARRIAGE THROUGH
FLOOR FRAMING.

(C) BOTTOM OF CARRIAGE/FLOOR
FREESPANNING STAIR

Finish landings must be at least as deep as the stairway is wide (automatic in the case of an L-shaped stair). Set the landing height so that the finish-floor level corresponds to the rise of the stair.

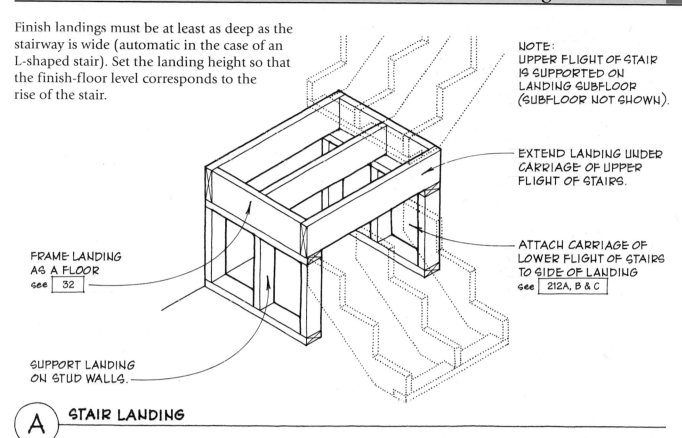

NOTE:
UPPER FLIGHT OF STAIR IS SUPPORTED ON LANDING SUBFLOOR (SUBFLOOR NOT SHOWN).

EXTEND LANDING UNDER CARRIAGE OF UPPER FLIGHT OF STAIRS.

ATTACH CARRIAGE OF LOWER FLIGHT OF STAIRS TO SIDE OF LANDING
see | 212A, B & C |

FRAME LANDING AS A FLOOR
see | 32 |

SUPPORT LANDING ON STUD WALLS.

A STAIR LANDING

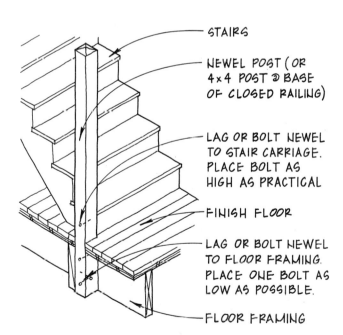

STAIRS

NEWEL POST (OR 4×4 POST @ BASE OF CLOSED RAILING)

LAG OR BOLT NEWEL TO STAIR CARRIAGE. PLACE BOLT AS HIGH AS PRACTICAL

FINISH FLOOR

LAG OR BOLT NEWEL TO FLOOR FRAMING. PLACE ONE BOLT AS LOW AS POSSIBLE.

FLOOR FRAMING

The newel post must be firmly anchored to resist the force of a person swinging around it. The most effective way to anchor the newel (or the framing of a closed rail) is to pass it through the subfloor and bolt or lag it to the floor framing.

B NEWEL POST

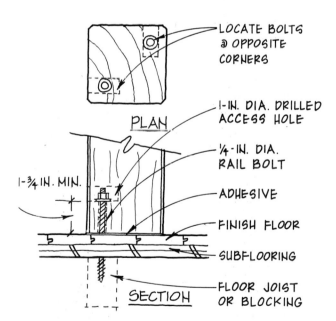

LOCATE BOLTS @ OPPOSITE CORNERS

PLAN

1-IN. DIA. DRILLED ACCESS HOLE

¼-IN. DIA. RAIL BOLT

ADHESIVE

FINISH FLOOR

SUBFLOORING

FLOOR JOIST OR BLOCKING

1-¾ IN. MIN.

SECTION

With solid flooring and/or subflooring, it is possible to firmly anchor the newel post to the surface of the floor by using rail bolts. The bolts are lagged into the floor surface, slipped into predrilled holes in the newel, and tightened with a special fitting through an access hole in the side of the newel. The access hole must be plugged to make a smooth finish surface on the newel.

C NEWEL POST
SURFACE ANCHORED

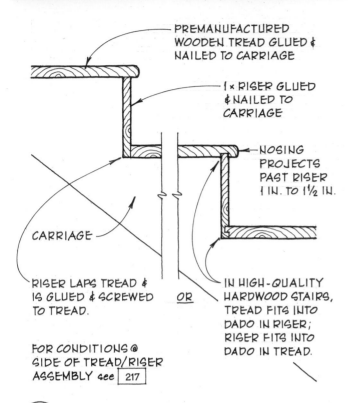

PREMANUFACTURED WOODEN TREAD GLUED & NAILED TO CARRIAGE

1 × RISER GLUED & NAILED TO CARRIAGE

NOSING PROJECTS PAST RISER 1 IN. TO 1½ IN.

CARRIAGE

RISER LAPS TREAD & IS GLUED & SCREWED TO TREAD.

IN HIGH-QUALITY HARDWOOD STAIRS, TREAD FITS INTO DADO IN RISER; RISER FITS INTO DADO IN TREAD.

FOR CONDITIONS @ SIDE OF TREAD/RISER ASSEMBLY see 217

A **EXPOSED FINISH TREAD & RISER**
2 ALTERNATIVES W/ NO SUB-TREAD

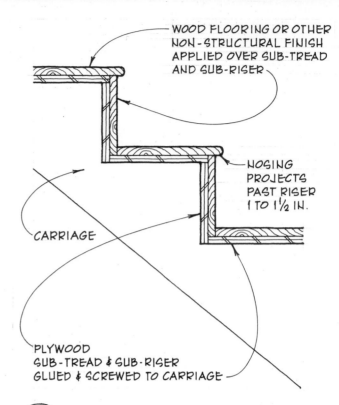

WOOD FLOORING OR OTHER NON-STRUCTURAL FINISH APPLIED OVER SUB-TREAD AND SUB-RISER

NOSING PROJECTS PAST RISER 1 TO 1½ IN.

CARRIAGE

PLYWOOD SUB-TREAD & SUB-RISER GLUED & SCREWED TO CARRIAGE

B **EXPOSED FINISH TREAD & RISER**
W/ SUB-TREAD

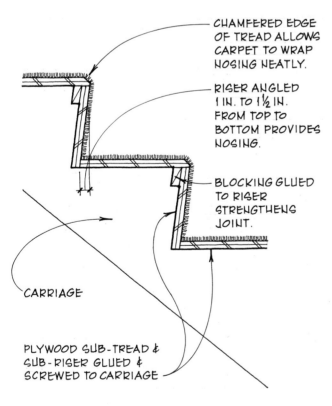

CHAMFERED EDGE OF TREAD ALLOWS CARPET TO WRAP NOSING NEATLY.

RISER ANGLED 1 IN. TO 1½ IN. FROM TOP TO BOTTOM PROVIDES NOSING.

BLOCKING GLUED TO RISER STRENGTHENS JOINT.

CARRIAGE

PLYWOOD SUB-TREAD & SUB-RISER GLUED & SCREWED TO CARRIAGE

C **CARPETED TREAD & RISER**

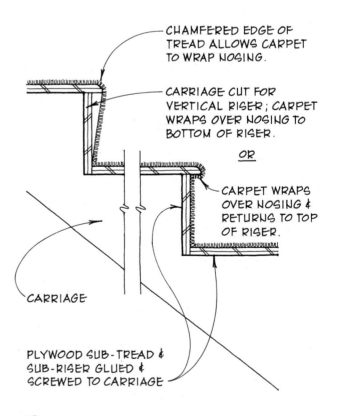

CHAMFERED EDGE OF TREAD ALLOWS CARPET TO WRAP NOSING.

CARRIAGE CUT FOR VERTICAL RISER; CARPET WRAPS OVER NOSING TO BOTTOM OF RISER.

OR

CARPET WRAPS OVER NOSING & RETURNS TO TOP OF RISER.

CARRIAGE

PLYWOOD SUB-TREAD & SUB-RISER GLUED & SCREWED TO CARRIAGE

D **CARPETED TREAD & RISER**
2 ALTERNATIVES

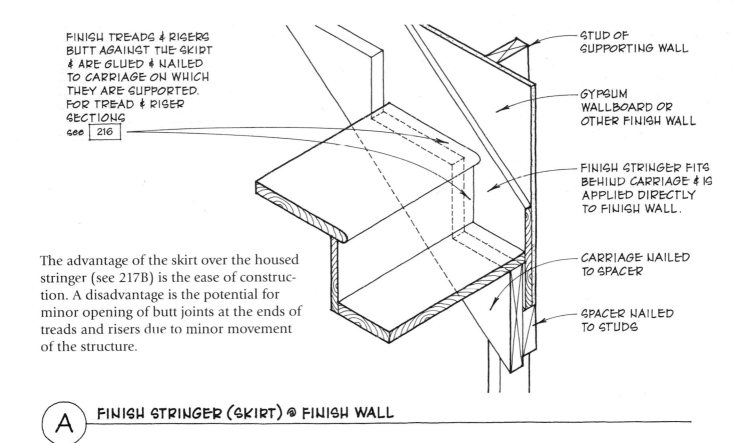

FINISH TREADS & RISERS
BUTT AGAINST THE SKIRT
& ARE GLUED & NAILED
TO CARRIAGE ON WHICH
THEY ARE SUPPORTED.
FOR TREAD & RISER
SECTIONS
see 216

STUD OF
SUPPORTING WALL

GYPSUM
WALLBOARD OR
OTHER FINISH WALL

FINISH STRINGER FITS
BEHIND CARRIAGE & IS
APPLIED DIRECTLY
TO FINISH WALL.

CARRIAGE NAILED
TO SPACER

SPACER NAILED
TO STUDS

The advantage of the skirt over the housed stringer (see 217B) is the ease of construction. A disadvantage is the potential for minor opening of butt joints at the ends of treads and risers due to minor movement of the structure.

A FINISH STRINGER (SKIRT) @ FINISH WALL

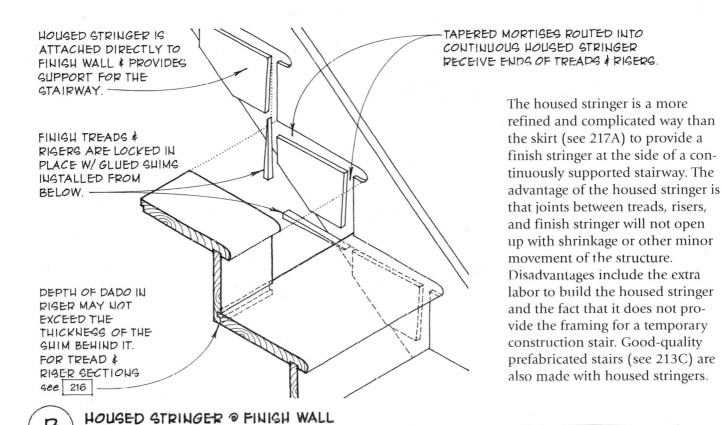

HOUSED STRINGER IS
ATTACHED DIRECTLY TO
FINISH WALL & PROVIDES
SUPPORT FOR THE
STAIRWAY.

FINISH TREADS &
RISERS ARE LOCKED IN
PLACE W/ GLUED SHIMS
INSTALLED FROM
BELOW.

DEPTH OF DADO IN
RISER MAY NOT
EXCEED THE
THICKNESS OF THE
SHIM BEHIND IT.
FOR TREAD &
RISER SECTIONS
see 216

TAPERED MORTISES ROUTED INTO
CONTINUOUS HOUSED STRINGER
RECEIVE ENDS OF TREADS & RISERS.

The housed stringer is a more refined and complicated way than the skirt (see 217A) to provide a finish stringer at the side of a continuously supported stairway. The advantage of the housed stringer is that joints between treads, risers, and finish stringer will not open up with shrinkage or other minor movement of the structure. Disadvantages include the extra labor to build the housed stringer and the fact that it does not provide the framing for a temporary construction stair. Good-quality prefabricated stairs (see 213C) are also made with housed stringers.

B HOUSED STRINGER @ FINISH WALL

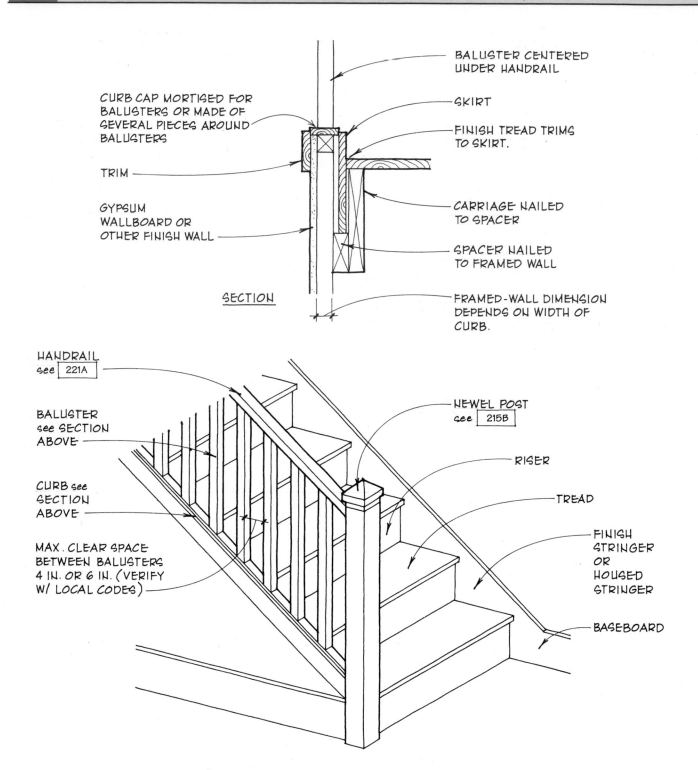

CURB CAP MORTISED FOR BALUSTERS OR MADE OF SEVERAL PIECES AROUND BALUSTERS

TRIM

GYPSUM WALLBOARD OR OTHER FINISH WALL

BALUSTER CENTERED UNDER HANDRAIL

SKIRT

FINISH TREAD TRIMS TO SKIRT.

CARRIAGE NAILED TO SPACER

SPACER NAILED TO FRAMED WALL

FRAMED-WALL DIMENSION DEPENDS ON WIDTH OF CURB.

SECTION

HANDRAIL see 221A

BALUSTER see SECTION ABOVE

CURB see SECTION ABOVE

MAX. CLEAR SPACE BETWEEN BALUSTERS 4 IN. OR 6 IN. (VERIFY W/ LOCAL CODES)

NEWEL POST see 215B

RISER

TREAD

FINISH STRINGER OR HOUSED STRINGER

BASEBOARD

In an open balustrade with a curb, the treads and risers are constructed on carriages and finished on both sides with a skirt, just as if the stairway were constructed between two walls. The skirt on the open side of the stairway forms one side of the curb. This simple construction has a similar aesthetic effect as the more technically difficult open balustrade without a curb (see 219).

(A) **OPEN BALUSTRADE**
W/ CURB

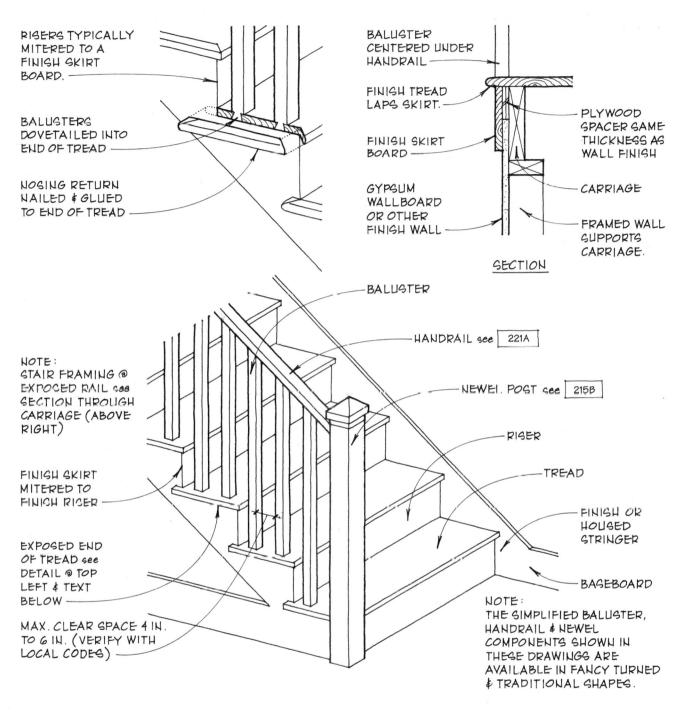

RISERS TYPICALLY MITERED TO A FINISH SKIRT BOARD.

BALUSTERS DOVETAILED INTO END OF TREAD

NOSING RETURN NAILED & GLUED TO END OF TREAD

BALUSTER CENTERED UNDER HANDRAIL

FINISH TREAD LAPS SKIRT.

FINISH SKIRT BOARD

GYPSUM WALLBOARD OR OTHER FINISH WALL

PLYWOOD SPACER SAME THICKNESS AS WALL FINISH

CARRIAGE

FRAMED WALL SUPPORTS CARRIAGE.

SECTION

BALUSTER

HANDRAIL see 221A

NEWEL POST see 215B

RISER

TREAD

FINISH OR HOUSED STRINGER

BASEBOARD

NOTE: STAIR FRAMING @ EXPOSED RAIL see SECTION THROUGH CARRIAGE (ABOVE RIGHT)

FINISH SKIRT MITERED TO FINISH RISER

EXPOSED END OF TREAD see DETAIL @ TOP LEFT & TEXT BELOW

MAX. CLEAR SPACE 4 IN. TO 6 IN. (VERIFY WITH LOCAL CODES)

NOTE: THE SIMPLIFIED BALUSTER, HANDRAIL & NEWEL COMPONENTS SHOWN IN THESE DRAWINGS ARE AVAILABLE IN FANCY TURNED & TRADITIONAL SHAPES.

In this traditional treatment of the open balustrade, the balusters rest on the treads, and the ends of the treads are exposed and finished. The balusters may be attached to the treads in four ways: toenailing, doweling, mortising, or sliding dovetail (see the detail at top left). The exposed ends of the treads may be finished in one of the following two ways. The treads may be cantilevered and rounded or chamfered like the nose of the tread (this will expose end grain). Alternatively, the treads may be capped with a finish piece called a nosing return, which is mitered at the corner and matches the profile of the nosing (see the detail at top left). This is the most refined finish treatment and is usually used in conjunction with mortised or sliding dovetail balusters.

(A) OPEN BALUSTRADE
WITHOUT CURB

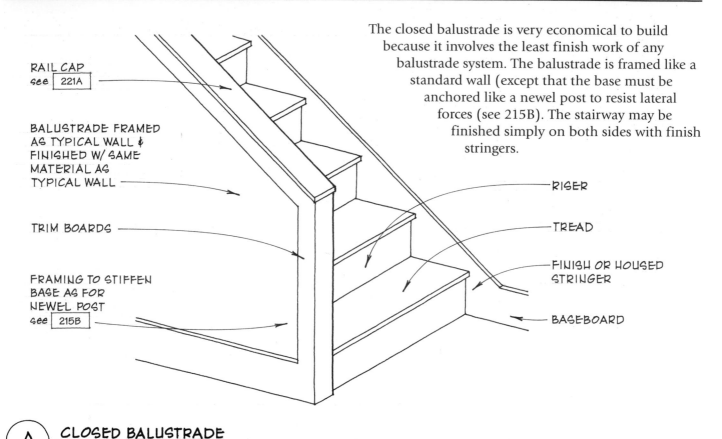

The closed balustrade is very economical to build because it involves the least finish work of any balustrade system. The balustrade is framed like a standard wall (except that the base must be anchored like a newel post to resist lateral forces (see 215B). The stairway may be finished simply on both sides with finish stringers.

RAIL CAP
see 221A

BALUSTRADE FRAMED AS TYPICAL WALL & FINISHED W/ SAME MATERIAL AS TYPICAL WALL

TRIM BOARDS

FRAMING TO STIFFEN BASE AS FOR NEWEL POST
see 215B

RISER

TREAD

FINISH OR HOUSED STRINGER

BASEBOARD

A CLOSED BALUSTRADE

HANDRAIL
see 221

BALUSTER

STRUCTURAL CARRIAGE

MAX. SPACE 4 IN. TO 6 IN. (VERIFY WITH LOCAL CODE)

FREESPANNING-STAIR FRAMING see 214B & C

CARRIAGE

TREAD see 214A

BASEBOARD IF STAIRWAY IS ADJACENT TO A WALL

The freespanning stair usually has a structural carriage to which the balusters may be attached. This arrangement allows the balusters themselves to be the structural support for the handrail. A newel post, if used, would typically be attached to the side of the structural carriage in the same fashion as the balusters.

B FREESPANNING-STAIR BALUSTRADE

Handrails provide stability and security for the young, the old, the blind, and the infirm. In addition, handrails are a safety feature for anyone who uses a stairway—one of the most likely and dangerous places for people to trip and fall.

In terms of safety, the most important design feature of a handrail is its ability to be grasped, especially in an emergency. The 1½-in. to 2-in. round rail is the most effective in this regard, as it allows the thumb and fingers to curl around and under the rail. Other shapes are allowable by code, but are less graspable.

The height of the handrail is usually specified by code. Most codes fall within the range of 29 in. to 36 in. above the nosing of the stairs. If the handrail is against a wall, a 1½-in. space is required between the handrail and the wall.

The tops and bottoms of handrails should be designed so as to avoid snagging clothing. For this reason, many codes require returning handrails to the wall at both top and bottom.

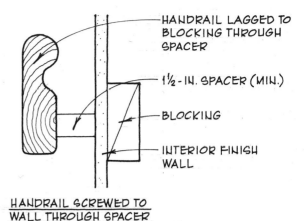

HANDRAIL LAGGED TO BLOCKING THROUGH SPACER

1½-IN. SPACER (MIN.)

BLOCKING

INTERIOR FINISH WALL

HANDRAIL SCREWED TO WALL THROUGH SPACER

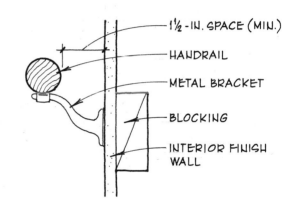

1½-IN. SPACE (MIN.)

HANDRAIL

METAL BRACKET

BLOCKING

INTERIOR FINISH WALL

HANDRAIL ATTACHED TO WALL W/ METAL BRACKETS

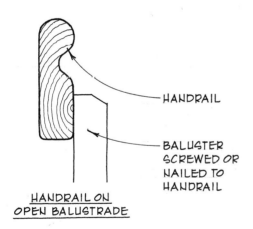

HANDRAIL

BALUSTER SCREWED OR NAILED TO HANDRAIL

HANDRAIL ON OPEN BALUSTRADE

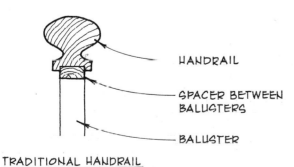

HANDRAIL

SPACER BETWEEN BALUSTERS

BALUSTER

TRADITIONAL HANDRAIL ON OPEN BALUSTRADE

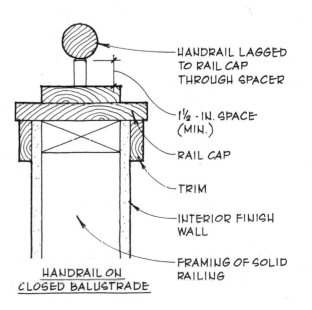

HANDRAIL LAGGED TO RAIL CAP THROUGH SPACER

1½-IN. SPACE (MIN.)

RAIL CAP

TRIM

INTERIOR FINISH WALL

FRAMING OF SOLID RAILING

HANDRAIL ON CLOSED BALUSTRADE

 A HANDRAILS

Exterior stairs made of wood should be built of weather-resistant species such as cedar or redwood or of pressure-treated lumber. Simple connections that minimize joints between boards are less likely to retain moisture. Where joints must occur, it is best to minimize the area of contact between pieces so that moisture will drain and the lumber can breathe.

Most exterior wood stairs are freespanning. For long runs of stairs, the continuous unnotched carriage is usually required for strength (see 222B & D). Short runs of freespanning stairs may be strong enough with a notched carriage (see 222C). The notched carriage is, of course, also suitable for wood stairs built between two parallel concrete or masonry walls.

Open risers are often employed in exterior wood stairs, but solid risers, common on traditional porches, are useful to stiffen the treads. For wood porches, and decks, see 52–60.

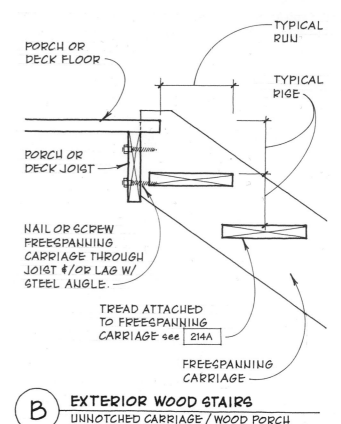

 EXTERIOR WOOD STAIRS
INTRODUCTION

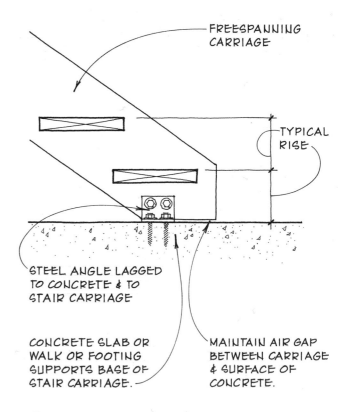

B **EXTERIOR WOOD STAIRS**
UNNOTCHED CARRIAGE / WOOD PORCH

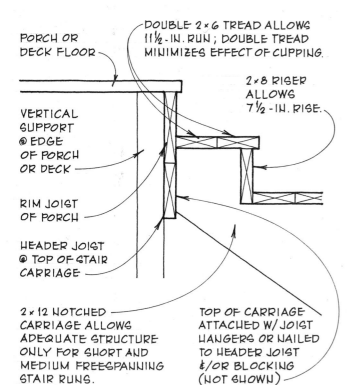

C **EXTERIOR WOOD STAIRS**
NOTCHED CARRIAGE / WOOD PORCH

D **EXTERIOR WOOD STAIRS**
FREESPANNING CARRIAGE @ GROUND

Dry-set brick steps are supported on a bed of compacted gravel and sand on the ground and are laid dry without concrete or mortar. The bricks must be contained at the edges or they will separate. A 2x decay-resistant header used as a riser will contain the bricks at each step.

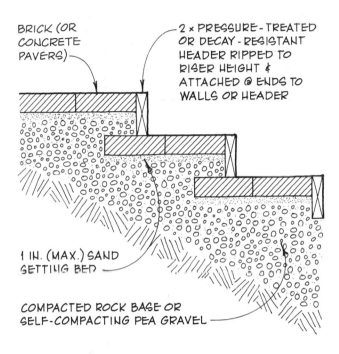

BRICK (OR CONCRETE PAVERS)

2 x PRESSURE-TREATED OR DECAY-RESISTANT HEADER RIPPED TO RISER HEIGHT & ATTACHED @ ENDS TO WALLS OR HEADER

1 IN. (MAX.) SAND SETTING BED

COMPACTED ROCK BASE OR SELF-COMPACTING PEA GRAVEL

The sides of the steps may be contained with 2x headers the same height as the riser, as shown below. These side headers may be staked to the ground so that they contain the step at the sides on their own.

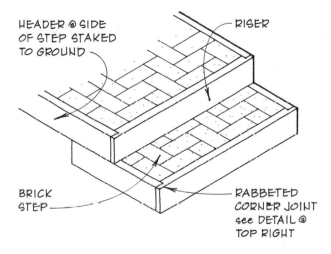

HEADER @ SIDE OF STEP STAKED TO GROUND

RISER

BRICK STEP

RABBETED CORNER JOINT see DETAIL @ TOP RIGHT

The rabbeted riser/side-header joint is nailed from two directions to lock the joint together.

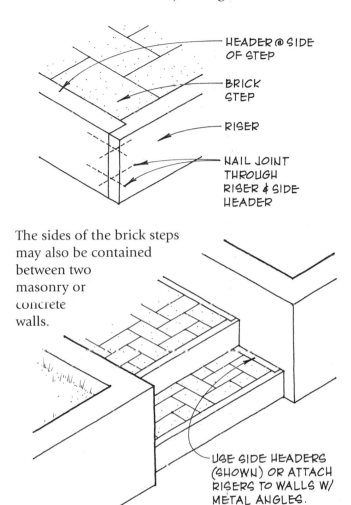

HEADER @ SIDE OF STEP

BRICK STEP

RISER

NAIL JOINT THROUGH RISER & SIDE HEADER

The sides of the brick steps may also be contained between two masonry or concrete walls.

USE SIDE HEADERS (SHOWN) OR ATTACH RISERS TO WALLS W/ METAL ANGLES.

A third alternative is to contain the sides of the steps with decay-resistant stringers at the slope of the steps. The risers may be attached directly to the stringers.

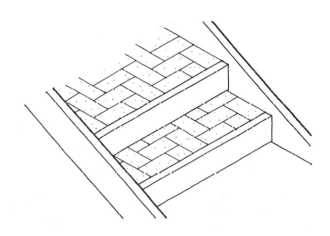

(A) DRY-SET EXTERIOR STEPS
BRICK

Dry-set concrete paver steps, like dry-set brick steps, are supported on a bed of compacted gravel on the ground and are laid dry without concrete or mortar. Because of their size, large pavers like the ones shown here are more stable than bricks. For this reason, paver stairs may be constructed without containment at the riser; some paver stairs are even constructed without containment at the sides.

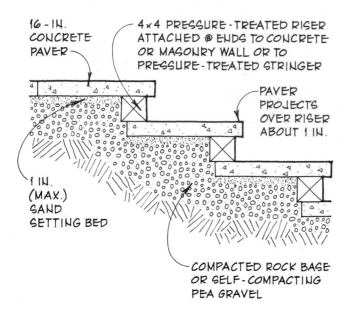

16-IN. CONCRETE PAVER

4×4 PRESSURE-TREATED RISER ATTACHED @ ENDS TO CONCRETE OR MASONRY WALL OR TO PRESSURE-TREATED STRINGER

PAVER PROJECTS OVER RISER ABOUT 1 IN.

1 IN. (MAX.) SAND SETTING BED

COMPACTED ROCK BASE OR SELF-COMPACTING PEA GRAVEL

Most paver stairs are contained at the sides with walls or stringers, as shown below.

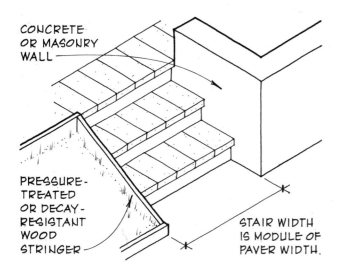

CONCRETE OR MASONRY WALL

PRESSURE-TREATED OR DECAY-RESISTANT WOOD STRINGER

STAIR WIDTH IS MODULE OF PAVER WIDTH.

Paver stairs may also be contained at all edges like brick stairs with 2x risers and side headers (see 223).

(A) **DRY-SET EXTERIOR STEPS**
CONCRETE PAVERS

Concrete steps are durable and can be reasonably inexpensive, especially if they are built along with other concrete work. They should be adequately supported on a foundation and should be reinforced. Handrails or handrail supports may be cast into the steps or into the walks, porches or terraces adjacent to them. The steps may be covered with a masonry or other veneer.

The main problem with concrete steps is that they are difficult to repair if anything should go wrong with them. The usual problem is settling due to the extreme weight of the steps themselves and to the fact that they are often constructed on fill. The safest way to avoid settling is to provide for the porch and steps a footing that is below the frost line, with a foundation wall above. This footing and foundation wall system may be an integral part of the foundation of the main structure (see the detail below), or it may be independent of the main structure with an expansion joint adjacent to the main structure that will allow the porch to move slightly without cracking (see 225A & B). Alternatively, concrete steps may be built independent of the main structure and adjacent to a wood porch (see 225C). All methods are expensive but will avoid costly maintenance in the long run.

For areas where building on backfill cannot be avoided, a wood porch with a lightweight wood stair that can be easily releveled is the most practical (see 222).

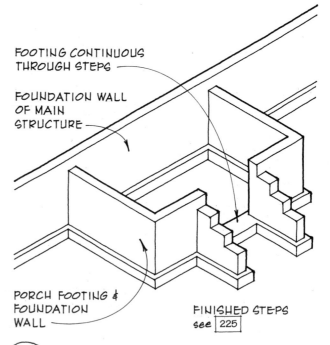

FOOTING CONTINUOUS THROUGH STEPS

FOUNDATION WALL OF MAIN STRUCTURE

PORCH FOOTING & FOUNDATION WALL

FINISHED STEPS see 225

(B) CONCRETE STEPS

NOTE:
ELEMENTS OF THE DETAILS ON THIS PAGE MAY BE COMBINED IN VARIOUS WAYS TO MEET THE NEEDS OF SPECIFIC SITUATIONS.

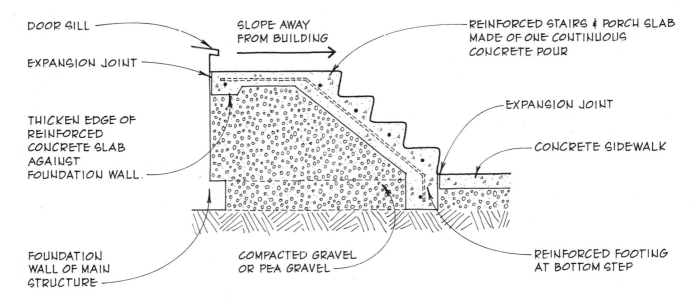

DOOR SILL

SLOPE AWAY FROM BUILDING

REINFORCED STAIRS & PORCH SLAB MADE OF ONE CONTINUOUS CONCRETE POUR

EXPANSION JOINT

EXPANSION JOINT

CONCRETE SIDEWALK

THICKEN EDGE OF REINFORCED CONCRETE SLAB AGAINST FOUNDATION WALL.

FOUNDATION WALL OF MAIN STRUCTURE

COMPACTED GRAVEL OR PEA GRAVEL

REINFORCED FOOTING AT BOTTOM STEP

A CONCRETE STEPS ON GRAVEL
@ CONCRETE PORCH

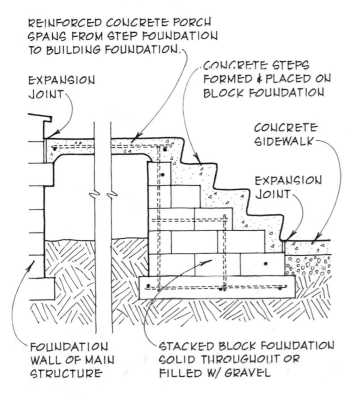

REINFORCED CONCRETE PORCH SPANS FROM STEP FOUNDATION TO BUILDING FOUNDATION.

EXPANSION JOINT

CONCRETE STEPS FORMED & PLACED ON BLOCK FOUNDATION

CONCRETE SIDEWALK

EXPANSION JOINT

FOUNDATION WALL OF MAIN STRUCTURE

STACKED BLOCK FOUNDATION SOLID THROUGHOUT OR FILLED W/ GRAVEL

B CONCRETE STEPS ON BLOCK
@ CONCRETE PORCH

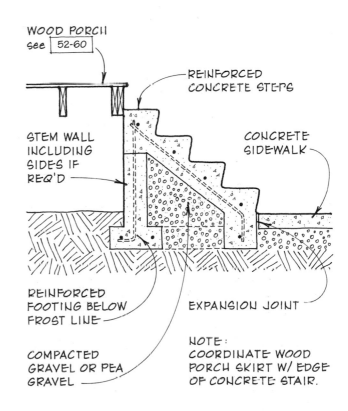

WOOD PORCH see 52-60

REINFORCED CONCRETE STEPS

STEM WALL INCLUDING SIDES IF REQ'D

CONCRETE SIDEWALK

REINFORCED FOOTING BELOW FROST LINE

EXPANSION JOINT

COMPACTED GRAVEL OR PEA GRAVEL

NOTE:
COORDINATE WOOD PORCH SKIRT W/ EDGE OF CONCRETE STAIR.

C CONCRETE STEPS @ WOOD PORCH
ON BLOCK OR GRAVEL

LEGEND

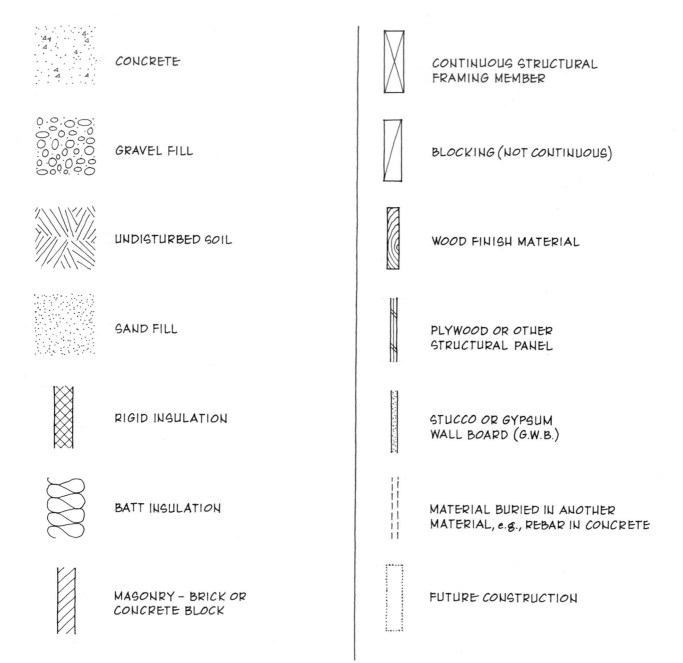

CONCRETE

GRAVEL FILL

UNDISTURBED SOIL

SAND FILL

RIGID INSULATION

BATT INSULATION

MASONRY – BRICK OR
CONCRETE BLOCK

CONTINUOUS STRUCTURAL
FRAMING MEMBER

BLOCKING (NOT CONTINUOUS)

WOOD FINISH MATERIAL

PLYWOOD OR OTHER
STRUCTURAL PANEL

STUCCO OR GYPSUM
WALL BOARD (G.W.B.)

MATERIAL BURIED IN ANOTHER
MATERIAL, e.g., REBAR IN CONCRETE

FUTURE CONSTRUCTION

LIST OF ABBREVIATIONS

&	AND
@	AT
APPROX.	APPROXIMATE(LY)
FT.	FOOT/FEET
F.F.L.	FINISH FLOOR LEVEL
H	HEIGHT
IN.	INCH(ES)
LSL	LAMINATED-STRAND LUMBER
LVL	LAMINATED-VENEER LUMBER
MAX.	MAXIMUM
MIN.	MINIMUM
#	NUMBER
O.C.	ON CENTER
‖	PARALLEL
⊥	PERPENDICULAR
LB.	POUNDS
PSF	POUNDS PER SQUARE FOOT
PSI	POUNDS PER SQUARE INCH
PSL	PARALLEL-STRAND LUMBER
P.T.	PRESSURE TREATED
REBAR	REINFORCING STEEL
REQ'D	REQUIRED
SQ. FT.	SQUARE FOOT/FEET
T & G	TONGUE AND GROOVE
TYP.	TYPICAL
W	WIDTH
W/	WITH
WWM	WELDED WIRE MESH

RESOURCES

TRADE AND PROFESSIONAL ASSOCIATIONS

ACI International
P.O. Box 9094
Farmington Hills, MI 48333
(248) 848-3700

American Institute of Architects
1735 New York Avenue NW
Washington, DC 20006
(202) 626-7300

APA-The Engineered Wood Association
P.O. Box 11700
Tacoma, WA 98411-0700
(253) 565-6600

American Society of Heating, Refrigerating &
Air-Conditioning Engineers
1791 Tullie Circle NE
Atlanta, GA 30329
(800) 527-4723

Brick Industry Association
11490 Commerce Park Drive
Reston, VA 20191
(703) 620-0010

Building Research Council
One East St. Mary's Road
Champaign, IL 61820
(217) 333-1801

Canadian Wood Council
1400 Blair Place, Suite 210
Ottawa, Ontario K1J9B8
Canada
(613) 747-5544

Energy Efficient Building Association (EEBA)
490 Concordia Avenue
St. Paul, MN 55103
(651) 268-7585

Forest Products Society
2801 Marshall Court
Madison, WI 53705-2295
(608) 231-1361

National Association of Home Builders
1201 Fifteenth Street NW
Washington, DC 20005
(202) 822-0200

National Concrete Masonry Association
2302 Horse Pen Road
Herndon, VA 20171-3499
(703) 713-1900

National Forest Products Association
1111 Nineteenth Street NW, Suite 700
Washington, DC 20036
(202) 463-2700

National Roofing Contractors Association
10255 W. Higgins Road, Suite 600
Rosemont, IL 60018
(847) 299-9070

Northeastern Lumber Manufacturers' Association
272 Tuttle Road
Cumberland Center, ME 04021
(207) 829-6901

Sheet Metal and Air Conditioning Contractors
National Association
4201 Lafayette Center Drive
Chantilly, VA 20151
(703) 803-2980

Southern Forest Products Association
P.O. Box 641700
New Orleans, LA 70064-1700
(504) 443-4464

Western Wood Products Association
522 SW Fifth Avenue, Suite 500
Portland, OR 97204
(503) 224-3930

FURTHER READING

Allen, Edward. *Fundamentals of Building Construction: Materials and Methods.* 3rd ed. New York: John Wiley & Sons, 1998.

Dietz, Albert. *Dwelling House Construction.* 5th ed. Cambridge, Mass.: M.I.T. Press, 1992.

Fine Homebuilding. Bimonthly magazine. The Taunton Press (P.O. Box 5506, 63 South Main Street, Newtown, CT 06470-5506).

Hoke, John Ray, Jr. *Architectural Graphic Standards.* New York: John Wiley & Sons, 1998.

Journal of Light Construction. Monthly magazine. Builderburg Partners Ltd. (1025 Vermont Avenue NW, Washington, DC 20005).

Riechers, A. F. J. *The Full Length Roof Framer.* Palo Alto, CA: Buccaneer Books, 1995.

PRODUCT INFORMATION

First Source for Products. Norcross, GA: Architect's First Source for Products; updated annually.

Sweet's Catalog File. New York: McGraw-Hill; updated annually. Sweet's also offers a CD quarterly with additional information.

Thomas Register of American Manufacturers: Products & Services and *Thomas Register of American Manufacturers: Catalog File.* New York: Thomas Publishing Company; updated annually.

GLOSSARY

This glossary is designed to clarify the concepts presented in the book. Words are included based on the frequency of their use and their absence from common language. Many of the words have other meanings not defined here for reasons of space.

Air-infiltration barrier A continuous layer at the insulated envelope of a building to prevent the entry of air.

Anchor bolt A metal bolt connecting the wood parts of a building to its foundation.

Apron Trim below a window sill or stool.

Backband Trim surrounding window or door casing, usually for the purpose of increasing depth.

Backer block Small plywood or OSB patch added to the web of I-joists where hangers are attached.

Backer rod An expansive material used to fill wide gaps behind caulk or sealant.

Backing Framing added for the purpose of providing a nailing surface where none exists.

Back-up clip A small metal or plastic flange attached to framing for the purpose of supporting gypsum wallboard.

Balloon framing The nearly archaic method of building with studs continuous from foundation to roof.

Baluster A single vertical component of a balustrade.

Balustrade A protective railing at a stairway, porch, or balcony made of numerous vertical elements.

Barge rafter The rafter at the edge of an overhanging gable roof; called fly rafter on the East Coast.

Batt insulation Fluffy insulation resembling cotton candy; usually made of fiberglass, either with a facing or unfaced.

Beam A large horizontal structural member spanning between two supports.

Bearing capacity The ability of soil to support the load of a building, measured in psf.

Bearing wall A wall that carries structural loads from above (as opposed to a partition wall which does not).

Bird's mouth A notch near the bottom end of a rafter made to form a level attachment with the top of a wall.

Bituminous Containing asphalt or tar.

Blocking Framing made of small pieces running perpendicular to or at an angle to studs, joists, or rafters. Blocking may support panel edges, prevent rotation of framing members, and retard the spread of fire.

Brick mold A deep exterior casing traditionally used with brick.

Bridging Bracing at the midspan of long joists or rafters to prevent their rotation.

Butt joint A joint in which the ends of two square-cut boards meet.

Buttress A compression brace of a masonry or concrete wall.

Cantilever The portion of a structural member that projects beyond its support.

Carriage The structure supporting a site-built stair; also called a jack or a stringer.

Casing The trim at head and jamb of a window or door.

Caulk Pliable viscous material used to seal gaps between materials. See also sealant.

Chamfer A bevel on the edge of a board or timber.

Chord The top or bottom component of a truss or I-joist where stresses are greatest; also, part of the structural perimeter of a diaphragm or shear wall.

Clad Covered for protection from the weather.

Cleat A concealed or exposed clip used to fasten flashing that does not penetrate the flashing itself.

Closed cell A type of rigid insulation that cannot be saturated by moisture.

Cold roof An insulated vaulted ceiling with a ventilation space above to isolate snow and prevent its melting.

Collar tie A horizontal tie between opposing rafters in order to prevent their spreading.

Concrete-rated The ability to be placed adjacent to concrete without deterioration due to chemical reaction.

Control joint A score line in a concrete slab, creating a weak point where cracking will likely concentrate

Cornerboard Trim boards at exterior corners for shingle or horizontal board siding.

Counterflashing Flashing that laps over another flashing.

Counterfort A buried tension brace of a masonry or concrete retaining wall.

Crawl space A usually unheated and uninhabitable space between the first floor and the ground.

Crib wall A short framed wall within a crawl space providing support for the first-floor structure.

Cricket A roof flashing above a chimney or other medium sized object to divert water around it.

Cross-grain shrinkage Shrinkage of wood perpendicular to its length due to moisture loss.

Curb A built-up edge such as to mount a skylight or to provide a base for a balustrade.

Dado A rectangular groove cut into a board.

Dead load The weight of the structure itself.

Decking Parallel boards providing the structural surface of a floor or roof.

Diagonal bracing Wood or metal structural member providing triangulation to brace a wall (or roof).

Diaphragm A structural plane acting like a beam between braced walls to resist lateral forces.

Dimension lumber Milled lumber cut to standard sizes.

Diverter A short flashing integrated with roofing to divert rainwater where a gutter is not practical.

Dormer A small building element that contains a window emerging from a roof.

Dovetail A locking finish joint shaped like the spread feathers of a bird's tail.

Downspout The pipe that conducts rainwater down from the gutter, also known as downpipe or leader.

Drag strut A structural tie connecting a portion of a diaphragm to braced walls that are not directly under it.

Drip A thin edge of material designed to direct the dripping of water away from the surface of a building.

Dry-set Masonry laid without mortar.

Dry well A hole in the ground filled with rocks, designed to collect and distribute storm water.

Duckboard A thin decking laid over a waterproof deck for the purpose of protecting the deck from abrasion.

Dummy A roof element such as an eave or rake that is discontinuous from the principal roof structure.

Eave The horizontal lower edge of a roof.

Edge nailing Nailing at the perimeter of a structural panel or larger structural element.

End-matched Boards having tongue and grooves at their ends.

Envelope The exterior insulated skin of a building

Expansion joint A flexible joint inserted into rigid materials such as concrete or brick to accommodate thermal expansion and contraction.

Exposure rating Rating that indicates the ability of composite panels such as plywood to withstand exposure to the weather.

Fascia Trim board at the eave of a roof.

Felt A heavy tar-impregnated paper used as a moisture barrier.

Filter fabric An underground textile that separates rock from soil and allows the passage of water.

Finish stringer The finish trim at the side of a stair.

Fireblock A block installed in a wood frame for the purpose of inhibiting the passage of fire from one section of the frame to another.

Firestopping See Fireblock.

Flashing A thin metal layer designed to divert water at the surface of a building.

Flat-grain A board with the annual growth rings oriented across its width.

Footing The spread portion at the base of a foundation.

Framing anchor A metal clip designed to add strength at the connection of framing members.

Frieze block Blocking between rafters at the eave of a roof.

Frost line The depth to which the ground freezes in a given locality.

Furring Strips of wood applied to a framed structure to adjust the plane of the finish surface.

Gable The triangular end wall of a building that has two equally pitched roofs opposed to each other.

Girder A structural member similar to a beam but larger.

Glue-laminated beam A composite beam made of 2x lumber stacked on one another and glued.

Grade beam A concrete beam at ground level that supports structure above.

Grout A mix of cement, sand, small aggregate, and water used to fill the cells of concrete block, locking reinforcing steel into the system.

Gusset A thin wooden plate attached to the surface, used to join two or more pieces of wood.

Gutter A horizontal trough used to collect rainwater at the eave of a building; also called an eave trough.

Handrail A safety device designed to be grasped by the hand while using a stair.

Head The zone at the top of a window or door.

Header A structural member over a window or door opening.

Header joist A joist that supports common joists at the edge of an opening in a floor or roof.

Hemmed edge A turned-over edge of a flashing.

Hip The outside intersection of two planes of a roof.

Hold-down A large steel connector used to anchor the base of sheer walls against overturning.

Housed stringer The side of a premanufactured stair, notched to receive the ends of treads and risers.

Hydrostatic pressure Water pressure in the ground.

Ice dam A buildup of ice, usually at the eave, caused when snow is melted by heat that escapes through the ceiling then refreezes when it reaches the cold eave.

I-joist A composite joist shaped like a steel beam to place most material where the stresses are greatest.

Interlayment A loose overlapping underlayment used with shake roofs.

Jamb The zone at the sides of a window or door, or the frame around a window or door.

Jamb extender An extension of a window or door frame to make it flush with the interior finish surface.

Joint reinforcement A method of placing horizontal reinforcement of masonry within the mortar joints.

Joist A relatively small repetitive horizontal structural member set on edge and spaced evenly.

Joist hanger A metal support used at the end of joists.

Kerf A shallow sawcut in wood.

Kiln-dried Wood dried in a large oven or kiln to 19% or 15% moisture content.

Lag bolt A relatively large screw used to make strong connections in wood; also known as lag screw.

Laminated strand lumber (LSL) A composite structural member used primarily for rim joists.

Laminated veneer lumber (LVL) Composite structural member used primarily for beams and headers.

Landing A wide level platform partway up a stairway, used as a turning point or resting place.

Lap joint A joint in which the ends of two boards are lapped, one over the other.

Lateral bracing The stabilizing of a building to resist horizontal forces.

Lateral force Any force such as a wind or earthquake that acts horizontally on a building.

Lateral load See Lateral force.

Ledger A horizontal member attached to a wall for the purpose of supporting other structural members such as joists or rafters.

Let-in Notching of one or more members so that another member such as a brace or ledger may be added flush with the original member(s).

Lintel A structural member over a window or door opening in masonry construction.

Live load The weight or force imposed on a structure by things other than the structure itself, such as furniture, occupants, snow, wind, or earthquake.

Load bearing Supporting a weight or force.

Lookout A cantilevered structural support of a rake.

Miter A butt joint made by bisecting the (usually right) angle between two intersecting pieces.

Moisture barrier A membrane designed to prevent the passage of water into a structure or space.

Moisture content The percent of the weight of wood that is water as compared to its bone-dry weight.

Mortise A rectangular cut into wood; the female receptor of a tenon in a mortise-and-tenon joint.

Mudsill The first wooden member bolted to a foundation forming the base of a wood frame.

Nailer A framing member added to a structure for the purpose of providing nailing for other members.

Nailing fin A continuous metal or plastic flange around the edge of a modern window or door to allow attachment to the wall and to seal the rough opening.

Nailing plate A nailer attached to a hard surface such as metal so other members may be nailed to it.

Neoprene A synthetic rubber.

Newel post A post at the top or bottom of a stair rail.

Nonbearing Not supporting any loads other than its own weight.

Nosing A rounded cantilevered edge of a stair tread.

Oriented strand board (OSB) A composite structural panel made of flakes of wood oriented for strength.

Parallel strand lumber (PSL) A composite structural member used primarily for short beams and headers.

Parapet The part of an exterior wall that projects above a roof.

Particle board A nonstructural composite panel made of small particles of wood.

Partition wall A nonbearing wall that does not support anything but its own weight.

Pea gravel A self-compacting fill material composed of pea-size rocks.

Perimeter insulation Insulation at the edges of a floor where the floor contacts the exterior environment.

Permeability The ability of a material to allow water vapor to pass through it.

Pilaster A vertical wall stiffener in masonry construction.

Pitch Roof slope expressed as a ratio, as in 4:12.

Plate A horizontal element that holds studs in place at the top and bottom of a framed wall.

Platform framing The common method of building with stud height limited to one floor.

Plumb Vertical.

Point load A concentrated load such as at a column.

Pony wall A framed wall at the perimeter of a building between the foundation and the first floor.

Portal frame A rigid frame consisting of two columns and a beam of similar dimensions.

Preformed metal Roofing metal manufactured to fit together in the field without special tools.

Prehung A door manufactured with hinges in a frame.

Pressure-treated Wood injected under pressure with chemicals that retard deterioration.

Protection board A cushion or shield that protects a moisture barrier from abrasion during backfill.

Purlin A horizontal structural element in a roof.

R-value The measure of resistance of a material to the passage of heat.

Rabbet A groove along the edge of a piece of wood.

Rafter The principal structural component in a sloped roof, including many types such as common, hip, valley, jack, barge, and verge.

Raised-heel truss A truss that is tall at the building edge to accommodate thick ceiling insulation.

Rake The sloped end portion of a roof.

Ridge beam A structural support at the top of rafters.

Ridge board A nonstructural board to which rafters are nailed.

Rigid insulation Any of a variety of insulative panels that retains its form through its own strength.

Rim joist A joist at the perimeter of a floor to which the common joists are attached; also known as band joist.

Rise The vertical distance between treads in a stair.

Riser A board that forms the vertical surface between treads in a stair.

Roof jack A roof flashing to allow plumbing vents to penetrate the roof surface.

Roof joist The principal structural element in a flat roof.

Rough opening An opening in framing made to fit a manufactured unit such as a door or window.

Run The horizontal distance between risers in a stair.

Sash A frame that holds glass in a window unit.

Scab A piece of wood on a surface of another piece.

Screed A straightedge used to level concrete.

Scupper A metal collector of rainwater at the edge of a flat roof to channel the water through a parapet.

Sealant A grade of caulk designed to prevent the passage of water, air, or other substance.

Setting block A small chunk of neoprene at the lower edge of glass that supports the weight of the glass.

Shake A wood shingle that is split from a bolt.

Shear wall A structural wall engineered to resist extreme lateral forces.

Sheathing The structural skin applied to the load-bearing surface of a wall, floor, or roof.

Shingle A thin, overlapping piece of material that will shed water; used for roofing or siding.

Sill The zone at the bottom edge of a door or window, or the sloped exterior base of a door or window.

Sill gasket A compressible material between mudsill and foundation or slab to inhibit air infiltration into heated spaces.

Single-wall A type of construction where the sheathing acts as the finish wall.

Slab-on-grade A concrete slab supported by the ground.

Sleeper A framing member laid flat across a series of joists or rafters to support other framing members.

Slope See Pitch.

Snow guard A small protrusion integrated with roofing to hold snow on the roof.

Soffit A horizontal surface at the eave, extending between fascia and wall.

Sole plate The bottom plate in a stud-wall assembly.

Spacing The distance between repetitive structural elements such as studs, joists, or rafters.

Span The horizontal distance between the two supports of a structural member such as a beam, joist, or rafter.

Splash block A concrete block designed to distribute rainwater at the base of a downspout.

Splash pan A metal flashing on a roof surface at the base of a downspout to direct rainwater over the roof.

Squash block A short block with grain oriented vertically, used where heavy loads could crush I-joists.

Stick-frame A colloquialism describing light wood frame.

Stool A horizontal shelflike trim at the interior base of a window.

Stop A protrusion around a window or door jamb that stops the hinged sash or door at the plane of the wall.

Storm drain A drain that carries rainwater runoff.

Storm sash A glazed unit applied to the exterior of a window as protection against storms and heat loss.

Storm sewer A large municipal drain for rainwater.

Strap A long piece of wood or metal used to tie one structural piece to another.

Strapping A layer of boards applied to the interior of framing to smooth the surface or to increase insulation.

Stringer *See Carriage.*

Strut Part of the structural perimeter of a diaphragm or shear wall.

Stud The principal vertical structural component in a framed wall, including many specialized types such as king, trimmer, and cripple studs.

Sub-fascia A structural fascia beneath a finish fascia.

Subfloor The structural plane supporting the finish floor.

Subflooring See Subfloor.

Superinsulation Insulation that significantly exceeds code minimums.

Tenon A rectangular extension of the end of a piece of wood, sized to fit a mortise in a mortise-and-tenon joint.

Termite shield A metal barrier to prevent termites from entering a wooden building.

Thermal bridge A component within an insulated assembly such as a wall or roof that conducts heat well and spans or bridges between the interior and exterior surfaces of the envelope, allowing heat to escape.

Threshold The weatherstripped transition between finish floor and sill at the base of a door.

Thrust block A block that is firmly attached to the floor at the base of a stair to prevent its horizontal movement.

Toenail A method of nailing diagonally through the end of one piece of lumber into another.

Tongue-and-groove An interlocking edge detail running the length of boards

Top plate The longitudinal uppermost member of a stud wall, usually doubled.

Tread The level plane that forms the steps of a stairway.

Trimmer joist An extra structural joist parallel to common joists at the edge of an opening in a floor or roof.

Truss An arrangement of structural members forming triangles that works efficiently to span long distances.

Turned-down slab A concrete slab with a thickened edge that acts as a footing to support a structure above.

Twist strap A metal strap with a 90-degree twist allowing surfaces perpendicular to one another to be tied.

Underlayment A moisture barrier located between roofing and roof sheathing.

Uniform load A load that is evenly distributed over a given area or length.

Valley The sloped channel formed when two planes of a roof meet at an interior corner.

Vapor barrier A membrane or other building element that retards the transmission of water vapor; more properly called a vapor retarder.

Vaulted ceiling A sloped ceiling following the roof pitch.

Vent channel A device that compresses insulation at the eave to allow ventilation of the roof assembly; also called a baffle.

Verge rafter A rafter attached to the building at the gable end; interchangeable with the term barge rafter.

Vertical grain A board with the annual growth rings oriented perpendicular to its width.

Waferboard A composite panel made of flakes of wood.

Warm roof A vaulted ceiling superinsulated with rigid insulation and with no ventilation space.

Weatherstripping A seal around doors and windows to reduce air infiltration.

Web The structural part of a truss or composite joist that holds the chords in position relative to one another.

Web stiffener An extra layer of plywood or OSB laminated to the web of an I-joist for stiffness.

Weep hole A small opening at the base of masonry construction to allow moisture to escape.

INDEX